ONE WEEK LOAN

Why Mothers Kill

Geoffrey R. McKee

Why Mothers Kill

A Forensic Psychologist's Casebook

OXFORD

UNIVERSITY PRESS

2006

OXFORD
UNIVERSITY PRESS

Oxford University Press, Inc., publishes works that further
Oxford University's objective of excellence
in research, scholarship, and education.

Oxford   New York
Auckland   Cape Town   Dar es Salaam   Hong Kong   Karachi
Kuala Lumpur   Madrid   Melbourne   Mexico City   Nairobi
New Delhi   Shanghai   Taipei   Toronto

With offices in
Argentina   Austria   Brazil   Chile   Czech Republic   France   Greece
Guatemala   Hungary   Italy   Japan   Poland   Portugal   Singapore
South Korea   Switzerland   Thailand   Turkey   Ukraine   Vietnam

Published by Oxford University Press, Inc.
198 Madison Avenue, New York, New York 10016

www.oup.com

Oxford is a registered trademark of Oxford University Press

Library of Congress Cataloging-in-Publication Data
McKee, Geoffrey R.
Why mothers kill : a forensic psychologist's casebook / Geoffrey R. McKee.
p.   cm.
Includes bibliographical references and index.
ISBN-13 978-0-19-518273-6
ISBN 0-19-518273-1
1. Filicide.   2. Infanticide.   3. Women murderers.   4. Mothers—Psychology.
5. Forensic psychology—Case studies.   I. Title.
HV6542.M38 2006
364.3'74—dc22   2005025827

9 8 7 6 5 4 3 2 1
Printed in the United States of America
on acid-free paper

For Sue Ann
and
mothers everywhere
doing the most important job
in the world

Preface

Few images are more symbolic of our sense of peace and security than a mother protectively holding her infant child. At a cultural level, the theme of maternal nurturing has been repeated in all known societies throughout history in stories, statues, plays, drawings, paintings, photographs, and films. The mothers in this casebook are tragic examples of the other side of the coin.

My motivation for writing this book has been to help medical and mental health clinicians, legal and protective services professionals, and the public anticipate and ideally intervene before these horrific events occur; that is, to prevent maternal filicide, infanticide, and neonaticide. Although I have included the most recent research findings and highlighted numerous practical methods of intervention within this book, I believe that it may ultimately be the mothers' stories that will help us all to better understand these fractured, fatal relationships. The chapters that follow introduce:

Cathy, a 14-year-old stepfather-incest victim, who threw her newborn against the wall after giving birth alone in her bedroom.

Edna, a college freshman, who suffocated her minutes-old baby in an act of delayed abortion.

Francine, age 22, who drowned her 5-month-old child so that she could return to her life of nightly parties.

Glenda, an exhausted 39-year-old obese mother of five, who ended her infant daughter's life by suffocation while nursing her in her bed.

Alcoholic Harriet, whose last physical abuse of her 4-year-old son resulted in his death.

Janet, who, in an isolated fit of frustration, shook her infant so violently that her baby expired.

Kaye, a mother with mental retardation, whose unattended toddler son drowned in the bathtub.

Barbara, whose perception of reality was so impaired by delusions that she believed her two demon-possessed children had to die so that she could save them and her husband.

Impulse-ridden Susan, who allowed the car carrying her two sons to sink into the waters of John D. Long Lake.

Chronically depressed Marilyn, who, following her favorite son's accidental death, killed herself on her second try after poisoning her two remaining children.

Olivia, who suffocated her toddler daughter to prevent her mother-in-law from gaining custody once again.

Pauline, who, with her equally greedy ex-convict boyfriend, drowned her preteen son in a staged accident to collect his inheritance from his deceased grandparents.

Samantha, a crack-addicted mother of a 9-year-old daughter whom she prostituted for drugs, who pushed her child down a staircase to keep her from revealing the sexual exploitation.

Rhonda, who, to obtain attention and sympathy from hospital staff, covertly created medical emergencies by serially suffocating and reviving her two sons until each died.

Many people have helped me along the way. Grateful appreciation is extended to Kirk Heilbrun for his wise counsel in the early stages of the book's formation and for his careful critique of an initial draft of the beginning chapters. Thanks, too, for Lita Schwartz's thoughtful comments and useful suggestions as the manuscript was taking shape. I was fortunate as well to have had many active discussions with George Holmes, whose probing questions helped me to clarify my goals and objectives for this project—his unselfish professionalism has made this a better book indeed. Joan Bossert, an exceptional editor, and her Oxford University Press staff created a nurturing environment that allowed this toddler author to learn how to walk. Special thanks go to Sue Ann, who has been an unfailing source of encouragement and support to me through 38 years of marriage.

I also thank my mother and father: a "good start"—finished.

Contents

Why Mothers Kill

1

Introduction

Barbara peeked out her living room window and stared at the strangers walking by. She knew what they were thinking. They were going to take away her children and put her in a mental hospital. She'd seen others in the neighborhood looking at her and making plans to abduct her. She felt exhausted, but a voice told her to stay vigilant. She knew her only place of safety was her house. She refused to allow her children to play outside.

Barbara's life had become confusing to her since the birth of her first child, Marcus, 4 years ago. She had become depressed after Marcus was born, but her doctor told her she was just having "baby blues" and would be better soon. Taking care of Marcus was more difficult than she anticipated: He rarely slept through the night and was often cranky and crying during the day. Although her husband, Tom, helped when he could, he was often gone on business trips, leaving her alone at home with Marcus. When Tom was out of town, Barbara would not get out of bed in the morning and would keep Marcus in the bedroom with her. For many weeks, she rarely showered and felt unable to clean, cook, and manage her household duties. Marcus would develop rashes on his bottom because Barbara was too exhausted to change his diapers. She began to have panic attacks and worried constantly about whether she was or could become a good mother. Tom became very concerned about her inability to care for Marcus and arranged for her to see a local psychiatrist, who recommended that she be hospitalized. Barbara was terrified about being sent to a mental hospital, believing that once she was admitted she would never be released. She refused to go to the emergency room but did accept medication that the psychiatrist prescribed.

The medications helped her become more energetic, and for a while she felt more optimistic and self-confident. She was able to take care of Marcus and was happy about her marriage. She had always wanted a large family with Tom, so they began discussing having another child. When she discovered she was pregnant, Tom was overjoyed and began organizing the second bedroom as a nursery for their new baby. Though Barbara was initially thrilled at being pregnant, her worries and anxieties soon returned.

When Tom was gone on business trips, she was unable to stop her recurrent panic episodes. She would awaken each morning with a sense of dread. She was nauseous with "morning sickness," but her frequent vomiting, due to excessive anxiety, continued into her second and third trimesters of pregnancy. Though depressed and despondent over her new maternal responsibilities, she did not have suicidal thoughts but often felt she was going to die during her attacks of panic.

Approximately two weeks after Heather was born, Barbara feared that she was losing her mind. She began to hear mumblings and noises in the house. A few weeks later, she believed she had clearly heard a voice telling her she was a bad mother. When she returned to her psychiatric appointment, she did not tell her doctor about the voice, because she was certain that he would put her in the hospital.

Barbara became fearful and excessively anxious around other people; then she began being suspicious of their reactions to her. The voice whispering in her ear was clearer and more frequent; occasionally she heard other "persons" talking to her. Though the voices initially scared her, as time went by she began to trust that they were protecting her from people wishing to harm her. She realized that Marcus, her 4-year-old son, and Heather, her 8-month-old daughter, had begun to act strangely and had stopped listening to her. They had become unruly and rebellious, and she felt unable to manage them. They looked at her strangely and resisted her attempts to comfort them. Marcus began to whisper to Heather about her, just like the others outside her home who talked about her.

A week before she killed them, Barbara was finally able to understand what had been happening to her: Marcus and Heather had become demonized by evil forces. They were crazy and had made her crazy, too—her children had to be stopped before they infected Tom. Today was the day she would do it.

Tom had left early for the office. He had seemed somewhat distant and distracted and had given her a funny look as he went out the door. Barbara knew that Tom would be safe from the children as long as he stayed at work. The house was quiet because Marcus and Heather were not yet awake. She went into the children's bedroom and watched them sleep. They looked so innocent, but she knew differently: They were sleeping to trick her into letting down her guard. A voice said "Do it, do it now!" She took a pillow from the floor and placed it over Marcus's face. He struggled for only a few minutes. When Barbara raised the pillow, Marcus's eyes were closed, and he looked to be at peace. She turned to Heather's bed with the pillow, and soon her daughter was also still. She knew her children were now in Heaven, safe from the demons.

She dressed the children in their favorite outfits, made their beds, and then laid them out with their hands crossed over their chests. Barbara smiled for the first time in months and walked downstairs. She called Tom at work to tell him that she had saved him from their children. She was alarmed by Tom's shock and disbelief. She was confused when Tom told her that he would call for the police and an ambulance. She then realized that she had been too late, that the children had already done their damage to him. Barbara was devastated and began to cry helplessly. When the police and ambulance arrived with her husband, she offered no resistance and was taken to the hospital.

Parental murders of children have occurred for centuries and have been documented in virtually every known society, from advanced, industrialized countries to indigenous groups. *Filicide* pertains to the killing of children older than 1 year of age. *Infanticide* refers to homicides of children who have not yet had their first birthdays. *Neonaticide* is reserved for children who are murdered on their first day of life.

Few crimes generate greater public reaction than that of a mother who murders her child. After cases such as those of Susan Smith and Andrea Yates are reported by the media, we ask: "Why? How could a mother do such a thing to her own child?" Our reactions vary from compassion and sympathy to rage and anger. We are repelled yet mesmerized by the emerging details of the case. We are morbidly curious about how a mother could destroy this first and most fundamental relationship we have all had in our lives. These crimes often evoke memories of our own childhoods, when we may have feared our parents' anger: We may wonder whether our mothers may have had intentions to kill, harm, or abandon us. For those of us who are parents, we may recall episodes in our lives when we felt so enraged at our children that our physical discipline went beyond accepted limits—we were shocked to learn that we were capable of such violence. We may also remember, with guilt, wanting to leave home to be free of the burdens of insistent, demanding children. In our deepest, most secret thoughts, however, we may be fearful of whether we too, as parents, might act on this darkest impulse of filicide.

The purpose of this book is to prevent maternal filicide, infanticide, and neonaticide. This casebook has been written to help mental health, medical, legal, law enforcement, and protective services professionals, as well as the general public, understand, analyze, and ideally intervene before these tragic events occur. The contents of the book derive from two sources: (1) my forensic psychological evaluations of 32 teenage girls and adult women who have been charged with killing their children; and (2) the professional literature relevant to the description, risk analysis, and prevention of maternal filicide.

Because this book comprises actual cases of maternal filicide from my evaluation work in numerous states over the past 26 years, a number of steps have been taken to mask the women's identities to conform to professional ethical standards. With the exception of Susan Smith, each woman was given a fictitious first name, and only first names are used. Many demographic characteristics (e.g., age, education, occupation, socioeconomic level, etc.) of the women have been altered. The names of the children and other family members have been changed in every case, and at times so have the ages, sexes, and number of child victims. Locations are described generically (e.g., university, hospital). To hide the women's identities, I have also exchanged information among cases within the same filicide category, a process described by Heilbrun, Marczyk, and DeMatteo (2002) as *hybridizing*. There is one exception, however. In 1994, I conducted a criminal forensic psychological evaluation of Susan Smith while she was awaiting trial for the murder of her two sons. Because the facts of her crime were so widely publicized, I was aware that I would be unable to hide her identity. With the endorsement of her attorney, I was able to obtain her written consent to use her name and case study.

In chapter 2, the current estimates of the prevalence of maternal filicide are described. Next, the difficulties in establishing true incidence rates are discussed in terms of the problems of discovering the bodies of abandoned children, determining the causes of the children's deaths, and prosecutorial decisions about whether to bring the cases to trial. Last, the demographic, historical, clinical, victim, forensic, and offense characteristics of maternal filicidal cases from the research and clinical literature are presented.

Chapter 3 illustrates the similarities, differences, and limitations of systems that have attempted to explain these tragic deaths. I first describe the existing classifications that encompass child killings by either the mother or father and follow with a discussion of those explanatory systems, limited to maternal filicide. The similarities among the models are then discussed in terms of their common emphasis on the mother's mental illness, lack of bonding to her child, or inadequate parenting. The chapter concludes with the description of my maternal classification system, drawn from my clinical experience and empirical research, comprising the categories of detached mothers, abusive/neglectful mothers, psychotic/depressed mothers, retaliatory mothers, and psychopathic mothers.

In chapter 4 I describe the scientific study of dangerous behavior and highlight clinical and everyday situations in which risk analysis is commonplace. The reader is introduced to the essential terms *target behaviors, signal behaviors, risk factors,* and *protective factors.* I then discuss my Maternal Filicide Risk Matrix, a model for analyzing maternal filicide risk and protective factors at five different time periods: prepregnancy, pregnancy and delivery, early postpartum (birth to 6 months), late postpartum (6 months to 1 year), and postinfancy (after 1 year). The risk and protective factors of the Risk Matrix have been drawn from the empirical and clinical maternal filicide research literature. A Maternal Filicide Risk Matrix for Barbara's filicide of Marcus and Heather is completed to further illustrate its utility to individual cases.

In chapter 5, the ongoing, interactive process of risk analysis and prevention is illustrated through everyday examples and situations from clinical settings. This chapter introduces the concept of *risk intervention points* (RIPs), behaviors or interpersonal situations that precede target behaviors. RIPs are signals that, if identified *and* modified, may neutralize risk factors or strengthen protective factors relevant to a maternal filicide case. The utility of RIPs is highlighted by extracting examples from Barbara's situation in which her husband recognized her at-risk status and attempted to intervene. Primary, secondary, and tertiary prevention methods are then described, with examples from the maternal filicide literature.

In chapters 6 through 19, the story of each filicidal mother is told in her own words, thoughts, worries, fears, and feelings, as each described the events that led her to commit this unthinkable crime. Through the case studies, the reader may begin to understand how these women arrived at the point at which they believed that their only course of action was to terminate the lives of their children.

Each of the case chapters begins with a narrative of the mother's ideas and emotions before, during, and/or after her homicidal act. Significant events from the mother's personal history before and after delivery identify those experiences that helped to shape her unique perceptions, attitudes, beliefs, and personality. Analysis of the case through the Maternal Filicide Risk Matrix describes the primary risk and protective factors that were unique to that mother. The research and scientific literature relevant to the mother's clinical circumstances is summarized to assist in understanding her behavior in the broader context of empirical findings and clinical knowledge. Suggestions for risk reduction and filicide prevention at various RIPs within the mother's case are presented to help the reader understand what might have been done to avert the tragedy. Each story concludes with an epilogue describing the legal resolution of the mother's case.

Chapters 6 through 9 describe filicide cases involving detached mothers, in which the bonding between the parent and newborn never adequately developed. Chapter 6 is based on *Cathy*, a 14-year-old girl so overwhelmed by her stepfather's repeated sexual assaults that she unconsciously eliminated any awareness of being pregnant until she gave birth alone in her bedroom. Chapter 7 tells the story of *Edna*, a college freshman so indecisive about ending her pregnancy or giving birth that she suffocated her minutes-old baby in an act of delayed abortion. Chapter 8 presents *Francine*, a 22-year-old single woman who drowned and then buried her 5-month-old child because she was angry, tired, and bored with motherhood and wished to return to her prepregnancy lifestyle of parties and recreational substance abuse. Chapter 9 is the case of *Glenda*, a 39-year-old obese mother of five children who was so overwhelmed by the demands of her numerous children that, while nursing her 3-month-old baby in bed, she rolled onto and suffocated the child.Chapters 10 through 12 describe filicides by abusive and neglectful mothers, accidental child deaths due to maternal physical discipline or inattention. Chapter 10 tells of *Harriet*, a chronically alcoholic woman whose repeated abuse of her 4-year-old son during periods of intoxication resulted in his death. Chapter 11 is based on *Janet*, who, in an isolated fit of rage, shook her 4-month-old daughter so violently that the child died. Chapter 12 depicts the story of *Kaye*, a woman of very low intelligence, whose unattended toddler son drowned in the bathtub.

Chapters 13 through 15 illustrate filicides by psychotic and depressed mothers, women whose mental illness was the most significant factor leading to their children's deaths. In chapter 13, *Barbara's* story is continued, exemplifying postpartum psychosis, and is described through the verdict in her insanity trial. *Susan Smith's* case is presented in chapter 14. Chapter 15 is based on *Marilyn*, a chronically depressed mother who, in an organized, deliberate manner, planned her own and her two remaining children's deaths by medication overdose.

Chapter 16 describes a retaliatory mother, *Olivia*, who killed her toddler to prevent the child's paternal grandmother from gaining custody once again.

Chapters 17, 18, and 19 present three cases of filicide by psychopathic mothers, situations in which the mothers, for exploitative and self-serving reasons, killed their children. Chapter 17 describes *Pauline*, who killed her son by staging an accident to cash in on his inheritance from his deceased grandparents. Chapter 18 describes *Samantha*, a crack-cocaine-addicted mother of a 9-year-old daughter whom she prostituted for drugs and then murdered after her child threatened to reveal her mother's sexual exploitation to the school counselor. Finally, Chapter 19 presents *Rhonda*, a woman with Munchausen syndrome by proxy (MBP), who repeatedly smothered and revived her two sons until each died.

The casebook concludes with an enumeration of recommendations for future research and clinical practice in maternal filicide.

2

Neonaticide, Infanticide, and Filicide Research

What Do We Know?

In this chapter, I address the question "What do we know?" by discussing filicide research in three areas. First, I present current estimates of the prevalence
of filicide. Second, I review the legal and medical problems in determining
true prevalence rates. Third, I summarize the demographic, historical, clinical,
victim, offense, and forensic characteristics of those mothers who have been
charged or convicted of murdering their children.

Filicide Prevalence Estimates

Over the past 40 years, many national studies have been conducted to determine the incidence, circumstances, causes of death, and demographic characteristics of children who are killed. For example, the U.S. Department of
Health and Human Services' (USDHHS) Office on Child Abuse and Neglect
estimated that in 2001, approximately 1,300 children under 18 died as a result
of abuse and neglect—a rate of more than three deaths per day, or one child
death every 7 hours (U.S. Department of Health & Human Services, 2003).
The USDHHS report indicated that almost all of the children killed by abuse
or neglect were very young: 85% were under 6 years of age, and 41% were under the age of 1. The 1,300 deaths represented 0.14%, or 14 per 1,000 victims of
the estimated 900,000 children in 2001 who were subjected to neglect, physical
abuse, sexual abuse, and/or emotional maltreatment. USDHHS reported that
over the past 30 years, the annual number of children under age 1 who have
died from physical abuse has more than doubled, to its highest rate in the year
2000. Most of the children were victims of filicide by one of their parents.

The U.S. Department of Justice (USDOJ) estimated that between 1976 and 1994, 13,774 children under age 10 were murdered in the United States, a yearly average of 765 filicides, or one child every 12 hours (Bureau of Justice Statistics, 1997). The USDOJ study also found that most of the victims were the youngest and most vulnerable children: 80% were under age 5, and 31% were less than 1 year old. These data are consistent with the studies of Overpeck that have found that approximately one child per day is killed before his or her first birthday (Overpeck, 2003).

Various studies have demonstrated that the most likely perpetrators of child homicide and abuse are the victim's biological parents (Bureau of Justice Statistics, 1997). The study determined that 61% of the children under 5 years old were murdered by their parents and that another 23% were killed by a male acquaintance of the mother, often acting as a de facto parent during her absence. Only 3% of the children died at the hands of a stranger. Biological mothers accounted for 30% of the child homicides between 1976 and 2000 at an annual rate as high as 256, or an average of one child death every 33 hours.

Difficulties in Establishing True Prevalence Rates

The principal causes of inaccurate prevalence rates involve legal and medical factors. To establish the true prevalence for filicide, at least three conditions must be met: (1) all deceased children's bodies must be discovered and examined; (2) the exact cause of each death must be determined; and (3) the circumstances of the death as accidental or intentional must be specified, and the parent must be convicted of killing his or her child.

Discovery of the Body

It is unknown how many babies die each year from filicide, because the documented filicide data is based on only those cases in which a body has been found (Crittenden & Craig, 1990; Overpeck, 2003). Once the federal government began to collect data on the number of abandoned newborns, in early 1990, the rates of known discarded babies have been astounding. In 1991, according to the U.S. Department of Health and Human Services' Administration for Children and Families (USDHHS, 2004a), over 21,660 newborn babies had been abandoned by mothers in hospitals or other public places. In 1998, the most recent year for which USDHHS has data, the number of abandoned babies had risen by over 9,400 infants to 31,000, an increase of more than 40%.

It is unknown how many babies abandoned by their mothers are never found because the newborns were discarded into community trash dumpsters, buried in remote locations, or left in unoccupied dwellings. For example, in 1999, Texas became the first state to pass a law that allowed mothers or fathers, under special conditions, to legally give up their infants. The statute was made after more than 800 babies were found discarded in a single year, including 50 who were discovered in dumpsters. Currently, 45 states have passed similar "safe haven" or "baby Moses" laws (National Conference of State Legislatures, 2003).

The mortality rate for discarded babies discovered in nonhospital settings has been staggering: In 1991, over 12% were found dead. By 1998, nearly 32% of the discovered babies were found deceased, an increase of almost 300% (U.S. Department of Health & Human Services, 2004a). In one sample of neonaticides, more than 64% of the newborns' bodies had been accidentally discovered on the beach or in trash bins (Crittenden & Craig, 1990). None of the newborns had been reported missing, thus confirming that the new mother had intended to conceal the delivery and abandonment of her baby.

Many researchers have found that an expectant mother's attitude toward her pregnancy is a strong factor in whether she emotionally bonds with her fetus and baby (Ainsworth, Blehar, Waters, & Wall, 1978; Bibring, 1959; Fonagy, Steele, & Steele, 1991). In 1987, 8% or 120,000 expectant mothers gave birth to babies they described as unwanted (Brown & Eisenberg, 1995). A high proportion of the 120,000 women with unwanted pregnancies, therefore, may not have had positive attachments to nor cared for the welfare of their newborn babies. Such negative maternal attitudes likely make undetected abandonment much more prevalent. These findings appear to support Meyer and Oberman's (2001) conclusion that many neonaticide (and first-week infanticide) victims are never found.

Establishing the True Cause of Death

Research estimating filicide is typically based on official reports such as death certificates or other state agency data. Causes of deaths in infants are often very difficult to establish even for highly experienced pathologists and medical specialists. In high-profile, well-publicized filicide cases, the issue of cause of death may lead to a vigorous "battle of the experts" for both the prosecution and the defense, especially if the defendant faces the death penalty for allegedly killing a very young victim. For example, infant deaths are often attributed to sudden infant death syndrome (SIDS), a diagnosis of exclusion; that is, a conclusion of an unknown cause of death after all other possible causes have been ruled out (Emery, 1993; Ewigman, Kivlahan, & Land, 1993). Although deaths attributed to SIDS have decreased dramatically due to medically recommended changes in sleeping procedures for newborns, the diagnosis is still widely recorded. Bacon (2004) estimated that undetected covert homicides of children may account for as many as 10% of sudden unexpected deaths in infancy. The high frequency of SIDS prompted the American Academy of Pediatrics in 1999 to recommend improved investigations of infants' abrupt deaths (American Academy of Pediatrics, 1999). Ominously, Overpeck (2003) has been widely quoted as stating that child homicides by mothers are among the least well-documented deaths in the United States.

Circumstances of the Child's Death and Prosecution

Even if the cause of death could be established, filicide research is further compromised by problems in determining whether the child's death was an accident or an intentional homicide by the alleged perpetrator-parent. Infants' deaths that are determined to be accidents are often not prosecuted or reported as instances of child abuse, and therefore the official number of infanticides may be underestimated (Bureau of Justice Statistics, 2000). Determination of the circumstances of the child's cause of death is particularly difficult when the victim is a newborn. For example, Meyer and Oberman (2001) found that 84% of the neonaticide cases they reviewed involved either suffocation or drowning. In suffocation cases, it is often difficult to establish whether the infant was intentionally smothered by the mother or died as a result of an accidental "layover suffocation" during nursing in bed. Glenda's case (chapter 9) turned on that issue: The coroner had declared the death as an accident, but after suffering 2 weeks of overwhelming guilt, Glenda admitted she had intentionally killed her child.

Research has indicated that, even when a medical examiner finds grounds for homicide, a police report might not be completed, resulting in an under-reporting of actual filicide rates (Overpeck, Brenner, & Cosgrove, 2002). For example, in one U.S. study of filicide, only 64% of 171 cases over a 30-year period were prosecuted by the local district attorneys (Crittenden & Craig, 1990).

Maternal Filicide Case Characteristics

Very little consistency across the studies was found regarding which variables of the mothers were measured and whether those data were quantitatively or qualitatively described. For example, only 10 of 30 study variables in McKee and Shea's cross-national comparison research (1998) were also measured in the findings of Resnick (1969), d'Orban (1979), and Bourget and Bradford (1990). Also, in maternal filicide studies based on secondary sources, such as newspaper reports or legal cases, the data may not be available to the researcher because the sources either did not report or had not known the mother's particular demographic or historical characteristics. The studies cited under each of the mothers' and victims' demographic, historical, and clinical characteristics provide the empirical underpinning for my Maternal Filicide Risk Matrix. For each characteristic, the specific percentages from the different studies are compared with one another in order to validate the utility of that characteristic in clinical decision making: the greater the differences in percentages, however, the less confidence the clinician may have in relying on that characteristic for risk analysis.

Demographic Characteristics

Age

Maternal age at the time of the child's death has been one of the most consistently reported statistics in studies of maternal filicide. Most of the research, after excluding neonaticide cases, has found that the mothers were typically in their 20s when the filicide occurred. Spinelli (2003) found that in 17 cases of infanticide, the mother's mean age was 23; however, women as young as 15 and as old as 40 have killed their children. Alder and Polk's (2001) sample of filicide-suicide cases reported that the mothers ranged in age from 18 to 35 years. Meyer and Oberman (2001) determined that in their cases of "assisted-coerced" and "neglect" filicides, the mothers were on average 25 years old. However, in the "abuse" filicide category, the women were slightly older, 27 years. Resnick (1969) found that, after excluding neonaticide cases, the average age of his sample of filicidal mothers was 31.5 years, compared with the mothers' mean age of 27.3 in the sample of Bourget and Bradford (1990), 24.6 years in the study by d'Orban (1979), and 29.3 years in research by McKee and Shea (1998). Lewis, Baranoski, Buchanan, and Benedek (1998) reported that the average age of filicidal mothers in their sample was 29 years.

Many studies have reported that the mothers in neonaticide cases are generally younger. For example, Meyer and Oberman's (2001) sample of 37 neonaticidal mothers had an average age of 19 years—though one woman was 39 years old when she killed her newborn baby. Overpeck, Brenner, and Trumble (1998) found that new mothers under age 15 were seven times more likely to commit neonaticide or infanticide than new mothers over age 25.

Intelligence

Subnormal intellectual functioning is frequently found as a demographic characteristic of mothers who commit filicide. In the general population, approximately 1% of adults and children are diagnosed with mental retardation (American Psychiatric Association, 2000). However, in maternal filicide cases, the prevalence appears to be much higher. For example, Meyer and Oberman (2001) found that 13% of their sample in the category of "abuse" filicides suffered from low intelligence, and Spinelli (2003) indicated that the majority of the infanticidal women in her study had limited IQs. McKee and Shea (1998) discovered, in their sample of filicidal mothers, that 5% were mentally retarded, which is consistent with the 4% prevalence found by d'Orban (1979).

Education

McKee and Shea (1998) reported that the filicidal women in their sample had an average of 11 years of education and that 20% had attended some college classes. Cummings, Theis, Mueller, and Rivara (1994) cited a lack of education (less than high school graduation) as a risk factor in cases of neonaticide: Only 7% of the new mothers had attended any college classes. Wilczynski (1997) found that almost 80% of the mothers in her sample had left school before age

16. Lewis et al. (1998) reported that 44% of their sample had not completed high school. Overpeck, Brenner, and Trumble (1998) found that infants whose mothers did not complete high school were eight times more likely to be killed than the infants of mothers who had completed more than 15 years of school.

Marital Status

Almost all of the studies found that most of the filicidal mothers (from 52% [Wilczynski, 1997] to 88% [Resnick, 1969]) were married or in an ongoing partnership at the time of the children's deaths. If the mother had committed neonaticide, however, she was unlikely to be married or in a stable relationship: 97% of Meyer and Oberman's (2001) sample of neonaticidal mothers were single. Unmarried status was also cited as a risk factor for neonaticide in the research of Cummings et al. (1994) and Emerick, Foster, and Campbell (1986).

Socioeconomic Status

The majority of studies have found that filicidal mothers came from impoverished situations at the time of their children's deaths. Many researchers have cited lack of financial resources as a common characteristic of the women who commit filicide or abandon their neonates. For example, McKee and Shea (1998) found that 80% of the mothers in their study had annual incomes of less than $20,000. Meyer and Oberman (2001) determined that 90% of the mothers who had fatally neglected their children lived below the poverty line. Crimmins, Langley, Brownstein, and Sprunt (1997) reported that only 29% of their sample were legitimately employed. The majority of the filicidal mothers reported by Holden, Burland, and Lemmen (1996) were unemployed at the time of their children's deaths. Wilczynski (1997) determined that 61% of the filicidal mothers in her sample reported having housing problems due to financial deficits and welfare allocations.

Historical Characteristics

Parental Divorce

Of the few studies that describe the marriages of filicidal mothers' parents, parental divorce was a common theme. In d'Orban's (1979) study, 57% of the mothers had come from broken homes, as had 80% of the mothers in McKee and Shea's (1998) sample. Crimmins et al. (1997) determined that 64% of the mothers in their sample had come from motherless homes.

Childhood Abuse

Filicidal mothers' childhood histories of victimization have been reported in many studies. Spinelli (2001) discovered that 53% of the infanticidal mothers she studied were victims of physical and/or sexual abuse. McKee and Shea (1998) indicated that 20% of their sample had been child abuse victims, as had 16% of the mothers in d'Orban's (1979) study. Crimmins et al. (1997) found that 74% of their filicidal mothers had reported histories of serious physical abuse or sexual molestation, which was somewhat higher than the 39% rate of childhood victimization found in the mothers in Wilczynski's (1997) sample. Korbin (1986) found that 78% of her sample reported histories of childhood physical or sexual abuse.

Abuse Victims as Adults

Many studies have reported that filicidal mothers are often in abusive, violent relationships at the time their children are killed. Crimmins et al. (1997) found that 52% of the mothers in their sample were living with abusive partners, compared with 18% of the mothers in Wilczynski's (1997) study. Meyer and Oberman (2001) indicated that criminal domestic violence was very prevalent in their sample of women who had committed "assisted/coerced" filicides: 40% had been abused by their partners. Of the women in McKee and Shea's (1998) study, 43% reported that they were in violent relationships, and half of those women also described abuse by former partners. These data were somewhat consistent with those of the women in d'Orban's (1979) study, in which 19% had reported being previously abused as adults.

Prior Arrest

Generally, filicidal mothers do not have histories of legal difficulties prior to their arrests for killing their children. D'Orban (1979) found that 20% of the sample had been previously arrested, compared with 5% of the mothers in the sample of McKee and Shea (1998). Holden et al. (1996) found that a small minority of their sample of filicidal mothers had been previously charged with crimes by the police. Of the mothers in Wilczynski's (1997) sample, 18% reported that they had been previously arrested. Meyer and Oberman (2001) discovered that of the mothers categorized as "purposeful" filicides, 16% had previously killed other children in their care, though it was unclear whether those mothers had been arrested for their prior crimes.

Clinical Characteristics

Prior Mental Health Services

A history of mental illness and treatment has been a common finding in many studies of filicidal mothers. In a 1979 study by d'Orban, 41% of the sample had been previously psychiatrically hospitalized, compared with 15% in the sample of McKee and Shea (1998). More than 64% of Wilczynski's (1997) sample reported that they had received prior psychiatric treatment, which was comparable to the 60% of filicidal mothers reported by Lewis et al. (1998). Crimmins et al. (1997) found that 59% of their sample had sought mental health care prior to their filicidal acts. Alder and Polk (2001) discovered that the majority of filicidal women in their study had been receiving psychiatric care at the time of their children's deaths, which was consistent with the findings of Sammons (1987) that 40% of filicidal mothers had been seen by psychiatrists shortly before committing their crimes.

Family Mental Illness

Psychiatric problems within the mothers' families also appeared to occur with higher frequency than in the general population. D'Orban (1979) reported that 25% of the sample indicated that one or more of their relatives were mentally ill, compared with 45% of the mothers in the sample of McKee and Shea (1998). Crimmins et al. (1997) found that in 38% of their cases, the filicidal mother reported that one or more family members suffered from alcoholism and 7% from serious mental problems. Lewis et al. (1998) indicated that 55% of the women in their sample declared that one or more family members had received psychiatric care. Wilczynski (1997) discovered that 23% of her sample of mothers reported that one or more of their family members had previously received psychiatric care and that 7% of the mothers had family members who had been arrested.

Psychological Testing

Only one published study (McKee, Shea, Mogy, & Holden, 2001) has assessed the personality characteristics of filicidal mothers through use of the Minnesota Multiphasic Personality Inventory, Second Edition (MMPI-2), a well-established psychological test. They compared the test results of women charged with filicide with those of women charged with the murders of either their spouses or nonfamily members. In contrast to the other two groups of women defendants, filicidal mothers' test results suggested that they were more likely to manifest symptoms characteristic of severe mental illness. Many of the filicidal women, however, did not share that overall test "profile," indicating that mothers who kill their children are a very diverse, heterogeneous group with many differences in personality and symptom characteristics.

Psychiatric Diagnosis

Many of the studies reviewed indicated that the mothers in their samples suffered from mental disorders. Resnick (1969) reported that 53% of the mothers in his sample had been diagnosed with a psychotic disorder, 13% had suffered from major depression, and 10% had experienced an adjustment disorder at the time of their crimes. Bourget and Bradford (1990) indicated that 8% of their sample had been diagnosed with a psychotic disorder, 31% suffered from major depression, 15% had an adjustment disorder, and 23% abused alcohol or drugs. In d'Orban's (1979) sample, 16% were psychotic, 21% experienced major depression, and 9% were diagnosed with substance abuse/dependence. McKee and Shea (1998) found similar results: 40% of their sample were diagnosed with psychosis or schizophrenia, 25% with major depression, 10% with an adjustment disorder, and 5% with substance abuse/dependence.

Lewis and Bunce (2003) discovered that 53% of the women in their sample had a psychotic diagnosis at the time of their commission of filicide. Lewis et al. (1998) found that 65% of their sample of filicidal women were diagnosed with schizophrenia, 20% had been diagnosed with bipolar affective disorder or schizoaffective disorder, and 30% had also reported a history of substance abuse/dependence. Wilczynski (1997) found that 90% of her sample had received at least one psychiatric diagnosis, primarily for depression (68%), suicide attempts (36%), and/or substance abuse (64%). These data were consistent with the findings of Crimmins et al. (1997), who discovered that 41% of their sample had had one or more prior suicide attempts and 64% had used alcohol or illegal drugs on a regular basis.

Holden et al. (1996) found that the majority of their sample of filicidal mothers suffered from severe mental illness. Few, however, were diagnosed with substance abuse. Meyer and Oberman's (2001) study of filicidal women found that in the "neglect" filicide category, 41% of the mothers were diagnosed with either mood disorders or substance abuse/dependence but that only 3% of the mothers in the "neonaticide" category had a mental illness. Alder and Polk (2001) found that the majority of mothers in the "filicide-suicide" category in their sample had been involved in mental health treatment before their arrests for murder of the children.

Victim Characteristics

Many studies of maternal filicide focus only on the characteristics of the mother rather than describing the features of the children they have killed. Of the studies that have indicated victim characteristics, the most frequently reported data have been the circumstances of the victim's birth, the number of child victims killed, child's age at death, and child's gender.

Circumstances of Child Victim's Birth

Many studies indicate that the location of the child's delivery, especially in neonaticide and first-week infanticide, is an important offense characteristic. Emerick et al. (1986) reported that a mother's delivery in a nonmedical setting is a significant risk factor in neonaticide, a finding also endorsed by Overpeck et al. (1998) and Cummings et al. (1994). Meyer and Oberman (2001) found that almost all of the women in the "neonaticide" category killed their newborns in bathrooms, bedrooms, or other nonmedical settings. Wilczynski (1997) reported that 94% of the maternal filicides in her sample occurred in the home and that 44% of the women delayed notifying the authorities. When a mother delivers alone, the possibility of an undetected neonaticide through direct action (suffocation, beating, etc.) or passive neglect (abandonment in a remote location) greatly increases. As described in other sections of this chapter, the mortality rate of newborns delivered and then discarded in nonhospital locations has been found to be very high (U.S. Department of Health & Human Services, 2004a).

Number of Child Victims

Most maternal filicides involve only one victim, primarily because neonaticides and infanticides are typically committed by first-time mothers. Some mothers, however, do kill more than one victim when they commit filicide.

For example, approximately 15% of the mothers in the studies by McKee and Shea (1998), Resnick (1969), and d'Orban (1979) killed more than one of their children. Lewis et al. (1998) discovered that 20% of the mothers in their sample had killed more than one child. Meyer and Oberman (2001) found that in their category of "purposeful" maternal filicides, 39% of the mothers had killed two or more children. Often, however, there were sibling survivors of maternal filicide: McKee and Shea (1998) found that 78% of the families with more than one infant had at least one surviving child. Meyer and Oberman (2001) reported that although two-thirds of the families in their "abuse" category had more than three children, in those cases only one had died at the hands of his or her mother.

Child's Age at Death

The majority of children killed are under the age of 6; indeed, the victim's age is typically used to differentiate neonaticides, infanticides, and filicides. All neonaticides occur on the first day of the newborn's life. Because of the very young age of most victims of maternal infanticide and filicide, their ages at death are typically reported in months rather than years. For example, Resnick (1969) found that the mean age of the child victims in his study was 41 months, compared with 36 months in McKee and Shea's (1998) research, 28 months in d'Orban's (1979) sample, 40 months in Crittenden and Craig's (1990) study, and 34 months in the cases reported by Bourget and Bradford (1990).

These data were highly consistent with the findings of Meyer and Oberman (2001), who indicated that in their "assisted-coerced" category, the mean age of the child victims was approximately 31 months, but it was 24 months in their "neglect" category of maternal filicide. Only 22% of the children in the sample of Crimmins et al. (1997) were older than 3 years. None of the child victims was older than age 12 in the studies by McKee and Shea (1998), d'Orban (1979), or Bourget and Bradford (1990), and only 5% of the children in Resnick's (1969) sample were younger than 13 when they died at the hands of their mothers. Alder and Polk (2001) discovered that the age of the child victims varied with the type of maternal filicide: In their cases of "filicide-suicide," the average age of the child was 10 years, but it was only 4 years in their cases of "fatal assault."

Gender of Child Victim

Most of the maternal filicide studies have indicated that the child victims are not predominantly either male or female. Certain studies have, however, indicated that there is a relationship between victim age and victim gender in child homicides. Among children under age 9, boys are as likely to be killed as girls; but from ages 10 to 18, males are five times more likely to be murdered by their fathers during domestic disputes (Maguire, Pastore, & Flanagan, 1993). When the perpetrator is the mother, her sons and daughters are equally likely to be victims. For example, the research of Lewis et al. (1998), Resnick (1969), and Bourget and Bradford (1990) found that daughters were slightly more likely to be killed, but only 46% of the daughters were victims in the study by McKee and Shea (1998). In samples of maternal filicide cases reported by Crittenden and Craig (1990) and Crimmins et al. (1997), the majority of the victims were male.

Offense and Forensic Characteristics

Offense characteristics include the method of child homicide, such as the use of weapons employed in the crime and the presence of a coperpetrator. Forensic characteristics include whether the woman confessed to her crime following her arrest and whether she was determined to be legally insane at the time of her murder of her child.

Method of Neonaticide, Infanticide, and/or Filicide

How the mother commits the homicidal act has been the subject of many studies. The method of killing the child has been found to vary widely depending on the age and vulnerability of the mother's victim.

Many mothers likely use the "hands on" methods of suffocation or drowning because the victims are most often very young children, under 5 years of age, who are incapable of presenting a physical threat to their mothers. Crittenden and Craig (1990) found that 79% of the maternal filicides in their sample involved suffocation or drowning. Meyer and Oberman (2001) discovered that in their sample of neonaticide cases, 70% of the newborns were smothered, 14% were drowned, and 11% died of exposure; however, in the infanticide and filicide cases in the "neglect-commission" category, almost 60% of the children were shaken, beaten, or thrown to their deaths.

Meyer and Oberman's (2001) data are consistent with the findings of Resnick (1969), who reported that 37% of the child victims died from suffocation or beatings, compared with 51% of the victims in d'Orban's (1979) study, who expired by similar means. McKee and Shea (1998) found that 70% of the victims of maternal filicide died either by suffocation or by physical assaults.

Weapons such as guns or knives are rarely employed by mothers, as illustrated by the research of McKee and Shea (0% of cases reported; 1998), d'Orban (4%; 1979), and Resnick (17%; 1969). Crittenden and Craig (1990) found a relationship between the victim's age and method of filicide. Neonaticides were committed by suffocation (27%), drowning (22%), or exposure (14%). By contrast, 65% of all children between the ages of 1 month and 5 years died from beatings, and most of the children older than 5 had been shot or stabbed.

Kunz and Bahr (1996) discovered a similar relationship between victim vulnerability (young age) and filicide method: 55% of the victims less than 1 week old had been suffocated, strangled, or drowned; but 83% of victims over 10 years of age had been either shot or stabbed. Lewis et al. (1998) also confirmed a relationship between victim age and filicide method: Younger children were suffocated (30%), beaten (13%), starved (12%), or drowned (8%), but older children were killed with guns or knives. Notably, Lewis et al. (1998) found that psychotic filicidal mothers were significantly more likely than nonpsychotic mothers to use a gun or knife to kill their children. Finally, Smithey (1998) confirmed that as the age of the victim increased, the level of violence of filicide also increased: Mothers were most likely to kill victims less than 4 months of age using suffocation or exposure/abandonment. However, head trauma perpetrated by the mother's boyfriend or child's stepfather was most common among older victims of filicide.

Arson has also been found to be a method of filicide for some mothers. Meyer and Oberman (2001) indicated that fire was employed in 37% of the cases in their "purposeful" category and in 16% of the cases in their "neglect-omission" category. McKee and Shea (1998) found that arson was involved in 20% of their cases, often being committed after the victims were asleep or had been sedated. Crimmins et al. (1997) reported that 11% of their cases involved fire—slightly higher than the 8% and 5% rates found by Smithey (1998) and Lewis et al. (1998), respectively.

Confession Following Arrest

Even though most maternal neonaticides, infanticides, and filicides are committed by women acting alone (McKee & Shea, 1998; Meyer & Oberman, 2001; Resnick, 1969; d'Orban, 1979), few studies have investigated the rate of confessions given by the mother once she has been arrested. In McKee and Shea's (1998) study of filicidal mothers, only 65% admitted culpability for their crimes when they were interrogated by the police. Wilczynski (1997) reported that 70% of her sample confessed to their crimes, but in the sample of Crimmins et al. (1997), only 38% of the mothers confessed to their filicides.

Insanity at the Time of Filicide

Legal insanity is generally defined as whether, *at the time of the crime,* the perpetrator did not know right from wrong because of severe mental illness (Melton, Petrila, Poythress, & Slobogin, 1997). Barbara's case, introduced in chapter 1, is an illustration of this legal issue: At the time she suffocated her children, did she know that she was breaking the law? Or, in her psychotic mental state, did she believe that she was saving her husband from becoming infected by her children? The insanity defense has been estimated to be successful in less than 0.1% (1 in 1,000) of all criminal trials (Melton et al., 1997; Turner & Ornstein, 1983).

Maternal filicide studies have found insanity to be a frequent verdict compared with the 0.1% standard in other criminal trials. For example, Bourget and Bradford (1990) reported that 15.4% of their maternal filicide cases ended in a decision that the mother was legally insane. In d'Orban's 1979 research, 27% of the maternal filicide defendants were acquitted on grounds of insanity, compared with 20% of the sample reported by McKee and Shea (1998). Lewis et al. (1998) discovered that 65% of the filicidal mothers in their sample had been adjudicated as not guilty by reason of insanity.

Wilczynski recently commented that "the first major limitation of the research on child homicide is simply its paucity" (1997, p. 11). Echoing her concerns, Alder and Baker declared: "Clearly we need to know much more before we can hope to understand these events" (2001, p.159). In this chapter I have presented the existing maternal filicide research to help to answer the questions "What do we know?" by identifying *who* (mothers, fathers, de facto parents, children under 5 years), *how* (suffocation, abandonment/exposure, beating, drowning, stabbing, shooting), *when* (at birth, early postpartum to age 1 year), and *where* (nonmedical settings, bedrooms, bathrooms, and public toilets) these tragedies occur.

3

Classification of Maternal Filicide

What Do We Know?

Parents kill their children for many different reasons under a variety of circumstances. Media reports, clinical case studies, and criminal justice statistics have amply demonstrated that neonaticide, infanticide, and filicide cannot be explained through a single construct, as though these unthinkable killings were homogeneous events. However, the clinical and academic research of the past few decades has suggested that similar patterns of parental filicide can be detected. In an effort to understand why parents kill their children, many researchers have developed classification systems to clarify communalities and differences among filicide cases.

Classification of cases is an important early step in the study of parental filicide: Systematic categorization facilitates communication among clinical and academic professionals in the same and related fields by providing a common, descriptive language to identify, analyze, and ideally prevent these events from occurring. Classification also improves the clinician's assessment and treatment of the filicidal parent, which in turn may enhance the validity and reliability of the explanatory system.

The first section of this chapter presents a review of the existing classifications of parental and maternal filicide, along with a discussion of the similarities among the systems. The limitations of the classification systems are then highlighted. Finally, I describe my maternal filicide classification system. Each category of my system is compared with the previous systems and then illustrated with a summary of the primary features of the mothers' characteristics for that category of the classification scheme.

Parental Filicide Classification Systems

Although filicide has been known to societies throughout history, the systematic and scientific study of these horrific acts has been a relatively recent phenomenon. In the first review of the world's literature on filicide, American forensic psychiatrist Philip Resnick (1969) found only 155 published case reports from 1751 through 1967. He developed the first classification of parental filicide based on the mother's or father's most apparent motive: altruism, acute psychosis, unwanted pregnancy, accident, or revenge against a spouse. Because Resnick's (1969, 1970) classification is still the most widely cited model and is the starting point for many subsequent systems in the literature, I discuss each of his categories in detail.

A parent's motive in "altruistic" filicide is to relieve the child of his or her current suffering, caused by a real or imagined condition, or to relieve the child's anticipated suffering caused by the parent's suicide. For example, a parent may suffocate her infant son to save him from a life of agony after learning that he has been diagnosed with an incurable disease that will result in prolonged pain. To the mother, her terrible act is not murder; rather she believes her filicide is born from compassion and love for her infant child. An example of Resnick's "altruistic" filicide is found under my category of psychotic/depressed mothers, suicidal type, in chapter 16: Suicidal Marilyn killed her children because she believed that they would experience lifelong emotional damage by growing up without her. To save her children from that terrible fate, she realized that they would have to join her in death.

Resnick's (1969) category of acute-psychosis filicides comprises parents who kill their children under the influence of severe mental illness, such as postpartum psychosis, bipolar affective disorder, or schizophrenia. In such cases, the parent's contact with reality has been significantly distorted through development of paranoid delusions and/or command auditory hallucinations of violence against the child. Barbara (whose story began in chapter 1 and is completed in chapter 13) is an example of this category of parental filicide due to her development of postpartum psychosis after the birth of each of her children. Barbara's case is an example of my category of psychotic/depressed mothers, delusional type.

In unwanted-child filicides, Resnick (1969) found that the murder occurred because a parent no longer desired to care for the child for reasons that were not psychotic ones, such as illegitimacy or uncertain paternity. This category is distinguished from the previous types in that the parent is not mentally ill, nor is the child killed for noble purposes; rather, the infant is murdered because the parent's bonding with the baby was insufficient or nonexistent. Notably, Resnick's research covered all filicide cases recorded between 1751 and 1967, a span of time during which social sanctions against unwed mothers and illegitimacy were much more severe.

Although today there are likely some children who are killed because of illegitimacy and/or uncertain paternity, our current cultural mores are not as socially punitive as in earlier years. These days, other reasons seem to negatively influence parent-infant attachment. In this casebook, unwanted-child homicides are included within my category of detached mothers, as illustrated by the cases of Cathy (denial type, chapter 6), Edna (ambivalent type, chapter 7), Francine (resentful type, chapter 8) and Glenda (exhausted type, chapter 9).

Resnick's (1969) category of "accidental" filicides described unintentional deaths that occur because of a parent's neglect or physical abuse of the child from excessive punishment. In contrast to the three previous categories, the parent's motive is not to kill. Instead, a filicide occurs by parental neglect, such as failure to adequately supervise the child, or by extreme physical discipline, such as shaking or hitting. The prevalence of child abuse and neglect in the United States described in chapter 2 and the high mortality rates that result from those situations attest to the commonness of "accidental" filicides. My category of abusive/neglectful mothers is represented by the cases of Harriet (recurrent type, chapter 10), Janet (reactive type, chapter 11), and Kaye (inadequate type, chapter 12), which illustrate the characteristics and circumstances that may precede a mother's accidental or neglectful killing of her child.

Finally, in spouse-revenge cases, Resnick (1969) believed that a parent's homicidal impulse was directed onto the child as a deliberate attempt to make his or her spouse suffer. For example, feeling outraged that his wife would dare to leave him, a father might kill his child, knowing that the toddler's death will result in lifelong agony for his estranged wife. Resnick (1969) considered this type of filicide to be very uncommon, and subsequent research has shown that often spouse-revenge or retaliatory cases are the smallest category in the classification system. Although some authors have noted that there has been little empirical support for such filicides by mothers (Meyer & Oberman, 2001), Resnick found that 2% of his sample were of this type, which was consistent with the results of McKee and Shea (1998), d'Orban (1979), and Bourget and Bradford (1990). In this casebook, a single case in the retaliatory mothers category is described in the story of Olivia in chapter 17.

Resnick's research sparked the development of many other explanatory systems of parental filicide (Baker, 1991; Bourget & Bradford, 1990; Scott, 1973; Wilczynski, 1997). These studies have found that the reasons for filicide by fathers and mothers are often quite different.

In 1973, British psychiatrist P. D. Scott, drawing heavily on Resnick's typology, suggested that parental motives in filicides included not wanting the children, the belief in "mercy" killings, gross mental pathology in the parent, parental revenge, or victim-precipitated parental frustration (e.g., child abuse). The definitions and characteristics of his categories were highly similar to those in Resnick's (1969) system.

Canadian psychiatrists Dominique Bourget and John Bradford, in their 1990 study of 13 parental filicides, found four likely motives: "accidental" homicides due to abuse and discipline, "pathological" homicides due to the parent's mental illness, "neonaticide" homicides occurring within 24 hours of birth, and "retaliating" homicides due to a parent's wish to punish his or her spouse. Notably, Bourget and Bradford (1990) were unable to classify any fathers within their four categories, and thus they established a single category of "paternal" filicide. In contrast to Resnick's (1969) finding that mental illness characterized the largest number of filicidal participants, Bourget and Bradford (1990) found that fewer than one-fourth of their cases fell into the "pathological" categories. They reported that almost half of their cases were categorized as "accidental" filicides, unlike Resnick's relatively small group of similarly labeled cases. Bourget and Bradford's (1990) smallest group was that of "retaliating" filicides, similar to the findings of Resnick (1969, 1970).

In 1991, Australian researcher June Baker developed a classification system of parental filicide that reflects six major motives: altruism, spouse revenge, jealousy and rejection, unwanted child, discipline-related cases, and self-defense. Baker (1991) found that mothers and fathers were not equivalent in their reasons for filicide: "Unwanted" child cases (neonaticides) were committed only by mothers, whereas fathers were the only perpetrators of spouse revenge, jealousy/rejection, and self-defense child homicides.

The explanatory system of parental filicide with the highest number of categories was authored by Ania Wilczynski in 1997 and based on her samples of English and Australian parents convicted of child homicide. She based her classification scheme on the parent's alleged motive, which she found to be the only way to give meaning to seemingly senseless filicidal acts. She proposed that cases could be classified on the basis of the parent's primary and secondary motives, because the parent's reasons for their crimes do not always fit neatly into only one category of motive.

A primary motive was defined as the predominant, relatively enduring reason or cause for the filicide. Secondary motives were described as reasons that were of lesser importance to the explanation of the filicide. For example, if a mentally ill mother were having auditory command hallucinations telling her to punish her son, who then died from the beating, the primary motive would be "psychosis," and the secondary motive would be "disciplinary." However, if the mother's mental illness were under control through medications and did not appear to be directly relevant to her filicidal punishment of her son, then "disciplinary" would be the primary motive and "psychosis" the secondary motive.

Wilczynski (1997) identified 10 categories of parental motives: retaliating, unwanted child (including neonaticide), altruistic, disciplinary, psychosis in the parent, no intent to kill or injure (e.g., neglect), jealousy of or rejection by the child victim, ritual or sexual abuse of the child, Munchausen syndrome by proxy, and unknown (insufficient data) reason. Her definitions of retaliating, unwanted child, altruistic, disciplinary, psychosis in the parent, no intent to kill or injure, and unknown reasons are similar to those already described. Her proposal to include filicides based on parental motives of jealousy of or rejection by the child victim, ritual or sexual abuse of the child, and Munchausen syndrome by proxy warrant further explanation, because they are relatively rare categories in the research literature of parental filicide.

Wilczynski's (1997) category of jealousy of or rejection by the child victim comprises those cases in which the parents killed their children because they believed that they were not the biological parents, because they were angered that the child was unresponsive to them because of previous parental abuse, or because they thought the child was a financial impediment to their careers. This category also contained cases in which the parent was jealous of the attention the child received from or gave to the other parent or was angered because the child had altered their marital/partner relationship. Parents in this category tended to have a narcissistic, insecure relationship with their spouses or partners: Filicide removed the children as rivals for their partners' affection. Wilczynski (1997) found, consistent with the research of Baker (1991), that fathers were the predominant perpetrators of this type of filicide.

The parents in Wilczynski's (1997) category of ritual or sexual abuse of the child killed their children inadvertently during a sexual assault, murdered the children to prevent disclosure of the molestations, or committed filicide as part of an organized satanic ritual. Although she proposed this category as part of her classification scheme, Wilczynski was unable to find any cases in her review of coroner, prosecution, social service, and police files in London from 1983 to 1984 and in Australia from 1989 to 1991. Wilczynski suggested that the reason for not discovering any cases in this category was perhaps the lack of professional awareness (and documentation) of child sexual abuse during the time period of her records review.

Wilczynski (1997) also suggested that some filicides were the result of Munchausen syndrome by proxy (MBP), a psychiatric disorder in which the parent repetitively, but covertly, induces illness in his or her child to gain for him- or herself the attention and sympathy of medical personnel (Schreier & Libow, 1993). The disorder is very difficult to detect because the perpetrator often abruptly leaves medical care if suspicions are raised. Also, many medical personnel may be reluctant to engage in the ethically delicate investigatory procedures needed to validate criminal charges, such as covert videotape recordings of mother-child interactions in the hospital. I have seen a number of MBP cases, one of which (Rhonda, chapter 20) resulted in a filicide placed in the psychopathic mother, narcissistic type category.

Consistent with results of Resnick (1969, 1970), Bourget and Bradford (1990), and Baker (1991), Wilczynski (1997) found that some categories were predominantly more descriptive either of fathers or of mothers. Filicides based on retaliation and on jealousy or rejection almost exclusively involved fathers. Mothers, in contrast, were the parents who most likely committed filicide because the child was unwanted, because of Munchausen syndrome by proxy, or because of psychotic motives. She found that fathers were slightly more likely than mothers to kill their children for disciplinary reasons (Wilczynski, 1997).

Maternal Filicide Classification Systems

Other classification systems have focused exclusively on filicides perpetrated by mothers, perhaps because their motives appear to be more varied, complex, and perplexing than those of fathers. The first maternal filicide model was developed by British psychiatrist P. T. d'Orban and based on a review of 89 women incarcerated for child homicide. D'Orban (1979) found that the women's motives could be classified into six groups: battering, mentally ill, neonaticide, retaliating, unwanted, and mercy killings. The model incorporated neonaticides and was a modification of Scott's (1973) system based on the source of the impulse (e.g., emanating from the parent, child, situation, etc.) for the mother's homicidal act. The definitions of each category were similar to those of other researchers, as described previously in this chapter. In d'Orban's sample, 40% of the mothers had battered their children, 27% were mentally ill, 12% had committed neonaticide, 11% had retaliatory motives, and 9% had not wanted their children; only 1 of the cases was categorized as a mercy killing (d'Orban, 1979).

Alder and Polk (2001) reviewed 32 mother-perpetrated filicides and found three primary types: filicide-suicide, fatal assaults, and neonaticide. They described mothers in the filicide-suicide category as women who killed their children, then attempted or completed their own deaths because they were so overwhelmed by their personal and familial circumstances. They found that mothers in the fatal-assault group often had histories of abusing their children but did not intend to commit murder. Alder and Polk (2001) discovered that the neonaticidal mothers killed their children because they never psychologically adjusted to pregnancy and dreaded the consequences that would follow their children's births. Though Alder and Polk (2001) had, to date, developed a classification system with the fewest categories, they noted that mothers' motives for filicide are likely much more varied and complex.

The maternal filicide system that is based on the largest number of cases was developed in 2001 by Americans Cheryl Meyer, a psychologist, and Michelle Oberman, a professor of law. The coauthors and their research team reviewed maternal filicide cases reported from 1990 to 1999 in the NEXIS news database, which provided complete text articles from American news magazines, regional and national newspapers, newsletters, trade magazines, and abstracts, in addition to transcripts of television and radio broadcasts (Meyer & Oberman, 2001). The resulting 219 cases were condensed into five categories of maternal filicide: ignored pregnancy (17% of the sample), abuse-related filicides (7%), neglect (35%), purposeful filicides (36%), and assisted/coerced filicides (5%).

Ignored-pregnancy cases were exclusively neonaticides, committed principally by young women who denied or concealed their condition. Abuse-related cases were committed by mothers who, during the course of discipline, accidentally killed their children. In neglect cases, the children died either as a result of the mothers' failure to provide adequate nutrition, health, or safety (e.g., the child died of dehydration in an enclosed car) or by an irresponsible act such as shaking a crying infant. The largest category, purposeful cases, included mothers who were experiencing emotional distress, personality disorders, or major mental illness (e.g., postpartum psychosis) prior to and at the time of the children's deaths. Assisted/coerced filicides involved cases in which mothers either helped their partners or were forced by their partners to kill their children.

Similarities Among Classifications of Maternal Filicide

Although many of the classification systems of maternal filicide have been based on cases from countries other than the United States, a number of the explanatory models have identified the same or similar motives (see table 3.1). In particular, the various systems highlight the mother's mental illness (e.g., "pathological," "mentally ill," "acutely psychotic"), lack of bonding with the child ("neonaticide," "unwanted child," "ignored pregnancy"), or inadequate parenting ("accidental," "discipline-related," "neglect").

In addition to the commonality of motives cited in maternal filicide classification systems, researchers have found comparable frequencies of cases within similar categories. For example, McKee and Shea (1998) compared the characteristics of their sample of 20 pretrial defendant-mothers charged with killing their children with the maternal filicide samples of Resnick (1969), d'Orban (1979), and Bourget and Bradford (1990). The samples were compared in terms of similarities in classification categories, as well as of the mothers' historical, clinical, offense, forensic, and victim characteristics. Remarkable consistencies were found in the relative frequencies of mothers classified in common categories. Each of the samples contained very few cases of neonaticide, ranging from approximately 18% (Resnick, 1969) to 8% (Bourget & Bradford, 1990). Cases that reflected retaliation were found to be the smallest category in each of the samples, from 8% in Bourget and Bradford's (1990) study to 4% in the study by Resnick (1969). Although the samples revealed different percentages in the categories of "pathological" (mentally ill) filicides and "accidental" filicides, these two categories were either the largest or second largest in each of the four studies.

Meyer and Oberman's (2001) sample of filicidal mothers revealed similar results in the relative sizes of their classification categories. Combining their neglect and abuse-related cases into a single category would account for 42% of their sample. Their "purposeful" category, which included 36% of the mothers, was equivalent to the "pathological" motive cases found in the samples of McKee and Shea (1998), Resnick (1969), d'Orban (1979), and Bourget and Bradford (1990). Similar to those studies, Meyer and Oberman (2001) discovered that less than 20% of their sample involved cases of neonaticide.

A cross-national comparative study by Cheung (1986) found consistency between the frequencies of d'Orban's (1979) maternal filicide categories and

Table 3.1

Comparison of Maternal Filicide Classification Systems

Author	Emphasis				
	Rejection	Unintended	Mental/Illness	Retaliation	Antisocial
Resnick (1969)	Unwanted	Accidental	Acute Psychosis	Spouse Revenge	None
d'Orban (1979)	Unwanted	Battering	Mentally ill	Retaliating	None
Adler & Polk (2001)	Neonaticide	Fatal assault	Filicide–suicide	None	None
Meyer & Oberman (2001)	Ignored	Abuse/neglect	Purposeful	None	Assisted
McKee (2006)	Detached	Accidental/neglectful	Psychotic/depressed	Retaliatory	Psychopathic

those of his own sample of 35 Hong Kong women who had killed one or more of their children. Cheung (1986) reported that the majority of filicidal women were either battering or mentally ill mothers, categories that comprised 67% of d'Orban's group and 71% of Cheung's sample. Comparable frequencies were also found in neonaticide (12% and 17%, respectively) and retaliatory (10% and 9%, respectively) cases.

Most recently, Oberman (2003) has explored the research literature on maternal filicide in India, Fiji, and Hungary and found notable contrasts to the data from the English-speaking countries. For example, she noted that in one study in India, female newborns were three times more likely to be victims of neonaticide than boys. In another study from the same country, 570 of 600 female babies were killed within days of their births, with 80% dying at the hands of their mothers (Oberman, 2003). In contrast to psychological motives that might underlie maternal neonaticide and infanticide in the United States, Oberman found that in India the female newborns were selectively killed by their mothers, principally for economic and familial reasons. She reported that most women in that country are poor and undereducated and rely on their husbands for safety and food. Thus, when a girl is born, the mother is often encouraged by the impoverished family to end the child's life.

In Fiji, Oberman (2003) found similarities to the United States in terms of young, unmarried prospective mothers concealing their pregnancies and giving birth alone as a prelude to neonaticide. She also noted that in maternal filicide cases, spousal domestic violence is a common theme and that many mothers, for altruistic reasons, commit suicide and filicide out of concern for their children's welfare. In Hungary, Oberman (2003) found that many newborns are abandoned by their mothers each year. She noted that economic and punitive legal reasons often underlie these neonaticides: The Hungarian government has nearly doubled cost of a legal abortion and has quadrupled the maximum prison sentence if a filicidal mother is convicted.

A New Classification of Maternal Filicide

The new classification system described within this casebook is based on my numerous forensic psychological evaluations of adolescent and adult women who had been criminally charged with the deaths of their children. The mothers were examined individually with multiple clinical interviews and psychological testing, either in response to a court order or at the request of the mother-defendants' attorneys.

Each evaluation comprised an extensive inquiry into the mother's personal, familial, clinical/mental health, educational, vocational, interpersonal, marital, medical, substance abuse, and criminal histories. These clinical interviews were conducted over many sessions of several hours' duration. The mother's family members were interviewed; additionally, I reviewed records, reports, and other documents from prior clinical/mental health, medical, legal/correctional, and/or educational services. As part of the evaluation I also reviewed records and reports of police officers, detectives, and medical examiners who had investigated the children's deaths.. The broad array of information from every case that detailed each mother's preoffense thoughts, emotions, perceptions, and behaviors became the foundation for my classification system and the chapters in this book.

The classification includes the following categories: detached mothers, abusive/neglectful mothers, psychotic/depressed mothers, retaliatory mothers, and psychopathic mothers, a new category not previously described in prior systems.

In the detached-mothers category, the bonding of the mother to her child has either not developed or is unwanted. This category is illustrated by two cases of neonaticide and two cases of early postpartum (birth to age 6 months) infanticide. The category is subdivided into four types—denial, ambivalent, resentful, and exhausted—that reflect the mothers' underlying motivation.

The abusive/neglectful mothers category reflects the condition that the mother-child relationship is characterized by either excessive or nonexistent discipline and behavioral limit setting. The category is subdivided into three types—recurrent, reactive, and inadequate—that describe the nature of the mothers' failed parenting.

The psychotic/depressed mothers category is characterized by maternal mental illness that negatively influences the mothers' perceptions of and relationship to their children. The category is subdivided into three types—delusional, impulsive, and suicidal—that reflect the mothers' most descriptive diagnoses or symptom patterns.

The retaliatory mothers category highlights the mother's wish to punish others' interference in her relationship to her child through the commission of infanticide or filicide. Because of its singular motive, the category is not divided into types.

The category of psychopathic mothers describes mothers whose relationships to their children are characterized by maternal exploitation and self-indulgence. The category is subdivided into three types that reflect the primary reasons for their self-serving use of their offspring—financial, addicted, and narcissistic.

The new classification system has been developed along relational, contextual, and developmental dimensions to help explain maternal motivations. The name of each category describes the nature and quality of the relationship of the mother with her child or children. For example, the women within the abusive/neglectful mothers category may have achieved bonding with their children, but the nature and quality of their relationships are aggressive or inattentive. In the psychotic/depressed mothers category, the parent-child relationship is most aptly depicted as irrational and/or hopeless. The hallmark of this type of maternal filicide is the mother's distorted view of reality due to incapacitating mental illness that is characterized by delusions, hallucinations, and/or a despondent, unchanging perception of the future. In the retaliatory category, the mother-child relationship is fused into a single hyperdefensive nonpsychotic "us against the world" entity wherein the mother obsessively believes that loss of her child is equivalent to loss of her own identity and existence. The women in the psychopathic mothers category have an unempathic, insensitive relationship with their children and use their sons or daughters to satisfy or indulge their own needs and wishes.

The types within each category illustrate the contextual dimension and indicate the most probable circumstances that led to the mother's commission of child homicide. Many of the types are defined in terms of primary psychiatric symptoms or diagnoses, consistent with numerous research studies that highlight the influence of mental disorders in maternal filicide. Other types are descriptive of mothers' typical emotional reactions (e.g., impulsive, reactive, resentful, etc.) or preoffense situational circumstances (e.g., exhausted, financial, etc.). The identification of categories and types provides likely explanations for the mothers' actions and also suggests what changes might have been made to prevent the children's deaths.

The basic classification of the acts of neonaticide, infanticide, and filicide are based on the child's age at death. The primary limitation of this type of classification is that the categories do not illuminate the characteristics of the mother-perpetrator from which an understanding and sufficient explanation of these horrific acts could be developed. Further, a classification model based only on age of death does not inform risk analysis and prevention strategies that might be undertaken by the mother herself, her family and community, or the attending clinician.

Although a large minority of maternal filicides occur within the first year of the children's lives and although almost all victims are under the age of 5 at the time of their deaths, research indicates that a number of children of elementary school and prepubertal age are also killed by their mothers. A classification of maternal filicide must therefore address the developmental changes that occur over the course of the child's life, as well as explain the demands on the evolving mother-child relationship imposed by those chronological changes.

The developmental dimension is demonstrated in this book by the emphasis on issues of pregnancy and initial maternal bonding, exemplified by the detached-mothers category. The demands on the primary child-care provider (the mother) to cope with the infant's immaturity in communication and continuing need for supervision is exemplified principally by the abusive/neglectful mothers grouping. The category of psychotic/depressed mothers highlights the tremendous emotional impact of pregnancy, delivery, and subsequent adjustment to parenting on the mother's psychological well-being and mental health. The cases included in the retaliatory and psychopathic categories illustrate long-term maternal personality disorders that have created deficient parenting relationships between these mothers and their older children.

My Maternal Filicide Risk Matrix (chapter 4) and the case studies in chapters 6 through 19 further amplify the developmental dimension of the classification system. The Risk Matrix illustrates stages in the mother's life: prepregnancy, pregnancy/delivery, early postpartum (to 6 months), late postpartum (6 months to 1 year), and postinfancy (more than 1 year from birth). A Risk Matrix assessment of every mother's risk and protective factors is completed to the appropriate stage. For neonaticide and infanticide cases, the Risk Matrix analysis terminates in the pregnancy/delivery or early or late postpartum stages, respectively. The risk matrix analyses for filicide cases are completed through the postinfancy stage.

Through the new classification system, the maternal filicide risk matrix, and the subsequent case study chapters, I hope that the reader will find answers to the question that drives this book. Why do mothers kill their children?

4

Risk Analysis and the Maternal Filicide Risk Matrix

In the last quarter century, research and clinical methods of violence assessment have been extended to many areas of human interaction, including marital and family violence (battered women, child abuse, parricide), interpersonal conflict (stalking, date rape, sexual harassment), workplace violence, criminal sentencing and the death penalty, inmate aggression, adolescent delinquency, postincarceration civil commitment of sexually dangerous inmates, involuntary psychiatric hospitalization of mentally ill citizens, and terrorism (Reid & Stout, 2003). This casebook broadens the professional literature of risk analysis to the areas of maternal neonaticide, infanticide, and filicide.

Key Terms of Risk Analysis

Target and Signal Behaviors

In risk analysis of violence, the outcome or *target behavior* is the act that is of ultimate concern. For cases of risk analysis in neonaticide, infanticide, and filicide, the target behavior is the homicide of a child by his or her parent. Because the ultimate purpose of risk analysis is to prevent a target behavior from occurring, it is important to identify *signal behaviors,* those acts by the perpetrator that precede and that may be predictive of the target behavior. The alteration of these precipitating behaviors through various interventions (e.g., medications, psychotherapy, hospitalization, etc.) might reduce the likelihood of the target behavior occurring.

Barbara's case, which was introduced in chapter 1, illustrated many signal behaviors that preceded her murder of Marcus and Heather. After her son was born, she had her first episode of postpartum depression, which her physician, unfortunately, dismissed as only "baby blues." Her difficulty in caring for Marcus, indifference to her personal hygiene, and inability to maintain the household were examples of signal behaviors of a major depressive episode that her husband, fortunately, recognized.

The psychiatrist's prescription of antidepressant medication was an example of the identification *and* alteration of her signal behaviors: With Barbara's major depression under control, she was less likely to harm Marcus or herself. When she became pregnant with Heather, Barbara's major depression returned, accompanied by recurrent, severe panic attacks. These signal behaviors, which occurred prior to her daughter's birth, illustrated even further mental deterioration. Barbara's postpartum fearful, anxious paranoid behavior, social isolation, and inability to manage her children—clear indications that something was seriously wrong with her—were signal behaviors that foreshadowed the tragic end of her children's lives.

Risk and Protective Factors

Risk factors are characteristics, conditions, circumstances, and/or signal behaviors that are associated with an *increased* likelihood of the target behavior occurring. The source of risk factors may be within the individual (e.g., demographic characteristics, current mental status and emotional functioning, mental health history, etc.) or may stem from the individual's family of origin relationships and characteristics (e.g., parents, siblings, relatives, family mental health history, etc.) or from the individual's immediate situational circumstances (spouse/partner relationships, child-care responsibilities, health care access, employment obligations, etc.). Examples from Barbara's case prior to the deaths of her children included the risk factors of her paranoid delusions and auditory hallucinations, her history of postpartum depression, her fears of being hospitalized, and her exhaustion from her daily responsibilities as the sole caretaker of two very young children.

Protective factors are characteristics, conditions, and/or circumstances that are associated with a *decreased* likelihood of the target behavior occurring. As with risk factors, the source of a protective factor may be within the individual or may arise from the individual's family of origin or from the individual's immediate situational circumstances. Risk analysis involves the systematic assessment of both risk and protective factors to provide a thorough, balanced evaluation of the individual's likelihood of committing signal and target behaviors. The consideration of protective factors is an extremely important step in risk analysis that has been often overlooked by clinicians (Rogers, 2000).

A protective factor may be the absence of a risk factor (e.g., no history of prior violence), the opposite extreme of a continuum (e.g., sobriety versus intoxication), or a middle range of a factor (e.g., normal mood vs. major depression or mania). For example, a 14-year-old single mother with a childhood history of physical abuse victimization (risk factors) may be more likely to physically abuse her own child (a signal behavior of filicide) than a 26-year-old married mother who employs "time out" or restriction of privileges when her child misbehaves because she was raised by parents who disciplined their children with nonviolent methods (protective factors). In Barbara's case, protective factors included her older age, two intended pregnancies, post—high school education, and stable marital status. Additional protective factors were her husband's ongoing support and concern about her mental well-being, his continued employment and financial stability, and the ready availability of medical and psychiatric care.

Table 4.1 illustrates the array of risk and protective factors that have been drawn from the worldwide empirical and clinical research on maternal neonaticide, infanticide, and filicide, as described in chapter 2. The factors have been organized into the individual, family of origin, and situational domains to reflect the principal sources for risk and protective markers. Examples, which are designated with an asterisk (*), have been cited in the professional literature as relevant risk or protective factors for child homicide by a mother. The smaller list of empirically based protective factors reflects Rogers's (2000) concerns that researchers too often emphasize only risk factors in their analyses of violent behavior.

The Maternal Filicide Risk Matrix

The acts of maternal neonaticide, infanticide, or filicide are complex, multi-faceted occurrences emanating from many different sources that may operate simultaneously. The Maternal Filicide Risk Matrix described in this section organizes a mother's risk and protective factors along two dimensions: domain (individual, family of origin, and situational) and stage (prepregnancy, pregnancy/delivery, early postpartum, late postpartum, and postinfancy). An example of the Risk Matrix as applied to Barbara's case in shown in table 4.2.

The Risk Matrix is not yet an empirically validated risk assessment instrument and thus should not be used as the sole basis for making significant clinical or agency decisions (e.g., foster care placement of a child of an abusive or neglectful mother). By specifying stages before, during, and after pregnancy, however, the Risk Matrix can be employed by the clinician to identify risk and/or protective factors that have preceded the current risk analysis and can plan interventions to maximize protective factors in subsequent stages.

For example, suppose an evaluating clinician knew that an unexpectedly pregnant teenage mother in her third trimester had a prepregnancy stage history of substance abuse, childhood physical abuse victimization, parental abandonment, and suicide attempts and a pregnancy/delivery stage characterized by frequently missed prenatal health care appointments and an unsupportive partner. By organizing the combinations of her risk and protective factors with the Risk Matrix, the clinician might begin planning interventions such as ensuring another's presence at delivery, arranging for hospital birthing, informing the mother about the state's "safe haven" laws, making appoint-

Table 4.1
Maternal Filicide Risk and Protective Factors

Factor	Risk	Protective
Individual		
Age	< 16*; teenage*	Over 21; 25+*
Intelligence	Low IQ,* mental retardation*	Average or above average
Education	< 10th grade*; < 12th grade*	College graduate*
Medical status	No prenatal care*; HIV/AIDS*	Prenatal care in first trimester*
Emotional status	Postpartum mood disorders* psychosis* Substance abuse* Suicide attempt history*	No mental disorder diagnoses
Trauma history	Physical or sexual abuse* Childhood loss of mother*	No prior trauma*
Maternal attitudes	Denial of pregnancy* Negative attitude to pregnancy* Unassisted birth* Nonhospital delivery* Abuse, neglect of prior child* Plans to abandon child at hospital* Edinburgh Postnatal Depression Scale score < 10* Difficult birth*	Intended pregnancy* Positive attitude to pregnancy* Prenatal, postnatal care* Hospital delivery* Edinburgh Postnatal Depression Scale score > 10*
Family of Origin		
Mother as parent	Poor bonding with child* History of mental illness,* substance abuse* Child abuse perpetrator* Absent or abandoned family*	Intended pregnancy* Positive bonding with child*
Father as parent	Child abuse, spouse abuse, incest perpetrator* Mental illness,* substance abuse* Absent or abandoned family	Nonviolent parenting Sufficient as provider Positive bonding with child
Marital/family	Frequent parental separations* Marital violence* Divorce* Financial instability, relocations	Nonviolent relationship Nurturing to all family

continued

Table 4.1
continued

Factor	Risk	Protective
Situational		
Marital/partner	Single parent*; abusive partner*	Nonviolent to mother/baby
	Partner substance abuse*	Absence of substance abuse
	Nonbiological father as parent*	Supportive to mother/baby
Financial status	Unemployed/poor,* Low SES*	Adequate income, resources
Child-care status	Having 2 or more children if under age 17*	Supportive, helpful partner
	Sole caretaker*	Supportive, helpful parents
	Sibling abuse*	Supportive, helpful relatives
	Many children in mother's care*	
	Baby youngest of many in care*	
Infant's temperament	Child difficult to care for*	Positive, secure attachment with baby
	Lack of sleep for mother*	Healthy child
	Prior abuse of infant/child*	Child has calm, quiet demeanor

Note: * = factor cited in empirical research

ments for outpatient counseling in anticipation of postpartum depression, and enrollment in parent education classes.

Another unexpectedly pregnant third-trimester mother, however, might be seen as having a much lower need for interventions. In this case, the clinician knew that the mother had faithfully attended prenatal medical appointments, delayed pregnancy until she finished high school, abstained from substance abuse, arranged for a hospital delivery, and had supportive parents who would assist her with child care. Because her individual, family of origin, and situational elements at the prepregnancy and pregnancy/delivery stages reflected fewer risk factors and more protective factors, there would likely be less need for nonfamily public agency interventions after her child was born.

As illustrated by the case of Barbara and other filicidal mothers of multiple children in subsequent chapters, the Risk Matrix may also be implemented to assess the risk and protective factors impinging on a woman's earlier pregnancy, delivery, and mothering as a guide to the clinician's current analysis. Her prior personal experiences with her other children, her family of origin's reactions to her mothering of the children, and the situational factors that

Table 4.2
Maternal Filicide Risk Matrix: Barbara (for Heather)

Factor	Pre-P	P/D	EP	LP	PI
Individual					
Age at current pregnancy	P	P	P	P	
Intelligence level	P	P	P	P	
Education level	P	P	P	P	
Medical status	P	P	P	P	
Emotional status	R	R	R	R	
Trauma history	P	P	P	P	
Maternal attitudes	P	R	R	R	
Family of Origin					
Mother's parenting	R	R	R	R	
Father's parenting	P	R	R	R	
Marital/family stability	P	P	P	P	
Situational					
Marital/partner status	P	P	P	P	
Financial status	P	P	P	P	
Child-care status	R	R	R	R	
Infant's temperament	P	P	P	P	

Note: R = Risk; P = Protective; Pre-P = Prepregnancy; P/D = Pregnancy/delivery; EP = Early postpartum; LP = Late postpartum; PI = Postinfancy.

occurred previously would be assessed within her current prepregnancy stage, and they would have a significant impact on her behavior and attitudes when she became pregnant again.

If a previously implemented intervention had successfully remedied a prior risk factor, that information would help the clinician to structure current prevention efforts if that factor again should pose a risk to the new baby's welfare. For example, if a woman had become suicidal during the postinfancy stage with a previous child but had then responded well to antidepressant medication and individual psychotherapy, the clinician might arrange for a series of counseling sessions during her early and late postpartum stages to prevent a relapse in her emotional functioning after she gives birth to her current child.

Individual Domain

Age at Pregnancy
The mother's age has been a consistently studied variable in filicide research. Studies have generally shown that the younger the mother is, the higher is her

risk of neonaticide or infanticide. Young, first-time mothers, especially girls under age 16, have often become pregnant unexpectedly either because of ignorance of effective contraception or because of immature, impulsive decision making characteristic of adolescents. Because most girls under 16 are still living at home, their fear of their parents' reaction to their pregnancy might lead them to take desperate steps to avoid discovery of their condition. Their fear of disclosure of their pregnancy by others may cause them to avoid regular prenatal medical care and result in their giving birth in a nonmedical setting such as a bedroom or a bathroom.

In contrast, unexpectedly pregnant adult women are most likely free of parental supervision and have the legal authority to implement decisions (e.g., abortion, adoption) that allow them to avoid neonaticide or infanticide. As indicated in chapter 2, Overpeck, Brenner, and Trumble (1998) found that the neonaticide/infanticide base rate of new mothers under 15 years of age was seven times higher than the base rate of new mothers over age 25.

> Barbara was over 25 years old during all stages pertaining to her second pregnancy, suggesting that this element was a protective factor for her.

Intelligence

A mother's intellectual capacity has a direct bearing on her decision-making and help-seeking abilities before, during, and after pregnancy. Many studies have cited low intelligence as an individual characteristic in maternal filicide cases. Girls and women of lower intelligence are likely to be less well informed about contraception, pregnancy care, or postpartum maternal obligations, and thus they may be less able to manage their lives once they become unexpectedly pregnant. Though teenage girls of limited intelligence are particularly vulnerable to unprotected sexual activity, so too are adult women with mental retardation who live without supervision in the community. Persons of limited intellect may have difficulty reading and comprehending written material or learning and retaining new information; thus they may incorrectly apply sex education, parenting education, or baby safety programs provided by schools, child protection agencies, or pediatric medical staff.

In contrast, girls and women with normal or above-average intelligence generally have the capacity to consider various alternative solutions to problems, comprehend educational material, retain information, and anticipate long-term consequences of acts. In sum, they are more able to draw on a wider array of resources in their decision making about pregnancy and parenting.

> Barbara was neither mentally retarded nor of below-average intellect; thus this element was a protective factor for her.

Education

Many studies have shown that low educational levels are a characteristic of neonaticidal, infanticidal, and filicidal mothers. For example, the rate of high school dropouts among filicidal mothers was as high as 80% in one sample (Wilczynski, 1997). The new mothers have often become pregnant while still in school, raising their risk for neonaticide. Even among older women, however, lower education levels are associated with lower socioeconomic status, lower rates of employment, and fewer financial resources. Thus these women are often struggling to adequately manage their own lives, along with the obligations of new motherhood (McKee & Shea, 1998). One systematic comparative study of education as a risk factor found that the base rate of filicide by mothers who did not complete high school was eight times higher than the filicidal base rate of mothers who had completed at least 15 years of education (Overpeck et al., 1998).

> Barbara was a high school graduate with some college credits at the time of the birth of her first and second babies; thus this element was a protective factor for her.

Medical Status

Medical status as a risk or protective factor encompasses the mother's health prior to, during, and following pregnancy. There have been few maternal filicide studies that specifically investigate a mother's medical health status per se except in terms of use of prenatal care. Neonaticide cases of abandoned babies are frequently found to be the result of hidden or denied pregnancies, cases in which the mother has avoided prenatal medical care as a way of preventing discovery of her condition. In one comparative study of birthing location, the base rate of neonaticide and infanticide was eight times higher in mothers who gave birth in nonmedical settings than in mothers who delivered in hospitals (Overpeck, 2003).

A mother's medical status might also include such conditions as morbid obesity. This condition carries risks of accidental late-postpartum infanticide and postinfancy filicide because of exhaustion that results in negligent maternal supervision or "layover suffocation" of babies nursed in bed. A mother's newly discovered terminal illness might indicate an increased risk of a filicide-suicide outcome, especially in a single mother without family or partner support.

The presence of sexually transmitted diseases (STDs) discovered during a prospective mother's prepregnancy stage may signal a pattern of careless or uninformed sexual activity that might foreshadow an unexpected or unwanted pregnancy and thus an increased risk of neonaticide. The prevalence of HIV/AIDS is especially high in studies of mothers who have abandoned their babies (U.S. Department of Health and Human Services, 2004a). If a pregnant mother discovers she has HIV/AIDS, she might be at increased risk for committing neonaticide or infanticide because she cannot bear the thought of her child being ravaged by the same disease. Another medical risk factor might be occasional recreational illegal drug use (e.g., cocaine, etc.)—the mother's fear of felony charges for possessing and using illicit drugs and/or of infecting her baby with drugs may result in a hidden neonaticide or infanticide as a means of escaping arrest and prosecution. Notably, studies of babies abandoned in hospitals have indicated an extremely high prevalence of maternal drug use (U.S. Department of Health and Human Services, 2004a).

In contrast, prospective mothers who are medically healthy, who obtain regular prenatal care, who are free of illicit drug use, and who give birth in hospital settings are generally at much lower risk for baby abandonment, neonaticide, infanticide, and filicide.

> Barbara appears to have been in reasonably good medical health prior to the birth of Heather and, 4 years earlier, of Marcus. There was no indication that she had suffered from any serious medical illnesses or had contracted any sexually transmitted diseases. She had not engaged in episodic illicit drug use before or during her pregnancy with either child. She apparently had good prenatal care with Marcus and Heather, and thus this element was a protective factor for her.

Emotional Status

As indicated throughout this casebook, numerous studies have found the presence of maternal mental and emotional disorders to be a significant risk factor in filicide. Many maternal filicide classification systems, including mine, have highlighted categories that reflect psychiatric illnesses. Emotional status would include risk factors such as psychotic and depressive diagnoses, as well as substance abuse/dependence and personality disorders.

At the prepregnancy stage, preexisting severe mental illness may be significantly exacerbated by conception and birth. For example, one study found that among psychotic women the base rate of psychiatric hospitalization during pregnancy was more than two times higher than it was prior to conception and that among mothers of newborns the relative risk of a psychiatric admission with a diagnosis of psychosis was almost 25 times higher in the 30 days after delivery (Kendell, Chalmers, & Platz, 1987). The American Psychiatric Association's endorsement of a "postpartum onset specifier" that may be applied to diagnoses of major depressive episode, bipolar disorder, or brief psychotic disorder attests to the impact of childbirth on a mother's emotional status (American Psychiatric Association, 2000).

Legislative confirmation of the influence of pregnancy and delivery on a woman's emotional status, for example, was provided in the English Infanticide Act of 1922 (modified to its present form in 1938). The act provided that a woman who committed infanticide prior to her baby's first birthday could be tried on a lesser charge than murder because of her diminished mental capacity stemming from childbirth (Dobson & Sales, 2000). The presence of psychosis and major depression, along with filicidal-suicidal plans during the postinfancy stage, has also been widely cited by many studies and maternal filicide classification systems, as indicated in chapters 2 and 3, respectively.

A mother's emotional status as a risk or protective factor also includes the presence of alcohol and drug abuse/dependence at the prepregnancy, pregnancy/delivery, early postpartum, late postpartum, and postinfancy stages. Frequent intoxication due to alcohol and drug abuse at the prepregnancy stage may place a woman at higher risk for an unintended conception, forcing her to consider issues of abortion or giving birth to a possibly unwanted child. In the postinfancy stage, alcohol and drug abuse/dependency have been associated with physical child abuse as significant precipitants of accidental deaths in children. Personality disorders, especially those associated with paranoid, narcissistic, antisocial, and borderline patterns, are also descriptive of a mother's emotional status and have been seen in many instances of maternal filicide, particularly in retaliatory cases.

> Barbara's mental health after Marcus was born was seriously impaired, with the development of a major depressive episode, postpartum onset, and panic disorder. Although there was no indication of psychotic symptoms prior to Heather's birth, Barbara clearly had delusions and hallucinations in the months preceding the children's deaths. Thus this element was a significant risk factor for maternal infanticide (Heather) and filicide (Marcus) in the early postpartum and late postpartum stages.

Trauma History
As indicated in chapter 2, many studies have pointed to childhood physical abuse, sexual abuse, and neglect as a common feature of mothers who have committed infanticide and filicide. For example, Spinelli (2003) found that more than half of the infanticidal mothers in her sample had been victims of either physical or sexual assaults as children. Cummings, Theis, Mueller, and Rivara. (1994) determined that three-fourths of their sample showed similar childhood victimization, a number that was highly consistent with the prevalence of 78% in a sample of filicidal mothers reported by Korbin (1986).

A number of studies have shown that physical abuse is often transmitted from one generation to the next; thus women with childhood histories of parental abuse often employ the same methods of discipline and behavior control with their children. Other studies have shown that childhood sexual abuse can have long-term effects on girls' mental and emotional functioning as they grow into adolescence and young adulthood. Such victims may become more promiscuous and indiscriminant in their sexual activity, which, at the prepregnancy stage, would place them at much higher risk for unintended and likely unwanted conception, as well as sexually transmitted disease.

The loss of a parent, especially a mother, during childhood is an especially traumatic experience: Motherless girls are deprived of their primary role model for learning how to be mothers in the future. Parental divorce is also a common theme in studies of filicidal mothers, with a per-sample incidence of 57% (d'Orban, 1979), 64% (Cummings et al., 1994), and 80% (McKee &

Shea, 1998), respectively. A woman's trauma history may also include adult domestic abuse by a previous partner, as cited in many studies of maternal filicide (d'Orban, 1979; McKee & Shea, 1998; Meyer & Oberman, 2001;).

In contrast, the absence of prior trauma as children or adults is likely to be a protective factor against maternal filicide. These mothers had positive, nonviolent childhoods and adulthoods and had been shown by parents and others how to raise children without resorting to excessive physical discipline.

> Barbara appeared to have a relatively trauma-free childhood, adolescence, and adulthood; thus this element was a protective factor for her at all stages.

Maternal Attitudes

At the prepregnancy, pregnancy/delivery, early postpartum, late postpartum, and postinfancy stages, no factor within the Maternal Filicide Risk Matrix is likely to be more important than the mother's attitudes toward her fetus, baby, infant, toddler, preschool, or school-age child.

During the prepregnancy stage, a prospective mother's attitudes toward conception and pregnancy significantly influence her choices regarding sexual activity, contraception, and selection of an intimate partner. Intended pregnancies are clearly a protective factor against neonaticide and infanticide in that the mother deliberately chose to produce an outcome she has desired, childbirth. Such women are much more likely to maintain a healthy medical status during pregnancy and to ensure that they obtain regular prenatal care. They are much more likely to abstain from alcohol and other drugs that might harm their fetuses.

In the early and late postpartum stages, mothers who give birth to planned children are much more likely to have secure bonds with their infants, and, in turn, the babies are much more likely to have positive attachments to their mothers. Women with intended pregnancies are much more likely to carefully schedule their conceptions so that they have sufficient energy and availability for each child they bear. Their positive maternal attitudes are a protective factor that gives them resilience, patience, and optimism as they manage the stresses and obligations of parenting their children.

In contrast, an unintended pregnancy resulting from careless risk taking during the prepregnancy stage is more likely to result in negative attitudes toward the fetus because the mother is now unexpectedly confronted with issues of abortion, adoption, or birth and long-term child-care duties. At the pregnancy/delivery stage, prospective mothers who deny being pregnant or who hide their conditions from others are at much greater risk for baby abandonment, neonaticide, or first-week infanticide, as indicated by the numerous studies cited in chapters 2 and 3. Among the mothers who left their babies in the hospitals, an alarming number did so because they did not wish to be responsible for maternal care (U.S. Department of Health and Human Services, 2004a). Though these mothers' choices were better than neonaticide or infanticide, the newborns are vulnerable to inadequate attachment because they are cared for by nonbiologically related, alternating substitute caretakers. This situation may likely result in a much higher risk for long-term childhood emotional and mental health problems.

In the early postpartum and late postpartum stages, new mothers with negative, resentful maternal attitudes are much less likely to seek nurturing, positive bonds with their children. Correspondingly, the children are much less likely to have secure attachments to their mothers. Babies who have avoidant, resistant, or disorganized attachments because of maternal indifference, resentment, or hostility (Ainsworth et al., 1978; Main & Solomon, 1986) are likely to be much more vulnerable to physical abuse, neglect, and accidental infanticide or filicide. Mothers with Munchausen syndrome by proxy (MBP), who intentionally harm their children because of their own narcissistic needs for public and/or medical staff attention, display the most heinous form of negative maternal attitudes.

> Barbara and her husband, Tom, had carefully planned to conceive Marcus, and, until he was born, she appeared to have a very optimistic and positive attitude toward her pregnancy and impending delivery. When she developed major depression after his birth, her inability to care for him was not due to negative, resentful maternal attitudes; indeed, she worried constantly about whether she was a good mother. After she began taking antidepressant medication, her mood improved, and her energy increased enough so that she and Tom chose to have another child. When Barbara became pregnant with Heather, she was initially happy, but she became depressed and anxious during the second and third trimesters and dreaded her maternal duties. Though her maternal thoughts emanated from her psychotic delusions and hallucinations, the content of the symptoms was highly negative toward her children; thus, in the early and late postpartum stages with Heather, this element was a risk factor for infanticide and filicide.

Family of Origin Domain

Factors in the family of origin domain include the new or prospective mother's: (1) mother's status and parenting attitudes; (2) father's status and parenting attitudes; and (3) parents' marital and family stability. During the prepregnancy stage, family of origin factors are historical markers in that they consist of prior positive or negative experiences of the prospective mother. During the pregnancy/delivery and later stages, however, these factors are better characterized as dynamic factors that may change or be changed through interventions as the mother and child develop.

Mother's Status and Parenting Attitudes

This factor is an assessment of the role and influence that the new or prospective mother's mother, the new baby's grandmother, had and continues to have in the mother's life. The individual factors described earlier are now applied to the grandmother, and, in the next factor, to the grandfather. This family of origin factor comprises the nature and quality of the grandmother's bonding to her own children, including the new or prospective mother, and would also include whether the grandmother enjoyed sufficient medical and mental health to nurture every child in her family.

At the prepregnancy stage, new and prospective mothers who have fearful, resistant, or disorganized attachments to their own mothers because of their mothers' indifferent, negative parenting attitudes may be more likely to carry those dysfunctional attitudes toward their own fetuses and children. At the pregnancy/delivery stage, negative grandmaternal attitudes may likely result in a lack of support for the prospective mother, which in turn may lead to her having poor prenatal care and negative attitudes toward her own fetus. If the conception was unintended and the prospective mother is fearful of her mother's angry, rejecting reaction to her pregnancy, the likelihood of a denied or hidden pregnancy is much higher and leads to a greater risk for neonaticide and baby abandonment. Even if the prospective mother wants the baby, if her own mother opposes the unplanned pregnancy, the predelivery period will likely be very stressful and conflicted, perhaps resulting in the new mother having negative attitudes toward the fetus.

At the early and late postpartum stages, the new grandmother's support or lack of support for the new mother will likely have a direct bearing on the nature and quality of the newborn's attachment and emotional development. A new mother who is forced to be the sole caretaker because her own mother has abandoned her is much more likely to be anxious, worried, depressed, and overwhelmed and thus to have a child whose attachment may be insecure and damaged.

At the postinfancy period, though the new grandmother's influence might lessen somewhat, the new mother's "ghosts of the nursery" (Fraiberg, Adelson, & Shapiro, 1975), derived from her own postinfancy childhood memories of her mother, will still likely have an impact on the nature and quality of the mother and child's lifelong interactions. In the most extreme form of negative grandmaternal attitudes, for example, mothers with MBP who induce illness in one or more of their children may produce daughters who develop MBP (Rosenberg, 1995; Schreier & Libow, 1993).

> Barbara and her mother enjoyed a close, secure relationship. She had reported growing up feeling loved and cherished by her parents; thus in the prepregnancy stage prior to the birth of Marcus, this element was a protective factor. After her son was born, Barbara's mother became ill and infirm, which prevented her from traveling across country to help with Marcus's care. Because of her deteriorating medical status,

Barbara's mother was unable to help Barbara when Heather was bo: Therefore, in the early and late postpartum and postinfancy stages w.... Marcus, and in all the stages with her daughter, this element became a risk factor for Barbara.

Father's Status and Parenting Attitudes

The new or prospective mother's relationship with her father is also a significantly influential family of origin factor. A father is a young girl's first role model of how adult males think, feel, and behave. This factor may also apply to stepfathers, especially if the mother's mother remarried during the girl's preschool or prepubertal years.

If a woman's father was unsupportive, violent, emotionally unstable, and/or absent, these experiences would likely foster his daughter's fearful, insecure attachment to him during her infant and toddler years. In her school-age and early adolescent years, her father's (and/or stepfather's) behavior and attitudes would have colored how she interacted with teenage boys and young adult men as she matured. Many studies have indicated that women who have come from abusive families in turn enter into abusive adolescent and adult heterosexual relationships, another common feature of filicidal women.

Biological fathers who are mentally ill or who suffer from substance abuse or dependence often transmit these disorders to the next generation. Their daughters may become mentally ill and/or chemically addicted and therefore be at higher risk for committing infanticide and filicide. Even daughters of fathers who are mentally healthy but absent and who grow up with psychiatrically impaired or chemically dependent stepfathers would still likely be at greater risk for these disorders and thus in greater danger of harming or killing their offspring.

As indicated earlier, many filicidal mothers report histories of childhood abuse, often perpetrated by domestically violent fathers (and/or stepfathers). If the new mother had experienced excessive though inconsistently applied physical discipline from her father, she may be more likely to consider such methods as "normal" ways of dealing with a child's noncompliance, thus placing her infant at greater risk for accidental filicide due to recurrent or reactive child abuse.

Paternal and stepfather incest and sexual abuse are especially devastating to a daughter's self-esteem, emotional stability, and psychosexual development. It is not uncommon for sexually abused daughters to become sexually provocative and promiscuous adolescents as a way of acting out their intimacy conflicts with teenage boys and young adult men. Their imprudent sexual behavior would place them at much higher risk for unintended pregnancies and sexually transmitted diseases that might lead to greater chances of baby abandonment, neonaticide, and infanticide. These children who have children at such a young age often do not have sufficient parenting knowledge and emotional resiliency to manage the child-care demands of newborns. If the new mother's own father has abandoned the family, he will likely be unavailable to provide emotional and financial support to the new mother at the pregnancy/delivery and subsequent stages.

In contrast, if the new mother grew up with a father who was dependable, supportive, emotionally stable, and available, she is much more likely to have a secure attachment to her father. Because of her father's positive role modeling and nurturance, she is much more likely to subsequently seek out a similar adult male partner with whom she might create a stable, nonviolent family. When she enters the pregnancy/delivery and later stages, her father would be much more likely to be a resource for her, emotionally and perhaps financially if necessary. Emotionally healthy grandfathers and grandmothers are much more likely to relish their new roles as alternative caretakers of their daughter's baby, which in turn allows the new mother to rest and recuperate in the weeks and months following delivery.

> Barbara enjoyed a close relationship with her father. He had been a kind, nurturing influence in her childhood, adolescence, and young adulthood. Prior to the birth of Marcus, this element was a protective factor; however, Barbara's father was obligated to care for his ailing wife in the years preceding Heather's birth. Even if he had been physically available to help with child care, he did not have the energy and stamina to manage two rambunctious infants; thus this element became a risk factor in Barbara's case through all of Heather's stages and Marcus's postinfancy stage.

Marital and Family Stability

This factor considers whether the new or prospective mother's parents, siblings, and relatives were and are a source of nurturance, security, consistency, and support. If she grew up in a home in which her parents were frequently arguing, separating, divorcing, and/or marrying other partners, she and her siblings likely had a very stressful, anxiety-ridden childhood and adolescence. These experiences would likely create expectations of unstable, volatile, chaotic relationships with adult intimate partners she selects. If she had an older sister who became pregnant before finishing high school as a way of escaping their turbulent family of origin, she may adopt a similar strategy, with unfortunate consequences for her and her baby.

Family instability may also be measured by the frequency of residential relocations. If a young woman's family moved often during her prepubertal and teenage years, she may be vulnerable to childhood and adolescent depression due to her inability to develop close, supportive, dependable, long-lasting friendships with other female schoolmates. Adolescent females with such histories are often at greater risk for alcohol and drug use, in part to self-medicate their despondent moods but also as a means of making new acquaintances with similar substance-abusing teenagers. Substance abuse, in turn, increases the chances of high school dropout, poorer medical health, less stable mental health, and unexpected teenage pregnancy—all factors associated with increased risk of neonaticide and infanticide.

Instability in the new mother's parents' marriage and chaotic relationships with her siblings during the pregnancy/delivery stage would likely make her pregnancy much more difficult, particularly if the family members see her condition as yet another stressor in their dysfunctional lives. Under such circumstances, it might be less likely that the parents and siblings would arrange baby showers and other predelivery rituals that might generate more optimistic, positive family attitudes toward the infant's arrival.

After delivery, her family's instability during the early and late postpartum and postinfancy stages would likely make the new mother's adjustment to motherhood much more anxiety provoking, perhaps resulting in less patience with her newborn. Such conditions are often a prelude to frustration-induced reactive child abuse and accidental infanticide or filicide. Her anxiety and uncertainty about parental and sibling support may make her bonding to her child more difficult and may produce an infant who is insecurely attached to its mother.

In contrast, daughters who grow up in homes with psychologically stable, nonviolent, and emotionally supportive parents and siblings are more likely to become emotionally healthy, resilient adolescents and adults. If the teenage girl becomes unexpectedly pregnant, her history of family support might make it more probable that she will disclose her condition earlier. Immediate discovery of her pregnancy is more likely to result in a deliberate, considered parent-adolescent decision about abortion or can at least eliminate the possibility of neonaticide, abandonment, or early postpartum infanticide. If the new mother decides to keep her baby, a supportive network of parents and siblings can provide respite child care and facilitate her finishing her education or enhancing her self-sufficiency through regular employment.

> Barbara's parents had a long, conflict-free, nonviolent marriage, which, prior to becoming mentally ill, Barbara had successfully duplicated in her relationship with Tom. She was an only child. Her parents' mutual support and encouragement had given her sufficient resiliency to weather the periodic arguments she had with her husband over his frequent absences due to business trips. Barbara's recovery from major depression after Marcus was born and her initial optimism in conceiving a second child was in part due to her parents' long-distance supportive telephone calls and periodic letters. All in all, this element therefore was a protective factor for her.

Situational Domain

Marital/Partner Status
This factor comprises the nature and quality of the mother's relationship with the father or prospective father of her child. At the prepregnancy stage, this

factor is defined in terms of the woman's current male partner(s) or husband with whom she is having intimate relations. At the pregnancy/delivery, early and late postpartum, and postinfancy stages, this factor is defined in terms of the nature and quality of her relationship with her child's biological father.

At the prepregnancy stage, marital/partner status as a risk factor might be illustrated in many ways. The partner's unwillingness to use contraceptive devices would increase the woman's risk of unintended pregnancy. His infidelity with other women would jeopardize her sense of relationship stability and increase her risk of contracting a sexually transmitted disease that might be transmitted to her fetus. His unwillingness to provide child-care support after her pregnancy might contribute to a greater risk of maternal infanticide and filicide due to the emotional and physical stresses of trying to manage a child alone. Last, he might use reactive and/or predatory violence and coercion to intimidate and subjugate her to his wishes. As indicated in chapter 2, large percentages of filicidal mothers reported that they were in abusive partner relationships, from 43% in the sample of McKee and Shea (1998) to 52% in the study by Cummings et al. (1994). In addition to enduring domestic abuse, a new or prospective mother may be physically or emotionally abandoned by her baby's biological father because the man did not want to have a child and resented becoming "entrapped" by his partner.

In contrast, partners and husbands who actively intend to have children, who are supportive throughout the pregnancy/delivery to postinfancy stages, and who are not domestically violent are resources who significantly decrease the chances of maternal filicide.

> Barbara's husband, Tom, appears to have been a consistently supportive figure for her. When she became so depressed after Marcus was born, he arranged for medical and psychiatric care to help his wife; had he not been so frequently absent on work-related travel, he might have sooner realized how impaired Barbara had become. To his credit, however, he did not disparage the value of mental health treatment and actively supported her medication compliance. When she recovered in the years preceding Heather's arrival, they did discuss having another child, so their daughter's conception was intended. Although Barbara may have felt a bit overwhelmed by Tom's immediate reorganization of the second bedroom as a nursery on news of her pregnancy, his reaction was positive and encouraging. In all, this factor was a protective factor throughout the Maternal Filicide Risk Matrix stages for both of their children.

Financial Status

This element is defined in terms of the mother's economic self-sufficiency, that is, her capacity to provide for herself and her children without reliance on her family of origin or the biological father of her infant(s). This element becomes a risk factor when a new or prospective mother lives in poverty, relies on public assistance, or is required to depend on others for subsistence. Numerous studies cited in chapter 2 indicate the high percentages of filicidal mothers who were on welfare, from more than 50% in the sample of Holden et al. (1996) to more than 90% in a sample of Meyer and Oberman (2001). Impoverished mothers are less likely to have money available for adequate prenatal and postnatal health care at the pregnancy/delivery, early and late postpartum, and postinfancy stages. Women who are financially dependent may be more vulnerable to domestic abuse and exploitation, which may include additional unwanted pregnancies caused by coerced sexual activity by a violent partner. Such conditions often produce maternal depression and despair, which place their children at an increased risk for a suicidal-filicidal outcome.

Financially self-sufficient women, though they may have to work outside the home, may be more able to direct the course of their lives and control the number of children they have. This element would also be a protective factor to mothers in partner relationships and marriages in which there has been a mutual decision for the biological father, stepfather, or adoptive father to be the sole financial provider for the family.

> Barbara's relationship to Tom would be an example of this latter financial arrangement. For her and the children, this element was a protective factor throughout the Maternal Filicide Risk Matrix stages for Marcus and Heather.

Child-Care Status

This factor is defined in terms of the prospective or new mother's parenting obligations for children other than the fetus or newborn. Many studies of filicidal mothers have pointed to situations in which the woman had "one too many" children: The newborn overwhelmed her resiliency and capacity to provide adequate care. McKee and Shea (1998) found that 78% of the families of filicidal mothers included one or more surviving siblings, and Meyer and Oberman (2001) reported that 90% of multiple-child families in their "abuse" category included one or more surviving siblings.

Additional duties to perform child care for a newborn are especially risk-filled for teenage mothers who already have at least one child: Their infanticidal base rate was more than 10 times higher than that of mothers over 25 giving birth to their first children (Overpeck, 2003). Single mothers who are the sole caretakers of many children are more vulnerable to being exhausted and over-stressed by their maternal responsibilities. Exhaustion and stress place them at higher risk for negligent supervision of their infants and/or for impulsive, reactive child abuse that may lead to an accidental infanticide or filicide.

This factor also includes whether or not the mother has a history of per-petrating child abuse, which may indicate a tendency to resort to physical discipline once their babies enter the early postpartum, late postpartum, and postinfancy stages. It is a well-known axiom of clinical mental health practice that previous violence is a risk factor for subsequent violence. In 1998, approximately 1,110 children under age 18 died from child abuse, a base rate of approximately 1.6 fatalities for every 100,000 children. However, when the number of fatalities is compared against the 1998 total of more than 2,972,000 investigated cases of child maltreatment, the filicidal base rate jumps to 37 fatalities per 100,000, a relative risk 23 times higher (U.S. Department of Health and Human Services, 2004b). Clearly, previous child abuse, confirmed by an agency, may be a risk factor for filicide.

In contrast, mothers who do not have preexisting child-care duties prior to giving birth are more able to devote their full energies to raising their babies and thus do not have this element as a situational risk factor.

> At the prepregnancy stage with Heather, Barbara had child-care responsibilities only for Marcus. However, for much of Marcus's early postpartum, late postpartum, and postinfancy stages, she was overwhelmed by her maternal duties due to major depression. Although her depression was subsequently mediated by medication, managing both Heather and Marcus during Heather's postpartum period became too much for Barbara and likely exacerbated the severity of her psychotic depression. Though her severe mental illness was the "root cause" of her maternal filicide, it is possible that had she had only one child, her family's tragedy might never have happened. In her case, this element was a risk factor for infanticide and filicide throughout each stage of Heather's life.

Infant's Temperament

This element is defined in terms of whether the child's demeanor, moods, attitudes, or behavior might have been a precipitant to the maternal filicidal act. Incorporation of this factor in a risk assessment of filicide does not diminish a mother's culpability nor shift the blame onto the child victim. Rather, analysis of this element recognizes that some infants and children are easier to manage than others.

Studies of infant attachment have demonstrated that certain babies were unbothered by their mother's temporary absences and ignored the mothers when they returned, an example of an avoidant attachment style. However, other infants were highly distressed when alone and unable to be comforted after their mothers reappeared, exemplifying a resistant attachment style (Ainsworth et al., 1978). The children in the latter category might be more frustrating for a mother to parent.

A number of studies of filicidal mothers have described such victim-child characteristics as "difficult to care for" and "disobedient," suggesting that the infant's predispositions may be a precipitant to physical child abuse that leads to death (Wilczynski, 1997). For example, Levitsky and Cooper (2000) found that 26% of the mothers in their study admitted to thoughts of killing their children during their infants' colic episodes, and 70% reported having aggressive feelings and thoughts when their children would not stop crying. Descriptions of developmental periods of the "terrible twos" and similar designations highlight the fact that children at certain ages might be more difficult to parent. Many studies of children with attention-deficit hyperactivity disorder (ADHD) indicate that parent-child conflicts are very common and can result in physical altercations (Abidin, 1995).

> Although Barbara described her children as unruly and rebellious during the early and late postpartum stages of Heather's life, her interpretation of their behavior was based on delusions and not actually caused by Heather and Marcus. Therefore, this element was a protective factor in her case and would not have contributed to filicide if Barbara had not been actively psychotic.

The Maternal Filicide Risk Matrix, as employed in this chapter, is an example of a clinical assessment instrument that may provide a more organized case-by-case analysis of the risk of maternal filicide. Although Barbara's few risk factors overwhelmed her numerous protective factors, the Maternal Filicide Risk Matrix helped answer the question, "Could the deaths of Marcus and Heather have been anticipated?"

In the next chapter I address the question, "Could the deaths of Marcus and Heather have been prevented, and if so, how?"

5

Prevention and Risk Intervention Points

The preceding two chapters of this book have focused on the research results and clinical practice methods of risk analysis as applied to maternal neonaticide, infanticide, and filicide. It is extremely important to understand the risk and protective factors that might identify at-risk new and prospective mothers, because the ultimate purpose of risk analysis is prevention through intervention. When applied to maternal filicide, risk prevention is the implementation of one or more procedures that will reduce or eliminate the contribution of a risk factor to either the reoccurrence of maternal filicide signal behaviors (e.g., denial and concealment of pregnancy, child neglect, etc.) or the target behavior, a mother killing her child or children.

As indicated in chapter 4, the research literature and clinical practice in the assessment and analysis of violent behavior have grown significantly over the past 25 years. The explosion in risk analysis, however, has not been matched by a corresponding increase in the research and clinical practice literature on the risk management or prevention of maternal filicide. Indeed, many of the studies of and texts on maternal filicide that have been highlighted in this book provide little, if any, discussion of what could have been done to intervene prior to the tragic events occurring. The purpose of this chapter is to describe and classify various risk prevention methods from the research and clinical literature so that the procedures may be applied to at-risk cases of maternal neonaticide, infanticide, and filicide.

Effective intervention against maternal filicide (or any other target behavior) depends on the recognition of those circumstances, situations, and/or signal behaviors that indicate opportunities to use one or more prevention methods. These occurrences are designated in this book as risk intervention points (RIPs), similar to the description of "missed opportunities" suggested by Spinelli (2003). Prevention methods are of little value if it is unknown when, where, how, and to whom they should be applied.

For example, when Barbara's husband, Tom, observed that she was repeatedly unable to adequately care for Marcus or for her own hygiene (risk intervention points), he contacted a psychiatrist to evaluate his wife as a first step to prevent further deterioration in Barbara's child care and personal functioning. His recognition and disclosure of those RIPs led the psychiatrist to prescribe medicine that effectively reduced Barbara's maternal filicide risk, at least until Heather's birth. The importance of RIPs in maternal filicide cases cannot be overstated. Numerous examples of RIPs are illustrated in the case studies in the remaining chapters, along with descriptions of both simple and complicated prevention approaches that might have prevented the mother's act of neonaticide, infanticide, or filicide.

In the professional literature, prevention programs are generally specified as either primary, secondary, or tertiary methods (Campbell, 1995).

Primary Risk Prevention Programs

Primary risk prevention programs are implemented for those groups and individuals who may possibly, at some point in their lives, commit a particular target behavior such as neonaticide. In these programs, there are no immediate signs or indications that the persons receiving the intervention are presently at risk; rather, the procedures are designed to broadly inform individuals of future risks and consequences. In the area of maternal filicide, primary prevention programs would be directed at those girls and women who might someday become pregnant and give birth but who may presently not even be sexually active or past puberty. Primary prevention programs are most typically educational efforts designed to highlight potential risks and consequences of certain acts and circumstances, such as sexual intercourse without contraception, before such behaviors and situations occur. In terms of my Maternal Filicide Risk Matrix (see chapter 4), primary prevention methods would be those procedures implemented at some point during the female's first prepregnancy stage; that is, prior to her initial conception of a fetus.

Maternal filicide primary prevention methods need not be elaborate and might include something as simple as a mother giving her daughter a prepuberty "birds and the bees" talk about how babies are made. In contrast, public school sex education programs are examples of much more complex, far-reaching primary prevention programs for both girls and boys. Schwartz and Isser (2000) highlighted the political controversy of such programs, noting that despite highly charged debates at school board meetings about course content (e.g., masturbation, homosexuality, varieties of sexual behavior, etc.), philosophy (e.g., abstinence vs. contraception, etc.), initiation (e.g., elementary grades or later) and attendance rules (e.g., only with parental permission), most states allow for some form of sex education in junior or senior high school classes.

The key to effective primary prevention of pregnancy in young, unprepared teenage girls, however, may be in implementing long-term programs at the start of their elementary school years. Brody (1999), for example, reported that girls who began a 12-year-long program of problem-solving skills, assertiveness training, and parent-child involvement in the first grade were less likely to engage in sexual intercourse, to have multiple sex partners, or to become pregnant at age 18.

Secondary Risk Prevention Programs

These interventions are similar to primary risk prevention methods in that they are implemented before the occurrence of the target behavior (e.g., neonaticide); however, efforts are focused on those persons who are seen as being at more immediate, imminent risk for committing a target or signal behavior (Campbell, 1995). In the area of maternal filicide, secondary prevention efforts would be programs designed for adolescent and young adult women who have become pregnant or have recently given birth. In terms of the Maternal Filicide Risk Matrix, these programs would be implemented during the pregnancy/delivery, early postpartum, late postpartum, and/or postinfancy stages.

One recent secondary prevention approach to neonaticide and infanticide has been the development of abandoned-infant acts and "safe haven" laws at the federal and state levels. The intent of these laws, now found in 45 states, has been to encourage mothers of newborns who might otherwise secretly abandon or discard their babies to leave their infants at a hospital or similar public agency without legal punishment if there is no evidence of child abuse or neglect. The origin of "safe haven" laws may be found in the high numbers of known public abandonment of babies: 17,400 infants in 1998 were left in hospitals by their biological mothers, a 46% increase from 1991 (National Abandoned Infants Assistance Resource Center, 2003). Unfortunately, these programs have rarely been employed by new mothers who do not wish to parent their babies. Since the passage of Illinois's legislation in 2001, for example, only two children have been dropped off at safe havens (National Conference of State Legislatures, 2003).

Secondary prevention programs would also include school- and community-based educational and counseling programs that attempt to reduce risk in new mothers by helping them to delay second and subsequent pregnancies and deliveries. For example, Seitz and Apfel (1993) demonstrated that pregnant teens who were permitted to remain in school while participating in a program that stressed prenatal and postnatal health counseling were significantly less likely to have second children within the following 5 years.

Secondary prevention programs additionally include case-by-case clinical interventions with new mothers who develop serious postpartum mood disorders or have difficulty adequately bonding with their newborns. When mothers develop mood disorders after giving birth, secondary prevention methods are often a combination of psychotherapy (e.g., O'Hara, Stuart, &

Gorman, 2000), antidepressant medications (e.g., Appleby, Warner, & Whitten, 1997), and/or support groups (e.g., Rosenberg, Greening, & Windell, 2003). For example, parent-infant psychotherapy with high-risk dyads, developed by Fraiberg (1980) and others (e.g., Stern, 1995), focus on changing the mothers' negative attitudes toward their newborns by enhancing their capacity for empathy and positive responsiveness. The sessions typically entail face-to-face mother-child play, which is videotaped for review with the mother's therapist (McDonough, 1993).

Similar to primary prevention programs, however, interventions of this type need not be elaborate nor involve highly trained professional staff. A mother who asks her teenage daughter if she is sexually active, then checks for signs of pregnancy is engaging in secondary prevention efforts. If it is discovered that the teen has been concealing her condition, the mother's recognition of the risk intervention point and her simple procedure would reduce the likelihood of tragedy for both women and the newborn. Though her daughter might be enraged at her mother's invasion of her privacy, the prevention of a neonaticide would be worth the cost of the teenager's ruffled feelings. The mother's discovery may open communication between them for discussions about pregnancy termination, prenatal care, adoption, or continuing motherhood—much better outcomes than the death of a newborn and the incarceration of a parent.

Tertiary Risk Prevention Programs

These procedures are designed to stop the reoccurrence of the signal and/or target behaviors of concern. In tertiary prevention programs, the person or persons who are the focus of the procedures have already demonstrated that they are at higher risk by their acts of commission or omission. Many examples of tertiary prevention programs come from the child protection literature, examples in which a parent has been found to have engaged in physical abuse, neglect, sexual assault, or other improper management of one or more children. Often these procedures result in the temporary removal of the vulnerable children, combined with court-ordered parent education classes, mandatory mental health counseling, and a protective services worker's development of a family reunification plan (Campbell, 1995; Sattler, 1998). Examples of tertiary prevention programs are illustrated in the cases in the abusive/neglectful mothers category, including Harriet (see chapter 11), Janet (see chapter 12), and Kaye (see chapter 13), wherein each displayed signal behaviors of abuse or neglect prior to the commission of filicide.

A Classification of Maternal Filicide
Risk Prevention Procedures

This section describes a classification of prevention procedures based on two dimensions: resource and complexity. The first dimension, resource, concerns whether the resources for the intervention are drawn from within or outside the family system: family-based and community-based, respectively. The low, moderate, and high levels of the second dimension, complexity, involve the difficulty of organizing and implementing the intervention in terms of number of people (e.g., family relatives, hospital staff, attorneys, judges, etc.) and/or systems (clinicians, agencies, hospitals, courts, etc).

As illustrated in table 5.1, my maternal filicide categories are integrated into the classification of prevention procedures to illustrate how different types of interventions might be employed. The assignment of maternal filicide types to certain risk-prevention types is neither exhaustive nor mutually exclusive; that is, a number of different interventions of varying complexity and resources might be brought to bear on a particular case, as is illustrated in chapters 6 through 19. The schema presented here, using Barbara's case once again, suggests intervention approaches that the clinician might use initially before proceeding on to more complex family- or community-based prevention methods.

Family- Versus Community-Based Risk Prevention Methods

Family-based risk-prevention methods are those procedures that employ resources found within the mother's immediate or extended family system (e.g., parents, siblings, in-laws, relatives, spouses/partners, etc.). Family-based prevention methods are familiar to all of us. For example, a mother standing next to her preschool child might watch for signs of whether he remembers to look both ways before crossing the street. If he steps off the curb without looking—a risk intervention point—the mother will likely either yell out or pull him back to reeducate him about the traffic risk. The example is an indication of a family-based intervention because the mother deals with the situation herself instead of, for instance, calling over a school crossing guard (a community-based intervention) to explain to her child the value of safely crossing the street.

Table 5.1
Classification of Risk Prevention Procedures by Maternal Filicide Type

Complexity	Family	Community
Low	Detached—denial	Psychopathic—financial Psychopathic—addicted Abusive/neglectful—inadequate
Moderate	Detached—ambivalent Detached—exhausted	Abusive/neglectful—recurrent Psychotic/depressed—suicidal Psychotic/depressed—impulsive
High	Abusive/neglectful—reactive Detached—resentful	Psychotic/depressed—delusional Psychopathic—narcissistic

In Barbara's case from chapter 1, Tom's efforts to help his wife with child care after observing her difficulty with housekeeping and personal hygiene (risk intervention points) were examples of family-based secondary prevention methods. His actions were designed to interrupt her maternal neglect, which might have led to an accidental filicide of Marcus. When Tom contacted a psychiatrist to evaluate and possibly medicate his wife, the intervention shifted from a family-based to community-based prevention method.

Complexity of Risk-Prevention Methods

Prevention methods may also be organized in terms of their complexity; that is, the level of difficulty and/or number of people (inside or outside the family system) needed to implement the intervention. Low-complexity methods are implemented by simple actions and/or conversations. To return to the example of the preschool child at the curb, the mother's action is a very simple prevention method involving only one word, "Stop!" If she decides that her son will not listen to her, she might employ a community-based risk prevention method of low complexity by asking the crossing guard to give her child a brief lecture on sidewalk safety. A low-complexity family-based intervention against neonaticide might consist of a mother demanding that her teenager take a home pregnancy test to alleviate or confirm her fears that her daughter has been engaging in unprotected sexual intercourse. Tom's arrangement of a psychiatric appointment for his wife was an example of a community-based risk intervention of low complexity in that it involved only a single phone call.

Moderately complex risk intervention methods, whether family- or community-based, are more difficult to implement because they involve more people for longer periods of time. For example, Tom arranged for Barbara's mother to stay with his wife for the first few weeks after their son, Marcus, was born so that she would have help during her early postpartum stage. His intervention was a very common family-based procedure of moderate complexity that many families use to ensure that the newborn is adequately cared for and that the mother is spared the energy-draining chores of housekeeping and cooking. Because the mother is free to devote her time and effort to infant care, the likelihood of secure attachment and bonding is increased.

After her mother's visit, Tom recognized that Barbara was increasingly unable to care for their son, a set of circumstances and signal behaviors that suggest a variety of RIPs. When he continued to find the dishes and laundry undone and his wife unkempt, Tom realized that his wife was depressed and implemented a community-based prevention method of low complexity by making an appointment for her to see a psychiatrist. The psychiatrist recommended that Barbara be hospitalized, a much more complex community-based prevention method, but she refused to be admitted. The psychiatrist then negotiated for the implementation of a moderately complex community-based intervention by recommending outpatient treatment comprising medications and periodic office checkups.

Risk interventions of high complexity are the most difficult to implement because they entail significant disruption to the daily life of the at-risk person and others. Family-based highly complex risk-intervention methods may employ relocation as the means for preventing signal or target behaviors. For example, if the parents of a young, single new mother found evidence that their grandchild had been physically abused when they saw bruises on the infant's legs (a risk intervention point), the baby might be placed temporarily with them or other relatives as a way of protecting both the child and its mother. They might arrange that method to keep the problem within the family so that their daughter would not become the subject of another community-based risk intervention, a Department of Social Services investigation.

The psychiatrist's recommendation that Barbara be psychiatrically hospitalized was an example of a highly complex, community-based risk intervention because it would have involved multidisciplinary admission evaluations (psychiatry, nursing, social work, psychology, activity therapy, etc.), as well as ongoing around-the-clock inpatient monitoring of her course of treatment on the ward. Because Barbara refused to be admitted, the psychiatrist might have then required an emergency involuntary psychiatric civil commitment. This procedure involves the additional complexity of court hearings within 72 hours of placement in the hospital to validate the necessity for admission. At the hearing, the psychiatrist would testify that Barbara needed continued hospital treatment because of the significant risk she posed to herself and her children. When the psychiatrist agreed to treat Barbara on an outpatient basis, his decision reflected an assessment that her filicidal risk did not yet warrant the more complex intervention of involuntary psychiatric inpatient commitment.

Because of her mother's ailing health, Barbara did not have assistance before and after Heather was born, which in turn placed the children at much greater risk once her psychosis became more severe and debilitating. After Barbara began to have clear auditory hallucinations involving paranoid themes, she was certain that her psychiatrist would hospitalize her. She kept silent about her growing suspiciousness, increasingly intrusive hallucinations, and delusional perceptions of her children's behavior. Her psychotically induced secrecy prohibited Tom and her psychiatrist from gaining a true and complete understanding of her late-postpartum emotional status, which led, tragically, to the deaths of Marcus and Heather.

Had Barbara's mother been able to stay with her after Heather was born, it is much more likely that Barbara's mental illness would have been detected, because her mother would have observed Barbara's increasingly odd, paranoid behavior and failure to maintain even minimal personal hygiene. With information about her bizarre daily activity, the psychiatrist would have been more certain of the necessity of either changing her medicine to an antipsychotic drug or implementing an involuntary hospitalization over Barbara's objections; either intervention would have significantly reduced her risk of maternal filicide.

6

Detached Mother, Denial Type
Cathy

Fourteen-year-old Cathy awoke on her bedroom floor after midnight and began screaming when she saw she was covered in blood. Her mother, Amanda, rushed to her room and found Cathy, her only child, huddled in the corner trembling and terrified. Amanda gasped and nearly fainted: The still body of a newborn baby lay on the floor beneath a wall that was splattered with blood. Amanda tried to comfort her daughter, but Cathy kept rocking back and forth moaning with her eyes closed. As Cathy's stepfather, Keith, looked into her room, he too was shaken, but for different reasons.

When her mother had remarried 11 months earlier, Cathy was ecstatic. Keith appeared to be so different from her alcoholic, violent father, who had abandoned them when she was 7 years old. Shortly after Keith and Amanda began dating, he wanted Cathy to go with them to restaurants or the movies. Keith would help prepare dinner at their apartment and play card games with them after the dishes were done. Cathy would smile when she saw her mother and her new boyfriend together, as they seemed to be a perfect match. Keith would buy presents and arrange trips to the beach or tickets to concerts. He would occasionally stay overnight in Amanda's room, which made Cathy uncomfortable, like the times when Keith would hug her too closely or brush against her developing chest.

When Amanda had talked with Cathy about menstruation and puberty last year, they were too embarrassed to talk about sex, intercourse, and pregnancy. A few months before, her mother had given her an illustrated book from the library, but Cathy was too nervous to ask questions about what she had seen and read. Amanda had not thought she needed to discuss boys with her daughter because Cathy had never shown any interest in dating and was too shy to talk with other teenagers when they went to church. When Keith would spend the night or touch her bust "accidentally," Cathy would not say anything to her mother because she was afraid he would get angry and no longer date Amanda.

After a few weeks of dating, Keith suggested to Amanda that he could pick up Cathy after school while Amanda was at work. He was a car salesman who could rearrange his work hours as needed. When she saw how enthusiastic her daughter was about his offer, Amanda agreed. Cathy was happy that she could ride home with Keith because she had no friends at school or in the neighborhood. A large-boned, awkward, and self-conscious 13-year-old girl, she was often teased and laughed at when riding on the school bus. After her parents divorced, Cathy and her mother had moved frequently as Amanda jumped from one low-wage job to another in an effort to make ends meet. As the "new kid" in each school she entered, Cathy was always anxious in class and had never learned how to make or keep friends.

When Keith would show up at school in a new luxury car, Cathy saw the looks of surprise and envy in her classmates' eyes. At first, Keith simply dropped Cathy off at her apartment, but he soon suggested that they stop for a Coke or ice cream, which he called their "little dates." Cathy had never had another adult take such a strong interest in her. Her grandparents had died many years ago, and she had no aunts or uncles. Though Cathy felt close to her mother, Amanda had always seemed too tired after work to talk with her in the evenings. Cathy began hoping that Keith would marry her mother and daydreamed about having a new father who would love and protect her.

After dating Keith for 4 months, Amanda told Cathy about their plans to wed. Cathy and her mother moved into Keith's home, and for the first time in her life, Cathy felt secure and safe. Rather than a small, two-bedroom apartment, they now lived in a large three-bedroom house with two bathrooms.

Shortly after the wedding, Amanda was offered a job promotion that would require her to work until 10 P.M. Keith encouraged her to take the position because the new family needed the additional income, and he volunteered to cover Amanda's duties in helping Cathy with her homework after school. Amanda's new job was more demanding than she anticipated, and soon she was coming home later and later each night. Cathy felt that her mother was less interested in her because she always seemed to be at work or thinking about work; as a result, her stepfather became more and more important in her daily life. Keith was always willing to talk with her during the dinners they shared, and over time their "little dates" expanded to movies and watching television together. At bedtime, Keith would ask for a good-night hug; then he began giving her a kiss on the cheek. Though these rituals made Cathy anxious, she did not complain because she enjoyed her stepfather's attention.

One night Cathy was preparing for bed, and Keith "accidentally" entered the bathroom while she was drying herself after showering. He did not immediately leave but apologized for seeing her naked. They never discussed the incident, but two nights later, while Cathy was doing her homework at the kitchen table, Keith came up behind her and began to fondle her breasts. Cathy was paralyzed with fear and was unable to speak; though she tried to get up, he continued until his hands were inside her shirt. He abruptly stopped and told her not to tell her mother. He then went into the living room as if nothing had happened and called to her to watch television with him. Cathy entered the room in a trance, feeling like a zombie. When he later kissed her good night and fondled her between her legs, she offered no resistance. After her mother came home that night and tucked her in bed, she pretended to fall asleep quickly to avoid talking with her. Cathy stayed awake almost all night crying into her pillow.

The next morning, a Sunday, Keith made breakfast and proposed a day trip to the beach because, he said, they had not vacationed as a family since Amanda's promotion. Amanda was enthusiastic about his plans, though Cathy remained quiet. She complained to her mother of a stomachache but agreed to go with them. Cathy wore an ankle-length cover-up and remained under the beach umbrella all day, saying that she did not want to get sunburned; in truth, she did not want Keith to see her in her swimsuit. Listening to her radio with headphones during the day-long trip kept her from having to talk with either parent. When she went to bed that night, Amanda was in the room, and Keith did not attempt his good-night hug and kiss.

The following evening, while Amanda was at work, Cathy tried to avoid having any contact with Keith by coming home from school on the bus and then staying in her bedroom. Keith entered her bedroom incensed because he had waited for her at school. As she tried to leave her room, he grabbed her and pushed her onto her bed. He ripped her shirt and digitally penetrated her vagina. He then unzipped his pants and held her hand on his penis. After he climaxed quickly, he angrily told her not to tell her mother, that the episode would be their secret. Cathy nodded blankly, unable to speak.

The next night, Keith undressed Cathy, removed his clothes, and forced her to have intercourse. She screamed in pain as he entered her, but he did not stop. After he finished, he told her to throw out her bloodstained bedsheets. He threatened to put them back on the street and harm her mother if she told anyone. Cathy, stunned again by his violence, obeyed wordlessly. Keith raped Cathy four more times that month, waiting each time until Amanda left for work. Cathy would never speak while she was being assaulted but would close her eyes and picture herself hiding in her closet, just as she had done as a child when her drunken father would beat her mother.

One night, Amanda arrived home early from work and saw Keith rapidly leaving Cathy's bedroom dressed in his shorts and a T-shirt. She questioned him, but Keith denied he had done anything wrong. When she asked Cathy what happened, her daughter hesitantly confirmed her stepfather's lie. Amanda then angrily told her husband she would call the police if he ever touched her daughter sexually. Keith left Cathy alone after nearly getting caught and also stopped his nightly ritual of hugs and kisses. Amanda, still worried about her daughter's welfare, arranged to return to her day schedule at work.

Cathy was happy to have her mother back in her life and once again felt safe and secure. She was now able to avoid being alone with her stepfather, and Keith did not object when Cathy began taking the school bus home in the afternoons. Her dread of her stepfather's nighttime visits began to recede, and her memories of his attacks dimmed. When thoughts about being raped would unexpectedly enter her mind, Cathy found that she calmed down if she distracted herself by playing her stereo or daydreaming alone in her room. Whenever Amanda had errands to run, Cathy would always volunteer to go with her to avoid having to be at home with Keith. Amanda noticed that her daughter seemed to be going through a childish phase, as she would now want to snuggle next to her mother on the couch when they would watch television with Keith in the evenings.

Cathy was not concerned when she missed her period because her menstrual flows had been very irregular and scanty since she had started the preceding year. She was nauseous many mornings in the following weeks, but she thought she had contracted a persistent flu bug that had been circulating at school. Feeling tired more frequently throughout the day, Cathy would often fall asleep in the early evenings and have difficulty getting up in the mornings. She continued to wear bulky sweaters, skirts, and slacks to be less appealing to her stepfather and to escape the taunts of the schoolboys, who would make comments about her growing figure. She believed she was gaining weight because she was having junk food snacks after school and second helpings at dinner. Amanda thought Cathy was going through an adolescent growth spurt. As the school year continued, Cathy seemed to regain her energy during the day, but she occasionally experienced abdominal pain, which she thought was indigestion. Her menstrual periods did not return, but she gave it little thought; she never considered that she might be pregnant.

Though she remained wary of Keith and did not like the way he looked at her at times, she was happy that her mother and stepfather appeared to be renewing the affection they'd had when they first married. Her parents began going out to dinner and the movies on weekends, often returning home shortly before midnight to find Cathy asleep in her room. She did not object to her parents being gone at night because she enjoyed being alone at home. Cathy was pleased that her mother did not think she was a child who needed a babysitter.

Approximately 8 months after she was raped by Keith, Cathy awoke one morning with strange feelings in her abdomen. She thought that she had a stomachache, but she had never felt like this before—her stomach would become tense, then stop, then become tense again a few minutes later. She told her mother she was not feeling well, and Amanda let her stay home from school. She knew that her parents were going out to dinner and a movie that night, but she assured her mother that she would be all right at home alone.

Throughout the day, Cathy continued to feel stomach pains, which became stronger in the early evening. When Cathy's water broke as she lay on her bed, she panicked, then briefly passed out.

When she awoke sweating and soaked, she felt as if she were having a huge bowel movement. She tried to get to the bathroom but fell to the floor, exhausted. Her pains were now so intense and prolonged that her mind went blank. She had never been so terrified in her life; everything was a blur. She felt as if she were dying from the pains in her stomach. She screamed as the baby emerged. She passed out again, then awoke to the baby's crying. Cathy screamed again at the sight of all the blood and tried to push herself away from the mess on her floor. As the baby cried louder, Cathy became more frightened and panicky. She clamped her hands to her ears and closed her eyes, but the noise would not stop. The next thing Cathy remembered was that the noise had stopped. She fell asleep exhausted. When she awoke, she began screaming again, then realized that she was in the arms of her mother.

Case Analysis

Cathy's experience is a good example of numerous case reports of very young, unprepared first-time mothers who have refused to believe that they were pregnant despite obvious signs and symptoms. Cathy's psychological blindness to her pregnancy is actually a very common pattern in young women who subsequently commit neonaticide. For example, in one study of 47 neonaticides, 40% of the mothers had denied their pregnancies (Oberman, 1996). A number of classifications have described this category of maternal homicide as an extreme reaction to pregnancy and fear of childbirth.

Denial-based neonaticides often result from unattended births in nonmedical settings such as bedrooms, hotel rooms, and bathrooms. A recent, widely reported example was the teenage "Prom Mom" who in 1997 gave birth in the women's rest room, then returned to her school's annual dance (Meyer & Oberman, 2001). Using bathrooms as nonmedical birthing places has resulted in at least one commentator describing these highly risky episodes as "porcelain deliveries" (Gruskin, 2001).

Because they are alone when giving birth, have not sought prenatal medical care due to their denial of pregnancy, and are afraid people will discover their condition, these mothers are often at very high risk for hiding their deliveries and discarding their babies in undetected locations (National Abandoned Infants Assistance Resource Center, 2003). Studies of mothers who do abandon their babies at hospitals (e.g., U.S. Department of Health and Human Services, 2004a) seem to share many of the demographic characteristics of the cases in the detached-mother, denial type, category.

Maternal Filicide Risk Matrix Analysis

The risk matrix for Cathy is displayed in table 6.1.

Table 6.1
Maternal Filicide Risk Matrix: Cathy

Factor	Pre-P	P/D	EP	LP	PI
Individual					
Age at current pregnancy	R	R			
Intelligence level	P	P			
Education level	R	R			
Medical status	P	R			
Emotional status	R	R			
Trauma history	R	R			
Maternal attitudes	R	R			
Family of Origin					
Mother's parenting	P	P			
Father's parenting	R	R			
Marital/family stability	P	R			
Situational					
Marital/partner status	R	R			
Financial status	R	R			
Child-care status	—	—			
Infant's temperament	—	—			

Note: R = Risk; P = Protective; Pre-P = Prepregnancy; P/D = Pregnancy/delivery; EP = Early postpartum; LP = Late postpartum; PI = Postinfancy.

Prepregnancy Stage

At this stage, Cathy faced numerous individual, family of origin, and situational risk factors. In terms of individual factors, young age and limited education have been well-documented markers associated with neonaticide and infant abandonment. Cathy's preadolescent experiences of family instability and impoverishment due to parental divorce and marital violence were very damaging to her emotional well-being and made her vulnerable to subsequent physical and/or sexual assaults. Research has shown that exposure to abuse in childhood is associated with higher risks of victimization at later ages (Pizarro & Billick, 2003; Sattler, 1998).

Her dissociative reactions to her father's violence and her stepfather's sexual assaults may have predisposed her to remaining silent and in denial of her pregnancy. Dissociation and denial are highly similar defense mechanisms for escaping stressful reality: In essence, Cathy's thinking and reasoning became paralyzed, causing her to be unable to act directly on the source of trauma. Her lifelong difficulties in developing interpersonal skills led to a failure to establish secure, supportive peer relationships after her mother remarried. Had she had at least one close friend in whom she could confide, Cathy might have been able to summon the courage to tell her mother (or teacher or school counselor) of her stepfather's sexual abuse prior to being raped and impregnated.

In terms of family of origin and situational factors, Cathy's lifelong secure attachment to her mother was a strong protective factor for her throughout her biological parents' crises and instability. Her mother's consistent care for her gave her a sense of stability and love that allowed her to weather her own prepregnancy adolescent problems of frequent readjustments to new schools and classes. Her mother's improved emotional stability after she married Keith was a protective factor for Cathy. However, her mother's change in work schedule and job responsibilities reduced her energy to attend to the crises in Cathy's life due to Keith's sexual assaults.

Pregnancy/Delivery Stage

Cathy's neonaticide risk during her pregnancy remained very high, as she completely denied the reality of her physical symptoms and medical condition. Keith's sexual assaults continued during this stage and did not stop until her mother accidentally discovered him leaving Cathy's room. Her medical status became a risk factor in that her denial of pregnancy prevented her from obtaining prenatal care and support that might have helped her cope in ways that would have protected her and the life of her baby. Discovery of her pregnancy would have very likely led to mother-daughter discussions and counseling about abortion, planning for the baby's birth, adoption, or keeping the baby in the family. The discovery would have also led immediately to investigations of paternity, which would have stopped her stepfather's rapes and other sexual assaults.

Because of her denial of pregnancy, Cathy was deprived of any positive bonding with her fetus. As a result, her trauma-induced absence of maternal attitudes toward motherhood became another risk factor for neonaticide. Though her mother's wedding had briefly provided more marital, locational, and financial stability to Cathy and her mother, these protective factors evaporated in the shocking aftermath of her baby's delivery and death. Amanda's soothing, nurturing holding of her blood-soaked daughter on that tragic night validated that she was Cathy's rock of support.

If Amanda or others had recognized some of the risk intervention points (discussed later), Cathy's victimization and pregnancy might have been avoided. Even when Cathy became pregnant, if Amanda had realized her daughter's condition, she would have been present at the baby's birth, the most effective intervention against neonaticide and infant abandonment.

Relevant Research: Posttraumatic Stress Disorder After Rape

Posttraumatic stress disorder (PTSD) is a disabling psychiatric condition resulting from exposure to and/or directly experiencing an event of actual or life-threatening serious injury during which the victim's immediate reaction is helplessness, intense fear, or horror (American Psychiatric Association, 2000). Studies of rape victims have shown that up to 94% develop significant, enduring, and intrusive anxiety-related symptoms in three areas: (1) persistent unexpected reexperiencing of the trauma through distressing recollections, dreams, and/or feelings that the assault is recurring; (2) persistent avoidance of situations, thoughts, activities, or persons that arouse memories of the trauma; and (3) persistent symptoms of anxiety, such as startle responses, sleep disturbance, concentration difficulties, and outbursts of anger. The severity, duration, and degree of impairment from rape is dependent on many factors; however, the most vulnerable victims are, like Cathy, young, sexually inexperienced, and previously traumatized females (Briere, 1997).

Research has demonstrated that almost every rape victim reports significant symptoms following the sexual assault (Burgess & Holmstrom, 1979; Nadelson, Notman, & Carmen, 1986). The majority have been found to progress through three sequential but overlapping phases of response to sexual assault: acute reaction, outward adjustment, and integration/resolution (Sutherland & Scherl, 1970). Symptoms seen in the first and second phases may be repeated in the last phase. The acute-reaction phase is characterized by shock, disbelief, and disruption of normal functioning. The victim is often mute and unable to think. Like Cathy, immediately after rape, victims frequently look and act as if they were robots, mechanically responding to their surrounding environment.

Cathy's shock and disbelief were deepened because her perpetrator was her stepfather, a man whom she had trusted and who had given her a sense of security for the first time in her life. Previous studies have shown that the impact of trauma is often higher when the perpetrator and victim have a preexisting relationship (American Psychiatric Association, 2000; Briere, 1997). When Keith acted as though nothing had happened after he first fondled her, Cathy's ability to acknowledge or understand his attacks was further disrupted—if he acted as though nothing happened, maybe nothing did. But something had happened, and she had no one to help her because she believed that Keith, like her biological father had, would harm her mother. Keith's repetitive sexual assaults and threats of physical violence terrorized her into keeping their "secret" secret.

The second phase, outward adjustment, often begins within several days or a few weeks after a sexual assault (Sutherland & Scherl, 1970). During this stage, through denial of her anxiety and the impact of the rape, the victim often attempts to reassure herself that all is well. She may appear to be normal to others as she returns to her daily routines. Her outward adjustment, however, is superficial and fragile because the reality of her victimization has not been emotionally acknowledged and/or processed through discussions with a close friend, therapist, pastor, family doctor, or family member.

Cathy's silence reflected a common reaction of rape victims: Research has estimated that as few as 5% of sexual assaults may be actually reported to authorities (Koss, 1993). Though Amanda recognized that her daughter was more childishly clingy, Cathy gave few other outward signs of her victimization. She continued going to school and doing her homework. She did not express anger or rage toward Keith because those actions would make her stepfather angry and might prompt renewed inquiries by her mother, thus jeopardizing Amanda's safety. Cathy's docility, consistent with the behavior of many other rape victims during this phase, was an attempt to avoid the intrusive, disruptive fear and anxiety she experienced. Her denial of rape was facilitated and further consolidated by the cessation of Keith's nighttime visits after her mother altered her work schedule. Though her psychological amnesia for the attacks reduced her immediate feelings of fear and anxiety, her denial blocked her consideration of the longer term consequence of rape: pregnancy.

In the months following Keith's assaults, Cathy did not seek or acknowledge the need for prenatal medical care and interpreted her pregnancy signs and symptoms as due to other causes. When her menstruation, abdominal pain, and morning sickness subsided and she began having more energy during her second trimester, it was easier for her to forget her stepfather's assaults. Like other rape victims, she eventually reached the final, long-term yet overlapping third phase, integration/resolution.

The integration/resolution phase, which essentially continues throughout the lifetime of the rape victim, is an ongoing process of incorporating the trauma into her perceptions of herself and others (Sutherland & Scherl, 1970). Because rape is such an extreme violation of one's most private, intimate space through violence and loss of personal control and autonomy, virtually every rape victim experiences psychological and physical symptoms. Cathy's integration/resolution phase became significantly more complicated when she became pregnant, denied the signs and symptoms of her condition, and kept her pregnancy secret.

Cathy's inability to recognize her pregnancy was the result of denial, a defense mechanism by which she overcame the traumatic memories of being raped by refusing to acknowledge that such actual events ever occurred (Valliant, 1988). Denial is a developmentally primitive form of amnesia that involves the unconscious blocking of the perception, memory, and/or emotional associations of the terrifying event or events despite overwhelming evidence that the trauma occurred (Blackman, 2004). For Cathy, denial was likely reactivated whenever she reexperienced anything associated with her unexpected victimization, such as anxious feelings and ideas about the attacks or certain actions and words by her stepfather.

Denial worked for Cathy for many reasons. By believing the rapes never happened, she experienced immediate relief from intense fear and anxiety; she did not have to reveal the sexual assaults, thus protecting her mother from Keith's threats of violence; and she was able to emotionally tolerate living in the home of her terrorist-rapist. Cathy was apparently no stranger to the use of denial to overcome fear and anxiety. She had used this defense mechanism as a child when she saw and heard her father assault her mother.

When her baby emerged from her, Cathy could no longer deny the reality that she was pregnant. Though she had been thinking and acting for months as though nothing significant were happening to her, she was overwhelmed by the blood, pain, and presence of this child that she had produced. She was alone and terrified, and her baby's screaming further accelerated her confusion and panic. Her months-long fear of Keith's attacks and feelings of helplessness exploded onto her newborn infant. Her terrible act was not made in a fully conscious manner. During her evaluation interviews, she was unable to remember throwing her child. She recalled being alone during her delivery and her newborn's crying, indicating that she was the only possible perpetrator. Selective amnesia—remembering some but not all events—is a common reaction to trauma (Briere, 1997).

The extent of the infant's fatal head injury revealed the depth and intensity of Cathy's bottled-up rage at Keith. The severity of her distress, panic, and anger was also evident in her reports of frequently passing out, likely due to emotional exhaustion, the terror of unattended labor and delivery, and blood loss. Had her mother been home when she entered the final stages of delivery prior to the infant's birth, Cathy's screams would have certainly brought Amanda to her bedroom, and her mother would certainly have called for an ambulance.

Suggestions for Prevention at Risk Intervention Points

The stories in this casebook have been chosen because they are valuable teaching cases. This section is not intended to criticize parents, husbands, or others for not recognizing risk intervention points (RIPs) but to highlight and discuss those points as a mechanism for preventing the situations that lead to increased risks for neonaticide, infanticide, and filicide. RIPs are presented in chronological order based on the theory that the earlier intervention occurs, the more likely it is that current and future risk factors may be reduced, neutralized, or altered into protective factors.

1. *When Amanda had talked with Cathy about menstruation and puberty the previous year, they were too embarrassed to talk about sex, intercourse, and pregnancy.*

Mother-daughter talks about "coming of age" are excellent times to discuss an array of anatomical, gynecological, and sexual matters. Certainly a mother needs to proceed at a pace her daughter is comfortable with; however, she should not rely solely on the school's health and sex education classes to answer all the questions or worries her adolescent may have. Amanda's use of an illustrated book was a good self-initiated intervention as a method of education. Had she followed up with discussions, she might have given Cathy a forum in which she felt comfortable to talk about boys, men, and what to do if she ever experienced unwanted touches.

If Amanda or Cathy were too embarrassed to discuss these issues with each other, Amanda might have asked for help from the school's counselor, sex education teacher, or physical education teacher—a community-based intervention of low complexity. She might have also discussed the matter with her minister or her family doctor or asked for referral to a public health nurse or mental health center clinician. If Cathy had been armed with this information, it might have been easier for her to express her complaints about Keith's behavior to her mother.

> 2. *Though Cathy felt close to her mother, Amanda had always seemed too tired after work to talk with her in the evenings. . . . After her mother came home that night and tucked her in bed, she pretended to fall asleep quickly to avoid talking with her (about Keith's sexual assault).*

Parent-child bedtime discussions are a very important, therapeutic, and nurturing process for family relationships. Nighttime talks provide less hectic opportunities for review of the day's activities, as well as hugs and snuggling that make children feel safe and secure. When children are little, reading a bedtime story is a cherished tradition in many families. As the children get older, however, these rituals are often overcome by the distractions of television, computer games, homework, and other diversions. These nighttime episodes do not need to be lengthy. They may amount to just tucking in. But children—even adolescents—do not lose their need for such focused, physical contact with their parents. At this point in Cathy's life, she felt that her mother was drifting away from her. Cathy had attempted a self-initiated intervention by taking the bus home from school and staying in her room, but Keith's rage and dehumanizing digital rape of her made her realize that she was defenseless. She wanted to reach out to her mother, but Amanda did not immediately respond because of fatigue and the continuing demands of her job, a common dilemma for swing-shift working parents. By the time Amanda did renew their bedtime ritual, it was unfortunately too late.

> 3. *Cathy wore an ankle-length cover-up and remained under the beach umbrella all day.*

This RIP signaled a change in Cathy's behavior at the beach. Though she was a large-boned, awkward teenager, she had previously not been bothered by wearing a swimsuit in public. Adolescents are often very moody and verbally uncommunicative with their parents and often use changes in appearance and behavior to indirectly announce problems they are having. If Amanda had, for example, encouraged or pestered Cathy to get into the water and been rebuffed by her daughter's anxious, demonstrative refusal, she might have been alerted that something significant was bothering her child and that a serious mother-daughter discussion was needed.

> 4. *One night, Amanda arrived home early from work and saw Keith rapidly leaving Cathy's bedroom dressed in his shorts and a T-shirt. She questioned*

him, but Keith denied he had done anything wrong. When she asked Cathy
what happened, her daughter hesitantly confirmed her stepfather's lie.

When this event occurred, Amanda was confronted with the reality of the damaging changes Keith had brought into her and Cathy's lives. She recognized that Keith may have been sexually inappropriate with Cathy. She questioned both but did not pursue her inquiry further after her daughter's answer in Keith's presence. Had she asked the same question in private, Cathy might have told her the truth. By now, Cathy was older, and Amanda could have talked much more frankly with her about sexual matters. Sometimes, however, we do not see what we are afraid to see and do not hear what we are afraid to hear. Amanda may have been too overwhelmed by the incident's implications that Keith was raping her daughter.

When sexual abuse occurs within a family, disbelief is a common reaction. Amanda was fortunately able to change her job schedule, another example of a good self-initiated intervention, though this intervention protected her daughter only from future danger. If Amanda had taken Cathy for an appointment with their family doctor, explaining to her that a budding teenage girl needs an annual physical examination, routine blood tests would have revealed her pregnancy and likely prompted prosecution of Keith for his sexual assaults. These revelations would have initiated regular prenatal care, rape-crisis therapy for Cathy and mother-daughter counseling sessions, and preparations for the baby's arrival. Through these community-based interventions of low to moderate complexity, many risk factors would have been neutralized and become protective factors as Cathy's pregnancy continued. Most important, neonaticide would have been prevented.

> 5. *When Cathy's water broke as she lay on her bed, she panicked, then briefly passed out. When she awoke sweating and soaked, she felt as if she were having a huge bowel movement.*

Technological changes have provided new opportunities for risk management and prevention of tragic events such as neonaticide. This case occurred well before the advent and widespread use of cell phones and pagers. As Cathy was entering labor in her bedroom, Amanda and Keith were out for the night and not immediately reachable while traveling in their car or sitting in the movie theater. If pagers and cell phones had been available, Cathy might have been able to contact her mother on that tragic night before her baby was born, then died.

Epilogue

Amanda dialed 911, and soon both the police and emergency medical technicians were at their house. She angrily confronted Keith, who quickly confessed to raping his stepdaughter. The police arrested Keith and notified Amanda that charges would also likely be brought against Cathy for the murder of her baby.

Cathy was transported to the emergency room and remained in the hospital for a week until she was medically stable to be released into the custody of her mother.

Because of the circumstances of Cathy's pregnancy and Keith's confession, the county prosecutor decided not to transfer her case to adult criminal court. As a minor, Cathy was entitled to be judged in family court, where treatment and rehabilitation, rather than punitive confinement, were more likely to be the dispositions of her case. In accordance with state law, Cathy was placed for 90 days in the Department of Youth Service's assessment center for completion of psychological and psychiatric presentence evaluations. She was also examined by defense-retained experts in forensic psychology and psychiatry. The clinicians for the prosecution and defense attorneys came to similar conclusions in recommending individual, group, and mother-daughter psychotherapy, as well as psychotherapy with medication for Amanda, who had become severely depressed because of her guilt and shame at failing to protect Cathy.

Cathy was allowed to plead guilty to the lesser charge of manslaughter. She was confined in the juvenile detention facility until her 16th birthday, then released to her mother's custody and placed on probation until age 19.

Keith pled guilty to one count of first-degree criminal sexual conduct with a minor and was sentenced to 15 years in prison.

7

Detached Mother, Ambivalent Type
Edna

Edna watched as the two detectives walked toward her front door. She knew why they were coming to see her. They had called from the police station that morning and said they needed to ask her some questions about a case they were investigating. She met them on the front porch so that her parents would not know they were there. The men showed her their badges and asked to see her driver's license to confirm her identity and age. Edna tried not to show how anxious she felt, but she began sobbing shortly after the detectives started questioning her. She quickly confessed to what she had done in her university dormitory room just 5 days earlier.

When she had graduated from high school the previous June, Edna could not wait for the fall semester to start at the university located nearly 5 hours away from her home. She would finally be on her own, free from her parents and the rural town in which she had lived all her life. Edna saw the university as her only opportunity to see the world she had seen in movies and read about in books.

Edna was the oldest of three children, born to parents who never finished high school after they had married at age 16. Both parents worked full time in the local textile mills. Because of their limited educations, they had encouraged Edna and her siblings to do well in school so they could graduate from college, and then return home to higher paying local employment. Her mother and father had been raised in a small rural Appalachian town and had known each other almost all their lives. They had few friends before or after marriage, because they were and always had been shy and uncomfortable in social situations outside their close-knit, very conservative, deeply religious families.

Edna's grandparents had been founding members of the community's church, and her mother and father still regularly attended twice-weekly services, as they had when they were children.

Her parents had been raised strictly with the frequent use of spankings and physical discipline on the basis of "spare the rod and spoil the child." Though they had not been abusive to Edna, they were very restrictive with her throughout her childhood and adolescent years. Her mother and father had rules that were to be followed to the letter; infractions resulted in an angry banishment to her room, loss of playtime outside, and/or additional household chores. It was unthinkable to Edna to rebel against her parents' regulations, because they could get so upset if she broke a rule. Her parents expected her to get excellent grades, and they checked that she had completed her homework each day until she entered the 7th grade. Thereafter, they could no longer understand the class material.

Though her parents were good providers financially, they preferred to spend the evenings and weekends at home watching television. The family rarely went to the movies or ate at restaurants because such activities were considered a waste of money. Edna could remember only two times when her parents took her on vacations. The only times she had visited large cities were on school-sponsored day trips to the state capitol in the 5th grade and to the state museum in the 6th grade. Each time, her father grumbled about the additional expense the school charged for the excursions, but he allowed her to go for the educational value of the activities.

Edna was quite different from her mother and father. Even before she entered kindergarten, she was outgoing, inquisitive, and extroverted. As the first grandchild, she was the center of attention at each family event. When she went to school, she was very popular with the other children—at recess she was the one most likely to be chosen first for playground games and activities. Edna rarely visited her classmates in their homes or went to pajama parties with her girlfriends because her parents worried about her safety when she was not with them or family relatives.

When Edna was around 12 years old, she had counted the months from her parents' wedding to her birth date and realized that her mother had been pregnant with her prior to their marriage. She never asked either parent about her discovery, knowing that they would be embarrassed to know that she was aware that they had violated their own rules about premarital sexual activity. Edna was not allowed to date boys as a teenager, even though many of her school friends were going steady. Her parents refused to let her out of the house on weekends unless it was a family or church youth group outing. Edna did not openly rebel against her parents' rules, but by the time she was a senior in high school, she had had enough of her parents' restrictions.

Rather than confronting her mother and father directly, Edna developed a "double life" that she had learned from her more adventurous classmates. She would be compliant and obedient in her parents', family's, or teachers' presence. When her parents would allow her to stay overnight with her friends, however, she began experimenting with alcohol, marijuana, and sexual fondling with adolescent senior boys. Edna found these new experiences to be very exciting and impatiently looked forward to the next time she could be with her friends at one of their secret parties. By the end of the summer before she went to the university, Edna had gotten drunk and hung over on alcohol, been high on pot, and lost her virginity with an 18-year-old boy in his car. She could not wait until she got to the university to continue her great adventure into adulthood.

Shortly after she arrived on campus, she went to a local bar with some of the other first-year young women who lived on her dormitory floor. They drank beer until 1 A.M., and Edna got so drunk that she vomited in the women's restroom, and then once again when she got to her room. Though she was hung over and felt physically ill the next day, by afternoon she was ready to go again and climbed in another student's car to go to a fraternity party. Edna again drank beer, but also had mixed drinks that were offered to her.

While at the party, she met Bob, who was in his senior year at the school. She was a little awestruck that a senior would want to spend time with her, but as they continued talking, she found that she was very attracted to Bob. Though she was tipsy from alcohol, she eagerly kissed Bob when he embraced her, then went with him to his room in the fraternity house. They began fondling each other on his bed, and she asked him to lock the door. They were soon naked and made love quickly and excitedly.

They had not stopped to use a condom, and afterward Bob asked if she was taking birth control pills. Edna lied and said she had a prescription so that she would appear to be a more sophisticated woman than she actually was. She had never been on birth control pills because she would have been terrified to ask for her mother's permission and so expose the "double life" she had so carefully concealed for the previous 8 months. Edna would never have considered asking their long-time family physician for the pills; if her doctor had told her parents what she wanted, she knew they would not have allowed her to go to the university. They would have kept her at home to attend the nearby 2-year community college.

For the next week, Bob and Edna continued to have unprotected sex whenever they could, often missing class to be alone in his room. As she became a more skilled lover, Edna thought that she was finally a woman in full control of her life, her independence, and her emerging sexuality.

Late one evening, Bob dropped the bomb: He told her that he had a fiancée at another school whom he would marry after his graduation. Edna was not completely surprised, because her roommate had told her that Bob had been dating someone else before they had begun seeing each other. Though she was upset that he had not been truthful with her, she accepted his revelation as a learning experience on her way to adulthood. When one of Bob's fraternity brothers asked her out, she agreed without hesitation.

Edna then began seeing a number of Bob's other fraternity brothers over the next few weeks. She had intercourse without condoms with three of the young men. Though she sometimes thought that her dating was getting out of control, she quickly dismissed such ideas because she was having so much fun.

The carousel stopped turning when she missed her period in early October. After a few sleepless nights waiting to see whether she was just late, she finally went to a drugstore and purchased a home pregnancy kit. She slowly read the directions and carefully followed the procedures. The test was positive. She anxiously disposed of the strip and repeated the process—positive again. Edna stared at the second strip not believing her eyes; she felt like she was going to faint. She repeated the procedure for the third time, but the same results appeared. She collapsed on the bathroom floor, then wobbled back to her room and fell into bed.

Edna stared at the ceiling with a million disconnected thoughts running through her mind: "What am I going to do now? How can I ever tell Mom and Dad? Who is the father? Maybe I'll miscarry, but if not, what do I do then? Will I have to drop out of school? Will the father marry me? What will my friends say when they see I'm pregnant? Who is the father? How can I ever tell Mom and Dad? Maybe I should just go somewhere, but where? What am I going to do now?"

Edna had few solid memories of the next few days. She stayed in her room and missed nearly a full week of classes. Her roommate asked her if there was anything wrong, and Edna told her that she was just depressed because she had broken up with her newest boyfriend and was having her period. She barely ate anything and had trouble keeping down what she had consumed. She slept poorly and fitfully at night, her mind racing with anxiety and dread.

As she adjusted to the reality of being pregnant, other, more serious long-term considerations emerged. She sometimes had fleeting thoughts of suicide to escape her panic, but she never developed a plan to end her life because of her religious upbringing. She felt paralyzed with indecision.

As the days blended into weeks, Edna ended up doing nothing. She was too embarrassed to confront the fraternity boys and terrified that she would be branded a slut. She believed she could not claim that she had been "date raped," because others had seen her willingly go into bedrooms at the fraternity house during parties and had seen her kissing her dates afterward. She did not go the university health center to see a doctor because she did not want her pregnancy confirmed by another person who would ask her what she wanted to do about the fetus.

She was afraid of what her parents and family would say to her and what they would do to her if she told them she was expecting a child. Her indecision was amplified by her guilty realization that she had enjoyed having sex and likely would have continued if she had not become pregnant. She was on an emotional roller coaster, occasionally even having pleasant daydreams about being a mother.

Eventually, Edna did what she had always done when in a crisis—she focused on her academic studies to keep herself from thinking about her dilemma. She found that it was easy to prevent her roommate from discovering her condition by wearing sweatshirts to class and full-length oversize flannel pajamas to bed. In fact, Edna's typical response to anxiety was to stop eating; thus during her first trimester she actually lost weight. As her nausea and fatigue lessened, she returned to being outgoing, talkative, and sociable.

When her friends asked her why she was not drinking alcohol or dating anymore, she told them she needed to work on her classes to maintain her university scholarship. Indeed, when midterm grades were posted, Edna had been able to achieve three B's and two A's because she had done so well on her last few tests. She called her parents to report her success and thanked them again for letting her come to the university. She was so convincing in her manufactured joy that they never suspected her condition.

Edna came home for the Thanksgiving holiday and had pangs of homesickness when she was surrounded by her family and relatives. Her parents were shocked to see that she had lost weight while at school and asked if she was getting enough to eat. She told them she sometimes missed meals in the cafeteria because she was studying in the library. Her pregnancy was never far from her mind, and she almost told her mother one evening as they were setting the table for dinner. Fortunately, because of the chillier late autumn weather, Edna was able to continue wearing baggy sweaters and slacks to hide her changing figure from her family.

Though she knew her first trimester would soon be over, she still did not know what she would do about the fetus, and she remained unable to resolve or even prioritize the options she had. As before, she found that avoidance was preferable and less anxiety provoking than facing the anticipated consequences of revealing her condition to others. During her time at home, she did come to one decision: She would decide what she would do before Christmas, if she had not miscarried by then. Guilt overwhelmed her as she realized that she had been hoping for a miscarriage as a solution to her dilemma.

After the long weekend holiday, she returned to campus and renewed her focus on her studies. She found that the university was no longer the scary place it had been when she first unpacked her bags. She quickly fell into the routines of attending class, studying, writing papers, and staying up late. One morning as she was showering, she noticed that her stomach was thicker and that the pregnancy was beginning to show. She had never forgotten that she was pregnant, but this discovery raised her anxiety and forced her once again to consider what she would do. Her options remained unchanged: tell her parents, determine paternity and settle child support and custody, give the baby up for adoption, or terminate the pregnancy.

True to her academic predisposition, she had begun reading pamphlets and articles about the alternatives before her. Though her efforts increased her knowledge and temporarily reduced her anxieties, her research did not bring her any closer to a resolution. Each choice required her to face the reality of the wrath of her parents and the identified father, as well as her own lifelong guilt if she chose adoption or abortion.

As the weeks passed, the pressure on her to make a decision increased. By now, she knew it was unlikely that she would have a miscarriage, as she was close to finishing her third month of pregnancy. She realized that it would be more difficult to conceal her condition when she went home for Christmas vacation. She began plotting how she would deceive her parents into letting her stay on campus for the semester break or shorten the amount of time she'd be at the family home.

In mid-December, she called her parents and told them that she would have to stay at the university over the Christmas and New Year's holidays to research and finish major papers she had due in each of her four classes. She felt awful not being entirely truthful with them and almost blurted out her true condition when her parents sounded so disappointed. It would be the first Christmas family gathering she would miss. She quickly offered an alternative plan of coming home on December 24th but returning to school on December 27th. Her parents reluctantly agreed, and Edna hung up feeling guiltier than she had ever been in her entire life.

After Christmas, which passed without incident except for her parents' continued concerns about her lower weight, Edna returned again to campus and began working on the four term papers she actually did have due in mid-January. As always, she enjoyed being a student and reveled in the discoveries she made as she spent long hours at the library. Soon it was clear that she had finished her first trimester, and she knew by her research that she could no longer legally terminate her pregnancy. She was shocked to realize that she had considered abortion as a reasonable solution to her dilemma.

Though she twice approached the university health center to make an appointment to see a doctor, she was too anxious to stay in the student waiting room. She feared the questions she would be asked by the doctor: Why hadn't she come in earlier? What prenatal care had she had? and so forth.

She had always known that the longer she delayed telling her parents, the more questions she would have to answer: Why hadn't she told them sooner? How had it happened? How could she have done this to the family? Who was the father? What do you mean you're not sure?

She also now dreaded the furious threats the identified prospective father might pose: She had lied to him about taking birth control pills. It wasn't his baby; he knew she had had sex with at least three other guys. She was trying to trap him.

Faced with such terrifying alternatives, Edna finally made a decision. She realized that now, alone and without any family ever finding out, she would take care of her problem as best she could. She was surprised at the temporary relief from anxiety she felt with this resolution of her crisis. Though she had gained some weight in the past few weeks, she was never very uncomfortable physically and was able to sleep soundly at night. When her roommate did not return for the second semester because of failing grades, Edna did not have to conceal her condition while in her room.

Edna made excellent first semester grades and, as an honors student, was asked to become more actively involved in a faculty member's laboratory research. She would often spend late evenings and weekends working as a lab assistant. When spring break came, her parents accepted that she would have to stay on campus to continue her work. Though she was still able to conceal her pregnancy from those who saw her on a daily basis, she knew her family would be alarmed at her larger size. At the end of the semester, almost all of the women in her dormitory had left campus; Edna, however, stayed an extra week to finish up a laboratory experiment.

She recognized the early signs of labor because she had read carefully about giving birth. She had prepared to deliver alone in her room when the time came. Edna anticipated each step of the process but was unprepared for the intense pains she felt during the final stage of delivery—it was one thing to read about the experience and another to actually live it. Though her dormitory was nearly empty, she bit on a towel to muffle the sounds of her screams. With the baby at her feet, she again realized that she could not face the questions and criticism of family and others as she went through the process of adoption.

Sobbing and distraught, she hugged the baby to her chest until he stopped breathing then wrapped the newborn in the bloody towels and sheets. She struggled across the hall and deposited the body down the garbage chute.

She never left her room for the next 3 days. Though exhausted, she rested fitfully, often crying herself to sleep. When awake, she tried to block her recent memories from her mind, without success. When she arrived home on the train, she explained to her parents that her exhaustion was due to the heavy academic and work load she had carried for the past few months.

When the detectives called, she knew that the baby had been discovered.

Case Analysis

Prior to her baby's death, the salient feature of Edna's case had been her fear of disclosing her pregnancy to someone else: her parents, a university doctor, a friend, or the prospective father. Her reluctance to tell others is a very common pattern in neonaticide cases and is illustrative of Oberman's (1996) analysis that neonaticide is more likely due to poor communication than a lack of financial resources.

Although Edna was very intelligent, studious, and outgoing, there were indications that she might have difficulty if she became pregnant. She was outwardly compliant and submissive with authority figures (e.g., parents, teachers, etc.) but could express socially unapproved impulses such as sexual feelings and actions only through the deception of a "double life." She was very sexually inexperienced, having begun intercourse less than a year before she became pregnant. She had numerous sexual partners, which made it difficult to identify the father and increased her guilt at being a promiscuous woman when she got pregnant. Her fear and apprehension about confronting others kept her from requiring her partners to use condoms and led to her lying about her use of birth control pills.

She was too embarrassed, even once on the university campus, to seek birth control pills from a physician; her reticence ultimately became her undoing. Though she thought of herself as a modern American woman, in many ways she was still a little girl who had not sufficiently mastered the personal independence issues of adolescence and young adulthood. Had she been a more directly rebellious youth with her parents, she might have learned better, through parent-adolescent arguments, how to accommodate her impulses of independence and develop the more mature adult skills of problem anticipation and solution.

There were other indications that she would likely have difficulty adjusting to an unintended pregnancy. She was away from her primary support group of family and friends, and, though she found the independence liberating, she was too embarrassed to seek their help when she got pregnant. She knew that her parents had been sexually active prior to marriage, but she never felt she could mention it to them, fearing their anger and embarrassment. She never had any meaningful discussion with either parent about premarital pregnancy other than to agree that it was morally wrong and that abortion was against their family's religious beliefs.

Additionally, Edna had very strong, clear, but secret career aspirations. She had never told her parents that she wished to go on to graduate school and live in a large city rather than return to her hometown. These plans for her future became threatened by the pregnancy and might have increased the chances of abortion or neonaticide. Her prolonged ambivalence about legally terminating her pregnancy also contributed to her case's outcome, as it removed an option that, although unpleasant, would not have had the long-term consequences of a murder conviction.

Maternal Filicide Risk Matrix Analysis

Prepregnancy Stage

Table 7.1 depicts the analysis of Edna's matrix of risk and protective factors at the prepregnancy and pregnancy/delivery stages. In contrast to the very high prepregnancy risk severity for Cathy (chapter 6), Edna's substantially lower risk was due to the higher number of individual and family of origin protective factors that characterized her much less traumatic childhood and adolescence.

Although Edna's young age was a risk factor, her intelligence level and educational achievements were superior to Cathy's. Edna's social and interpersonal skills were also a protective factor for most of her life until her senior year in high school. At an early age, she had developed the ability to attract many classmates into her personal circle with her extroverted demeanor; in contrast, Cathy simply lacked any ability to make or retain friendships. Edna's maternal attitude during her prepregnancy stage was a risk factor in that she gave little thought to birth control or identification of paternity. Pregnancy

Table 7.1
Maternal Filicide Risk Matrix: Edna

Factor	Pre-P	P/D	EP	LP	PI
Individual					
Age at current pregnancy	R	R			
Intelligence level	P	P			
Education level	P	P			
Medical status	P	R			
Emotional status	P	R			
Trauma history	P	P			
Maternal attitudes	R	R			
Family of Origin					
Mother's parenting	P	R			
Father's parenting	P	R			
Marital/family stability	P	P			
Situational					
Marital/partner status	R	R			
Financial status	R	R			
Child-care status	—	—			
Infant's temperament	—	—			

Note: R = Risk; P = Protective; Pre-P = Prepregnancy; P/D = Pregnancy/delivery; EP = Early postpartum; LP = Late postpartum; PI = Postinfancy.

simply became a very unwelcome, disruptive surprise to her life plans for a professional career.

Her family of origin factors were all protective elements for her prior to getting pregnant. Though her parents were relatively uneducated, somewhat socially avoidant people, they provided her with a stable, predictable, and safe environment, as well as a model for long-term marital stability. Her parents' close ties to relatives and Edna's siblings also served as protective factors during her prepregnancy period.

Edna's relevant situational factors—marital/partner status, financial status, and peer relationships—in the year before her pregnancy/delivery stage were all suggestive of increased risk of neonaticide or infanticide. Her partner status and peer relationships were very dangerous in that she had engaged in the indiscriminate use of alcohol and illegal drugs and promiscuous, unprotected intercourse, which made her vulnerable to an unplanned pregnancy with an unidentified partner. Her financial status was a risk factor in that she, by herself, did not have steady employment or income to live on if she were to become pregnant.

Pregnancy/Delivery Stage

When Edna entered the pregnancy/delivery stage, her emotional status changed from a protective to a risk factor due to her extreme ambivalence and indecision about her condition. Her medical status became a risk factor in that, like Cathy, she failed to obtain prenatal care for herself and her fetus, placing her in significantly greater jeopardy of various illnesses. She avoided alcohol and drugs while pregnant, which seemed to be a positive maternal attitude factor to protect her fetus. In truth, however, she became sober and clean in order to raise her grades and avoid being academically expelled from the university. Her reasons for abstinence were personal more than for her baby—on balance, a risk factor for neonaticide or infanticide. During this stage, her intelligence level and education level remained protective factors, and she used both to learn about her options as a pregnant woman. Her extreme anxiety-driven indecision and repetitive failure to resolve her dilemma through legally or medically appropriate ways indicated that, despite her intellectual and academic resources, she lacked effective judgment.

Some family of origin elements shifted from protective to risk factors due to her anticipation of her parents' explosive and rejecting reaction to her out-of-wedlock pregnancy and her inability to identify the baby's father. Both conditions would significantly strain her parents' mental stability and perhaps reveal that their love for Edna was highly conditional on her displaying proper, socially approved behavior to her siblings, relatives, and community.

Edna's situational factor of partner status continued to be a risk, as she failed to confront any of her prior lovers to establish paternity and avoided discussing her condition with her roommate or other classmates who might have been sympathetic and helpful in her dilemma. Though she did obtain a laboratory assistantship during her pregnancy, her reward was academic rather than financial. Thus her economic situation remained a risk for neonaticide, infanticide, or abandonment as an alternative to raising her baby on her own impoverished resources.

Relevant Research: Adolescent Sexuality and Abortion

Adolescent Sexuality

Edna's story of unprotected sex, unanticipated pregnancy, and ambivalent indecision is a common pattern among sexually active young women and adolescent girls (Cates, 1991; Poppen, 1994). A number of studies have shown that although the levels of adolescent sexual activity in the United States is not higher than in other countries, the United States has the highest rate of teenage pregnancy in the Western world (Braverman & Strasburger, 1994; Jones et al., 1985). Approximately 1 million unmarried adolescent American girls become pregnant each year (Pistella & Bonati, 1998; Roye & Balk, 1997). From this group, 40% will terminate their pregnancies and another 10% will have spontaneous miscarriages or stillbirths, leaving approximately 500,000 babies carried to term (Braverman & Strasburger, 1994; Glasser, Dennis, Orthoefer,

Carter, & Hollander, 1989; McGrew & Shore, 1991). Compared with women who give birth after age 20, pregnant teens tend to have more health complications and higher prenatal and infant mortality rates, primarily due to absent, inconsistent, or inadequate medical care (Bright, 1987; Roye & Balk, 1997). Although adoption is a resolution to an unexpected pregnancy, more than 95% of adolescent mothers decide to keep their babies (Stevens-Simon & White, 1991).

Despite all the national, regional, and local public advertising and education about male and female contraception, research has consistently demonstrated over the past 30 years that many teenage men and women still engage in unprotected sexual intercourse at alarmingly high rates (Poppen, 1994). Adolescent and young adult couples who are sexually inexperienced often use contraceptive methods incorrectly, which also increases their risk of pregnancy (Orr et al., 1992). Although adolescents and young adults are aware of HIV/AIDS and other sexually transmitted diseases, their reported sexual practices have not changed substantially (Clark, Brasseux, Richmond, Getson, & D'Angelo, 1998; Sieving et al., 1997), and many unwanted pregnancies still occur. More permanent methods of pregnancy prevention, such as tubal ligation and vasectomy, are extremely rare with young people due to cost, reduced reversibility, and absence of medical necessity.

Abortion

This section is not intended to advocate for or against abortion, but only to highlight the relevance of the issue when an unwanted pregnancy occurs. Most, if not all, women faced with an unexpected, unwanted pregnancy are placed in the position of having to decide whether to abort the fetus. It is not a choice made easily, and it is typically fraught with anxiety, ambivalence, and uncertainty (Connell, 1992; Stone & Waszak, 1992).

Elective abortions occur in 25% of all U.S. pregnancies, and most are completed by unmarried, low-income women under age 25 (Gober, 1997). Although the debate about abortion has raged on since the *Roe v. Wade* ruling was made, research has indicated that women faced with abortion do not ask themselves about the abstract political arguments. Rather, they rely on practical, interpersonal, and emotional matters to make their decisions (Crooks & Bauer, 1999). Among the factors they consider are the quality of the relationship with the baby's father and the woman's capacity to provide economically for her child; rather than a public policy debate, "these are the real-life dilemmas each woman struggles with in deciding what to do" (Crooks & Bauer, 1999, p. 357).

Suggestions for Prevention at Risk Intervention Points

> 1. *Edna was not completely surprised, because her roommate had told her he'd been dating someone else before they had begun seeing each other.*

Though she was upset that he had not been truthful with her, she accepted his revelation as a "learning experience" on her way to adulthood.

It was unfortunate that Edna did not take the opportunity to talk with her roommate about how to protect herself in sexually intimate relationships. By discussing her sex life with her roommate, she might have found out that the university health center was sensitive to issues of sexuality in their female students, and it might have arranged a referral for her for contraception counseling from one of the center's staff or nurses. These sessions might have prevented Edna from eventually becoming pregnant. Talking frankly with her roommate at this point might have later facilitated Edna's obtaining prenatal care, as well as facing the critical decisions about medically supervised abortion or delivery and adoption. Edna did not make a self-initiated intervention at this RIP, when she became pregnant, but instead shrank from her roommate's concern for her. It was another example of Edna's not trusting that she would get support if she were honest and forthright, a pattern traceable to her early childhood.

2. *After a few sleepless nights waiting to see whether she was just late, she finally went to a drugstore and purchased a home pregnancy kit.*

Edna was capable of some independent action about the consequences of her sexual behavior. This RIP suggests a possible commercial—public health alliance as a low-complexity community-based primary prevention method against neonaticide, infanticide, and undetected abandonment in cases of unplanned pregnancies. If the public health department had acquired free shelf space next to the drugstore's home pregnancy kits for pamphlets about the state's Abandoned Infant Act and the county's problem pregnancy services, an intervention similar to public service radio and television "spots," perhaps Edna would have learned viable alternatives and resources to facilitate her earliest decisions about her pregnancy.

3. *She did not go the university health center to see a doctor because she did not want her pregnancy confirmed by another person who would ask her what she wanted to do about the fetus.*

Had Edna talked frankly with her roommate, as suggested earlier, she might have had a supportive ally to go with her to the health center, to ensure that she did not nervously bolt from the waiting room, to comfort her during her interview with the center's medical staff, to encourage her to schedule follow-up appointments, and to accompany her when she discussed her prenatal and postpartum options. If the center were required to notify Edna's parents, her roommate might have been able to help her talk with a university health center physician or a university counseling center clinician who could act as an intermediary during her discussions with her parents.

These professional resources, for example, might have helped Edna write a "therapeutic letter" to her parents about her pregnancy. Therapeutic letters allow the sender to safely explain and, as needed, apologize for shameful behavior and allow the recipient to explode in rage and/or tears in private. After the smoke clears, both parties have the opportunity to resolve their conflicts with less heated emotion.

> 4. *She recognized the early signs of labor because she had read carefully about giving birth. She had prepared to deliver alone in her room when the time came.*

At this point, believing that all of her options were gone, the likelihood of neonaticide was extremely high unless someone happened to walk by her room during her labor and assisted her unattended delivery. Any of the interventions suggested for the preceding RIPs would have likely eliminated the target behavior of neonaticide because someone else would have known and then been available to help Edna get safely through her unwanted, though self-induced, ordeal.

Epilogue

Edna was charged with the murder of her baby, and the county prosecutor considered filing a death penalty notice against her because of the callous manner in which she discarded her infant victim. After she was arrested, her parents went to the prosecutor to beg for Edna's life. They persuaded him not to file the murder as a capital offense, but he insisted that the charge of murder, not manslaughter, be retained.

Forensic psychologists and psychiatrists for the state and the defense agreed that Edna was able to understand the legal proceedings against her and to assist her attorney in her defense. The judge found her competent to stand trial. Because neither set of experts determined that she suffered from a psychotic disorder, an insanity defense was not raised, and plea negotiations began. Because of Edna's young age and absence of prior arrests or convictions, the judge accepted her plea of guilty to manslaughter but sentenced her to 10 years in prison to be followed by 5 years of probation.

8

Detached Mother, Resentful Type

Francine

Francine put down her crying 5-month-old son, Bobby, to answer the telephone. It was Jimmy calling again to tell her about a party the next night. Jimmy had been Francine's boyfriend, though not Bobby's father, and he wanted to rekindle their relationship. Bobby was a mixed-race child. Francine's parents had never forgiven her for dating Larry, her son's father, who left town when she told him she was pregnant. She knew that her parents did not accept her new baby. Neither did Francine.

Francine was the youngest of her parents' four children, but she had been born 10 years after her next-closest sibling, Helen. Francine had been an unplanned child, born when her parents were in their early 40s. As the baby of the family, she was spoiled with toys, clothes, and dolls. Her mother had returned to full-time work less than 3 months after giving birth. Francine was raised by a series of nannies and babysitters. Her parents were demanding employers—many of the caretakers were fired or quit because of her mother's frequent insistence that the caretakers were negligent, lazy, or stealing. In later years, Francine had difficulty remembering the names and faces of her nannies, because there had been so many before and after she entered public school.

Francine was not sure when she began to feel unwanted by her parents, but she did remember that they seemed to become more distant as she entered her preteen years. Because her parents were so much older than her friends' parents, she often went in her friends' cars to school activities, Girl Scouts, and the parks. She saw how her friends' parents would snuggle and hug their children and actively participate in their games—she was jealous, then angry at her parents' emotional and physical coldness.

In ninth grade, Francine tried out for cheerleading and won a spot on the junior varsity squad. Her social life exploded. She began attending after-game parties with other students and was offered alcohol, marijuana, and cocaine, which she tried so that she would be accepted. At 15, she and her boyfriend began experimenting sexually with mutual fondling, deep kissing, and masturbation to orgasm. When they decided to have intercourse, she was surprised that it was not as painful as she had imagined. It was not the first time for her 18-year-old boyfriend, Sam. He was a gentle, considerate lover.

Francine had a number of boyfriends over the next 2 years, often being intimate with each soon after the first date. None of the relationships lasted more than a few months, because Francine would get bored or restless and then pick an argument with the young man so that he would leave her. Francine would already be on the lookout for her next partner.

When she went on to college, her social life increased significantly. Now that she was away from home, she could go out every night, and she easily found first-year women and men to accompany her. Not surprisingly, Francine was placed on academic probation at the end of the first semester. It was during her second semester that she met Larry.

When Francine realized that she was not going to escape academic probation, she decided to have as much fun as she could before she was kicked out of school. She stopped going to classes and would often sleep in late, recovering from the party she'd gone to the night before. She was seeing Larry almost every day and often sleeping at his off-campus apartment, which was the site of many of their parties. She never introduced her parents to Larry because she knew they would not accept her relationship with an adult man of a different race.

Shortly after failing the second semester and returning home, Francine moved into an apartment at her parents' insistence. They told her that because she had thrown away her opportunity for college, she would have to support herself by getting a job to pay her own bills. Francine found work at a local restaurant as a waitress on the afternoon and evening shifts. The restaurant and bar closed at midnight, and as a new employee she was often scheduled to stay until all the customers had left. Francine did not mind, because after the restaurant closed, she would go out to a party with her fellow employees. At the parties, alcohol, marijuana, cocaine, and other drugs were available in copious quantities; the partygoers were all employed, young, single adults.

When she finally got around to getting her employment medical examination, her doctor told her she was pregnant. Francine was stunned and did not receive the news with joy. She realized that Larry was the only one who could be the father. She called Larry, who at first sounded optimistic and supportive. When the weekend came, however, Larry did not show up. Francine called his apartment and his cell phone, only to discover that both phones had been disconnected. She knew that she was on her own.

Another 2 weeks went by before Francine summoned the courage to tell her parents. As she had expected, they were furious. When she raised the possibility of abortion or adoption, her parents became more enraged and lectured her on her failure to take responsibility for the choices she had made in her life. However, they told Francine that they would help her out financially once she could not work because of her advanced pregnancy. They expected her to continue working for the next few months to support herself for as long as she could. Her parents said that after the baby was born, the child would be her responsibility, although they would still give her money for bills and other baby-related expenses. When her parents saw a picture of Francine and Larry, they realized the baby was a mixed-race child. Her mother told her not to expect baby showers or gifts because they wanted to keep her condition a secret from their friends and neighbors.

Francine continued to work at the restaurant throughout her first trimester. She went to the after-hours parties and found that cocaine gave her energy to overcome her recent fatigue. A month after her talk with her parents, Francine's routine did not seem to be different from that of her prepregnancy state. She worked until late in the evening, often stayed out until the early morning hours, then slept in until noon. At times, she forgot she was pregnant: Her mother twice had to remind her of prenatal appointments with her doctor. When Francine did think of her pregnancy, she would become irritated and sullen, angry that her parents were forcing her to carry the baby to term.

She gained a lot of weight in the second and third trimesters. She felt that her body was unattractive. She worked as a hostess at the restaurant because it required less effort and allowed her to sit on a stool while she waited for new customers. After work, she'd go to her apartment and watch TV until she fell asleep in the early evening. Occasionally, her friends would visit and tell her about the parties she was missing. She felt left out and again resented being pregnant.

Her labor was painful and long, but she finally was able to deliver in the early morning hours while her parents waited at the hospital. She was exhausted after giving birth so late at night and slept most of the next day, awakening only when the nurses would bring her baby into her room. These visits were short and unpleasant. Bobby cried loudly, and Francine became impatient when he would not stop. She did not want to nurse her baby because she was afraid that her breasts, which she considered one of her best features, would become disfigured.

Francine's parents hired a daytime nanny for the first month that she was back in her apartment. She spent the day either sleeping or watching TV while the nanny fed, changed, and bathed Bobby. Francine seemed to have little interest in caring for her baby and would often leave the child alone in his crib in the evenings. When he would not stop crying as she watched television, she'd put on headphones until he fell asleep. After the nanny's employment was over, Francine became the sole caretaker for Bobby. Over the next few months, Francine's life was, to her, a boring routine of feeding, changing, and bathing her son. She found little satisfaction in these duties and dreaded having to clean up Bobby after he had produced a very messy diaper. Sometimes, he would get rashes because she would neglect to change him when he needed it.

When Jimmy began calling her, she would invite him over to her apartment to talk, watch TV, and stay overnight. She missed being around her friends and thought about how lonely she had been since Bobby was born. Some nights, Jimmy would stay over, and they would engage in sexual play. Frequently, Bobby would wake them in the middle of the night with his crying, Jimmy would get angry and tell Francine to take care of her child, and Francine would sullenly get out of bed, feed or change her baby, and wonder again whether this drudgery would ever end.

When Bobby was 5 months old, Francine took him to a weekend party with her old friends. Her girlfriends clustered around Bobby and passed him from one to another. Francine was happy to be back with the crowd. She temporarily forgot she had brought Bobby there as she renewed old friendships, danced, flirted, and took some drugs. When Bobby's crying competed with the party's music, her friends suggested that she should go home so that her son could sleep in his own crib. Francine left, angry that Bobby had kept her from having a good time. At home, she put him in his crib, closed the door, and listened to her stereo with headphones clamped over her ears to block the noise coming from the bedroom.

The next morning, Francine awoke with a hangover from her mixture of alcohol, marijuana, and cocaine. She heard Bobby crying in the bedroom. When she went into the room, she found that the baby had completely wet and soiled his diaper, clothes, sheets, and blanket. She had put a new diaper on him the night before, but in her intoxicated state she had not fully secured the adhesive on one side. As a result, excrement was everywhere—in his crib, in his hair, on his fingers and his face. She felt physically ill from the stench. She picked him up as he screamed and took him into the bathroom to clean up. She saw the dirty dishes piled high in the sink and the magazines and clothes strewn about the living room, and she believed that this was a life from which she could not escape.

She ran some water in the bathtub because the sink was filled with dishes. She placed Bobby in the tub and began to wash his face and hands. He continued to cry. She put him on his stomach to wash his back and legs, but then held his head down into the shallow water and looked away from the tub. She continued pushing on the back of Bobby's neck until he stopped moving. Conflicting emotions flooded her. She briefly cried as she thought about what she had done to her baby, yet also felt relief, as if the burden was gone. She took the body out of the tub and wrapped it in a towel. Francine found an empty bag in her closet and put Bobby in it.

She took the bag to her car, then drove to a wooded area about a mile from her apartment complex. After parking at the end of one of the dirt roads, she carried the bag behind a large tree. She dug a shallow hole with her hands in the soft moist ground, put the bag down, then covered it with dirt and leaves.

She sat next to the tree, crying and trying to pray, but no words would come to her mind.

For the remainder of the day, Francine stayed in her apartment watching television and sleeping. About 9 P.M., she went to the restaurant bar where she used to work and spent the evening drinking and talking with her friends. When they asked where Bobby was, Francine told them that her mother and father had volunteered to keep him overnight. After the restaurant closed, she went along with her friends to a party that lasted until the early morning hours.

Awakening about noon, she called her mother to tell her that Bobby was missing. She told her that she had put her baby in the stroller to take him for a walk in the park but had left him in the lobby briefly to return to her apartment to get his bottle and baby wipes. Francine said that when she went back to Bobby the stroller was there, but he was gone. Her mother called the police to report her missing grandson. The police were immediately suspicious of Francine's account of Bobby's disappearance.

At the station, Francine was introduced to a woman detective who asked to hear her story in her own words. She listened patiently, then told Francine that no one the police officers interviewed remembered seeing a stroller near the entrance nor recalled any strangers in the lobby. Francine insisted that she was telling the truth. The detective brought out a tape recorder and told her that she was under arrest for the murder of her son. Francine started to cry. She told the true story of what she had done. She went with the detectives to show them where Bobby was buried.

Case Analysis

Many women report that when they become pregnant for the first time, the experience stimulates memories of their early relationships with their mothers, who served as their first role models of parenting. If their childhoods were recalled as times of emotional security, warmth, and love, they are likely to have positive bonding with their babies, even in spite of limited financial or material resources. However, if their childhood memories of their mothers are unpleasant, fearful, and anxiety-ridden, described as the "ghosts of the nursery" (Fraiberg et al., 1975), their nurturing capacity may be diminished. Indeed, research has demonstrated that a woman's attitudes toward her pregnancy are predictive of later mother-child attachment (Meesand & Turchin, 2003).

Maternal Filicide Risk Matrix Analysis

The risk matrix for Francine is shown in table 8.1.

Prepregnancy Stage

Francine's age of 18 prior to pregnancy was a risk factor, as maternal age under 20 years has been shown to be associated with increased likelihood of neonaticide and infanticide. Francine's average intelligence and high school-

Table 8.1
Maternal Filicide Risk Matrix: Francine

Factor	Pre-P	P/D	EP	LP	PI
Individual					
Age at current pregnancy	R	R	R		
Intelligence level	P	P	P		
Education level	P	P	P		
Medical status	R	P	P		
Emotional status	R	R	R		
Trauma history	R	R	R		
Maternal attitudes	R	R	R		
Family of Origin					
Mother's parenting	R	R	R		
Father's parenting	P	R	R		
Marital/family stability	P	P	P		
Situational					
Marital/partner status	R	R	R		
Financial status	R	R	R		
Child-care status	—	—	—		
Infant's temperament	—	—	R		

Note: R = Risk; P = Protective; Pre-P = Prepregnancy; P/D = Pregnancy/delivery; EP = Early postpartum; LP = Late postpartum; PI = Postinfancy.

level education were not risk factors because she was neither mentally retarded nor a high school dropout prior to the 11th grade. Francine did not have any known illnesses at this stage. However, her prepregnancy patterns of indiscriminate sexual activity put her at much higher risk for HIV/AIDS and drug dependence, characteristics of mothers who may abandon their babies.

Francine's emotional status was certainly a risk factor. Her behavior and attitudes were suggestive of a reactive attachment disorder, disinhibited type (American Psychiatric Association, 2000), characterized by impairments in impulse control and judgment in social situations. These deficits interfered with her developing a tolerance for frustration, a vital skill for any new mother. Francine's interpersonal skills were poor in that prior to pregnancy she had not developed the ability to maintain an enduring, mutually beneficial, and nurturing relationship with another person who might be a source of support after she became pregnant. As a heterosexual woman, she displayed little desire to form a lasting, satisfying relationship with a man with whom she'd been intimate.

Francine showed little interest in becoming a mother, even though her recurrent risky sexual behavior put her at risk for pregnancy. Her negative maternal attitudes became readily apparent during the pregnancy/delivery and early postpartum stages described later.

Within the family of origin domain, her mother's dismissive parenting attitudes throughout her childhood and adolescent years placed Francine at higher risk for negative reactions to her own pregnancy and motherhood. Her mother delegated her child-care responsibilities for Francine onto a constantly changing series of nannies; she did not appreciate how damaging such unstable parenting was to her daughter's emotional well-being. Francine's father appears to have been, on balance, a stable, predictable figure during the prepregnancy period of her life, suggesting a protective factor. However, he was quite emotionally distant from her in delegating his parenting duties to his wife and other nannies. He was particularly absent as an emotional support to his daughter during her pregnancy/delivery and early postpartum stages. Francine's parents were residentially, financially, and maritally stable before, during, and after Bobby was born, which were protective factors. Notably, Francine's older siblings were not involved in her life. Their absence kept them from being a supportive, protective factor for her, especially once she became pregnant.

Within the situational domain prior to pregnancy, Francine did not have an enduring relationship with a man who might have been a protective factor as a husband or partner. The transient quality of her relationship with Larry, Bobby's father, was evident once she became pregnant—he disappeared. Francine's financial status, based on her own resources, was also a risk factor. Though employed, she appeared to have been spending her income as fast as she was earning it and was unable to support herself without her parents' assistance.

Pregnancy/Delivery Stage

Within the individual domain, being pregnant before age 20 placed Francine at higher risk for neonaticide and infanticide. Her medical status emerged as a protective factor in that she received regular prenatal care, principally at the urging and insistence of her mother. Her delivery of Bobby in a hospital was a protective factor against neonaticide in that others were present at his birth. Because of her resentment at becoming pregnant, Francine likely would have avoided medical care if she had not told her parents. Francine's emotional status and interpersonal skills continued to be risk factors. She displayed little change in her ability to inhibit her impulses or her preference for substance abuse after she became pregnant. During this stage, it appeared that Francine's trauma history was still a risk factor: Her parents' emotionally dismissive and highly judgmental reaction to her pregnancy seemed to be a repetition of the conditional love they gave her during her childhood. Francine's very negative maternal attitude was a significant risk factor for neonaticide or infanticide.

From her first notification of pregnancy until she delivered Bobby, she felt trapped, angered, and resentful about her impending motherhood.

Within the family of origin domain, Francine's mother's parenting continued to be a risk factor in that she persisted in her hypercritical, dismissive judgments of her daughter. Her mother's indication that there would be no baby showers or announcements to the neighbors and family friends was a narcissistic reaction to Francine's pregnancy. That is, she believed that her daughter had done something deliberately harmful to her. Historically, Francine's mother always expected her to fail, and once again, she had. Her mother's negative response to her grandchild may also have encouraged Francine to see her fetus as an "it," thus significantly increasing her risk for neonaticide and infanticide.

Francine's father's stability, measured in terms of emotional support and assistance, appeared to have turned into a risk factor after she became pregnant. He was more remote during this stage, and his absence from her life also conveyed to her that her future child was not acknowledged as a positive event in the family's history. These parental reactions deepened Francine's frustration with her pregnancy, made her feel more trapped, and focused her anger onto her baby. Though both parents provided financial and residential stability as protective factors for Francine, their support was not emotionally nurturing.

Within the situational domain, Larry's disappearance clarified her marital/partner status as a risk factor: Young, single mothers are at greater risk for neonaticide and infanticide. When she realized that he had abandoned her, she was enraged—an ironic contrast to her preemptive pattern of manipulatively severing relationships. She transferred her anger and resentment onto her fetus. Francine's financial status deteriorated after she became pregnant. Though employed, she could not afford health insurance, thus making her more dependent on her parents. Once she entered her third trimester, then gave birth, she was unable to continue earning a living on her own and unable to afford child care.

Early Postpartum Stage

After Bobby was born, Francine's individual risk and protective factors remained essentially unchanged, indicating that little effective intervention had been accomplished. Her negligent, passive, indifferent approach to her personal responsibilities and household duties and her active rejection of her baby suggested the onset of a postpartum depression. However, her behavior and attitudes during this stage were essentially the same as in they had been in the pregnancy/delivery stage, indicating that her personal and maternal neglect was not activated by the birth of her baby.

Her factors within the family of origin and situational domains also remained unchanged during the brief span of Bobby's life. Her parents' refusal to assist her with Bobby reflected their continuing reluctance to welcome their grandson into the family. The marital/partner element was a risk factor in that Larry remained absent and Jimmy had little tolerance for Bobby's crying.

Francine's unstable financial status continued to be a risk factor. It was unclear whether her baby's temperament contributed to her thoughts of infanticide. Her negligent, rejecting maternal behavior might have made even the most placid baby cranky and noisy. Though it was the baby's messy, soiled condition that ostensibly precipitated Francine's crime in the bathtub, her wishes to escape her entrapment had been forming for many months.

Relevant Research: Attachment and Maternal Bonding

At the heart of Francine's case is the impaired infant, childhood, and adolescent relationship she had with her own mother (and father) and her subsequent difficulty in developing a nurturing, loving, caring, and emotionally supportive involvement with her fetus and newborn baby. The relationship between a mother and her child begins with her first awareness of pregnancy and continues throughout the life of both. *Bonding* refers to a mother's feelings for her fetus and infant, whereas *attachment* is the developmental process of the baby's relationship with its mother. The terms are often used interchangeably.

Because humans have the capacity to visualize their babies in the womb, a mother's bonding with her child begins before it is born and is influenced by prenatal experiences (medical examinations, sonograms, etc.), as well as prenatal social rituals (baby showers, purchases, naming, announcements, etc.). An infant's attachment to its mother occurs as it attempts to find physical and emotional security from the fear and anxiety it has as a helpless newborn being (Bowlby, 1973, 1980). The mother's ability and willingness to relieve an infant's distress is fundamental to attachment to her and to the ongoing quality of their relationship (Bell & Ainsworth, 1972). If the mother's feelings toward her baby are positive and if she has the emotional capacity to provide comfort and security for the child, the infant's attachment to her is more likely to be enhanced and secured (George, Kaplan, & Main, 1985).

The process of attachment is not automatic and does not occur instantaneously. Rather, research has shown that attachment and bonding gradually develop over time, though it is substantially consolidated in the first 6 months after birth (Ainsworth et al., 1978; Main, Kaplan, & Cassidy, 1985). The quality of the mother and baby's relationship to each other is the result of the "goodness of fit" between the baby's temperament and the mother's personality (Chess & Thomas, 1986).

Studies of newborns have suggested that, in general, babies' temperaments range from "difficult" (about 10%)—children who react intensely to situations with crying and distress, are difficult to comfort, eat at unpredictable times, and sleep poorly—to "easy" (about 40%)—children who are adaptable to changing situations and who eat, sleep, urinate, and defecate with regularity (Kaplan & Sadock, 1990). The remaining 50% are a mixture of both temperaments and are not able to be categorized as distinctly "difficult" or "easy." Not surprisingly, difficult children place more physical and emotional demands on their mothers and thus require parents to have above-average caretaking capacities to produce successful, secure attachment.

Studies have shown that one measure of the nature of an infant's attachment to its mother is the infant's reaction to her absence (Ainsworth et al., 1978). Infants with *secure* attachment to their mothers become concerned when their mothers leave briefly but are easily comforted and relieved when their mothers return. Babies with *avoidant* attachment do not display distress when their mothers leave and ignore them when they return. Infants with *resistant* attachment are greatly distressed when left alone and are unable to be comforted by their mothers' nurturing when they return.

Similarly, research on mothers of newborns has distinguished three types of maternal bonding to their babies: secure, dismissing, and preoccupied (George et al., 1985). Securely bonded mothers have emotionally balanced, empathic, nurturing relationships with their children. They are capable of perceiving their babies' worlds through the babies' eyes and thus anticipate how their behavior and surrounding situation might affect their children's well-being. Mothers with dismissing styles tend to be indifferent to their children's immediate and daily functioning and welfare. Though not necessarily neglectful, these women provide for their babies' physical comfort but are less likely to be emotionally nurturing through talking, cooing, snuggling, singing, or rocking their infants. Preoccupied mothers tend to have histories of past or current unsatisfying relationships with their mothers, fathers, and/or significant others—such as the babies' fathers—that interfere with their ability to provide a secure, nurturing environment for their infants.

The widely held belief that all mothers love and become bonded to their babies, the "myth of maternal bliss," has not been supported by research (Spinelli, 2003). Unfortunately, not all mothers have positive, nurturing thoughts about the babies they carry during pregnancy, as seen in the cases of Cathy, Edna, and Francine. Research suggests that approximately 1 in 10 mothers will have a delayed attachment to their infants and that nearly 1 in 100 will have specifically negative or hostile thoughts about their fetuses and/or newborn children (Spinelli, 2003). The cases of Cathy, Edna, Francine, and Glenda (chapter 9) illustrate how a mother's inability to bond with her baby may result in disastrous, tragic consequences.

The difficulty that Francine had in bonding with Bobby likely had its origin in her relationship with her own mother. Francine was an unexpected baby born 10 years after her mother's previous child. Her mother's quick return to work less than 3 months after she was born and her employment of a continuous line of different nannies suggested that she might have had negative or ambivalent feelings toward her youngest daughter. Francine's memory of her childhood was that she did not feel cherished or loved by her mother or father. She recalled that those early years were unpleasant and unfulfilling until she went to public schools.

Francine's inability to securely bond to Bobby was clearly evident in the inadequate, indifferent care she gave her son. Her recollections of her pregnancy suggested that she was one of those unfortunate mothers who had negative, hostile feelings for her fetus. Her dismissive feelings toward Bobby did not change during the course of his brief life. She appeared to be incapable of empathy for her son, of appreciating how scared Bobby felt when he was left alone in his crib for hours at a time. It is likely that even when Bobby was as young as 6 weeks old, he may have been capable of perceiving his mother's indifference to him (Brazelton, Koslowski, & Main, 1974).

Suggestions for Prevention at Risk Intervention Points

Francine's risk intervention points (RIPs) began with the first discovery of her pregnancy. The interventions suggested are almost all community-based, moderately complex methods because of the family's significant dysfunctional history and Francine's extremely negative, resentful reaction to her pregnancy.

> 1. *When she finally got around to getting her employment medical examination, her doctor told her she was pregnant. Francine was stunned and did not receive the news with joy.*

Problem pregnancies are a too-common occurrence with adolescent girls. It is important for family physicians to have educational and reference materials available to help young women who are newly discovered to be pregnant process their unexpected crisis. Francine's reaction of displeasure was likely an important sign that she would have trouble accepting her fetus.

As indicated in Edna's case, women faced with decisions about whether to terminate their pregnancies eventually, after many tears, take a pragmatic approach to their conditions. Because Francine was stunned by this disruption to her carefree lifestyle, she might have then been more receptive to an impromptu session of crisis counseling wherein she could express her anger and fear about her pregnancy. After the session, Francine could have been given a referral for follow-up services with a public health service program, the community mental health center, or a private sector mental health practice specializing in women's services. Coordinating those services with the physician's subsequent prenatal care might have led to a more positive resolution for Francine and the baby.

> 2. *Francine's routine did not seem to be different from that of her prepregnancy state. She worked until late in the evening, often stayed out until the early morning hours, then slept in until noon . . . her mother had to twice remind her of prenatal appointments with her doctor . . . she would become irritated and sullen, angry that her parents were forcing her to carry the baby to term.*

Francine's unchanged behavior during her pregnancy might have been avoided by more proactive interventions, as described earlier. Her mother's reminding her of medical appointments indicated that she was somewhat involved in her daughter's life at this time. If she had told Francine's doctor about Francine's continued irresponsible behavior, the physician might have arranged for a psychiatric or psychological consultation, which would likely have resulted in ongoing prenatal and postnatal mental health care. Involving clinicians at this point might also have defused some of the ongoing mother-daughter arguments that jeopardized Francine's bonding and Bobby's attachment to her.

As a community-based intervention of low complexity, Francine might have been placed on the lunch and dinner shifts at the restaurant during her first trimester rather than in her 7th month of pregnancy. This change in schedule would have resulted in steady income and also likely would have made her too tired for late-night carousing—a medical benefit for her and her fetus. A family-based, moderately complex intervention—having Francine move into her parents' home during her pregnancy—might also have lowered infanticide risk. Though the move would have exacerbated their conflicts, their daily contact might have produced an uneasy truce and a practical pregnancy care plan. Living with her parents would have made late-night carousing more difficult for Francine in that her parents would have known when she left and returned home.

Both of these simple changes, made in conjunction with the professional interventions described earlier, might have positively altered Francine's relationship with her parents *and* with her fetus and decreased the likelihood of infanticide. These interventions might have also stimulated Francine's siblings to take a more active role in helping the family through this crisis. For example, Helen and her brothers might have offered to have Francine stay briefly with them as weekend respite care for their parents—a family-based moderately complex intervention.

> 3. *She spent the day either sleeping or watching TV while the nanny fed, changed, and bathed Bobby . . . Francine seemed to have little interest in caring for her baby and would often leave the child alone in his crib in the evenings. . . .*

If Francine's parents had arranged for her to live with them while she was pregnant, these signs of her maternal rejection of Bobby would have been more apparent and more readily stopped. Further, these episodes (and the resultant parent-daughter eruptions) would have been rich fodder for resolution during family therapy sessions. Having Francine at home would have made it more difficult for her parents to avoid helping her with the baby and thus would have given her parents opportunities to develop a relationship with Bobby. If Francine lived with her parents after delivery, her parents would also have had to address their fears of their neighbors' and friends' reactions to their mixed-race grandson. They might have discovered that their acquaintances were less judgmental than they expected.

4. *Over the next few months, Francine's life was, to her, a boring routine of feeding, changing, and bathing her son. She found little satisfaction in these duties and dreaded having to clean up Bobby after he had produced a very messy diaper.*

Many new mothers relish the repetitive tasks of caring for their babies; unfortunately, some do not. When the mother is the sole provider of infant care, especially if she is living alone, her days and nights may become as Francine described hers. Her negative, resentful reactions to motherhood might have been decreased by the interventions of living at home, sharing child-care duties with her parents and thus getting temporary relief, and reuniting with her older siblings during family visits.

Some research suggests that a variety of different mother-infant therapy approaches may also help to overcome maternal rejection of her child and to promote positive attachment (Stern, 1995; Cramer et al., 1990). In the sessions, the mother interacts directly with her infant to stimulate maternal empathy and responsiveness. The mother reenacts routine child-care tasks during each appointment. The sessions provide a forum to express her fears, anxieties, frustrations, and irritations, allowing the therapist to give continuing education regarding infant-parent development.

Epilogue

After Francine confessed to killing her son, she was arrested and detained in the county detention center until trial. Because of the gruesome facts of her case, her partying after the murder, and concerns about her risk of leaving town, the court denied her bail. Though her parents came to see her in jail occasionally, she spent most of the time alone. Other women inmates rejected her with insults and threats of physical harm. Jimmy did not visit, nor did her other friends from the restaurant. She never heard from Larry. Francine agreed to plead guilty to second-degree murder and was sentenced to 10 years in prison followed by 5 years of probation once she left the penitentiary.

9

Detached Mother, Exhausted Type
Glenda

Glenda trudged upstairs when she heard the loud argument between her two young sons, Dan and Peter. She knew that if she did not get between them they would begin to fight and damage each other's toys. It was harder for her to climb the steps since she gave birth to her fifth child, Emma, 5 weeks earlier. She'd gained a lot of weight in her last pregnancy, as she had with her four other children, Elizabeth, age 11, Peter, age 9, Dan, age 7, and Molly, 20 months. As Glenda approached her sons' bedroom door, she heard Emma crying in her bassinet downstairs and Elizabeth yelling at her brothers to stop arguing.

Later, as she was rocking Emma to sleep, Elizabeth entered the room to complain again about her brothers' fights and noisemaking while she was trying to talk on the phone with her friends. Glenda patiently tried to explain to her daughter about Dan's attention-deficit hyperactivity disorder (ADHD), but Elizabeth, like her father, John, believed that he just needed more discipline to control his behavior. Glenda jumped up from the rocking chair when a crashing sound came from the living room. Rushing there, she found that Molly had knocked a lamp down as she'd pulled herself up from the floor. She was unhurt, but Emma began crying again from her crib, drawing Glenda back to her room. The events of that afternoon were not unique.

Glenda had not foreseen that her life would turn out quite this way. She had been raised as an only child by parents who provided a stable, secure home. Glenda remembered her childhood as a happy period in her life. She loved the trips her mother would plan for the two of them but also enjoyed learning how to sew, knit, and cook by her mother's side. Glenda had been a good student in school but had no desire to enter college; she hoped to have the same life her parents had lived, just with more children.

After she had graduated from high school, she'd met John at the restaurant where she'd worked as a waitress until she was 24 years old. They found they had many dreams in common: a house filled with children, close ties with each other's parents, and a peaceful, slow-paced journey through life to retirement. When John proposed marriage after they had dated for 2 years, Glenda readily accepted. She continued to work at the restaurant until she became pregnant, as planned, with her first child, Elizabeth. Peter, another planned pregnancy, was born about 2 years later. John and Glenda felt that their life plan was progressing nicely. Their third child, Dan, arrived on schedule.

Although Glenda had been able to manage her household well in the years before Dan was born, the 7 years after had been a pattern of constant stress. A year after Molly's arrival, Glenda's mother had died in an automobile accident, a devastating loss for both families and their children. Glenda continued to keep in touch with her father, but he never seemed to recover from his wife's untimely death.

As Dan got older, his hyperactive behavior became more pronounced. When Glenda had taken him to day care after she'd started a part-time waitress job to supplement their income, Dan had started fights with the other children and rebelled at the staff's efforts to discipline him. The day-care owner finally asked Glenda to find another placement for Dan. Glenda tried two other day-care centers without success; Dan had quickly become a terror to the other children.

When Dan was expelled from the last place, Glenda realized that she would have to quit her job to stay home with her son. Her husband, John, was not happy with her decision because it meant that he would have to take overtime work to make up for Glenda's lost wages. John told her that Dan just needed more discipline. Their family's stability had been disrupted 2 years previously when Glenda discovered she was pregnant with Molly. John was happy to see their family expand; however, Glenda was less enthusiastic. She was aware that the demands of a new infant would draw her attention away from Dan. She knew that Dan's behavior would likely deteriorate once Molly was born.

When Glenda brought Molly home, Dan became more insistent and demanding as she tried to rock her new baby to sleep. She explained to her son that Molly needed her attention, but Dan would become sullen and break the toys she'd purchase for him. One day she heard Molly scream. She entered the room to find Dan standing over her daughter's crib. He denied that he had hit her, but Molly's face showed a red welt on her cheek.

In the following weeks, Glenda made sure that she was always present to protect Molly when Dan was near. Her son continued to be sullen and almost hit her when he was frustrated. Her worries about Molly's safety took a toll on Glenda's energy and resilience. She felt that she could not take a nap when Molly napped because she was afraid that Dan might strike her baby again.

With her attention given to Molly, Dan's behavior became more unruly and uncontrolled. Glenda was unable to sleep through the night because Molly did not sleep through the night. In her sleep-deprived state, Glenda had even less tolerance for Dan's tantrums and angry, destructive explosions. She felt guilty as she saw her son become more withdrawn and remote from her.

When Glenda became unexpectedly pregnant with Emma, the news hit her very hard. As Glenda walked out of her doctor's office, she barely acknowledged the office staff. She felt no happiness, because she dreaded the immediate and long-term implications of her new pregnancy on her, her marriage, and her other children. She had been hopeful when she was pregnant with Dan, but less so with Molly. Now, she only felt numb. The following day Glenda became so distraught that she even briefly contemplated ending the pregnancy.

John was joyful when she gave him the news of her pregnancy. He'd always wanted to have more children. The factory where John worked had recently won a large government contract, which meant more opportunities for lucrative overtime. He now accepted working extra hours each day and on some weekends because their family expenses kept increasing. Glenda appreciated how hard he worked and was thankful for the fringe benefits that allowed them to afford their frequent medical expenses. Though she wished he would help her more, she did not feel she could complain; his additional wages did cover their expenditures well enough. John slept soundly the night he heard he was to be a father again. Glenda stared at the ceiling until Molly awoke crying, needing to be fed and changed.

During her first trimester Glenda hoped that she would become optimistic about her fetus, as she had with her other children, but she did not. She kept her bothersome thoughts to herself, not even discussing her worries with her female family doctor. She trudged through each day. She seemed to have less energy for Dan's outbursts and less interest in keeping the house clean and neat. Glenda found that she spent more time sitting on the living room couch nibbling on snacks and sweets while letting the children run wild. John was often angry at the disarray of the living room and kitchen when he came home from work.

He would once again tell her of his mother's excellence at motherhood and housekeeping. His frequent references to her mother-in-law made Glenda feel angry but also guilty. They drifted apart into sullen silence. Glenda also became aware that her children seemed to sense that she was less attentive and interested in them. For a woman who had taken pride in motherhood, these insights also drained her resilience. The laundry and dishes began piling up. Glenda would make a concerted effort to keep the house neat for John's arrival home from work, but she'd then be exhausted for the next few days as the dishes, laundry, and household mess would pile up again.

As the weeks went by, Glenda was disturbed that her numbed, empty feelings persisted. She felt little connection to the baby growing inside her and saw that its arrival would mean more drudgery for her. She continued to keep these thoughts and worries to herself. Fortunately, her pregnancy continued without additional complications other than increasing obesity and difficulties regulating her gestational diabetes.

Emma's delivery was uncomplicated. Glenda stayed in the hospital only 3 days after her birth, but it was the only time she had had alone in the past 18 months. She nursed Emma as she had with all her other children. Glenda believed that she always drew closer to her newborns during these feeding times, but with Emma, she felt no such joy. Her newest daughter had some difficulty learning to nurse despite Glenda's efforts.

When Glenda came home with Emma, her children gathered around them, happy to see the newest addition to their family. Glenda was briefly optimistic that perhaps her marriage and family life would become less stressful. Soon, however, her family returned to their previous patterns of sibling squabbling, opposition to her requests for help, and marital silence when John came home from work in the late evenings. Glenda would get up from bed many times each night to care for Emma, and often Molly would be wet and hungry as well.

At 39 years of age, Glenda found that her body did not recover from the delivery as rapidly as it had done before. Her aches and pains did not decrease with the medication her physician had prescribed, but Glenda did not complain. She was afraid of the side effects she might have with a stronger prescription. Glenda began bringing Emma into their bed for nighttime nursing in an attempt to get more sleep each night. Her infant still had some problems feeding, and her crying sometimes woke up John. He would grumble and tell her to take Emma back to her bassinet, but there the baby would begin crying again. Glenda had no other bed in which she could rest while she fed her baby, so she would use the rocker to keep Emma quiet. Though her daughter would eventually fall asleep, Glenda would not. If she tried to get up to go back to bed, Emma would awaken again.

Overwhelmed, hopeless, and exhausted, Glenda brought Emma to bed to nurse. She felt as if she was at her wits' end and saw no change in her circumstances for many years. She received no joy from feeding Emma; it was just another task on her unending to-do list. She looked numbly at her daughter and sighed with fatigue. After a few minutes, she closed her eyes, prayed briefly for forgiveness, and then smothered Emma with her body. She stayed on her stomach for only a few minutes before rolling onto her back. John, sleeping beside her, had not moved. The house was quiet. Emma had stopped breathing.

Two hours later, John awoke and went to the bathroom to get ready for work. Glenda arose, then shrieked as she saw the cold, lifeless body of her daughter lying on the bed. John ran to his wife's side and stared in disbelief. He demanded an explanation from Glenda, who could only babble that it had been a terrible accident: She had fallen asleep nursing Emma and somehow her daughter became trapped beneath her. John immediately dialed 911, but it was clear to them before the paramedics arrived that their daughter had died. One week later, a coroner's report declared that the child's death was accidental.

Another 2 weeks passed before Glenda, riddled with guilt and remorse, confessed to the police that she had killed her daughter. She went to the station house alone after asking her mother-in-law to take care of her children on the ruse that she had a follow-up medical appointment with her doctor. Glenda had often thought of telling the truth to John or her doctor, but she was unable to reveal her crime to them face-to-face. She decided to go to the police primarily because she did not know them at all.

Glenda completed the report form the desk sergeant gave her with tears in her eyes and gave it to the policeman. As she silently cried, he asked her if she wanted to make a telephone call before he arrested her. Glenda asked him to call John.

Case Analysis

Glenda's case illustrates how an infanticide can occur in a mother with a highly protective and secure personal history when situational factors become overwhelming. Her story is instructive in showing that adult resilience can be worn down by the demands of larger families, especially when one or more children have behavioral difficulties. In contrast to the other cases discussed previously in this category, Glenda's advanced maternal age, multiple children, and significant medical problems demonstrate that infanticide is not only a problem involving young, inexperienced, new mothers with single children.

Maternal Filicide Risk Matrix Analysis

The risk matrix for Glenda is shown in table 9.1.

Prepregnancy Stage
Glenda's age of 39 prior to pregnancy was a risk factor, as maternal age over 35, and particularly over 40, has been associated with increased risk of infant death in the first postpartum year (Visscher & Rinehart, 1990). Her average intelligence and completion of high school were protective factors and likely did not increase her risk of infanticide. In the years and months before Emma was born, Glenda's medical condition had deteriorated significantly, and her obesity decreased her energy, resilience, and stamina to manage her children and household. Her medical condition was further complicated by her recent unplanned pregnancy and delivery of Molly. Glenda's emotional status, although not indicative of a specific, severe major mental disorder, was nonetheless at risk from recurrent stress, unexpected pregnancies, severe parent-child problems with Dan, and the devastating loss of her beloved mother. Her trauma-free childhood, adolescent, young adult, and adult history were strong protective factors for her. Glenda's maternal attitudes had deteriorated somewhat in the years before Emma was born. When she was first married, she and John looked optimistically toward a houseful of children; her maternal attitudes were positive protective factors for the births of Elizabeth, Peter, and

Table 9.1
Maternal Filicide Risk Matrix: Glenda

Factor	Pre-P	P/D	EP	LP	PI
Individual					
Age at current pregnancy	R	R	R		
Intelligence level	P	P	P		
Education level	P	P	P		
Medical status	R	R	R		
Emotional status	R	R	R		
Trauma history	P	P	P		
Maternal attitudes	R	R	R		
Family of Origin					
Mother's parenting	P	R	R		
Father's parenting	P	R	R		
Marital/family stability	P	—	—		
Situational					
Marital/partner status	P	P	P		
Financial status	P	P	P		
Child-care status	R	R	R		
Infant's temperament	—	—	P		

Note: R = Risk; P = Protective; Pre-P = Prepregnancy; P/D = Pregnancy/delivery; EP = Early postpartum; LP = Late postpartum; PI = Postinfancy.

Dan. Dan's ADHD took its toll on her self-esteem as a mother. When she conceived Molly, Glenda had her first negative, problematic feelings toward pregnancy.

Glenda had many protective factors from her family of origin. She described her mother and father in glowing terms for their warm, nurturing parenting of her during her childhood and adolescence. Glenda had hoped to duplicate their lives in her marriage, an example of the protective influence of a stable parental history. However, her mother's death became a risk factor because she was not available to assist Glenda in child care and/or household obligations after Molly was born.

During the prepregnancy stage, Glenda's relationship with John was, on balance, a protective factor. Though there were some stresses and strains, as described earlier, they never separated, nor did their arguments result in physical violence. Their intimacy was infrequent but still existent. At this stage, Glenda's overwhelming child-care obligations and Dan's threats to his siblings', especially Molly's, welfare were serious risk factors contributing to Glenda's less optimistic maternal attitudes when Molly was conceived.

Pregnancy/Delivery Stage

As described in the previous section, Glenda's advanced age of 39 at her pregnancy with Emma was a risk factor contributing to her newborn's death. Glenda's obesity during pregnancy increased, and her medical condition was worsened by development of gestational diabetes and hypertension. Though she actively sought prenatal medical care, she was not able to follow her physician's diet plans, a fact that appeared to contribute to her sense of helplessness and incompetence in managing her life. Her emotional status was also a risk factor due to her unexpected, unplanned pregnancy with Emma and the unavailability of her mother to help in managing her conflicts with Dan. Glenda's maternal attitude soured during her pregnancy with Emma, most clearly indicated by her willingness to consider abortion of her fetus, to her a previously unthinkable solution to her problems.

Glenda's family of origin elements were, on balance, risk factors during the pregnancy/delivery and early postpartum stages due to her mother's death and her father's extended bereavement. However, in contrast to the cases of Cathy, Edna, and Francine, who needed parental help, Glenda and John were fully self-sufficient adults who were capable of making decisions for themselves and their own family. After her mother died, Glenda's mother-in-law became a more prominent person in her life and at this stage was supportive of her pregnancy. It did not appear that their relationship became significantly conflicted until after Emma was born and Glenda's resiliency collapsed.

As in the previous stage, Glenda's marital/partner status and financial status remained protective factors, as John was supportive of the pregnancy and took additional work to keep their finances under control. Her pregnancy with Emma, however, complicated her abilities to deal with her child-care obligations.

Early Postpartum Stage

Glenda's medical status, emotional status, and maternal attitude did not improve after Emma was born. Indeed, each of these factors worsened, placing her at much greater risk for infanticide. In the weeks after Emma's delivery, Glenda felt less able to manage herself, her children, and the household. Her mother's death and her father's prolonged depression continued to be risk factors because they were not available to help Glenda. Unfortunately, her relationship with her mother-in-law deteriorated even while she was in the hospital with Emma. Though her mother-in-law moved in to help with the children, Glenda perceived the assistance as a subtle message that she was not as able as her husband's mother to manage the burdens of multiple children.

As in the earlier stages, the marital/partner status and financial-status factors continued to be protective. Emma's temperament was not problematic: Had she been the first child, Glenda would have had the resilience to manage her baby's normal postpartum behavior. Her birth significantly added to Glenda's child-care obligations and to sibling temperament conflicts, which soon took her to the breaking point of infanticide.

Relevant Research: Postpartum Adjustment

The challenges and joys of welcoming a new baby into the world have been well documented through the centuries. Sleep deprivation, fatigue, diminished sexual drives, and rearrangement of parental priorities are universal experiences recounted from culture to culture in family stories, memories, and jokes.

Normal postpartum adjustment occurs over a period of weeks and months of physical, emotional, and hormonal changes. The new mother's uterus decreases in size and weight from almost 3 pounds to less than 3 ounces (Curtis & Shuler, 2001). After-birth pains caused by the uterus's contractions are common, as are the continuing discomforts of vaginal discharges and the healing of the episiotomy incision. Constipation and hemorrhoids occur after almost all deliveries, as well as discomfort in the mother's breasts (Curtis & Shuler, 2001). The American College of Obstetricians and Gynecologists highlights increased risks for a variety of symptoms, including nausea and vomiting, high fever, painful urination, atypical vaginal bleeding, leg pain or swelling, chest pain or cough, tender breasts, or persistent perineal pain and tenderness (Visscher & Rinehart, 1990).

Emotional changes can be very disturbing to new mothers, despite warnings from their families and physicians that such events are typical. In later chapters, postpartum depression and postpartum psychosis are discussed in the context of Marilyn's and Barbara's cases, respectively. Even when the mother does not experience such severe reactions after delivery as these mental disorders, typical psychological/emotional feelings in both new and experienced mothers may entail postpartum distress syndrome (PDS), the "baby blues." PDS symptoms may include anxiety, ranging from mild to severe levels; unexplained crying; exhaustion; impatience; irritability; lack of self-confidence; lack of feeling for the baby; low self-esteem; oversensitivity; and restlessness (Rosenberg et al., 2003). Studies have found that "baby blues" occur in 50–80% of women and that PDS symptoms tend to be at their highest approximately 4 to 5 days after delivery, commonly resolving without medical treatment (Wisner, Gracious, Piontek, Peindel, & Perel, 2003).

Glenda's descriptions of her feelings and emotions in the weeks preceding Emma's death were very suggestive of PDS. She reported similar reactions following Molly's birth 18 months earlier. Mothers with histories of PDS tend to reexperience such symptoms in subsequent deliveries, often with increased severity (Curtis & Shuler, 2001; Rosenberg et al., 2003). It is not uncommon for new mothers to hide their depressed and guilty feelings after giving birth, as Glenda had with Molly and then Emma. Even a very intelligent, highly educated woman with medical training subsequently reported that during her postpartum adjustment she kept her depression a secret from others (Jamison, 1999).

Many women have fears that if they express their real thoughts their babies may be taken from them, that their families and friends won't understand what they are going through, that they may learn things about themselves that will frighten them even more, and that their relationships with their husbands or partners will be damaged or severed (Rosenberg et al., 2003). PDS is temporary and treatable, especially through simple methods of arranging support from family and friends, temporary housekeeping, moderate exercise outdoors, and nutritious meals. Unfortunately, these interventions were not made after Glenda's delivery of Molly or, more tragically, Emma.

Suggestions for Prevention at Risk Intervention Points

Glenda's case is an excellent illustration that the path to infanticide may begin well before the pregnancy and delivery of the baby who dies. Three events that significantly contributed to Glenda's postpartum adjustment to Emma were her mother's death, the children's unruly and disruptive behavior, and the deterioration in her bonding to Emma.

1. *A year after Molly's arrival, Glenda's mother had died in an automobile accident, a devastating loss for both families and their children.*

Glenda indicated that after her mother's unexpected death, she did not seek psychological or psychiatric care, believing that her feelings were "just normal after a parent dies." The unexpected death of a parent is among the most stressful and devastating events that any of us can experience. A family physician's or pastor's referral for a psychological or psychiatric evaluation would have determined whether Glenda's symptoms were indicative of (in order of increasing severity) bereavement, adjustment disorder with depressed mood, major depressive episode, emerging dysthymic disorder, or recurrent major depressive disorder (American Psychiatric Association, 2000). Community-based interventions of outpatient psychotherapy and antidepressant medications might have resulted in Glenda having more energy to manage Dan's oppositional behavior and given her the fortitude to gain control of her obesity.

2. *Glenda found that she spent more time sitting on the living room couch nibbling on snacks and sweets while letting the children run wild. John was often angry at the disarray of the living room and kitchen when he came home from work.*

As her pregnancy with Emma progressed, Glenda's fatigue increased substantially. Glenda may have been able to better manage the clutter of the children's toys and games through use of the "Friday box." With this method, the children are informed that if a toy is not put away as requested, the object will be locked in a box that will not be opened until Friday evening after the child is in bed. Though children initially complain, they readily learn to put away their possessions when asked. To cut down on repetitive laundry, Glenda might have had a second "Friday box" for the children's clothes left on the floor, which would be opened only once a week when the laundry would be done. The "Friday box" might have been located near the kitchen and living room for use just before John came home so that his first impression was that the house was orderly. In time, John might have even commented on how well Glenda was managing the house. At that point, she could have encouraged him to join her in obeying the "Friday box" rules for his clothes and possessions.

> 3. *Glenda stayed in the hospital only 3 days after her birth, but it was the only time she had had alone in the past 18 months. . . . Glenda believed that she always drew closer to her newborns during these breast-feeding times, but with Emma, she felt no such joy.*

Although she had only 3 days due to her managed health care policy, there were interventions that could have been made to enhance her bonding with Emma. Sears and Sears (2001) suggest a number of simple, yet important procedures: holding the baby skin to skin immediately after delivery, attending closely to the baby's quiet alertness, touching and stroking the baby's whole body, gazing into the baby's eyes during the first hour after birth while breast-feeding, and talking softly to the baby. To accomplish these critical tasks in complete privacy, Sears and Sears (2001) suggest that the mother (and father) should ask the hospital staff for an hour's delay of routine procedures. If John had been encouraged to do these procedures with Emma while Glenda was resting and sleeping in the hospital, his bonding with his new baby would have been enhanced, and he might have been more supportive to Glenda and Emma once they came home. Repeating these procedures throughout the 72 hours Glenda and Emma (and John) were in the hospital would likely have started their attachment-bonding pattern on a much more positive foundation for the prevention of infanticide.

> 4. *Glenda had no other bed in which she could rest while she fed her baby, so she would use the rocker to keep Emma quiet. Though her daughter would eventually fall asleep, Glenda would not.*

Rest is critical for new mothers, especially those who are older and have the demands of other children. It was important for Glenda to have a regular bed in which to sleep so that she'd be available to both daughters. She and John could have told their sons that they would be camping out on the living room floor for a while so that Glenda could have their bedroom. Because of Glenda's obesity, having her own bed, the rocker, and Emma within reach in her bassinette would have made it easier for her, and she and her new daughter would have gotten more consistent sleep over the following 2 months. Glenda would have had much more energy to face her other family obligations during daylight hours, bonded more closely to her new daughter, and ultimately eliminated the despair and exhaustion that led her to infanticide.

Epilogue

Glenda was arrested and charged with felony homicide by child abuse. When her attorney described her family situation, she was allowed to live with her father but to have only supervised visitations with the rest of her children. John and his mother were not sympathetic and resisted any efforts by Glenda to reunite with them or the children. They did not visit her in prison after Glenda was allowed to plead guilty in exchange for a reduced sentence of 2 years of incarceration, 5 years of probation, and mandatory mental health treatment, as recommended by psychological and psychiatric experts retained by her attorney. While in prison late one night, she committed suicide by choking herself with a cord hung from an unoccupied upper bunk in her two-person cell.

10

Abusive/Neglectful Mother, Recurrent Type

Harriet

Harriet awoke groggily from the living room couch and saw her 4-year old son, Johnny, lying still beside the coffee table. It was 11:30 in the morning, yet she was wearing the same clothes from yesterday. Once again she'd passed out on the couch while watching television. She called to her son but received no reply. She vaguely remembered that he had talked with her about getting up earlier that morning and recalled that she had angrily hit him because he would not stop pestering her about making breakfast. When Johnny still did not move after she raised her voice, she began to get very worried. She got off the couch and went to his side. His skin was cold, and she could see that he was not breathing. Panic set in as she tried to piece together the events of the morning. She shook her son in an attempt to arouse him; however, it was clear to her that he was dead. She called her mother at the family's furniture store and told her that there had been a terrible accident with Johnny. Her mother demanded to know what happened but Harriet could only repeat "I don't know, I don't know" and continue crying.

Her mother dialed 911, and soon paramedics were knocking on Harriet's front door. She greeted them frantically and begged them to help her son, but it was clear there was nothing they could do. Harriet went to the hospital in the back of the ambulance, sobbing while she held Johnny's lifeless hand. At the emergency room, the physician pronounced her son dead and began his examination of the corpse. After inspecting his body, the doctor told one of the nurses to contact the police and the county's child protection services office. Within 2 hours, Harriet was arrested on charges of homicide by child abuse and booked into the county detention center.

111

Harriet was the youngest of four children born to parents who were self-employed in a furniture business that had been owned by the family for two generations. She had been raised by a live-in nanny because her mother and father worked full-time at the store 6 days a week. To the community, her family appeared to have everything: a large house overlooking a pond, the newest cars in the driveway, and a thriving business. Her parents had been married for 30 years without ever separating.

Harriet and her siblings knew the true story. For as long as she could remember, Harriet had seen her parents' nightly arguments and altercations, fueled by their ritual of predinner cocktails and nightcaps. She had witnessed her parents hitting each other in drunken rages. It was not uncommon to come downstairs for breakfast and find broken dishes left on the kitchen floor.

When Harriet was a child, her favorite time of the day was just before dinner. Her parents would be home from work, and they would frequently have a new toy or surprise for her. Often she would be the only child at home at this time of the day, because her two teenage twin sisters and brother, all in high school, would claim that they had after-school activities or part-time jobs that kept them out of the house until 9 or 10 each night. Actually, her siblings' schedules kept them from being the targets of their parents' rages. Though Harriet looked forward to her parents coming home each night, once they began drinking she would become anxious and afraid. Soon her parents would be yelling and swearing at each other and occasionally turn on her. Harriet's mother slapped her for the first time when Harriet was 9 years old. She had told her mother that she did not like her drinking and that she was scared when her parents would fight.

Harriet tried alcohol for the first time when she was 13 years old. She was at a friend's house for a sleepover and took a sip of beer from the can her friend held. She found that she liked the taste and took another sip. After that night, Harriet realized why her parents liked to drink and looked forward to the next time she could get a "buzz" from beer. She began sneaking beers from her parents' well-stocked refrigerator and would drink in her bedroom after telling them she had homework to do. Her parents never discovered her alcohol use until, at age 13, she came home drunk from a party she'd attended after a school football game.

By the time Harriet was 16, she'd lost count of the number of times she'd drunk to the point of intoxication; she estimated that it was in excess of 20 occasions. She reported that she had had blackouts two or three times. She'd once awakened to find herself naked in bed with a boy she knew from high school. She could not recall how she'd lost her clothes or whether they had had sex. She had lost her virginity at a party when she was 15, and afterward she found that she enjoyed having sex after a few beers so that it did not bother her to awaken in a strange bed. Although Harriet developed a regular pattern of weekend alcohol use, she did not gravitate to other drugs.

She became pregnant for the first time at age 16, when her boyfriend wanted to try sex without a condom. Harriet was somewhat drunk when they were in bed and did not object. She told her sisters that she was pregnant, and they agreed that their parents should be told. They selected a time prior to dinner, when their parents would be beginning their "happy hour" cocktails. Harriet was happy when her sisters agreed to be with her. Surprisingly, her parents took the news rather well, in part because they liked Harriet's boyfriend and his parents. For the next few evenings, Harriet and her parents discussed her options and also met with her boyfriend's parents. They all agreed that a baby would disrupt the college plans each had for their children. Harriet had her pregnancy terminated at an out-of-town clinic.

Harriet was 19 when she was arrested for the first time for driving while intoxicated (DWI) on the way home from a party. Her father arranged to have the charge dismissed, and Harriet's only punishment was a lecture from the judge. Harriet received her second DWI 2 years later, at age 21. She was ordered to pay a fine and attend a 10-week outpatient alcohol treatment class taught by the county's community mental health center. It was during this time that she met the man who would eventually become the father of her son, Johnny.

Harriet was introduced to Jake while both were in a bar celebrating a birthday for one of their friends. Both got drunk that night and ended up in bed together. The next morning they made plans to see each other again and soon were dating almost every night. After she had been seeing Jake for about 6 months, Harriet moved from her parents' home into her own apartment. Jake moved in 2 weeks later. Jake and Harriet talked about getting married but never seemed to actually set a date. Harriet was reluctant to commit to marriage because she found that they would often get into loud, violent arguments when they were drinking.

Harriet was 22 when she became pregnant with Johnny. She was excited to be having a child. Jake was less enthused. He saw her pregnancy as an impediment to their lifestyle and suggested that they arrange for a termination. Harriet refused vehemently, telling him that she had had one abortion and had promised herself that she would never have another.

She decided that one of the first things she had to do was to stop drinking. She was able to maintain about 2 weeks of sobriety, but then Jake brought home her favorite beer, and Harriet split a six-pack with him. She'd intended to have only half a bottle. Though she was chagrined that she had slipped, she was pleased that she had not become intoxicated. The next morning she vowed again to remain sober until her baby was born.

As she maintained her abstinence from alcohol, her relationship with Jake began to sour. He would want to go out in the evenings and party with their friends. Harriet would want to stay home and knit booties. As she entered her second trimester, her tolerance for Jake's substance abuse evaporated, and she gave him an ultimatum to get sober or leave. Jake left and moved out of state when a lucrative job opportunity arose.

Harriet kept her promise of sobriety for approximately 3 months, until she was invited home to celebrate her father's birthday. Though they began the evening with cautions about drinking while pregnant, her parents told her that "one wouldn't hurt." She sipped a glass of wine. One glass led to another and, with her parents consuming martinis, they all became drunk. Surprisingly, they did not argue or fight; rather, they ended the evening happily, with her father giving her a ride home. He was able to avoid his third DWI that night. The next morning, Harriet renewed her commitment to sobriety, and for the remainder of her pregnancy she was able to abstain from alcohol.

Prior to Johnny's birth, Harriet and her mother would shop at various stores for baby clothes and other paraphernalia. Harriet's sisters and brother also reentered her life. It seemed as though her pregnancy was bringing the family closer together in hopeful expectation of the third grandchild. Harriet's pregnancy was uneventful. She enjoyed her prenatal medical appointments, often accompanied by one of her sisters or her mother. Harriet's sisters arranged a baby shower, which provided her with the basic necessities for infant care. Her mother stayed sober that day.

Harriet's delivery of Johnny was uncomplicated. She stayed in the hospital a full week at her parent's insistence. After she came home with Johnny, her parents provided her with a nanny who would help her with household and child-care obligations. Johnny was a quiet, peaceful baby who would sleep through the night but awake in the morning to be fed.

When her mother would visit Harriet after the store closed, she would often bring along alcohol to make "happy hour" cocktails. At first, Harriet resisted drinking with her mother, but no longer being pregnant, she decided there was no medical reason why she couldn't have a drink. Soon her mother's visits were a regular occurrence, but they seemed to get along better once they were a bit tipsy.

Johnny was 7 months old the first time Harriet hit him in anger. It was early in the morning when he woke up crying. She had yelled and reflexively slapped her son on the face. She was shocked by what she had done and immediately tried to console Johnny, but he continued to cry for the next 10 minutes. For the next few months, Harriet did not change her pattern of alcohol use but did make an extra effort to be more tolerant with her child. Things seemed to go well. Johnny was not an oppositional child, and they had few episodes in which Harriet needed to discipline her son.

When Johnny was about 10 months old, however, Harriet hit him again. She had been in the kitchen with her son preparing food for her parents' wedding anniversary. Family gatherings were always fraught with anxiety because her parents were often intoxicated and insulting by the end of the evening. To calm her nerves, Harriet had been sipping wine for most of the morning and had consumed about half a bottle when Johnny accidentally spilled a bowl of cake mix onto the floor. Harriet became enraged and hit him on his bare leg with the spoon she held. Though he cried loudly, Harriet continued to yell at him and hit him once more. When she dressed Johnny for the party the next day, she covered her child's injuries with long pants.

Harriet was now drinking on a near-daily basis and would often join her parents at their home for their evening nightcaps. Often when the three would be drinking, they'd complain that her sisters and brother never visited anymore. Her siblings avoided the house because they realized how severe Harriet's and their parents' alcoholism had become. By the time Johnny was 4 years old, Harriet had hit him many more times using a spoon or her hand. Physical discipline had become a regular part of her management of her son.

When she had returned to full-time work at the family store, she had put her son in a child-care center with a full range of preschool educational and recreational activities. After one episode of abuse, the center's director asked Harriet about bruises she'd found on Johnny's arm. She explained that she had probably grabbed her son's arm too hard when he started to bolt across the street. She told the director that she'd never hurt her son before and promised that she would never harm Johnny intentionally. For the next 2 weeks, she was very cautious with her child and soon transferred him to another facility.

About 6 months later, she was asked why her son's finger was in a cast. She told that day-care director that Johnny's finger had been caught in a bedroom door. Actually, Harriet had broken her son's finger when she had hit his hand with a ruler's edge after he'd hit her on the face. The emergency room doctor had been suspicious of her explanation but, finding no prior reports of abuse and seeing that Harriet was well dressed, chose not to file a report to protective services. After the day-care director's questioning, Harriet again waited about 2 weeks before placing Johnny with a young woman who was babysitting children in her home.

When her parents had seen the bruises on Johnny and asked her about them, Harriet said that her son was going through a stage of not listening to her. She told them that he only responded to her requests when she would grab him or hit him. She told her parents that recently he was so oppositional that he went to his room only after she'd hit him with an extension cord. They agreed with Harriet that she was wise to keep Johnny out of day care for the next week so that their grandson would not be placed in foster care. They supported her discipline of Johnny, citing the maxim, "spare the rod, spoil the child." Harriet said that she would have been a much more rebellious child and teenager if they had not used similar disciplinary methods with her.

On the morning that Johnny died, the terrible consequences of their distorted beliefs came to fruition.

Case Analysis

Harriet's story aptly depicts the relationship between substance abuse and domestic violence in the form of recurrent child abuse. The case demonstrates that family of origin factors, especially involving alcohol and excessive corporal punishment of children, can be transmitted to future generations. In contrast to the cases in the detached-mothers category, wherein each filicide was a deliberate, if sometimes impulsive, act with the intent to terminate the child's life, Harriet's case is descriptive of an accidental filicide. She meant to stop Johnny from pestering her, but she did not mean to kill him. Although the legal aspects of the perpetrator's intention may be important for issues of criminal culpability and sentencing, the impact on the victim was the same: the child died.

Maternal Filicide Risk Matrix Analysis

The risk matrix for Harriet is displayed in table 10.1.

Prepregnancy Stage

As illustrated in table 10.1, prior to her conception of Johnny, Harriet had a number of protective factors suggesting a lower risk of filicide. She became pregnant at age 22 and by then had completed high school, as well as a number of college credits. She was an intelligent young woman who, apart from her alcohol use, was in reasonably good health. Her joy at discovering she was pregnant with Johnny indicated that her maternal attitudes were positive and protective. Indeed, when Jake suggested an abortion, she firmly informed him that she would never terminate a pregnancy again. She was financially self-sufficient and had her own apartment due to her full-time employment in the

Table 10.1
Maternal Filicide Risk Matrix: Harriet

Factor	Pre-P	P/D	EP	LP	PI
Individual					
Age at current pregnancy	P	P	P	P	P
Intelligence level	P	P	P	P	P
Education level	P	P	P	P	P
Medical status	P	P	P	P	R
Emotional status	R	P	P	R	R
Trauma history	R	R	R	R	R
Maternal attitudes	P	P	P	R	R
Family of Origin					
Mother's parenting	R	P	R	R	R
Father's parenting	R	P	R	R	R
Marital/family stability	R	P	R	R	R
Situational					
Marital/partner status	R	R	R	R	R
Financial status	P	P	P	P	R
Child-care status	—	—	—	—	—
Infant's temperament	—	P	P	P	P

Note: R = Risk; P = Protective; Pre-P = Prepregnancy; P/D = Pregnancy/delivery; EP = Early postpartum; LP = Late postpartum; PI = Postinfancy.

family's business. When she discovered she was pregnant, she did not attempt to deny or hide her new medical condition; in a mature fashion, she immediately informed her parents.

Despite these protective factors, Harriet had a number of risk factors evident in the months preceding her pregnancy with Johnny. Her emotional status was a risk factor due to her very problematic consumption of alcohol. Though she had abstained from illegal drugs and resisted Jake's efforts to expand her substance abuse pattern, she had already received her second DWI by her 21st birthday. Further, with Jake she had developed a pattern of steady drinking that put her at substantial risk for alcohol dependence before age 25. Their frequent substance-induced arguments, although not physically violent, did little to ensure that their relationship would endure over time.

One large cloud over Harriet was her parents' alcoholism, which was well established during her childhood. Their alcohol dependence placed her at a significantly higher risk for developing alcoholism and gave Harriet many traumatic memories of spousal violence and child abuse. Before she became pregnant with Johnny, Harriet was well aware that her parents' marriage was unstable.

Pregnancy/Delivery Stage

The news of Harriet's pregnancy appeared to have a beneficial, if temporary, effect on her and her family system. Harriet quickly decided to stop drinking as a protection against birth defects and focused on improving her medical and mental health. Though her sobriety was short-lived and she drank beer with Jake 2 weeks later, she did manage to avoid becoming intoxicated and remained abstinent for another few months. When she told her parents about her pregnancy, their response was positive and supportive of their daughter. Though Harriet got drunk at her father's birthday party, she was subsequently able to stay sober until Johnny was born.

Harriet's pregnancy did seem to bring her family of origin a bit closer together. Her mother and sisters would accompany her to prenatal doctor's appointments, after which they would shop for baby clothes. Her sisters arranged a baby shower, and her mother remained sober that day. Her parents' support continued when they arranged to have a nanny help her adjustment to new motherhood after leaving the hospital. Indeed, apart from the lingering effects of her trauma history of parental alcoholism and child maltreatment, the only other risk factor at this stage was Jake's decision to leave her. In retrospect, given his wish to continue to drink and take drugs, Harriet was likely better off without him.

Early Postpartum Stage

Harriet maintained positive maternal attitudes in the first 6 months after Johnny was born. Her bonding with her son was facilitated by her extended maternity leave from work, by her improved medical and emotional status from her uncomplicated pregnancy and delivery, and by Johnny's mild, quiet disposition as an infant. Her relationship with her parents continued to be positive, as her mother would often visit. Soon the family's long history of alcohol abuse and dependence asserted itself again. Harriet's mother began to bring alcohol and leave it at her daughter's apartment so that they could share the family tradition of "happy hour" cocktails.

Though her parents had tried to cut down on their drinking during Harriet's pregnancy, they returned to steady heavy consumption once the novelty of their grandson's birth began to recede. Harriet tried to resist her mother's encouragements to join her in drinking but soon succumbed to her parents' distorted beliefs that because she was no longer pregnant, Johnny was not at risk. The presence of alcohol in her apartment became too much of a temptation. By the end of this stage, Harriet had returned to her prepregnancy excessive drinking patterns.

Late Postpartum Stage

As Harriet's drinking became more pronounced and steady, the effects of her intoxication and hangovers became more problematic. It was during this stage that Harriet reported first hitting her son. Although her act was reflexive to his grabbing her hair, had she not been hung over and tired from her late-night drinking, she likely would have acted in a less aggressive manner. Though she tried to be more tolerant with her son in the next few months, she did not change her drinking habits.

Harriet hit Johnny again when he accidentally spilled food. By then she was drinking during the day to calm her nerves, an ominous sign that her alcohol use was getting out of control. It was during this stage that she began the pattern of deception of hiding her child's injuries and/or lying about the reasons for his bruises. Her parents were of little help to her during this stage as their alcohol dependence deepened. Harriet was the sole caretaker of Johnny, and as her drinking continued, her maternal attitudes toward Johnny worsened.

Postinfancy Stage

By the time that Johnny died, Harriet's medical and emotional health had deteriorated due to alcoholism. She had become her parents' drinking partner on a near-daily basis and had fully adopted their distorted views about her absent siblings. Physical discipline of her son was now routinely administered without guilt or remorse. Her positive maternal attitudes toward her son had long since disappeared, as she saw him being an early-morning irritant. He, however, appeared to be a typical 4-year-old child making normal demands of his mother.

Relevant Research: Women With Alcohol Abuse and Dependence

The research and clinical literature of alcohol dependence is vast and well beyond the scope of this case chapter. Alcohol is the most widely used psychoactive drug in the world. In the United States, approximately 5%, or 14 million persons, meet the diagnostic criteria for alcohol dependence (American Psychiatric Association, 2000). Approximately 13% of Americans will suffer from alcohol dependence or abuse at some point in their lives (Sadock & Sadock, 2003). Research has generally shown that the highest prevalence of alcohol use occurs between ages 18 and 34 for both sexes. In the age range between 26 and 34, only 12% report abstaining from alcohol (American Psychiatric Association, 2000). Studies of alcohol dependence and abuse may substantially underestimate prevalence (Hasin & Grant, 2004).

Alcohol dependence and abuse are common across all socioeconomic and education levels. Alcohol is the drug most commonly associated with violence and death. According to the American Psychiatric Association (2000), more than 50% of all murderers and their victims were likely inebriated at the time of the crime, and 55% of all traffic fatalities are alcohol-related. It is estimated that as many as 40% of all people in the United States will experience an alcohol-related vehicular accident at some point in their lives. Of all completed suicides, approximately 25% are alcohol-related (Sadock & Sadock, 2003).

Alcohol is the third leading preventable cause of death in the United States. Alcohol use substantially increases the risk for cirrhosis, cancer, heart disease, stroke, injury, and depression (Centers for Disease Control and Prevention, 2004). Some studies indicate that as many as 20% of all intensive-care admissions are attributable to excessive use of alcohol (American Psychiatric Association, 2000). Some studies have shown that alcohol may decrease life expectancy by as much as 10 years (Carlson, 1998).

Patterns of alcohol consumption vary by gender. Prevalence studies have indicated that alcohol dependence and abuse are much more common in men than women, perhaps by a ratio of 5:1 (American Psychiatric Association, 2000). Men generally start consuming alcohol at a younger age than women and begin to display the signs of alcohol dependence at an earlier stage in their lives, typically in the late 20s or early 30s.

Although women are less likely to be diagnosed with alcohol abuse or dependence, their course to dependence is often much faster (American Psychiatric Association, 2000; Carlson, 1998; Sadock & Sadock, 2003). Women tend to develop higher blood alcohol concentrations than males due to lower percentages of body water and slower metabolism of alcohol (American Psychiatric Association, 2000). Despite these differences, many researchers consider the course of alcohol dependence to be very similar in men and women.

Literature from the past 20 years has suggested that two types of problematic alcohol consumers can be distinguished by their patterns of drinking. Heavy or steady drinkers are generally defined as those who regularly consume more than 8 ounces of alcohol on a near-daily basis (American Psychiatric Association, 2000). These drinkers cannot abstain from alcohol and consume it consistently (Carlson, 1998; Cloninger, 1987).

In contrast, binge drinkers are able to abstain from alcohol for long periods of time but are unable to control their drinking once they start (Carlson,

1998). Heavy or steady drinkers (whether male or female) tend to develop alcohol dependence before age 25 and may organize their lives around the acquisition and consumption of alcohol. This type of alcoholic is much more likely to become involved with physical altercations such as domestic violence and to be the subject of police arrests for alcohol-related offenses (e.g., DWI, disorderly conduct, marital abuse, etc.). One recent prevalence study suggested that approximately 16% of adults reported a pattern of binge drinking, compared with 6% of adults who met the criteria for heavy consumption (Centers for Disease Control, 2004).

Steady drinkers are much more likely than binge drinkers to come from families with parental alcohol dependence. For example, the risk for alcohol dependence is three to four times higher in close relatives (e.g., daughters, sons) of alcoholics. Further, higher risk for developing alcohol dependence is correlated with the number of alcoholic relatives, the severity of their dependence, and the closeness of their genetic relationship (American Psychiatric Association, 2000).

Children of alcoholic parents have been found to display insecure and fearful-avoidant attachment patterns when young and to develop alcohol abuse as young adults (Vungkhanching, Sher, Jackson, & Parra, 2004). Parental alcoholism that leads to child abuse and domestic violence, especially by the abusive mother, has been shown to result in higher rates of alcohol abuse and dependence among the adult daughters of these parents (Downs, Capshew, & Rindels, 2004). Mothers who came from families with parental substance abuse problems and/or child maltreatment were found to have poorer parenting skills with their own children (Locke & Newcomb, 2004).

Harriet and her parents appear to be illustrative of the characteristics and patterns of alcohol dependence of steady, heavy drinkers. Her case demonstrates the downward spiral that may result from continuing alcohol use. Though she had periods when she abstained from drinking, for example during her pregnancy with Johnny, her resumption of alcohol use began when she thought that she was no longer at risk of harming him with her drinking. Harriet's parents clearly exemplified steady drinkers whose dependence became more severe after Johnny was born.

Suggestions for Prevention at Risk Intervention Points

Harriet's case illustrates the devastating effect alcohol abuse and dependence can have within generations of a family. Her parents' chronic alcoholism colored their interactions with her and interfered with their ability to recognize their daughter's early-onset development of substance dependence. As suggested in chapter 5, interventions for abusive/neglectful mothers, recurrent type, often need to begin with community-based methods as a way of breaking the dynamics of family dysfunction that underlie generational domestic violence.

1. *Her parents never discovered her alcohol use until, at age 13, she came home drunk from a party she'd attended after a school football game.*

It is unfortunate, though not surprising, that Harriet's parents did not recognize that their daughter was displaying the first signs of alcohol abuse by becoming intoxicated at such a young age. For most persons who subsequently develop alcohol dependence, the first episode of intoxication occurs during middle adolescence (American Psychiatric Association, 2000); thus Harriet's start at age 13 was a very troublesome signal.

If her parents had arranged for an outpatient assessment of Harriet's alcohol use, there might have been at least two benefits: Harriet could have begun an effective treatment program of brief therapy (Miller, Andrews, Wilbourne, & Bennett, 1998; Wilk, Jenson, & Havighurst, 1997), and her parents could have been encouraged to join their daughter for family therapy sessions. As part of a family-system approach to treatment, Harriet's siblings could have been incorporated into sessions to provide her with additional resources to maintain her sobriety. During the sessions, the family secret of her parents' alcoholism would have been revealed, which might have saved Harriet from the later tragedies in her life.

2. *Harriet was 19 when she was arrested for the first time for driving while intoxicated (DWI) on the way home from a party. Her father arranged to have the charge dismissed, and Harriet's only punishment was a lecture from the judge.*

Any DWI is likely a sign of problematic substance use in that many inebriated drivers are not detected and arrested. It is unfortunate that the judge agreed to dismiss the charge at her father's request. Harriet recalled later that she hardly listened to the lecture. Had she been required to enter outpatient substance abuse treatment as described before, she might have altered the downward course of her alcohol pattern. Her parents blamed the police department rather than focusing on Harriet's choice to drink and drive; thus they provided her with a rationalization that allowed her to avoid accepting personal responsibility for her actions.

3. *She had yelled and reflexively slapped her son on the face. She was shocked by what she had done and immediately tried to console Johnny; however, he continued to cry for the next 10 minutes.*

Harriet's reaction to her abuse of Johnny suggested that her bonding to him was still strong and empathic. She was remorseful that she had harmed her child. Her behavior was immediate and unplanned, an example of impulsive aggression rather than deliberate instrumental violence in which the parent feels justified in her discipline (Berkowitz, 1993; Dietrich, Berkowitz, Kadushin, & McGloin, 1990; Mammen, Kolko, & Pilkonis, 2002).

It is unfortunate but understandable that Harriet cancelled her appointment with her physician due to a fear of being reported to child protective services. Less than 0.5% of perpetrators of child abuse will report themselves to authorities (National Center on Child Abuse and Neglect, 1996). If she had kept the appointment, her physician might have been able to discuss and arrange for outpatient treatment services for her as an adjunct to a protective services investigation. In contrast to her attitude later in Johnny's life, Harriet was at this point much more amenable to being helped because of her concern for her child's welfare. An intervention might have also included assistance from her sisters or brother. For example, Harriet and Johnny could have visited her siblings for a week or more of family-based respite care and interaction with siblings who were alcohol-free.

> 4. *Rather than getting upset with their daughter's maltreatment of their grandson, they supported her discipline of Johnny, citing the maxim, "spare the rod, spoil the child." Harriet said that she would have been a much more rebellious child and teenager if they had not used similar disciplinary methods with her.*

Although Harriet was responsible for her maltreatment of her son, her recurrent abuse of him can, in part, be traced to her family history as an abuse victim of her parents. A number of studies have shown that stressed parents who strongly believe in corporal punishment of their children score higher on scales measuring child-abuse potential (Abidin, 1995; Crouch & Behl, 2001; Downs et al., 2004).

Child abuse is not only the actual physical acts of excessive discipline but also the beliefs that justify the parent's violent interaction with his or her child. Harriet's report of this episode with her parents reflects the distorted ideas held in many abusive families. Bugental's (1992) cognitive model of child abuse, which has been supported by many studies (Sattler, 1998), suggests that abusive caretakers tend to believe that: (1) children act in a way to make their caregivers angry; (2) the child's oppositional act is willful, rather than due to individual factors (e.g., fatigue, hunger, etc.); (3) caretakers have little control over their own disciplining behavior; (4) caretakers interpret the child's behavior as a threat to their authority; and (5) caretakers use physical discipline to regain control of the parent-child relationship. Had Harriet been actively involved in outpatient mental health care and substance abuse counseling following the initial signal behaviors of abuse, her distorted beliefs about discipline could have been challenged, and Johnny's life might have been saved.

Epilogue

Harriet pled guilty to homicide by child abuse and received a 10-year sentence of incarceration with court-ordered substance abuse treatment while confined.

11

Abusive/Neglectful Mother, Reactive Type
Janet

Janet was frazzled as she returned home from work that afternoon. Her day had been a disaster from the beginning. She'd arrived late for work again. Her supervisor had called her into his office to demand a reason that she had not completed a computer programming assignment he'd given her. Janet had accomplished little at work that day because of repeated telephone calls from her live-in boyfriend, Ted, who'd said that their 4-month-old daughter, Marcie, was cranky and irritable all day. Marcie was a slight, underweight child who had been born prematurely during a difficult delivery. Janet and Ted had spent many nights of disrupted sleep trying to manage their daughter's colic in the weeks after Marcie came home from the hospital. Her digestive system was very delicate, and she suffered from a number of allergies that caused her to cry out in pain.

Janet usually played with Marcie for a while before feeding her daughter an evening meal and giving her a bath before bed at 8 p.m. Today, however, Janet was worried about all that she had to get done. While Marcie was playing by herself on the living room carpet at her feet, Janet thought she could start her research paper, so she opened her laptop computer and began typing.

Soon, Marcie was crying and demanding her attention as Janet worked. When she put her daughter on the floor by her toys, Marcie began whining again. Janet tried to type with Marcie on the couch, but her daughter began reaching for the computer's keyboard. Janet put her on the floor again by her feet, and Marcie began crying once more. Janet checked to see whether her daughter's diaper needed changing, but the baby was clean and dry. Marcie continued to whine and demanded to be held in her mother's arms. When Janet tried to put her to bed, however, her daughter began crying once again.

Though Marcie was now quiet on her shoulder, Janet's worry increased as she realized that she still had so much work to complete that night. She hoped that if Marcie did fall asleep by 9 P.M., she could still study for her examinations and finish her paper by midnight, when Ted would be home from work. For the next 2 hours, however, Janet was unable to put Marcie in her crib. Each time she tried, her daughter would begin to cry and beg to be held again. She threatened to spank Marcie if she did not stop crying, something she and Ted had agreed never to do because they both were raised by physically abusive parents.

By 10 P.M., Janet had had enough. She put Marcie in her crib and let her yell. Marcie cried continuously for 30 minutes, until Janet could not stand the noise any longer. She tried counting to 10 and putting her fingers in her ears to calm her growing anger, but neither technique worked. Janet tried to concentrate on the paper she was typing, but her daughter's screams would not stop. She burst into the bedroom where Marcie's crib was and yelled at her daughter to stop crying. Marcie stopped briefly, shocked at Janet's explosion, but then began wailing even louder in fear of her mother's rage.

Janet then closed the door and stood outside the bedroom worrying about what she would do next. She went back to her computer and tried to type, but her daughter's noise continued. This time when she picked up her daughter from the crib, she shook Marcie in angry frustration, and the crying finally ceased. She laid her daughter back down, closed the bedroom door, and worked on her paper for the next 2 hours without interruption. Not hearing any sounds from Marcie, Janet thought that her daughter had finally fallen asleep.

When Ted came home at 1 A.M., he found Janet typing on her laptop computer with schoolbooks scattered around on the living room couch. He asked her how Marcie had been that night, and Janet told him that it had been a rough night for them both. Ted went into the bedroom, and as he bent to kiss his daughter good night, he felt her cold, clammy skin. He yelled at Janet to call 911 and told her they had to go the emergency room immediately. Janet was shocked and confused: What had happened to their daughter?

She ran out the door after Ted, who was carrying Marcie in his arms. As she drove them to the hospital, she did not think about work or school, only about the welfare of Marcie. They looked anxiously at each other as they sped along, but neither parent spoke: Both knew that Marcie was dead.

Janet and Ted had met 3 years before when both were students at the technical college. Janet was working on her 2-year degree in computer science, and Ted was completing his associate of science program in X-ray medical technology. At age 20 and 21, respectively, Janet and Ted were a bit older than many of the students at the technical school. Both were serious about their education and hoped eventually to finish 4-year degree programs at the local university.

They avoided parties with other students because neither had ever had much interest in alcohol and were afraid of illegal drugs.

It was in the following semester that they became intimate. By then, they were seeing each other as often as they could and decided to move in together. Though they discussed marriage, each was hesitant because of parental divorce, which had been so traumatic for them during childhood. When they discovered that Janet was pregnant, plans were quickly made for their child's arrival. Neither was surprised at the pregnancy. In retrospect, they realized that they had been ready for a more permanent relationship than they had been willing to admit to each other. Both were committed to seeing their relationship continue after their baby was born. They agreed that their child needed a mother and a father to have a more emotionally healthy family than they had had.

Janet and Ted were pleased and surprised when their parents asked how they could help ease the financial and child-care burdens that would soon be on them; they did not consider their mothers and fathers to be very good parents. They asked only for a series of 2-week visits after the baby's birth to assist their adjustment to the new infant.

As Janet's pregnancy continued, they discussed how they wanted to raise their child. Both had been victims of parental physical abuse. Even though Janet received regular prenatal medical care, Marcie arrived early. After their daughter was placed in Janet's arms, they tried to console Marcie, but she would not calm down. Janet was distressed that she was unable to successfully breast-feed her daughter. When she told Ted that Marcie would need to be bottle-fed, he was happy, because it meant he could be more involved in his daughter's care.

After Janet and Marcie came home from the hospital with Ted, the first week of their plan of sharing duties seemed to work well. Janet's mother had moved in for her 2-week visit and had helped with housework and meals as Ted worked the afternoon shift at the hospital. While Ted was at work, Janet and her mother had time to rebuild their relationship by discussing the difficulties her mother had had as a single parent when Janet was in elementary school. To Janet's surprise, her mother apologized for the times when she would beat her with a belt, explaining that her own mother had treated her the same way.

Ted's mother quickly adapted to the schedule Ted and Janet had developed. At dinner one evening, she told her son, in Janet's presence, that he was a better father than he had had. She also told him he was a better husband, even if unmarried, than his father had been to her.

For the first 2 weeks in which Ted and Janet were on their own as Marcie's parents, they managed rather well. They quickly noticed their mothers' absences as they tried to juggle their work, sleep, and household routines. On those days and nights when Marcie's colic was relatively mild, they found that their alternating shift schedule worked adequately. However, when their daughter's allergies and colic were more pronounced, they found that they became more short-tempered with each other and with Marcie. As the weeks progressed, they became more exhausted and stressed. Some nights each would pretend to be asleep in hopes that the other would get up to attend to Marcie's crying. On the weekends they would try to recover their energy by taking day trips. They discovered that Marcie would often fall asleep in her car seat—the resulting peace and quiet often prolonged their drives in the country.

When Janet's school semester began again, her weekends became devoted to catching up on term papers and studying. After 2 months of work, school, and caring for Marcie, Janet was exhausted. She talked with Ted about possibly dropping one or more of her classes, but she did not want to lose the course credits, because that would put her further behind in trying to finish her degree. They both knew that cutting back on her work hours was not possible: Even with their parents' occasional checks, their budget was tight. They finally decided that they would continue with their current schedule and hoped that Marcie would soon grow out of her crying, tantrums, and fussy temperament.

In the following week, Marcie did seem to be improving, which gave Ted and Janet renewed energy to keep going with their plan. A week later, however, Marcie's colic returned, and neither was able to sleep soundly at night. In the next few weeks, Ted and Janet plodded through their duties, increasingly worn out from their round-the-clock, unending obligations. The 3 days preceding Marcie's death were particularly difficult for both of them as their daughter's colic worsened.

At the point when Janet violently shook her child in exasperated frustration, she had reached the end of her rope. She was unaware of what terrible damage she'd done until she touched her daughter's lifeless cheek on the way to the emergency room.

Case Analysis

Janet's case and that of Harriet in chapter 10 illustrate two examples of fatal child abuse. However, each depicts how diverse may be the characteristics, histories, and circumstances of the filicidal mothers in this category. The child abuse displayed by Harriet occurred frequently over the course of her son's life. She was often suspected of physically harming her child, but her intentional discipline was not stopped prior to Johnny's death. Janet's case was quite different in that neither she nor Ted had mistreated Marcie; indeed, they were in complete agreement about how their child should be raised. The use of physical discipline on their daughter was abhorrent to them because they had both been victims of parental child abuse.

A number of researchers have considered interpersonal aggression, such as child abuse, to exist on a continuum of intentionality and premeditation (Berkowitz, 1993; Dietrich et al., 1990; Mammen et al., 2002). At one extreme is impulsive aggression; at the other extreme, instrumental aggression. Impulsive aggression, illustrated by Janet's abuse of Marcie, is characterized by strong emotion and a lack of premeditation. The parent's violent act is sudden and excessive in response to the immediate situation (Dietrich et al., 1990). Impulsive aggression has also been described as reactive or emotional aggression because of its immediacy and severity (Berkowitz, 1993).

In contrast, instrumental aggression, as illustrated by Harriet's actions, is characterized by a purposeful and deliberate use of force to resolve a particular situation or conflict. In cases of child abuse, instrumental aggression is displayed by parents who feel that the use of physical discipline is justified in response to the actions of the child. These parents often report that they do not feel remorse and would use the same methods if the situation occurred again (Mammen et al., 2002; Strauss & Mouradian, 1998). Harriet's abusive treatment of Johnny was recurrent and based in a justification, endorsed by her own parents, that her child would be spoiled if he was not often physically disciplined. Harriet was irritated when she fatally struck her son but apparently had no intention of killing him; thus his death was accidental. However, Harriet's repetitive, deliberate use of aggression to manage Johnny illustrated that her behavior was much more consistent with instrumental rather than impulsive or reactive aggression (Strauss & Mouradian, 1998).

Research on parental child abuse has found that most often aggression within the family is a mixture of emotion and attitude, of impulsive and instrumental aggression, respectively. For example, a retrospective analysis of parents undergoing child protective services investigations for physical abuse found that the adults' explanations for their actions could be equally categorized as primarily instrumental, primarily impulsive, or a mixture of the two (Dietrich et al., 1990).

Maternal Filicide Risk Matrix Analysis

In contrast to Harriet's predictably recurrent child abuse, Janet's case is important because of the unpredictability of her fatal assault of Marcie. As is illustrated in her Maternal Filicide Risk Matrix (table 11.1), Janet had very few risk factors and numerous protective factors. Indeed, her primary prepregnancy individual risk factors of childhood trauma and poor family of origin parenting were substantially resolved by the time she became pregnant and gave birth to Marcie. Janet's case is important expressly because it could happen to any parent.

Prepregnancy Stage

As illustrated in table 11.1, Janet's prepregnancy-stage individual factors were almost exclusively protective. She was a woman of above-average intelligence who had completed high school and some technical school training in computer programming. She was an emotionally and medically healthy young woman who abstained from substance use. She was not promiscuous, nor did she engage in other forms of risky behavior that might have increased her chances of contracting various diseases. She did become pregnant due to some impulsive passion with Ted, but by the time they began having intercourse,

Table 11.1
Maternal Filicide Risk Matrix: Janet

Factor	Pre-P	P/D	EP	LP	PI
Individual					
Age at current pregnancy	P	P	P		
Intelligence level	P	P	P		
Education level	P	P	P		
Medical status	P	P	P		
Emotional status	P	P	P		
Trauma history	R	R	P		
Maternal attitudes	P	P	P		
Family of Origin					
Mother's parenting	P	P	P		
Father's parenting	P	P	P		
Marital/family stability	R	R	R		
Situational					
Marital/partner status	P	P	P		
Financial status	P	P	R		
Child-care status	—	—	—		
Infant's temperament	—	R	R		

Note: R = Risk; P = Protective; Pre-P = Prepregnancy; P/D = Pregnancy/delivery; EP = Early postpartum; LP = Late postpartum; PI = Postinfancy.

they had a stable, well-founded relationship of shared goals and dreams. Their occasional mutual avoidance of birth control reflected a shared, though unspoken, willingness to accept the consequences of their unprotected intimacy.

Prior to becoming pregnant at age 21, Janet had successfully delayed motherhood until her teenage years were behind her. Although she was a victim of childhood physical abuse and parental divorce, a trauma history that was a risk factor, these early negative experiences did not appear to substantially affect her prepregnancy-stage emotional stability or her attitudes toward motherhood. When she discovered she was pregnant, her reaction was highly positive and nurturing toward the fetus within her.

Her positive maternal attitudes may have been the result of the changes in her family of origin elements toward the end of her prepregnancy stage. Janet did not consider either her mother or father to be a very good parent when she was a child and adolescent. However, it appeared that after Ted entered her life and she could discuss her abuse history with someone who'd had similar experiences, Janet and her parents reconciled their differences. Her mother and father were not models for marital stability, a risk factor that contributed to Janet's (and Ted's) reluctance to marry, but her parents wanted to make up for their shortcomings by helping their daughter and de facto son-in-law through emotional and financial support.

Janet's situational factors at the prepregnancy stage were very protective. She was financially stable and gainfully employed in a job with a bright future of increasing income. She had her own apartment and lived carefully within her income. Until she became pregnant, she was pursuing her education in computer science on a part-time basis, which would result in greater financial independence and security. Her relationship with Ted was stable and mutually satisfying. They had been friends with shared, well-articulated personal and familial goals before they became lovers. The quality and depth of their alliance was not measured by their decision to live together but rather in the similarity of their positive reaction to pregnancy and wish to build a family together.

Pregnancy/Delivery Stage
Inspection of Janet's Maternal Filicide Risk Matrix indicates that this stage was also primarily characterized by protective individual, family of origin, and situational factors. Janet became pregnant at age 21 and was not devastated by the discovery of her medical condition. Her emotional stability was evidenced by her careful planning with Ted about the course of her next 9 months. Further, she did not have a history of substance abuse, chaotic interpersonal relationships, or depressive and anxiety-related symptoms. Janet quickly affirmed her decision to continue her pregnancy until her baby's birth, a goal that Ted readily shared. Janet made sure that her medical status remained healthy by regularly attending her prenatal appointments, often accompanied by Ted. She continued to pursue her educational goals during her pregnancy, which signaled the persistence of her academic intentions. Although her trauma history remained a risk factor, her maternal attitudes during pregnancy were very positive and protective against the possibility of neonaticide. Janet appeared to welcome her unexpected pregnancy, which, though inconvenient, was the product of her loving, stable relationship with Ted.

In terms of family of origin elements, her parents' declaration of emotional support and financial assistance were significant protective factors for Janet. Her parents' marital/familial stability was not a protective factor and contributed to her reluctance to marry Ted during this stage. Janet's situational factors of marital/partner status and financial status were protective elements for her throughout her pregnancy and subsequent delivery. Ted's very positive response to her pregnancy and their joint planning kept Janet from having to manage this stage alone. Fortunately, Janet was able to keep working during her pregnancy, which ensured that her independent financial stability would continue to be a protective factor for her and the baby. Marcie's difficult, fussy temperament appeared to be evident within the first few days of her birth, a harbinger of the stresses that Janet and Ted would face in the next stage.

Early Postpartum Stage

Janet's family of origin elements during this stage were a mixture of protective and risk factors. Her mother's compliments about her parenting of Marcie and her father's continuing emotional and financial support were very positive experiences for Janet. However, because both grandparents lived out of town and were not more immediately available in the weeks preceding Marcie's death, Janet (and Ted) had fewer family resources to draw on when she became over-stressed by the infant's continuing colic and allergies.

Janet's situational factors changed slightly but significantly during the early postpartum stage. Her relationship with Ted continued to be strong and protective for her. The necessity for Janet to continue working, however, kept her from being able to devote her energies to helping her daughter weather her early-childhood medical problems. If their daughter had had a more placid, quiet demeanor, it is likely that Janet's and Ted's time with her would have been highly enjoyable and much less stressful. The likelihood of impulsive aggression by either parent would have been significantly reduced. In essence, these two situational factors of limited financial status in concert with colicky infant temperament increased Janet's risk of child abuse. Despite all the positive protective factors for Janet during the early postpartum stage, these elements were not strong enough to prevent the seconds-long act that caused Marcie's death.

Relevant Research: Fatal Child Abuse

More than 1,000 children die annually in the United States from maltreatment (Stiffman, Schnitzer, Adam, Kruse, & Ewigman, 2002). Child abuse is the leading cause of infant deaths and serious traumatic brain injury in young children (Berger, Kochanek, & Pierce, 2004). Despite these staggering numbers, however, the actual incidence of childhood deaths due to abuse may be substantially higher (Ewigman et al., 1993; Olsen & Durkin, 1996). For example, it has been estimated that in the United States between 1985 and 1996, the actual number of child deaths due to abuse may have been more than three times higher than the 2,973 cases reported by states' vital records systems (Herman-Giddens et al., 1999). In a review of states' death certificate data from 1979 to 1988, a study by the Centers for Disease Control suggested that approximately 85% of fatal child abuse cases are recorded as due to other causes (McClain, Sacks, Froelke, & Ewigman, 1993).

Child homicides are considered the most difficult cases for which forensic pathologists must establish cause of death and culpability, for many reasons: The events are typically not witnessed by others, explanations of an accident are commonly offered by the suspect, conflicting opinions are often found among investigating medical specialists, and the child may have had many caretakers during the period when the injuries occurred (Cordner, Burke, Dodd, Lynch, Ranson, & Robertson, 2001). Other researchers cite systemic problems that contribute to the inaccurate estimates of child homicide prevalence, including inadequate and incomplete investigations, lack of information sharing among investigative agency personnel, and poorly designed reporting systems that fail to acknowledge the contribution of maltreatment as a cause of death (Ewigman et al., 1993; Herman-Giddens et al., 1999; McClain et al., 1993).

Many investigators have attempted to identify demographic, historical, situational, and medical factors as markers of fatal child abuse. For example, Jason and Andereck (1983) found the highest rates of fatal child abuse cases in poor, rural, white families and poor urban families in which teenage mothers had children less than 2 years of age. In a 2-year study of fatal child maltreatment, children residing in households with adults unrelated to them were 8 times more likely to die from abuse than same-age children living in a household with two biological parents (Stiffman et al., 2002).

Fatal child abuse cases in the United States (McClain et al., 1993) have been found to vary widely by geographic region (highest in the South and West, lowest in the Northeast) and by metropolitan area (highest in Phoenix, lowest in Boston). Fatal child abuse has been found to occur more frequently in the home and on weekends and during the afternoon/evening hours of the day (Meadow, 1999). Schmitt (1987) indicated that early childhood situations involving colic and toilet-training resistance were the most common precursors to fatal abuse. Krugman (1983) found that inconsolable crying was the salient predisposing situation in fatal abuse in children less than 1 year old.

Because head injury and damage to the central nervous system have been found to be the most frequent causes of fatal child abuse (Willman, Bank, Senac, & Chadwick, 1997), many researchers have attempted to establish reliable medical and physical signs and symptoms as indicators of infant homicide. Pollanen and his colleagues (Pollanen, Smith, Chiasson, Cairns, & Young, 2002) found that although the "classic markers" of child maltreatment (rib and long-bone fractures) were relatively rare, 71% of their fatal child abuse cases had evidence of recent significant head injury with intercranial bleeding and more than two-thirds had blunt injuries of the skin and soft tissues.

Prior contact with child protective services regarding the child or another sibling is not uncommon. For example, Hicks and Gaughan (1995) found that 43% of their sample of fatal child abuse cases were previously known to the state's caseworkers. In another recent study (Vock et al., 1999), 71% of fatal child abuse cases between 1985 and 1990 displayed indications of repeated physical maltreatment.

Children may die from many forms of abuse other than head injuries, such as intra-abdominal injury and forced water ingestion as a disciplinary method (Arieff & Kronlund, 1999). Cases of fatal child abuse, though rare, have also been documented as due to anorectal injuries (Orr et al., 1995), foreign objects forced into the infant's esophagus (Nolte, 1993), pepper aspiration (Cohle et al., 1988), and caffeine toxicity (Morrow, 1987).

Relevant to Janet's case, one form of fatal child abuse that has received extensive examination and research is "shaken baby syndrome" (SBS). The victims of SBS are rarely older than 3 years, with most less than 8 months of age. SBS is caused by the caretaker's violent shaking of an infant, which results in damage to the infant's brain and spinal cord because of the baby's undeveloped neck muscles (Ide, 2001; Reece & Kirschner, 2004). After the shaking, ruptured blood vessels and tears in the brain's tissues cause swelling and enormous pressure within the skull, leading to death or severe injury. The signs and symptoms of SBS include a characteristic pattern of subdural hematomas, subarachnoid hemorrhages, and retinal hemorrhages (Atwal, Rutty, Carter, & Green, 1998; Case et al., 2001), with an absence of signs of recent external trauma such as facial bruising (Alexander, Sato, Smith, & Bennett, 1990; Atwal et al., 1998; Saternus, Kernbach-Wighton, & Oehmichen, 2000).

The severity of SBS, as with other forms of child abuse, varies along a continuum of brief episodes lasting less than 5 seconds to others of longer than 20 seconds. Even in mild cases, the child might experience as many as two to four shakes per second (Reece & Kirschner, 2004). The mortality rate of SBS victims is extremely high: Some studies (e.g., Ide, 2001) report that as many as 50% die from this type of child abuse, typically within a few hours after the shaking incident (Saternus et al., 2000). Among the children who survive, the resulting brain damage may produce coma, partial or total blindness, hearing loss, seizures, impaired intellectual and learning abilities, and significant developmental delays (Reece & Kirschner, 2004). The annual incidence of SBS in the United States has been estimated to range from 600 to 1,400 cases (Reece & Kirschner, 2004). However, as with other forms of fatal and severe child abuse, detection and identification of SBS is often difficult (Alexander et al., 1990).

Suggestions for Risk Prevention at Intervention Points

Janet's case is important because, although she had very few risk factors, her child did die at her hands. The suggestions here are presented to illustrate a number of family-based interventions of low complexity that can be implemented with colicky, crying infants, the ones most at risk for SBS.

> 1. *When Marcie was born, Janet and Ted were overwhelmed and exhausted by the process. After their daughter was placed in Janet's arms, they tried to console Marcie, but she would not calm down.*

Shortly after Marcie was delivered, Janet and Ted were confronted with a situation in which they were unable to comfort their newborn child. Although an infant's temperament and resistance to nurturing is not consistently predictive of its behavior during the early postpartum stage, Janet and Ted would have profited from the postdelivery bonding-attachment and postdischarge "baby wearing" procedures suggested by Sears and Sears (2001) that were described in chapter 9, the case of Glenda. Sears and Sears (2001) recommend that, in the first hour after the baby's birth and frequently over the next few days, the mother hold her newborn skin to skin, stroke her child's entire body, and talk softly while beginning breast-feeding. If, after Janet left the hospital, she had used a "baby wearing" sling during Marcie's first 6 months, Marcie's prolonged crying episodes might have been significantly reduced, which in turn would have decreased the likelihood of Janet's impulsive, reactive, fatal aggression.

2. *They asked only for a series of 2-week visits after the baby's birth to assist their adjustment to the new infant.*

Janet and Ted did display good judgment in asking for help from their parents after Marcie's birth. Virtually all pediatricians recommend that parents of newborns seek assistance from other family members to cope with the new responsibilities and stresses of parenthood. Their mothers' visits went better than either Janet or Ted expected; thus they may have underestimated the strain that Marcie's colic would have on them. In the following 3 months, however, they experienced the full effect of having to care for a child with persistent colic. Perhaps, in their eagerness to show each of their parents that they were better parents, Janet's and Ted's self-appraisals of their parenting capacity was overestimated. Their faulty confidence prevented them from asking their mothers to help again when Marcie was 3 and 4 months old. If Janet and Ted had arranged for return visits by their mothers, they would have likely been better able to weather Marcie's colic.

3. *When their daughter's allergies and/or colic were more pronounced, they found that they became more short-tempered with each other and with Marcie.*

When Marcie's intense crying was prolonged, neither Janet nor Ted seemed to have a well-planned approach to resolving their parenting crisis. Had they been aware of various methods for managing their colicky baby, Janet most likely might not have reached the breaking point that resulted in her reactive aggression on Marcie.

Sears and Sears (2001) have emphasized the importance of the parent recognizing the baby's "precry" patterns (signal behaviors) and responding to the initial cries as quickly as possible, before the noise becomes so bothersome that the parent avoids contact with the child. They noted that a baby's cry changes from beginning to end and that it can be divided into the "attachment" phase and the "avoidance" phase. During the attachment phase, the parent may quickly act to comfort the child. However, if the baby's crying persists, the avoidance phase develops, and the excessively frustrated parent may become angry at the baby. Sears and Sears (2001) suggested that using the postdelivery and "baby wearing" methods described here might prevent the avoidance phase from occurring. According to Sears and Sears (2001), if a newborn is not hungry, wet, soiled, or medically ill, an infant's cries are communications, not manipulations; thus the parent need not feel as if he or she is being controlled by the baby's actions.

As described in chapter 5, the website of the National Center on Shaken Baby Syndrome (2005) recommends a series of simple strategies that a caretaker can employ to prevent shaking or physically abusing a child who cries excessively. These procedures include swaddling the baby snugly in a soft warm blanket, laying the baby on its stomach across your lap and gently rubbing its back, creating music for the baby by singing or playing the radio, taking the baby for a walk in a stroller, or calling a relative to watch the baby for an hour so that you can regain your composure.

It is unfortunate that Janet felt that she was the only one who could take care of Marcie that night. If she had called Ted and told him to come home because she was at her breaking point, this strategy of "changing listeners" (Sears & Sears, 2001) might have provided her the emotional distance she needed at that point to overcome her anger and frustration with Marcie.

Epilogue

Janet pled guilty to homicide by child abuse after telling the investigating detectives that she had shaken Marcie in frustration. Medical examination of the baby did not reveal any other signs of prior parental abuse or neglect. Marcie's pediatric records confirmed her diagnosis of chronic infantile colic. Affidavits by neighbors attested to Janet's character as a loving, nurturing parent prior to the offense. Ted stood by Janet's side during the plea-agreement hearing and testified on her behalf. The judge sentenced Janet to a year's incarceration, followed by 5 years of probation.

12

Abusive/Neglectful Mother,
Inadequate Type
Kaye

Kaye, her 4-year-old daughter, Ann, and Kaye's mother entered the apartment where they lived together. They had been at the park for the past hour watching the child play on the swings and slide. Kaye's mother, Margaret, asked where Kaye's son, Sam, was. Kaye said that she had left him asleep on his bed after they had taken a bath. Neither adult checked to see if Sam was still in the children's bedroom. Margaret shrugged and turned on the television set. She liked to watch the children's shows with her granddaughter. Kaye went into the kitchen to get some chips and Coke. For the next half hour they sat together on the couch and watched cartoons. Unknown to all three, Ann's 15-month-old brother, Sam, floated face down in the bathtub.

Margaret went to the bathroom at the end of the television show, shrieked when she saw Sam, and pulled him out of the water. Kaye and Ann ran to the bathroom. Screaming at each other, Kaye and Margaret tried to decide what to do next. Kaye then remembered that her caseworker had told her to call 911 if something ever happened.

Kaye got through to the dispatcher after twice dialing the number. She told her that Sam had been in the bathtub and was dead. When the dispatcher asked where she was, Kaye answered "in the kitchen." The dispatcher then asked her where she lived and Kaye replied "at home." On the dispatcher's third try, Kaye told her the name of the building and her apartment number. Kaye had always been a little slow.

Kaye was placed in special education classes after the second grade, when she was diagnosed with mental retardation, like her mother, Margaret. Kaye had not attended kindergarten. She was often late to school in the mornings because she and her mother had overslept. Records indicated that in the first grade she had been tardy more than 50 days and absent more than 20 days. Her mother was investigated for educational neglect, but Kaye was allowed to stay with Margaret when her mother promised to be more diligent in getting her child to school.

When Kaye repeated the first grade, school officials thought that the reason that she was academically behind her classmates was that she had missed so many school days. An evaluation by the school district's psychologist, however, recommended that Kaye have remedial and special classes due to her limited intellect. Kaye enjoyed going to school and liked her elementary teacher. Margaret did make a better effort to get her to school on time, and protective services closed her case at the end of the year.

Kaye was her mother's only child and had been raised by Margaret alone after her father had left them. She never knew her father but did like her mother's live-in boyfriend, Steve. He had stayed with them for more than 2 years, until Kaye was about 8 years old. Steve had not been abusive to her or her mother, but he was often unemployed because he worked menial construction jobs. He would complain about Margaret's negligent care of Kaye but would help when he was not working. One morning, they awoke to find that Steve had packed and gone.

Margaret was investigated for child neglect a second time when Kaye came to school after a week's absence unkempt and wearing dirty, wrinkled clothes. When the child protective services caseworker arrived for her home visit, she found that Margaret's trailer was a mess. Food had been left out on the table, and unwashed dishes were in the sink. The refrigerator was nearly empty, and the cabinets contained few boxes or cans of food. The beds were unmade, and clothes were strewn on the floor. Dirty towels were found in the bathroom, and the bathtub looked as though it had not been cleaned after many uses.

Margaret made no excuses when the caseworker arrived and was angry that she was again being investigated. Kaye was placed in temporary foster care for 3 months until the agency documented that Margaret was able to independently care for her daughter again. Protective services kept Margaret's case open for another 12 months, then closed it when they did not receive any more reports from the school about Kaye's clothes or appearance.

Kaye was socially promoted each year and continued going to special education classes into her adolescent years. She and her mother subsisted on public assistance and rent supplements on the trailer where they lived together. During these years there were no further protective services investigations of Margaret, as she was not physically or emotionally abusive toward her daughter.

Margaret was content spending her days at home watching television or taking naps while Kaye was at school. In the afternoons they would go for walks around the trailer park. They'd walk to the store for groceries, which Margaret would pay for with food stamps. Margaret never had an automobile because she had never learned to drive. When Steve lived with them, he would sometimes take them for rides in his car, which they enjoyed very much. After he abandoned them, Margaret did not want to become involved with another man. She was happy having Kaye all to herself.

Kaye was 15 when she dropped out of school after becoming pregnant with Ann. Ann's father, Robert, was a 16-year-old boy who was another special education student at the school Kaye attended. She considered Robert to be her boyfriend, though they never actually had a date. They had had sex only a few times and never with the use of condoms or other forms of birth control. Kaye and Robert had educated themselves about sex by looking at a pornographic magazine Robert had been given by one of his friends. They thought sex was exciting, though they knew it was "wrong."

Kaye's pregnancy was discovered from blood tests during a routine examination by a doctor. Kaye told Margaret that Robert was the father and that she had liked having sex with him. Though Margaret was angry for a while, she soon became excited about the baby. Robert's family wanted Kaye to terminate the pregnancy because they did not want to financially support a baby with mental retardation. Kaye and her mother wanted to keep the baby. Robert's family relented when Kaye and Margaret told them they'd raise the child by themselves. Ann was delivered without complications.

Kaye was first investigated by the county's child protective services agency when Ann was almost 2 years old. She'd been reported when a neighbor in the trailer park observed that Ann was left unattended in the yard between their mobile homes. Kaye explained to the caseworker that she and her mother had been watching television and not noticed that Ann had gone outside. The caseworker noted that Ann did not appear to be dirty or underfed. Despite the disarray in the trailer, there was not enough evidence to warrant further action by the agency. She did tell Kaye not to leave her child unattended again and closed the case with her supervisor's agreement.

About 3 months later, Kaye became pregnant for the second time, this time by a man who had lived in the trailer park. She had met him while walking with Ann, and he'd invited them in for snacks and a soft drink. Kaye liked the attention he gave her and would visit him in the evenings sometimes, telling her mother she was going out for a walk. She liked how he talked to her and touched her.

Soon they became intimate. She believed him when he told her she could not get pregnant so soon after having Ann. Kaye kept her meetings with him a secret from her mother because she knew she'd be told to stop visiting him. She knew the man only as Carl. When it was evident that Kaye was pregnant again, Kaye did not want to have an abortion or give up her baby for adoption because she liked Carl so much. When she told Carl they were going to have a baby, he was quiet. By the next morning, the trailer he had been renting was deserted. Sam's father's actual identity was never established because Carl had also given a false name to the trailer park's manager.

Kaye's doctor and his staff managed her prenatal care once again. Sam was delivered easily in the hospital. Kaye and her mother now had two children to parent and had their hands full as Ann became more mobile. Kaye's daughter always seemed to be in motion. She exhausted her mother and grandmother by the end of each day. She would often explore under the bathroom sink and the lower cabinets in the kitchen area, sometimes pouring out the bottles she found. A visiting neighbor had once observed Ann crawling under the sink and playing with the bottles, and soon a protective services worker was investigating once again. This caseworker told Kaye to keep her cleaning bottles on top of the refrigerator so that Ann would not be harmed. The agency decided not to remove Ann from the home after being told by Kaye's doctor that Ann did not appear to be physically neglected and that her mother had not missed any pre- or postnatal visits. Also, the county's few foster care beds had to be prioritized for sexual and physical abuse cases.

During the months after Sam was born, Ann and her grandmother appeared to develop a closer bond, because Kaye was so involved with her newborn's needs. Sam rarely slept through the night, and during the day his naps were often brief. As the months went by and Sam grew, the trailer became too small for the four of them. Kaye mentioned it to her doctor during a postnatal well-baby visit, and he suggested they move into public housing apartments not far from his downtown office. After months on the waiting list, Kaye and her mother moved into a three-bedroom apartment shortly after Sam's first birthday.

Ann had been somewhat delayed in learning to crawl and walk, but Sam was soon scooting around, as active on all fours as his half-sister was on two legs. Kaye would often get up from the couch where she was watching television to find him rummaging on the floor of her closet or in the lower cabinets, as Ann had done. She did not scold him but would bring him into the living room to watch television with her. Soon, Sam would be off the couch and exploring alone once again. In the new apartment, there was no space above the refrigerator, so Kaye and Margaret kept the cleaning supplies under the kitchen and bathroom sinks. Fortunately, the children escaped injury or death from accidental poisoning. Sam was nearly 15 months old when he took his first tentative steps upright.

On the day that Sam died, Ann and Margaret had gone to the store as a special treat. Kaye had stayed home with her son. Both had slept late because Sam had been up late the night before watching television with his mother. While Margaret and Ann were out of the apartment, Kaye decided to take a bath. She filled the tub, removed Sam's diaper, and brought Sam into the water with her, as she had done many times before. He had long since outgrown the kitchen sink and his bassinet. Kaye liked to bathe her son in the tub and enjoyed his laughter, as he would play with his water toys. After a half-hour of bathing and playing, she got out with Sam in her arms and dried off. Sam yawned briefly, and Kaye thought that he wanted to go back to bed for a nap. She put a diaper and pajamas on him, got dressed, and took him into the bedroom he shared with Ann.

Sam rested quietly, and Kaye left the room to watch television. After a half-hour, she thought that she would surprise Ann and Margaret by meeting them on their way back from the store. She did not hear any noise from Sam's room, thought that he was still asleep, and left the apartment. When Kaye met up with her daughter and mother, Ann wanted to go across the street to the park to play on the swings. Kaye told Margaret that she'd left Sam sleeping in his bed. Other children came to the park and joined Ann in play, and Kaye and Margaret lost track of time. They were not aware that an hour had passed before Ann got tired and wanted to go home.

When they entered the apartment and did not hear any noise from Sam, Kaye thought that he was still asleep. She never checked his room and did not know what had happened to him until she heard her mother cry out. The toys that Sam had tried to get out of the tub were still bobbing in the water.

Case Analysis

It is obvious from the facts of this case that the primary issue of Kaye's story was parental neglect, which resulted in Sam's death. Neglect, defined as the failure of a parent or caretaker to provide for the child's basic needs (Sattler, 1998), is the most frequent form of child maltreatment (Melton et al., 1997; Sedlak & Broadhurst, 1996). Types of child neglect pertain to the child's physical, educational, or emotional needs. Examples of physical neglect include a parent's refusal or delay in seeking medical or dental care for the child, abandonment, or inadequate supervision of the child's activities. Educational neglect may entail failure to enroll a child in school or parental allowance of a child's truancy. Emotional neglect comprises parental disinterest in providing for the child's psychological needs for attention, love, and security, as well as exposure of the child to repeated marital/partner violence or drug and alcohol abuse.

Although neglect may be seen by some as more benign than physical child abuse or sexual molestation, severe forms of neglect include endangerment, wherein the child's life or welfare is at immediate risk, as in the case of Kaye and Sam. Additional examples of endangerment would be failing to use a child car seat, driving while intoxicated with the child as a passenger, or negligently allowing a child's access to loaded guns or illegal drugs (Sattler, 1998).

The impact of neglect has been documented by long-term studies of children who were raised by negligent parents. For example, Hildyard and Wolfe (2002) found that in comparison with physically abused children, neglected offspring displayed more severe cognitive and academic deficits, social withdrawal, and internalizing problems (e.g., anxiety, depression, etc.), particularly if the neglect began and continued early in the child's life. Hart, Brassard, and Karlson (1996) found that child victims of emotional neglect often developed problems in learning and relationships, unusual behaviors and feelings, anxiety and physical symptoms, and depression.

Maternal Filicide Risk Matrix Analysis

The Risk Matrix for Kaye's parenting of Sam is presented in table 12.1.

Table 12.1
Maternal Filicide Risk Matrix: Kaye

Factor	Pre-P	P/D	EP	LP	PI
Individual					
Age at current pregnancy	R	R	R	R	R
Intelligence level	R	R	R	R	R
Education level	R	R	R	R	R
Medical status	P	P	P	P	P
Emotional status	P	P	P	P	P
Trauma history	P	P	P	P	P
Maternal attitudes	P	P	P	R	R
Family of Origin					
Mother's parenting	P	P	P	R	R
Father's parenting	R	R	R	R	R
Marital/family stability	R	R	R	R	R
Situational					
Marital/partner status	R	R	R	R	R
Financial status	R	R	R	R	R
Child-care status	P	P	R	R	R
Infant's temperament	—	—	R	P	P

Note: R = Risk; P = Protective; Pre-P = Prepregnancy; P/D = Pregnancy/delivery; EP = Early postpartum; LP = Late postpartum; PI = Postinfancy.

Prepregnancy Stage

Prior to Kaye's pregnancy with Sam, she displayed a mix of individual risk and protective factors associated with maternal filicide. Kaye's adolescent age, very low intelligence level, and limited educational achievement were significant elements that would place Sam at higher risk for neglect and perhaps abandonment. At this point in her life, she was relatively emotionally stable in that she was not suffering from a severe mental illness that distorted her perceptions of reality (e.g., delusions, hallucinations, etc.), nor did she abuse alcohol or illegal drugs. Because of her physician's concern about Ann's well-being, Kaye's medical status was not problematic. Her doctor ensured that Kaye would attend Ann's postnatal appointments by arranging transportation for her through his staff.

Although Kaye's father deserted her when she was born and her mother's boyfriend abruptly left them, there was no indication in her history that she was a victim of physical or sexual abuse. Kaye was briefly placed in foster care because of her mother's failure to keep their trailer clean and safe, but there were no other indications of trauma in her life prior to her pregnancy with Sam. Kaye's pregnancy with Ann by Robert was not the result of coercion or force. Though her capacity to consent to sex with virginal Robert or exploitative Carl was diminished due to her limited intellect and judgment, neither partner appeared to physically abuse her; thus her life prior to Sam's birth was relatively trauma-free.

When Kaye was pregnant with Ann, she had very positive attitudes toward parenthood. She and her mother did not wish to end her pregnancy nor give her child up for adoption. Kaye did have an episode of neglect with Ann; however, the agency apparently did not consider its severity high enough to warrant removal of her daughter. On balance, therefore, she appeared to be adequately bonded to Ann, and her maternal attitudes were positive.

Kaye's family of origin factors at this stage were also mixed prior to her pregnancy with Sam. Margaret's parenting of Kaye, given her limited abilities, was generally protective, with only two prior episodes of neglect that resulted in action by the county's child protective services agency. Margaret's angry resentment of the agency's intrusion into her life when Kaye was a child, and later when Kaye had Ann, was not reflective of good parenting attitudes, as she did not see the risks posed by her neglect. Margaret's reactions to the investigations may have contributed to Kaye's subsequent neglectful supervision of her children. However, Margaret was never cited for physical abuse, nor was Kaye ever exposed to domestic violence or substance abuse during her childhood and adolescent years. Margaret's relationships with men, although not abusive, were not very stable: Both Kaye's father and Steve left them.

Kaye's situational factors were also mixed. When she got to an age at which she was developing heterosexual relationships, she appears to have duplicated her mother's pattern with men. Both Robert and Carl, though for quite different reasons, were not available to Kaye to help with her parenting of Ann or Sam. Financial stability was also a risk factor for Kaye, as her family relied on public assistance throughout her life. At the prepregnancy stage, Kaye was assisted by Margaret in her child-care obligations to Ann.

Pregnancy/Delivery Stage

Kaye's individual, family of origin, and situational risk and protective factors during this stage were essentially the same as they had been prior to her pregnancy with Sam. The major reason for this absence of change was that she and her mother led rather simple, uncomplicated lives of caring for Ann, watching television, and taking walks. Their limited finances and illiteracy did not allow for a broader array of life experiences. Though her pregnancy with Sam was unintended, Kaye still enjoyed the continuous support of her mother and the practical help of her family physician and his office staff. She continued to have problems finding a stable, reliable partner to help her with the children, as Carl abruptly left after hearing the news he was a new father.

Early Postpartum Stage

In the first 6 months after Kaye's delivery of her son, her situational risk factors increased. She was now a teenage mother with two children, and Sam's activity levels often left her sleep deprived. She was fortunate to live with her mother, with whom she could share her child-care duties. If she had been on her own, her individual and situational risk factors would likely have placed both children at much higher vulnerability for physical abuse or endangerment neglect. The children's risk of harm would have also increased as they became more mobile because of Kaye's patterns of inadequate supervision. In terms of individual factors, Kaye continued to receive good medical care from her physician, and she appeared to be trauma-free. There were no indications that her emotional status had deteriorated following her son's birth. As she focused on Sam's care while her mother took care of Ann, Kaye was able to develop a positive bonding with her newborn through shared experiences of breast-feeding and taking baths together.

Late Postpartum Stage

The most notable change in risk, as illustrated in Kaye's risk matrix, was her relative indifference to her children's explorations under the sinks in the kitchen and bathroom. As Sam overcame his colic, his temperament improved. His increased movement was indicative of normal activity and curiosity for a child between the ages of 6 and 12 months. However, given Kaye's television-distracted neglect at this stage, her inadequate supervision of Sam suggested that her maternal attitude was a risk factor. Also, her mother had her hands full with Ann; thus Margaret was less available to share child-care duties for Sam with Kaye.

Postinfancy Stage

During the postinfancy stage, when Sam could walk upright, he was able to see the toys in the bathtub, which Kaye had forgotten to drain. He fell into the tub while reaching for the toys, was unable to get out, and eventually drowned. It was undetermined whether had Sam left his bedroom while Kaye was watching television or after she had left the apartment to meet Ann and her mother. In either instance, her failure to drain the bathtub, to check on her son's location, or to foresee the consequences of leaving him unattended ultimately led to his death.

Relevant Research: Mental Retardation and Parenting

According to the American Psychiatric Association (2000), mental retardation is characterized by extremely low general intellectual functioning beginning before age 18 in combination with significant impairment in the person's adaptive functioning in communication, self-care, self-direction, home living, academic skills, social-interpersonal relationships, work skills, and/or judgment regarding one's health and safety.

Mental retardation varies in degrees of increasing impairment, categorized as mild, moderate, severe, and profound. The prevalence of mental retardation has been estimated to be approximately 1% of the general population. Of those, 85% are likely to be classified in the mild category, and another 10% in the category of moderate mental retardation. Those with mild or moderate mental retardation often live in the community, and some hold semiskilled or unskilled employment. Persons with mild mental retardation may acquire academic skills to a sixth-grade level and live independently or with minimum supervision. Persons diagnosed with profound and severe mental retardation are often placed in residential facilities.

Parental mental retardation has been found to be a risk factor for child maltreatment, especially neglect (Dowdney & Skuse, 1993; Tymchuk, 1992). In one study, mothers with mental retardation who were compared with a nonimpaired sample scored lower on measures of their decision-making abilities in parenting tasks (Tymchuk, Yokota, & Rahbar, 1990). Feldman, Ducharme, and Case (1999), for example, suggested that parents with mental retardation often have inadequate abilities in basic child-care skills such as diapering, treating diaper rashes, bathing, and safety. Seagull and Scheurer (1986) found in their longitudinal research with 64 children of parents with mental retardation that fewer than 20% were still living with their parents at the end of the 7-year study period. More than 76% of the children had been adopted or were living in foster care after the courts had terminated their parents' rights.

Although parents with mental retardation constitute a disproportionately larger percentage of child neglect cases, a number of investigators have argued that their neglect is not solely the result of limited intellect. Rather, the parents' neglect is due to poverty and limited resources or to additional problems such as substance abuse or co-occurring mental illness (Crittenden, 1985; Dowdney & Skuse, 1993). Dowdney and Skuse (1993) have commented that many studies have been poorly designed, with vague measures of parenting ability. However, a well-designed study that compared the children of impoverished mothers with and without mental retardation found that the offspring of the impaired mothers had more behavioral problems, lower intellectual functioning, and poorer academic achievement (Feldman & Walton-Allen, 1997).

When mothers with mental retardation have been neglectful or abusive with their children, remediation and education are key components to preventing their children's removal into temporary foster care. Traditional parent education programs for adults are often ineffective because parents with mental retardation have difficulty understanding, let alone reading, the course materials. As a result, many parents with mental retardation will fail to complete the agency's remediation program, which in turn may lead to termination of the parents' rights to their children (Bakken, Miltenberger, & Schauss, 1993; Ray, Rubenstein, & Russo, 1994; Seagull & Scheurer, 1986; Taylor et al., 1991).

The most effective parenting education for adults with mental retardation may be a combination of behaviorally oriented practical demonstrations of managing child-care situations. For example, Feldman et al. (1999)

demonstrated that 90% of mothers with mental retardation who were given self-instructional manuals containing pictures were able to acquire and retain basic child-care cleaning and safety skills. They reported that the mothers expressed high satisfaction with the training program. Bakken et al. (1993) found that behaviorally based child-care training presented in the parents' home was more effective than similar training given in a small-group format. Sattler (1998) suggested that, for neglectful parents, the most effective programs are those that help the adults to respond to children's signals that parental attention is required, situations that were repeatedly demonstrated by Sam and Ann.

Suggestions for Prevention at Risk Intervention Points

Because the similarity of Margaret's and Kaye's neglectful supervision reflects the generational aspects of inadequate parenting, RIPs from both women's histories are employed as examples.

1. The school district's psychologist recommended that Kaye have remedial and special classes due to her limited intellect. . . . Margaret did make a better effort to get her to school on time, and protective services closed her case at the end of the year.

When it was discovered that Kaye had mental retardation, it would have been helpful if the psychologist's recommendations had also included parenting education for Margaret about her daughter's special needs. Numerous educational resources exist for parents of children with mental retardation (Bakken et al., 1993). For parents of more limited intellect, picture books have been developed to describe the lives of children with mental retardation (Feldman et al., 1999). The school might have also invited Margaret into Kaye's classroom to observe how the special education teacher dealt with many situations that Margaret likely faced at home, such as responding to Kaye's requests for attention, the frequency of supervision "checks" of her daughter's behavior, and managing her oppositional tantrums. The family preservation programs for training parents with mental retardation described by Ray et al. (1994) might also have been helpful to Margaret.

2. When the child protective services caseworker arrived for her home visit, she found that Margaret's trailer was a mess. . . . Kaye was placed in temporary foster care for 3 months until the agency documented that Margaret was able to independently care for her daughter again.

This RIP might have been a good opportunity for the agency to arrange home-based health and safety child-care demonstrations, which could have been monitored by weekly checkup visits by an agency-sponsored community volunteer. Picture books showing the effects on a child from poisoning or infections from spoiled food or garbage, presented educationally, not punitively, to Margaret, might have helped her understand the long-term consequences of her neglect of Kaye. The combination of such community-based interventions of low to moderate complexity might have allowed the agency to keep Kaye at home with her mother and resulted in a more positive response from Margaret toward child protective services help. When Kaye became a mother, these more therapeutic interactions with the agency might have changed Margaret's reactions after her daughter was investigated.

> 3. *Kaye explained to the caseworker that she and her mother had been watching television and not noticed that Ann had gone outside. The caseworker . . . did tell Kaye not to leave her child unattended again and closed the case with her supervisor's agreement.*

One simple intervention that might have alerted Kaye and Margaret to Ann's leaving the trailer would be to install a doorbell that would sound off when the door was opened. This alarm might have easily alerted them to attend to Ann and might likely have had a more lasting impact on their supervision of the child than the caseworker's lecture. With Kaye and Margaret's permission, the caseworker's installation of the bell (which also works for nonimpaired parents of young, mobile preschool children) might have also improved Margaret and Kaye's reaction to the agency's child protective service investigation.

> 4. *This caseworker told Kaye to keep her cleaning bottles on top of the refrigerator so that Ann would not be harmed. . . . In the new apartment Kaye and Margaret kept the cleaning supplies under the kitchen and bathroom sinks.*

Many baby-proof door locks exist as simple interventions to keep crawling children out of lower cabinets that might contain dangerous substances. The agency's suggestion of such devices and demonstration of their use might have been effective in keeping Ann and Sam out of harm's way. Fortunately, neither was accidentally poisoned.

> 5. *Sam rested quietly, and Kaye left the room to watch television. . . . She did not hear any noise from Sam's room, thought that he was still asleep, and left the apartment.*

It was unfortunate that Kaye did not simply check for Sam's presence in his bedroom, but her history of inadequate supervision ultimately resulted in his death. One simple intervention that might have prevented his drowning would have been the installation of a slide lock on the outside of each of the apartment's interior doors. Sliding the lock on Sam's door would have kept him inside his bedroom, even if he got up after a short nap. Latching the lock on the bathroom door would have kept Sam out of the tub's water, even if he'd wandered out of his room after Kaye left the apartment. Though there are occasional reports of parents locking their children for long periods of time in their rooms as punishment, there was no indication in Kaye's or Margaret's history that they would be deliberately abusive to Ann or Sam. Even if they did not install such locks on the children's bedroom door, use of the devices on the kitchen and bathroom doors, which are the sites of most child accidents, might have kept Sam alive until he was big enough to get out of a tub full of water on his own.

Epilogue

Kaye was charged with homicide by child abuse and evaluated by both prosecution and defense experts. The examiners diagnosed her as having mental retardation. After hearing testimony and directly questioning Kaye, the trial judge ruled that she was competent to stand trial. She was sentenced to 10 years in prison. After the trial, the family court involuntarily terminated her parental rights to Ann on motion by the county protective services agency. Ann was not placed in Margaret's care because of Margaret's history of parental neglect of Kaye.

13

Psychotic/Depressed Mother, Delusional Type

Barbara

Barbara sat in the kitchen sobbing as the police searched her house. Her husband, Tom, sat next to her crying softly. He reached out to hold her hand, but Barbara jerked away and turned her back to him. Neither spoke of the children. Barbara kept mumbling and rocking in her chair as the police moved about their house taking photographs and collecting evidence. When the ambulance arrived, the paramedics were given permission to remove the children's bodies from the house. Marcus and Heather were brought down the stairs by two paramedics, each child wrapped in a blanket. As they passed through the kitchen, Barbara looked up and groaned loudly, and Tom burst into tears. The detective waited until the children were placed in the ambulance before she began her questioning.

Barbara was unresponsive as the police officer read her *Miranda* rights. The detective asked if she understood each of her rights, but Barbara would not reply. She continued rocking and mumbling in her chair. The detective told Tom that Barbara was now under arrest for the murder of their two children and that she would be taken to the county jail for booking and fingerprinting. Tom nodded quietly and got up to call their family attorney, a former public defender.

When Tom reentered the kitchen, he saw that the detective had handcuffed Barbara and was leading her to the police car. He followed them to the driveway and told Barbara that their lawyer would meet them at the jail. His wife did not react to his statements or look at him. She shuffled to the police car with her head down, mumbling to herself. Tom drove his car to the jail, not letting the police cruiser out of his sight.

At the jail, Barbara stood quietly, staring blankly as she was fingerprinted. A woman officer helped her change into an inmate's jumpsuit and then led her to her cell. While walking down the jail corridor, Barbara abruptly looked at the officer and stated, "I killed them because they were crazy." The officer immediately contacted the detective, who told her to bring Barbara back to the jail's interview room. Barbara's attorney asked the officers to leave the room while he consulted with his client for a few minutes.

When the detective returned, the attorney informed her that Barbara would not answer any of the detective's questions at this time. He requested that the police arrange for Barbara to be transported to the local hospital, where her psychiatrist would admit her to the facility's secure floor for prisoners with medical and mental illnesses. While they were discussing these plans, Barbara stared blankly at the wall. As they got up to leave, however, Barbara looked straight into the detective's eyes and said, "I killed them because they were crazy, but they are in heaven now."

The deaths of Marcus and Heather were the lead story on the evening television news and on the front page of the morning newspaper the following day. The county district attorney declined to answer reporters' questions other than to confirm that Barbara had been charged with two counts of murder. The district attorney reminded the reporters that their state did not have the death penalty but that he would seek a life without parole sentence when Barbara's case went to trial. Barbara's attorney refused to answer any reporters' questions and did not return their telephone calls.

The psychiatrist who had been treating Barbara met her in the emergency room of the hospital on the afternoon of her arrest. She looked up briefly as he entered the room but otherwise remained mute to his initial questions. During the interview, Barbara continued to rock slowly in her chair while hugging herself and staring at the floor. Tears ran down her face, but she made no effort to wipe them away. Her psychiatrist spoke softly to her, telling her that she was going to be admitted to the hospital and that he would see her again that evening. He did not attempt to complete a thorough psychiatric evaluation that afternoon, as Barbara appeared to be incapable of answering questions.

As she left quietly with a nurse, her psychiatrist wrote orders for increased dosages of the antipsychotic and antidepressant medication that she had been taking as an outpatient under his care. He also wrote an order placing Barbara on continuous-observation suicide watch. When the psychiatrist saw her later that evening, Barbara's condition had not changed. In accordance with the hospital's suicide-watch procedures, Barbara's door was left open, and a nursing assistant sat in the corridor to keep her in sight. The nurses on the floor reported to the psychiatrist that Barbara had not left her room and had not spontaneously requested anything from them. The nurse technician described Barbara as initially sitting on the edge of her bed and staring blankly, while her lips moved without speech. She told the psychiatrist that after about an hour, Barbara lay down on her bed and curled up into a fetal position, moaning softly. The patient's movements had not changed since.

The psychiatrist entered Barbara's room, and the nursing assistant resumed her post in the corridor. He tried without success to get Barbara to verbally respond, though she did sit up on the bed. She clasped her knees to her chest and began to rock gently while turning her face to the wall. The psychiatrist waited patiently for the next few minutes hoping that she would initiate conversation.

Spontaneously, Barbara said, "I killed my kids because they were crazy. They are in heaven now." When the psychiatrist asked if she wished to join her children, Barbara turned to face him and replied, "Yes, they need me there. I'm their mother." The psychiatrist then gently informed her that he had increased her medications and was going to continue his suicide precaution orders for her over the next few days. Barbara nodded in acknowledgement and stretched out on the bed. Over the next week, Barbara's condition slowly improved. She remained in her room for most of each day and minimally responded to the nurses' inquiries. She did occasionally walk up and down the corridor of the psychiatric wing under the continuing observation of the staff. Her demeanor remained unchanged: She never smiled nor displayed any emotion. Her face was devoid of expression, as she looked dully at persons who addressed her. When she would sit in the day room, she would remain by herself and avoid interaction with other patients. She never spontaneously requested any assistance from the staff and declined to participate in activity therapy sessions of mild physical exercise, crafts, and board games.

At the end of Barbara's first week of hospitalization, her defense attorney telephoned her psychiatrist to arrange a series of meetings with Barbara at the hospital. The attorney informed the psychiatrist that, within the next 4 weeks, it was likely that the district attorney would request that Barbara undergo evaluations by a psychiatrist and a psychologist from the state's forensic mental hospital.

During the next week, Barbara's attorney introduced her to the forensic psychologist and forensic psychiatrist he had retained for her case, who would be questioning Barbara about her personal, family, educational, vocational, marital, mental health, and medical history. The psychologist indicated that he would ask her to take a number of paper-and-pencil tests to help them understand her thoughts and emotions. The psychiatrist said that they would also be asking her to describe how she was thinking and feeling in the past few months and on the day that the children died. Barbara's attorney reassured her that he had worked with the two clinicians on other cases and that their evaluations might help him with her defense. Barbara gave her consent to the evaluations and to the clinicians' request to interview her husband and psychiatrist.

After the initial appointment with Barbara during the second week of her hospitalization, I, the defense attorney's forensic psychologist, interviewed Tom about his recollections of his wife's behavior since they got married and, in particular, since she became pregnant with Marcus, then Heather. Tom said that Barbara had become depressed after Marcus was born and that she had had great difficulty with her parental and household responsibilities for the first 6 months of their son's life. After his mother-in-law's month-long visit to help Barbara recover from Marcus' birth, he often came home from work to find her unkempt and exhausted. She often cried herself to sleep each night and appeared to have little interest in leaving the house when he'd suggest they go for a weekend drive in the country. Tom noted that his wife's mood improved substantially after she began psychiatric treatment and antidepressant medications.

He revealed that Barbara's psychiatrist then had initially recommended that she be hospitalized but had agreed to an initial trial of outpatient care, which seemed to work well. She seemed to be herself again, as she enjoyed motherhood and homemaking for their family. Tom said that, after a year's treatment, Barbara and her psychiatrist had agreed that she had fully recovered from her depression and no longer needed medication. He remembered that his wife's psychiatrist had moved to another city before she became pregnant with Heather.

Tom then told me that Barbara had never seemed to recover from Heather's birth. He described her increasingly bizarre, anxious behavior of looking suspiciously out the window and commenting about how people were talking about her. His wife would sometimes ask him to repeat what he had said, even though he had not spoken. Marcus had complained to him that Barbara never let him play outside—she would tell him and his sister to be quiet and hid with them in the locked bedroom closet. Tom said that his wife would always tell him she felt fine. However in the months before the children died, he had realized that his wife's depression had returned with symptoms that were worse than those he had seen after Marcus's birth. She rarely had dinner prepared when he came home from work, and she seemed to have little interest in eating. He would often find her still in her bathrobe and slippers in the afternoon, with her hair uncombed and disheveled.

He indicated that Barbara would often cry alone in their bedroom and tell him that the children no longer obeyed her. When he would try to encourage her and tell her that the children loved her, Barbara would say that Marcus and Heather had "changed." He remembered that when he had asked her how the children had changed, his wife looked at him oddly, then went to the window, saying, "somebody is listening." After the incident he knew Barbara needed professional treatment once more.

Tom stated that Barbara was very reluctant to see a new psychiatrist and went with him only after he insisted. Barbara went to every weekly session at the doctor's office only because Tom took her there. Her condition did not seem to change much with the new medicine, though she appeared to be less anxious and panicky. He never expected that Barbara would kill their children, because before she became ill again she seemed to be such a wonderful mother.

Over the next several weeks, the forensic psychiatrist and I interviewed Barbara. Barbara described her personal history to us and completed a variety of psychological personality tests that were consistent with her psychiatrist's diagnosis of major depression with psychotic features following Heather's birth. Her previous psychiatrist's records confirmed that after Marcus' birth she had suffered from nonpsychotic postpartum major depression and panic disorder but had responded well to medication and individual psychotherapy.

In the final two evaluation sessions, which occurred 6 weeks after her arrest, Barbara revealed to us that in the past few months she had been hearing voices telling her that she was a bad mother. She believed that the police would take her children away and put her in a mental hospital. She said that the voices told her that she needed to stay alert, especially at night, because that was when the police would come for her. Barbara described how she became increasingly unable to take care of herself or her children. She was often exhausted each day because she was getting very little sleep.

She remembered that the children began to look at her with strange expressions when they all would be hiding in the closet. She recalled that during those episodes, Marcus would whisper to Heather, then try to escape. She revealed that when she would grab the children to keep them from leaving the closet, they would begin to scream and cry. She thought they were trying to tell the police where she was so that they could put her away.

Barbara said that when Tom took her to the psychiatrist, she became aware that she had become "infected" by her children and that she was as "crazy" as they were. She knew then that she had to protect her husband from her "crazy babies." She said she was not surprised when the psychiatrist put her back on medicine, but she was confused when he did not call the police to put her in the hospital. She remembered that even though he often asked about auditory hallucinations, she always denied that she was ever hearing voices.

She stated that it was the night before their deaths that she realized that to save Marcus, Heather, and Tom, she had to "send the children to heaven." On the morning of the offense, Barbara remembered that she felt at peace, because soon her babies would be safe. She recalled that Tom had asked her before he went to work if she felt all right; however, before she could answer, a voice distracted her attention. When she finally answered that she was fine, she remembered that Tom looked at her with a strange expression before leaving for work. She said that as she heard him drive off, she knew that he was safe from harm.

She recalled climbing the stairs to her children's bedroom. She remembered a voice telling her to "do it" as she put the pillow over Marcus's face, then turned to Heather's bed. She said she felt a great relief after she dressed the children, then walked back down to the kitchen. She recalled her panic and confusion when Tom screamed at her, "What have you done? I'm calling the police!"

Barbara said she could remember very little after that except seeing her psychiatrist at the hospital. She remarked that over the past few weeks in the hospital she was feeling better because she believed she would soon be seeing her children again. On hearing this statement at the end of the evaluation session, we notified the head nurse that Barbara continued to be at risk for self-harm. The nurse said she would contact Barbara's psychiatrist for suicide precaution orders.

During our postevaluation consultation the next day, the forensic psychiatrist and I confirmed that we had separately arrived at a similar opinion. We agreed that in the weeks preceding the offense and at the time of the children's deaths, Barbara had suffered from postpartum major depression with psychotic features and that when she killed Marcus and Heather, she had a delusional belief that she was saving their souls from the Devil by "sending the children to heaven." Our opinion was consistent with the state's law defining legal insanity. We met with Barbara's attorney later that afternoon to discuss the results of our evaluations. The attorney asked us to draft our respective psychological and psychiatric reports and send the documents to his office.

While Barbara was hospitalized, both the county district attorney and her lawyer had been busy preparing for her trial. Barbara had been arraigned on two counts of murder. At a pretrial hearing, Barbara's lawyer entered a plea of not guilty by reason of insanity. On receipt of the defense attorney's notice of a plea of insanity, the county prosecutor filed a motion requesting that in accordance with state law, Barbara be ordered to undergo psychiatric and psychological evaluations at the state mental hospital. Barbara's attorney requested that the evaluations take place at the local hospital where she was a patient so that her psychiatric treatment would not be disrupted. The judge agreed.

Two weeks later—which was approximately 4 weeks after we, the experts retained by the defense, had completed our evaluations—Barbara was reexamined by the state's forensic psychologist and psychiatrist. Their procedures were very similar to those used in her previous evaluation: multiple clinical interviews, psychological testing, collateral interviews with Barbara's psychiatrist and Tom, as well as review of her medical and psychiatric records. Barbara's attorney sat in on every evaluation session conducted by the state's clinicians and took notes of their questions and his client's answers. The state's experts concluded that Barbara suffered from postpartum major depression with psychotic features and that she had delusional beliefs about her children, an opinion consistent with the state's definition of insanity.

Relevant Research: Postpartum Psychosis

The clinicians' diagnosis of Barbara illustrates a case of a new mother who experiences a debilitating, severe mental illness in the weeks and months following birth of a baby. Postpartum psychosis is a generic term often employed to describe a variety of psychiatric symptoms associated with major depression, bipolar (manic-depressive), and other unspecified psychotic disorders (Klompenhouwer & van Hulst, 1991; Nonacs & Cohen, 1998; Susman, 1996). Numerous studies have shown that postpartum psychosis is rare, occurring in approximately 0.2%, or 2 of every 1,000 mothers after live births (American

Psychiatric Association, 2000; Gale & Harlow, 2003). Though relatively infrequent, the incidence of postpartum psychotic disorders among the 3 million annual births in the United States would still constitute an estimate of 6,000 new cases each year.

Psychiatric disturbance in mothers of newborns often presents a diagnostic dilemma for the clinician because postpartum symptoms may vary in type (e.g., hallucinations, delusions, mood, and/or levels of alertness and orientation), onset after delivery (e.g., within days or weeks), course (daily or intermittent symptoms, spontaneous remission within weeks of onset), and levels of maternal awareness and insight. The psychiatric presentation of a new mother may also include a co-occurring spectrum of anxiety disorders, including panic attacks, psychosomatic complaints, social phobia, and obsessive-compulsive disorder (Rapkin, Mikacich, Moatekef-Imani, & Rasgon, 2002). Also, substance abuse in mothers during and after pregnancy may complicate the diagnostic picture for medical and mental health clinicians (Singer et al., 1995). Many new mothers are unwilling to disclose symptoms of intrusive, obsessive thoughts about and impulses toward infanticide from fear of legal consequences (Abramowitz, Schwartz, Moore, & Luenzmann, 2003; Brandes, Soares, & Cohen, 2004; McElroy, 2004). As a result of these numerous factors, many cases are undetected, underdiagnosed (e.g., major depression diagnosed as "baby blues"), or misdiagnosed (Gale & Harlow, 2003; Nonacs & Cohen, 1998; Seyfried & Marcus, 2003).

The first signs of postpartum psychosis tend to develop within the first week of the mother's delivery, though recognizable symptoms of the disorder do not typically emerge until the second month. The pattern for most postpartum psychotic mothers entails initial complaints of insomnia, fatigue, and fearful emotional fluctuation, in combination with not loving or wanting to care for the baby. Over the next few weeks, the mother displays increasing suspiciousness and irrational statements about the baby's safety and welfare, followed by delusional beliefs that the baby is defective. Command auditory hallucinations telling the mother to kill the baby occur in approximately a quarter of postpartum psychotic mothers (Sadock & Sadock, 2003).

Postpartum psychosis is recognized as a serious psychiatric emergency for a number of reasons. Research has demonstrated that postpartum psychotic mothers are at increased risk for suicidal ideation and harmful thoughts toward their babies (Comitz, Comitz, & Semprevivo, 1990; Seyfried & Marcus, 2003). In a recent study, Chandra, Venkatasubramanian, and Thomas (2002) found that among a sample of new mothers who were psychiatrically hospitalized, 43% reported infanticidal ideas, and another 36% displayed homicidal behavior toward their newborns. Sadock and Sadock (2003) reported that approximately 4% of mothers with postpartum psychosis may commit infanticide, then attempt or complete suicide.

Once new mothers are discharged from the hospital, their postpartum illness may severely interfere with their capacity to effectively manage their immediate child-care responsibilities. For example, Wisner, Peindl, and Hanusa

(1994) found that psychosis in many childbearing women was characterized by thought disorganization, bizarre behavior, delusions of persecution and reference, delirium, and self-neglect. Because of its onset during the first few months following delivery, postpartum psychosis also affects the mother's capacity for developing a healthy, nurturing bond with her baby (Murray, Cooper, & Hipwell, 2003). In a study of 82 postpartum mother-infant dyads, mothers with postpartum psychosis and mothers with nonpsychotic depression were found to have much more disturbed and insecure interactions with their babies than an individually matched group of normal mothers of newborns (Hipwell, Goossens, Melhuish, & Kumar, 2000).

Psychiatric treatment of pre- and postpartum mothers with psychosis may pose risks in the form of transmission of antipsychotic and mood-stabilizing medications to the fetus or to the newborn during breast-feeding (Chaudron, 2000; McElroy, 2004; Webb, Howard, & Abel, 2004). Even among new mothers who recover from postpartum psychosis, many will experience relapses of severe mental illness, with corresponding impairments in their parenting abilities, as their children age. For example, follow-up studies of new mothers who experience their first psychotic episode during or after pregnancy have shown that as many as 75% had psychotic episodes in later life (Robling, Paykel, Dunn, Abbott, & Katona, 2000).

Approximately two-thirds of postpartum mothers with psychosis will likely have a second episode within a year of the baby's birth (Sadock & Sadock, 2003). Schopf and Rust (1994) discovered that 66% of their sample of first-time postpartum mothers with psychosis had at least one more recurrence, a rate that was comparable to the relapse rate of 64% reported by Rhode and Marneros (1993). Videbech and Gouliaev (1995) found that 60% of the first-break postpartum psychotic mothers they studied had recurrences of their mental illness. In a similar study of new mothers who developed postpartum psychosis, the majority of the sample eventually had two or more subsequent psychotic relapses (Pfulman, Franzek, Beckmann, & Stober, 1999).

Research studies have indicated that some groups may be more vulnerable to these forms of severe mental illness. Mothers with a prepregnancy history of depression and psychosis, for example, have been shown in numerous studies to experience a relapse and/or exacerbation of their symptoms during and after pregnancy (Verdoux & Sutter, 2002; Oates, 2003). A family history of mental illness has also been found to be associated with psychosis during the postpartum period (Jones & Craddock, 2001). Obstetric complications (Verdoux & Sutter, 2002), lack of social support (Terp, Engholm, Moller, & Mortensen, 1999), cocaine abuse (Singer et al., 1995), and sleep deprivation (Ehlers, Frank, & Kupfer, 1998; Wisner, et al., 1994) have also been associated with increased risks for postpartum psychotic disorders in women.

Many researchers have emphasized the need for careful, early identification of and intervention with prospective mothers who may develop postpartum psychosis (Currid, 2004; Murray et al., 2003; Walther, 1997; Webb et al., 2004). Effective treatment of postpartum psychosis appears to be a multi-faceted approach consisting of psychiatric hospitalization (Guscott & Steiner, 1991; Hipwell & Kumar, 1996); antipsychotic medications (Burt, Suri, Altshuler, & Stowe, 2001; Kumar, McIvor, Davies, & Brown, 2003; Winans, 2001); psychotherapy (Friedman & Rosenthal, 2003; Sharma, 2003); ongoing consultation among obstetricians, pediatricians, and psychiatrists (Stocky & Lynch, 2000); and outpatient multidisciplinary care (Casiano, 1990). Electroconvulsive therapy (ECT) has been considered an effective treatment for cases of very severe postpartum psychotic disorders (Pedersen, 1999; Reed, Sermin, Appleby, & Faragher, 1999).

Epilogue

Barbara waived her right to a jury trial. After consultation with her attorney, she preferred to be tried by a circuit court judge whose long judicial experience would have given him or her more knowledge and understanding of defendants with mental illness. At the conclusion of her insanity trial, the judge noted that he had reviewed the psychiatric and psychological reports of the state and defense forensic mental health experts and listened carefully to their courtroom testimony.

The judge highlighted that the clinicians were in agreement that Barbara's most probable diagnosis following the birth of Heather was a severe, debilitating mental illness, major depression with psychotic features (postpartum psychosis). Further, he emphasized that each clinician had independently concluded and testified that, in his or her expert opinion, when Barbara smothered her children she had a delusional belief that she was cleansing Marcus and Heather of their infection, as well as saving her husband from mental illness. He noted that each of the clinicians had referenced Barbara's self-report of smiling and feeling at peace immediately after the children died, as well as her phone call to her husband, as evidence that she was unaware of the criminality of her homicides.

The judge concluded therefore that Barbara did not appreciate the wrongfulness of her actions that led to the death of her children and that she was thus, under the state's statutes, legally insane at the time of her crimes.

The judge declared that Barbara was not guilty by reason of insanity in the deaths of Marcus and Heather. In accordance with state law, Barbara was transferred to an inpatient ward of the state psychiatric facility for an indeterminate period until the circuit court authorized her release to outpatient mental health care. She remains hospitalized to this day.

14

Psychotic/Depressed Mother,
Impulsive Type

Susan Smith

Susan drove aimlessly through the night with tears streaming down her cheeks. The car was quiet now, with her two sons, 14-month-old Alex and 3-year-old Michael, asleep in their car seats. Thoughts raced through her mind in a jumbled confusion. She felt so panicky, desperate, and lonely that she was unable to concentrate. Although she was anxious and upset, she was also still angry with herself for yelling at her boys when Michael had cried out earlier that he wanted to go home. Everything seemed to be falling apart around her. She felt that her life was spinning out of control. Nothing was turning out as she had hoped it would. She was shaking uncontrollably and often felt as though she was going to throw up. She cried loudly, at times waking up her children in the back seat. She bit her nails and wiped the tears from her eyes as she turned from one road to another in a seemingly random pattern. At one point she almost went off the road because she was so distraught about her uncertain, terrifying future.

As she desperately drove on the rural roads of Union County, she felt alone and abandoned, with nowhere to go and no one to love her. She wanted the pain to stop immediately and realized once again that ending her life was her only solution for lasting peace. She found herself on a bridge over the Broad River and quickly stopped the car. She got out and looked out over the river as it moved silently under the bridge. She thought about jumping into the river and drowning. As she approached the railing, however, she realized that her sons were in the back seat of the car. She could not leave them alone and abandoned on a bridge in the middle of the night. She told herself that a good mother would not allow her children to grow up without a mom.

She got back in the car sobbing helplessly. She drove on in a daze, not knowing where she was going or remembering where she had just been. She could only think that she had to die to escape this worst catastrophe of her life. Shaking her head in confusion, she wondered once again why bad things always seemed to happen to her. She had no answers to her questions.

As she drove by John D. Long Lake, she stopped and exited the car once again. The children were asleep in their car seats, and the night was quiet as she walked around to the back of the car. She was consumed with thoughts of wanting her pain to end. She saw the lake's boat ramp and a plan quickly formed in her mind: She would drive into the lake and drown. She got back into the driver's seat. She released the hand brake and the car slowly, silently rolled down the ramp. She pulled up the brake abruptly, got out, and walked to the rear of the car in a panic, crying and thinking what she was going to do next.

She got back in the car and released the hand brake again, but as the wheels touched the lake, she jumped out of the car and ran back up the ramp with her hands over her ears, screaming "Help me!" She got to the top of a small rise by the lake and turned around. The car had sunk, with Alex and Michael still in their car seats. Susan cried out hysterically, then thought "I cannot tell anyone what happened. Everyone will hate me."

She saw a light from a house, went to the porch screaming, and banged on the door. When the woman inside opened the door, Susan breathlessly pleaded for help, telling her that her car had been highjacked by a black man who had taken her children. Over the next 9 days, despite intensive national and international media coverage and numerous interrogations by local and state law enforcement officers, Susan denied killing her sons. In Susan's words, "I just made it up as I went along." She finally confessed killing Alex and Michael to Union County Sheriff Howard Wells at the First Baptist Church on November 3, 1994.

Many months after the night when her sons died, Susan would remember that until October 15, 1994, everything seemed to be going rather well in her life. She had felt loved and desired by many men. During 1994, she had had at least four men winning her sexual favors: her stepfather, Bev, with whom she'd been having sexual intimacies since she was 15 years old; her husband, David; her lover and coworker, Tom; and Tom's father, who was the owner of the company where she worked. She had also been receiving calls from other men wanting to date her after they had found out she was separated from her husband.

During 1994, Susan's 3-year marriage was very unsettled and unstable. Although she and David had decided to divorce earlier in the year, they had briefly reunited in June. By August, however, they had amicably agreed to terminate their marriage on grounds of a year's separation. They would still occasionally have sex together, and sometimes David would stay at the house to play with their sons. He would often take care of the children when Susan went out at night. It made her happy to see David and her sons together.

Susan's sexual relationship with Tom had begun in January 1994 and had continued until mid-October. Susan was infatuated with him and had asked another coworker to invite her to after-work parties at a local bar so that she could see Tom more frequently. Shortly thereafter, Tom asked her out on a date. They quickly became intimate and had sex often. Susan believed that she and Tom were deeply in love because he was willing to be seen in public with her.

On October 15, 1994, Susan and others were invited back to Tom's residence for a party. They had all been drinking that night at a local bar and continued to consume alcohol once they arrived at his house. Soon everyone was naked and soaking in Tom's hot tub. Susan was very drunk and complied when Tom asked her to kiss a married man seated beside her. On the way home, Susan began thinking she had made a terrible mistake that would jeopardize her relationship with Tom, but he did not know that Susan had also begun an intimate sexual relationship with his father. Tom found out on the afternoon of October 25, 1994, the day that Alex and Michael died.

On October 18, 1994, Susan's fears that Tom would reject her were confirmed. Tom gave Susan a letter telling her that their sexual relationship was over. Though they would remain friends, he wrote that he was not ready for marriage to anyone. Susan was devastated and panicky: Who would love her now? Suicidal thoughts flooded her mind once again.

In the early morning hours of October 21, 1994, David confronted Susan about her adulterous relationship with Tom. He told her he had a copy of Tom's letter, which he would use at their divorce hearing. During the argument, Susan admitted her affair with Tom but told David she also knew of his infidelity because she had hired a private investigator to follow him.

On the evening of October 23, 1994, Susan called Tom in another attempt to rekindle their intimacy. During their conversation, Susan told him about her sexual relationship with her stepfather, Bev, hoping to gain his compassion. Susan was shocked by his disgusted reaction to her disclosure. After she hung up the telephone she was again flooded by panic that she had jeopardized her future with him. After work the next day, Susan desperately hoped to talk with Tom but was unable to locate him.

On October 25, 1994, Susan awoke worried and scared that David would publicly reveal her infidelity with Tom and Tom's father. She worried that the disclosure would cause her to be fired from work and also ruin any chance she would have at reuniting with Tom. When she called him that afternoon, Tom agreed to talk with her. During their conversation, Susan told him that her husband knew of their affair. She said David might also claim that she had had sexual intimacies with another member of Tom's family. At first, Tom did not believe her when she told him of her affair with his father. When she insisted that it was true, he looked at her with disgust and reaffirmed that they would never be lovers again. As he went back to his office, Susan began crying as she tried to figure out how she could talk to Tom again.

She told her supervisor that she needed to go home, then went to Tom's office once more. With tears in her eyes, she told him that she was still upset and said he might never see her again, a vague threat of suicide. Despite Tom's efforts to comfort her by telling her that things would be better tomorrow, Susan left in tears and picked up her children from daycare. She asked a friend to watch her children while she talked with Tom. Susan told her friend that she had played a practical joke on Tom by telling him that she had had an affair with his father. Susan asked her friend to tell Tom that her affair with his father had just been a joke. Her friend refused but agreed to watch Alex and Michael while Susan talked with Tom.

Susan carried Alex in her arms as she entered his office with her friend and Michael. Tom was surprised to see her and asked why she was there. Susan told him that her story of having sex with his father was a practical joke, then turned to her friend to confirm what she had said. Her friend declined any knowledge of her affairs and left the office. Tom told Susan that he did not believe her and asked why she had told him about her affair with his father. Susan replied that she wanted to find out how he, Tom, really felt about her. Tom then told her it was not appropriate for her to discuss their relationship in front of her children and her friend. He dismissed her by telling her he needed to get back to work.

Susan took her children home, fed them, and walked around the house in a daze. As she sobbed, her children became scared and also cried loudly. Susan thought she was having a nervous breakdown. As her panic increased, Susan again tried to reassure herself that her relationship with Tom could still be repaired. She called her friend at the local bar to find out if Tom was there and whether he was angry. Her friend told Susan that Tom had not said anything to her that evening about Susan. Her friend then hung up on Susan.

The phone call may have been the tipping point for Susan's downward spiral that night. She had called hoping that Tom was in despair, as she was, over their breakup. Susan found out that Tom was not wallowing in agony. He'd not said anything about Susan and appeared to be unfazed by the afternoon's events at work. His rejection of her was complete. Susan left her house with Alex and Michael and went by the local bar to see if Tom was there. As she drove past, she saw that his car was still in the parking lot. She did not stop but began crying helplessly again: While she was drowning in pain, Tom and her friends were going on with their lives without her. She was on the outside looking in. Susan drove on aimlessly until she arrived at John D. Long Lake.

How had she arrived at this last, desperate point in her young adult life?

From Susan's earliest days, her infancy, childhood, and adolescent years were filled with instability and uncertainty. In her book, Susan's mother, Linda, wrote that her 10-year marriage was on the rocks again when Susan, their third child, was born on September 26, 1971 (Russell, 2000). Linda's description of Susan in her book indicated that she displayed many early childhood signs of emotional insecurity (Russell, 2000). Linda recalled that Susan's temper tantrums and constant requests for her attention were extremely bothersome. Susan's behaviors, which were not observed by her day school teachers, were likely due to the chaotic home life with which she had to cope.

Susan's sense of security and stability was threatened at age 3, when her parents separated for the first time. Susan would recall years later that her parent's screaming matches and separations were very traumatic for her as a child. The abrupt loss of her father, Harry, was very upsetting to Susan because of her strong emotional attachment to him. When her parents reconciled and reunited, Susan thought that her father was home to stay. They lived together for 3 months before separating again shortly after Christmas.

Approximately 7 months later, Harry entered Susan's house armed with a shotgun, loudly threatening to kill Linda and commit suicide. Susan's parents never lived together again. In January 1978, shortly after their divorce was final, Susan's father shot himself after he had threatened her mother's life once again. Susan was 6 years old.

Susan did not believe her mother's assertion that her father had died and gone to heaven. She called his telephone number, letting it ring many times before concluding that he was not at home. Linda later recalled that her daughter told her that if her father was in heaven, she wanted to be there with him. Linda did not tell Susan how her father died because she wanted to keep the gory details from harming her daughter.

Shortly after the funeral, however, Susan's cousin found her crying. Susan told her cousin that her father had killed himself. Later that year, Linda's mother was hospitalized after an attempted suicide by overdose of prescription pills following the death a few months earlier of her husband, Linda's father (Andrews, 1995). These traumatic episodes were clearly significant losses for Linda and her young daughter, Susan. Suicide as a means of resolving grief, depression, and loss was a family lesson that young Susan was learning well. Within 4 years of these episodes, Susan, at age 10, had her first thoughts of ending her life.

The next unanticipated disruption to Susan's stability and security was her mother's impulsive, undisclosed marriage to Bev Russell less than 2 years after her biological father's death. Linda had been dating Bev for a number of months, and each had ambivalently backed out of the other's offers of marriage. When Bev proposed to her shortly before Christmas 1979, Linda finally agreed to elope. They decided not to tell Susan and her brothers, Michael and Scott, of the marriage until after the wedding (Russell, 2000). According to Linda's book, after they began living together as husband and wife, Susan would repeatedly ask Linda if her mother loved her (Russell, 2000). Susan even wrote a letter to Linda hoping to prove that she loved her and wishing her mother felt the same way. Later, Susan included a similar wishful sentiment on a Valentine's Day card to Linda. Susan would also write notes to other family members asking repeatedly, "Do you love me?" When Susan wanted to address her stepfather as "Daddy," however, Linda would not allow it (Andrews, 1995).

By the time Susan was 13 years old, her episodic suicidal thoughts, which had begun at age 10, became more frequent. During the 8th grade she was obsessively thinking of ending her life and had developed a plan of suicide. She began saving aspirin pills, a plan that she had disclosed to her stepsister, so that she could take more than 10 pills daily until she died. Susan gave a suicide note to her teacher, who then gave it to Scott for Linda to read. Linda was dumbfounded but also upset that Susan was talking to others about things that should be kept as family secrets.

After reading the note, Linda, Bev, and Scott agreed that they would not talk to Susan about her suicide plan (Russell, 2000). They would instead monitor her very closely by counting the family's aspirin pills each night and removing the bullets from the guns Bev displayed in the family den. Linda recalled that she and her husband relented and allowed Susan to have counseling at the school's request. They took Susan's threats seriously but did not think that she needed professional help outside of the family for a phase she was going through (Russell, 2000).

Susan became more rebellious toward Linda and Bev. During one angry argument with Susan, Linda declared that Harry had abandoned Susan by his own choice, by leaving the family and then committing suicide. Shortly thereafter, following another episode of Susan's sullen attitude, Linda threatened to place her daughter in a halfway house as a way of scaring some sense into her (Russell, 2000). She believed that the threat, which she never intended to carry out, improved Susan's attitude as she became more active in school-related activities.

In the ninth grade, however, Susan disclosed to a teacher that she continued to have suicidal thoughts. Linda reluctantly agreed with the teacher to let her daughter have weekly sessions with a school counselor. Linda had consented to the counseling on the stipulation of after-session feedback to her by the school counselor. However, she felt that she was excluded from any meaningful content concerning her daughter's treatment. Linda was subsequently asked to agree to the counselor's recommendation that Susan be evaluated by an experimental research program for depressed adolescents at the university's medical school. Linda refused out of concern that her daughter would be incorrectly labeled as mentally unbalanced (Russell, 2000). Linda believed that the counseling had helped her daughter, because Susan appeared to be happier as she continued her after-school volunteer work at the local hospital.

Her daughter's happiness and sense of safety was short-lived. Susan's stepfather had begun to molest her by fondling her breasts and kissing her on the lips as she sat on his lap watching television. Susan finally disclosed his unwanted intimacies to the same teacher to whom she'd revealed her recurrent thoughts of suicide. The teacher believed that Susan was suicidal. The teacher informed the school counselor, who told Susan to tell her mother.

When Susan disclosed the sexual abuse by Bev to her mother, Linda asked her daughter why she didn't stop him by leaving the room. Susan replied that she was testing her stepfather to see if she could trust him. Linda was confused and angered by her answer. She could not understand why her daughter did not defend herself. Linda confronted her husband, who confessed and promised to stop. Linda decided that although he was responsible for the molestation, her daughter's reluctance to prevent his actions contributed to the sexual assault. Linda arranged for psychotherapy for each of them with a licensed psychologist. The treatment sessions lasted for several months, ending at Susan's request. Shortly thereafter, Bev began to molest her again by entering her bedroom and fondling her while Susan pretended to be asleep.

Susan's next disclosure to the school counselor of her stepfather's continued sexual abuse resulted in a law enforcement and social service agency investigation. When Susan, Linda, the agency social worker, and the deputy sheriff met at Bev's attorney's office, however, the criminal charges were dropped with the approval of Linda and Susan, even though Bev confessed once again. Susan had asked her mother what she should do about the criminal charges against her stepfather. Linda replied that she did not want to see her husband prosecuted but told her daughter that it was her decision (Russell, 2000). Susan then complied with her mother's wish. Later, the Family Court substantiated Susan's allegations, and Bev agreed to leave the house to prevent Susan from being placed in foster care. The court's order was sealed to protect Susan's and the family's privacy. Linda, Susan, and Bev returned for counseling with the same psychologist.

After several months of counseling, Bev moved back into the house. He quickly resumed his molestation of Susan, but now she reciprocated by fondling him. Susan was only 16 years old.

Less than a year later, Susan lost her virginity to a middle-aged married man who managed the grocery store where she worked after school. When she informed her stepfather that she was no longer a virgin, Bev told Susan that he wished she had lost her virginity with him (Andrews, 1995). Bev and Linda once caught the store manager at their home with Susan, who was dressed in her pajamas; he left, embarrassed. Linda had known and confronted Susan about her relationship with the married man; however, she was unsuccessful in stopping her daughter from seeing him. Susan asked her mother if she could resume counseling sessions with the psychologist they had seen before, but she did not tell Linda why—Susan had become pregnant and had had an abortion (Rekers, 1996).

Shortly thereafter, Susan began a concurrent sexual relationship with the grocery store's assistant manager. The next day she told the store manager about her new lover. He was so angry at her revelation that he was unable to talk with her. Susan's reaction to her impulsive sexual promiscuity was to attempt suicide by ingesting two bottles of Tylenol and aspirin while walking alone late at night in a city park. Crying and scared, she returned home to wake her mother and stepfather.

She revealed that she had been having sex with both men. When she had told one about the other, she said she was so terrified that she had lost them both that she wanted to kill herself. After her stomach was pumped in the emergency room, Susan was hospitalized in the intensive care unit and received a week of inpatient psychiatric treatment. Her convoluted sexual intricacies and impulsive suicide attempt foreshadowed those she would have with Tom and his father less than 5 years later.

Seven months after being discharged from the hospital, Susan began dating David, who was an employee at the same grocery store where she worked. On their second date, they began having intercourse. They rarely used condoms or other forms of birth control. Despite their intimacy, David was still engaged to another young woman. A few months later, Susan told David she was pregnant. The same day, he told his fiancée about Susan's condition. His fiancée had not known about the relationship and terminated their engagement.

A few days later, David and Susan discussed what they would do. They decided to get married as soon as possible. They agreed that they were adamantly opposed to abortion, perhaps for similar reasons: When David was 17 he had impregnated a teenage girlfriend, who informed him later that she had terminated her pregnancy (Smith, 1995).

The wedding of David and Susan occurred on March 15, 1991. Susan told Linda that she had deliberately chosen the birthday of her deceased biological father. Susan and David were married in the same church where, just 2 weeks earlier, the funeral of David's older brother, Danny, had been conducted. Danny had unexpectedly died of Crohn's disease after contracting an infection during a routine operation.

Less than a month following their wedding, David's father attempted suicide by overdose. After Danny's death, he suffered a depression that was exacerbated when his wife left their marriage shortly after David and Susan's wedding. Susan had found her father-in-law semiconscious on the floor of his bedroom with blood pooling near his mouth; she'd been looking for him at David's request.

Michael was born on October 10, 1991, with David helping his wife through the delivery. The newborn had to wear an uncomfortable brace in bed to correct a congenital misalignment of his foot. The baby often cried himself to sleep despite his parents' efforts to comfort him. Six months after their son's arrival, David and Susan separated for the first time. Through the first year of marriage, their arguments had occurred with greater frequency.

During one argument David slapped Susan, dragged her onto their porch, and left her there (Smith, 1995). In the midst of another argument, David grabbed Michael, put him in his car seat, and drove off, yelling that Susan would never see her son again. He returned 10 minutes later and did not protest when Susan took their son to Linda's house to spend the night.

During their separation, David found Susan parked late at night with her former lover, the assistant manager who had been reassigned to the grocery store where both David and Susan worked. He pulled the man out of the automobile and beat him. A few weeks later, David discovered Susan at the man's house and beat him again. Though David and Susan were separated, they soon resumed their sexual intimacies. In December 1992, Susan discovered that she was pregnant with Alex.

They decided to make another effort to save their marriage and found a small, three-bedroom home to buy with Susan's parents' financial help.

Tension soon returned to their marriage. David began a close relationship with a young woman who had been recently hired at his store. Susan was soon accusing him of being unfaithful. Susan delivered Alex by caesarean section on August 5, 1993. She received around-the-clock help from her parents, siblings, other family relatives, and friends. Susan began working with Tom less than 2 months later.

Three weeks after Alex was born, David and Susan separated again. By January 1994, Susan had begun her affair with Tom. David's belief that Susan was unfaithful to him was confirmed when he overheard Susan talking to Tom on the telephone in June. David interrupted their call and told Tom to stop seeing Susan. A week later, David moved back into the house. Less than a month later, on July 27, 1994, following a dinner for David's birthday, Susan told her husband that she wanted a divorce. They decided to divorce on friendly terms. David moved out in August 1994. David renewed his relationship with the young woman, and Susan began seeing Tom again.

Though they each had the other's consent to be unfaithful, Susan filed papers in September on grounds of adultery. David was furious on receiving Susan's documents and felt betrayed by his wife. He retained a private investigator to follow Susan. When David discovered Tom's letter and had the evidence he believed he needed to contest Susan's claims of his adultery, he quickly made sure she knew by confronting her on October 21, 1994. Four days later, the convoluted web of intimacy Susan had orchestrated with Bev, Tom, Tom's father, and David culminated in her desperate journey to John D. Long Lake.

Case Analysis

Although Susan's childhood, adolescent, and adult histories were filled with depression and suicide, the hallmark of her relationships with her parents, spouse, and other adults was the recurrent fear of being abandoned and unloved. Susan's lifelong behavior is best viewed as borderline personality disorder, a long-standing pervasive pattern of marked impulsivity and instability in emotional functioning, self-image, and interpersonal relationships.

According to the American Psychiatric Association (2000), persons with borderline personality disorder (BPD) are characterized by: (1) making frantic attempts to avoid actual or imagined abandonment by others; (2) repeatedly developing intense but unstable relationships in which significant others are alternatively idealized and devalued; (3) a persistently unstable self-image; (4) impulsivity in self-damaging behavior patterns (e.g., promiscuous sexual activity, substance abuse, reckless driving, spending, gambling, binge eating, etc.); (5) recurrent suicidal behavior, gestures, threats, or self-mutilating behavior; (6) intense emotional instability (e.g. depression, anger/irritability, anxiety) lasting more than a few hours though less than a few days; (7) chronic feelings of emptiness (e.g., absence of self-assurance, self-esteem, and sense of personal contentment); (8) inappropriate, intense anger and/or difficulty controlling one's anger; and (9) transient, stress-related paranoid ideation or severe dissociative symptoms. The diagnosis of BPD requires at least five criteria to be met; Susan had many more. In the years, months, weeks, days, and hours leading to her sons' deaths, she was a very disturbed, emotionally volatile, and impulse-ridden young woman.

Maternal Filicide Risk Matrix Analysis

Susan's risk matrix is shown in table 14.1.

Prepregnancy Stage

Prior to Susan's unintended pregnancy with Alex, her life to that point was replete with instability and impulsivity. Although she did not become pregnant with Alex until she was 21, she had terminated an unintended pregnancy at age 18 and had another unexpected conception that led to her hasty marriage to David. Susan's intelligence was well within the high-average range, and her

Table 14.1
Maternal Filicide Risk Matrix: Susan (for Alex)

Factor	Pre-P	P/D	EP	LP	PI
Individual					
Age at current pregnancy	R	R	R	R	R
Intelligence level	P	P	P	R	R
Education level	P	P	P	P	P
Medical status	P	P	P	P	P
Emotional status	R	R	R	R	R
Trauma history	R	R	R	R	R
Maternal attitudes	R	P	P	R	R
Family of Origin					
Mother's parenting	P	P	P	P	P
Father's parenting	R	R	R	R	R
Marital/family stability	R	R	R	R	R
Situational					
Marital/partner status	R	R	R	R	R
Financial status	P	P	P	P	P
Child-care status	P	P	P	P	P
Infant's temperament	P	P	P	P	P

Note: R = Risk; P = Protective; Pre-P = Prepregnancy; P/D = Pregnancy/delivery; EP = Early postpartum; LP = Late postpartum; PI = Postinfancy.

education was also a protective factor. She easily graduated from high school and was pursuing further education at a branch campus of the state university. When she became pregnant with Michael, Susan received excellent, well-monitored prenatal care, which continued after her first son was born. There is no evidence that she developed obesity after Michael's birth. David Smith noted in his book that she regained her figure through diet and aerobics before Alex was conceived (Smith, 1995).

Susan's emotional status was a significant risk factor. Her life was an ongoing drama of multiple, conflicting sexual affairs, which she would impulsively initiate, then destroy through her self-defeating machinations. Because of her continuing panic over being alone and unloved, she could have conceived a child by any of a number of men during her separations from her husband prior to Alex's birth. During this stage, she had recurrent suicidal thoughts and had already been psychiatrically hospitalized at age 18. I have already described numerous traumas that Susan experienced throughout her life.

Susan's maternal attitudes during this stage, in sum, comprise a risk factor. Her husband and others describe Susan as a doting mother to Michael both prior to his conception and after his birth. However, her impulsive, unprotected sexual intercourse with men suggested that she had given little thought to the consequences of her liaisons if she were suddenly to become pregnant again.

Susan's family of origin factors during her prepregnancy stage reflect her family's long history of instability and marital discord. Her mother's parenting attitudes led Susan to doubt whether Linda loved her and whether she was worthy of her mother's love. Linda's questionable maternal attitudes were also suggested by her secret wedding to Bev without forewarning her children. Susan's disclosure of recurrent suicidal thoughts to her teacher, rather than to her mother, suggested that at age 10 she did not see Linda as a nurturing resource. Linda's immediate reaction in partly blaming Susan for her husband's molestation of her daughter was not a positive maternal response to a daughter's trauma. When Linda placed onto Susan the burden of whether to prosecute Bev for his renewed sexual assaults, she did not take responsibility for protecting her daughter. After Linda allowed Bev to return home, Susan disclosed to her therapist that she did not believe that her mother loved her.

When Susan told her mother that she was pregnant with Michael, Linda's maternal attitudes were significantly more positive. She actively assisted Susan in ensuring that she received excellent prenatal care with Michael and arranged for an array of relatives and friends to assist Susan with her postpartum adjustment. Linda was also highly active when Susan became pregnant with Alex by encouraging and assisting her to receive regular prenatal care. When Susan and David first separated, Linda opened her house to her daughter and grandson. Susan's mother would also provide additional financial support to her daughter's family when Susan and David were apart. Linda's emotional support to her daughter continued throughout this stage and persisted even after Susan confessed to killing her sons.

The parenting attitudes of Susan's father and stepfather were significant risk factors for the development of her recurrent depression and obsession with suicide. Although her biological father was described as a man who adored Susan, his alcohol-induced rages, abrupt disappearances, separations from his wife, recurrent suicide threats, and marital violence made Susan an anxious, insecure child. Her stepfather was equally inadequate as a father figure, repeatedly exploiting Susan for his narcissistic sexual gratification until 2 months before she killed her sons.

As illustrated throughout this chapter, from a very young age, Susan's perceptions of marital relationships were negatively influenced by Linda's marriages to Harry and Bev.

Prior to her unintended pregnancy with Alex, Susan's relationship with her husband was far from stable, as they had recurrent arguments, separations, and at least one episode of domestic violence. Though separated, Susan and David continued having sexual relations and decided to reunite only after discovering that they had conceived another child. Susan's financial status prior to her pregnancy with Alex appeared to be a protective factor in that she was fully employed, as was her husband. Her child-care responsibilities at this stage involved only Michael, and she received extensive free child-care help from her mother, relatives, and friends; in sum, a protective factor against filicide. Prior to her pregnancy with Alex, Michael's temperament did not appear to be problematic or difficult.

Pregnancy/Delivery and Early Postpartum Stages

Susan was just barely 20 when she gave birth to her second child, a risk factor for filicide as indicated by the research of Overpeck et al. (1998). Susan's medical status was excellent during her pregnancy with Alex, as she received continuous, careful prenatal care. After she delivered her baby by caesarean section, Susan's medical condition was monitored daily by the extensive support network her mother had arranged for a 6-week period after Alex arrived. Susan's emotional status was as unstable as it had been for virtually all of her life. She had been seeing another man when it was discovered that she was pregnant with Alex; David moved out 3 weeks after Alex's birth; and within 5 months thereafter Susan began her relationship with Tom.

During these stages, Susan did not experience any new traumas but continued to have contact with her stepfather, whose presence would be a constant reminder of her childhood sexual victimization. Susan's maternal attitudes appear to have been ambivalent at this point in her life. Her often unprotected sexual activity with her estranged husband and others put her at high risk for an unintended pregnancy, which suggested little forethought about the emotional impact of such an event on Michael. There are differing accounts of Susan's attitude toward her pregnancy with Alex. Her mother, Linda, described her as actively anticipating her impending delivery; however, David recalled that Susan would continuously complain about being pregnant again (Smith, 1995). Susan reported that although she was not initially pleased at discovering she had conceived another child with David, she did look forward to the birth of her second child. Once Alex was born, there was no evidence that Susan was abusive or excessively neglectful of her children.

Linda's maternal attitudes toward her daughter and grandchildren were a protective factor as well. After Susan became pregnant with Alex, Linda ensured that she received regular prenatal and postnatal medical care. Linda performed and coordinated around-the-clock postpartum assistance for Susan, employing family and friends as needed (Russell, 2000). Although Bev did agree to financially assist his stepdaughter, he apparently did not assist in child care for his newest grandchild. Her parents' marriage was so strained that Bev moved out of the house for a week before they reconciled (Russell, 2000).

Susan's marriage to David continued to be unstable and unfulfilling before and after Alex's birth, when they separated for the last time. Six weeks after delivering Alex, Susan returned to full-time work. Thus her financial status was unaffected during these stages. Even after she was reemployed, Susan had an array of family and friends, as well as David, willing to assist her with child care; thus this factor was a protective element. In the first 6 months following his birth, all accounts suggest that Alex was a happy, contented baby.

Late Postpartum and Postinfancy Stages
From 6 months after Alex's birth until his death at 14 months of age, Susan's individual factors reflected her personal impulsivity and instability. Her medical and educational statuses remained essentially unchanged and were positive elements. Her judgment, an intelligence factor, deteriorated as her reasoning was overwhelmed by her increasingly unstable emotional status. Her daily life and relationships became more chaotic and complicated. During these stages, her incapacity to control her sexual impulses and intense fears of abandonment were evident in her four conflicting and self-defeating intimate relationships. Susan drank alcohol to excess more frequently than she ever had in her life. The damaging influence of her trauma history was continued by her self-defeating sex with Bev. Her emotional impulsivity was also negatively affecting her maternal attitudes. Many nights each week she would place her sons with alternative caretakers while she partied with Tom and other coworkers at a local bar. When Susan would pick up her children after going to the local bar, she put her children (and others) at an increased risk for a motor vehicle accident due to her drinking.

Susan's family of origin factors during these stages remained essentially the same. Linda continued to assist her with child care, a demonstration of positive maternal attitudes, but Bev continued to victimize her. Although Bev and Linda continued to live together, their marriage was still unsettled. In terms of situational factors, Susan's financial, child-care, and infant-temperament factors remained protective, but Susan's relationship with David continued to be intense, unstable, and conflicted before and after the day their sons died.

Relevant Research: Women with Borderline Personality Disorder

Borderline personality disorder (BPD) is a long-term, chronic, pervasive emotional disturbance characterized by marked impulsivity, unstable and volatile interpersonal relationships, and distorted self-image (American Psychiatric Association, 2000). The initial symptoms of BPD are often seen in adolescence and become consolidated by early adulthood. As persons with BPD age, their high risk of suicide often decreases, as does the impairment from their disorder; but some will display symptoms throughout their lives.

In the United States, approximately 2% of the general population, 10% of the individuals treated in outpatient mental health clinics, and 20% of psychiatric inpatients have been diagnosed with BPD. The disorder has been identified in many other cultures than the United States. Females are much more likely to be diagnosed with BPD than males, at a ratio of approximately 3:1 (American Psychiatric Association, 2000). Although the American Psychiatric Association (2000) has highlighted nine diagnostic criteria for BPD, numerous studies have suggested that the core components of the disorder—amply demonstrated in Susan's case—are impulsivity, excessive emotional variability, and an inability to establish a stable self-concept (Bagge et al., 2004; Berlin & Rolls, 2004; Clarkin, Hull, & Hurt, 1993).

Many researchers have cited family of origin factors as contributing elements to the development of borderline personality disorder (American Psychiatric Association, 2000). For example, in a study of 445 psychiatric inpatients, BPD was found to be much more common among first-degree relatives (e.g., parents, siblings) of BPD patients than among comparison groups of patients with other personality disorders (Zanarini, Frankenburg, Hennen, Reich, & Silk, 2004). Linda's description of Susan's biological father, Harry, suggested that his emotional instability, erratic behavior toward her, and impulsive suicide were consistent with BPD symptom patterns.

A number of studies have indicated that persons diagnosed with BPD report significantly higher rates of negative childhood and adolescent family life experiences (e.g., insecure attachment, physical and/or sexual abuse) than persons diagnosed with other personality disorders, major depression, or schizophrenia (Agrawal, Gunderson, Holmes, & Lyons-Ruth, 2004; Byrne, Velamoor, Cernovsky, Cortese, & Losztyn, 1990; Pagano, Skodol, Stout, Shea, & Yen, S., 2004). As I have illustrated, Susan weathered repetitive family crises and traumas as a child and teenager.

When compared with other diagnostic groups, persons with BPD are particularly vulnerable to suicidal ideation, plans, attempts, and completions. Studies of suicide risk in BPD patients have routinely validated significantly higher rates of self-harm. A recent study found that more than 75% of BPD patients had made at least one suicide attempt and that approximately 10% subsequently completed suicide (Black, Blum, Pfohl, & Hale, 2004). In a 7-year follow-up study, Soderberg, Kullgren, and Salander (2004) discovered that persons with BPD who had been sexually assaulted in childhood, like Susan, were significantly more likely to engage in additional suicidal attempts and require more psychiatric support than similarly diagnosed patients without a history of childhood molestation. Comparable results were found in a 2-year prospective study of 621 psychiatric patients by Yen, Shea, Sanislow, Grilo, and Skodol (2004). In this research, patients with BPD were discovered to have higher suicide rates, suggesting higher levels of impulsivity and emotional instability, than patients with diagnoses of major depressive disorder or substance abuse disorder.

Because of their difficulty in establishing stable relationships with others, their impulsivity, and their myriad problems—such as depression, substance abuse, eating disorders, and chronic suicide risk—persons with borderline personality disorder have been consistently described as a very difficult clinical population to treat effectively (Brown, Newman, Charlesworth, Crits-Christoph, & Beck, 2004; Clarkin & Foelsch, 2005; Sadock & Sadock, 2003). In a review of psychiatric medication treatments for BPD, antidepressant, antipsychotic, and behavior/mood stabilizing agents have shown some promise in single-subject and small-group studies. The results from well-designed research, however, have yielded mixed results (Koenigsberg, Woo-Ming, & Siever, 2002).

Among psychological and psychosocial treatments for BPD, Linehan (1993), as well as Barley et al. (1993), has demonstrated lower rates of suicide attempts, self-inflicted injuries, overdoses, and psychiatric hospital admissions with the use of dialectical behavior therapy (DBT), a highly structured program of cognitive-behavioral treatment. Stevenson and Meares (1992) demonstrated substantial reductions in violent behavior, drug use, medical visits, and self-harm episodes following 1 year of twice-weekly outpatient psychodynamic therapy; 30% of the patients no longer met the criteria for BPD. Stevenson and Meares (1999) found that the patients' gains were maintained in a 5-year follow-up study.

Treatments of patients with BPD frequently combine medication, psychological, day hospital, brief psychiatric hospitalization, and group psychotherapy approaches (Lieb, Zanarini, Schmahl, Linehan, & Bohus, 2004; Paris, 2004; Ryle, 2004). Also, many therapists have successfully used discussion of videotape playbacks of the patient's behavior during social skills training as an adjunct to traditional treatment (Sadock & Sadock, 2003). Clearly, treatment of BPD is a complex, complicated, long-term undertaking that requires highly skilled and experienced mental health clinicians working in close consultation (Clarkin & Foelsch, 2005; Oldham, 2002; Sadock & Sadock, 2003).

Suggestions for Prevention at Risk Intervention Points

Because of the nearly lifelong duration of Susan's depression and suicidal thoughts and because of her unresolved sexual victimization by her stepfather, in this section I emphasize her early childhood and adolescent experiences. Interventions during those years might well have interrupted the development of borderline personality disorder. Her most important RIP, therefore, occurred before her marriage to David.

It is not my intention to blame Linda, David, Bev, Tom, or any other persons identified at her widely publicized trial (e.g., teachers, school counselors, agency social workers, mental health clinicians, etc.) for the tragic end to Michael's and Alex's lives. Susan was ultimately responsible for the deaths of her children.

1. *Susan did not believe her mother's assertion that her father had died and gone to heaven. She called his telephone number, letting it ring many times before concluding that he was not at home.*

The unexpected loss of a parent is a tragic, extremely upsetting event for anyone, but especially for young children, who have less developed cognitive ability and life experience to understand what happened. Linda wisely chose to keep the specific details of Harry's death from Susan. However, her daughter exhibited many signals (e.g., calling on the phone, wanting to be with him in heaven) indicating that she wanted to talk to and about her father.

Cassem (1988) has suggested that allowing the bereaved to express their feelings about their sense of loss and preoccupation with the deceased is essential to the survivor's short- and long-term adjustment. According to Bowlby (1961), a death, especially a sudden loss as in Susan's case, represents a rupture of the survivor's attachment to the deceased person. The bereaved child (and adult) often feels smaller, weaker, and more fragmented. When a parent dies, it is not uncommon for a child to feel at fault, believing he or she was a bad child or failed to live up to his or her parents' expectations. Young children experiencing loss of a parent need to find a substitute adult who is consistently available to them (Sadock & Sadock, 2003).

Had Linda at this point sought professional help for herself, Susan, and Susan's brothers, all might have managed Harry's suicide in a more self-fulfilling way. For Linda, the ripples from her estranged husband's death led to an impulsive decision to marry Bev, but shortly thereafter, she berated herself for remarrying so soon (Russell, 2000). For children such as Susan, numerous research studies have demonstrated that poorly managed grief reactions place these children at increased risk for clinical depression and suicidal impulses as adults (Sadock & Sadock, 2003). For example, one review of studies found nearly a twofold frequency of suicide attempts in adults with a childhood history of parental loss (Pope & Vasquez, 2005).

2. *When Bev proposed to her shortly before Christmas 1979, Linda finally agreed to elope. They decided not to tell Susan and her brothers of the marriage until after the wedding (Russell, 2000). . . . Susan would repeatedly ask Linda if her mother loved her.*

Susan's behavior after her mother remarried suggested that she was still reeling from the loss of her father. Linda's silence about the wedding indicated that she was concerned that her children would be upset with her. Many clinicians believe that in cases of remarriage, adjustment problems in the family are minimized if the children are prepared by parent-child discussions well prior to the new wedding. These preparatory discussions need not be in a therapist's office and do not require professional intervention. Children's fears and anxieties about a new family arrangement, however, do need to be expressed so that all parties can adjust smoothly—Susan was clearly trying to make her voice heard.

> 3. *After reading the note, Linda, Bev, and Scott agreed that they would not talk to Susan about her suicide plan. . . . They took Susan's threats seriously but did not think that she needed professional help outside of the family for a phase she was going through.*

Susan's suicidal thoughts, which had begun at age 10 and continued to age 13, clearly suggested that her threat was not a phase she was going through. Linda did arrange counseling. However, Susan's parental loss by suicide, suicidal ideation history, completion of a note, and development of a suicide plan by saving aspirins mandated a comprehensive intervention with psychiatric consultation and hospitalization.

Given Harry's suicide by shotgun, Linda and Bev were wise to remove the bullets from Bev's guns in the den: The most common method of completing suicide in children and adolescents is by firearms (Sadock & Sadock, 2003). Though it was not available in 1984, today Linda and Bev could have obtained extensive information about adolescent suicide risk through the Internet (Grohol, 2005).

> 4. *In the ninth grade, however, Susan disclosed to a teacher that she continued to have suicidal thoughts . . . Linda . . . felt as though she was excluded from any meaningful content concerning her daughter's treatment. Linda was subsequently asked to agree . . . that Susan be evaluated by an experimental research program for depressed adolescents at the university's medical school. Linda refused out of concern that her daughter would be incorrectly labeled as mentally unbalanced.*

Providing psychotherapeutic services to adolescents is a complicated task for mental health clinicians. On the one hand, it is important for the therapist to gain the teenager's trust by assuring a level of privacy and confidentiality to their sessions. On the other hand, the adolescent's parent is legally responsible for the child's welfare; thus the adult needs to be apprised of treatment progress. Most clinicians believe that involvement of parents in their treatment of adolescents is beneficial, though clear guidelines about disclosure of session information need to be fully discussed before the parent gives consent (Calzada, Aamiry, & Eyberg, 2005; Harris & Bennett, 2005; see, especially,

Rubenstein, 1998). From Linda's perspective, she wished to know more about Susan's sessions. A number of initial and midpoint parent-child-counselor sessions might have enhanced Linda's enthusiasm for her daughter's treatment, especially after the school counselor recognized the severity of Susan's emotional problems.

When a clinician decides that it is in the best interest of the client to be referred to another treatment specialist, the transfer of service needs to be completed with careful thought, planning, and sensitivity to the client's and parents' needs (Chasten, 1991; O'Leary & Norcross, 1998). Referral to more complex, intensive treatment programs is substantially facilitated, especially in serious cases involving depression and suicide, when a therapist plans and discusses an array of mental health service options with the adolescent and parent (Bongar & Sullivan, 2005).

> 5. *When Susan disclosed the sexual abuse by Bev to her mother, Linda asked her daughter why she didn't stop him by leaving the room. . . . She could not understand why her daughter did not defend herself. Linda confronted her husband, who confessed and promised to stop. . . . Linda arranged for psychotherapy for each of them with a licensed psychologist. The treatment sessions lasted for several months, ending at Susan's request. Shortly thereafter, Bev began to molest her again. . . .*

In the 18 years since Susan, Linda, and Bev entered psychotherapy because of his sexual assault of his stepdaughter, mental health clinicians have learned a lot about the predatory thinking and behavior of incest perpetrators. Linda partially blamed her daughter for contributing to her own abuse, possibly diminishing Susan's speed of recovery (Cohen & Mannarino, 1998; Kuehnle, 2005). However, she did obtain her husband's confession and did seek professional help outside the family; many cases of child sexual abuse go unreported (Baker & Hill, 2005).

Approaches to treatment in child sexual abuse cases are often characterized as child-focused, parent-focused, and parent-child-focused methods. Linda described their sessions as involving all three of them for a number of appointments, followed by individual treatment for Susan and marital therapy for her and Bev (Russell, 2000). Though many clinicians then would have developed similar treatment plans for the Russell family, current research suggests that the most effective models in child sexual assault cases involve child-focused approaches in combination with sessions involving only the child and the nonoffending parent (Kuehnle, 2005). Treatment for the offending parent is typically provided by a different clinician (Deblinger, Steer, & Lippman, 1999).

> 6. *The Family Court substantiated Susan's allegations, and Bev agreed to leave the house to prevent Susan from being placed in foster care . . . Linda, Susan, and Bev returned for counseling with the same psychologist. After*

several months of counseling, Bev moved back into the house. He quickly resumed his molestation of Susan, but now she reciprocated by fondling him. Less than a year later, Susan had lost her virginity to a middle-aged married man. . . .

For Susan, Bev's removal from her home reenacted her father's abandonment of her. After numerous episodes of sexual victimization by her stepfather, she had learned that she could ensure his continued attraction to her by complying with his sexual requests. Had the Family Court ordered or had the Department of Social Services (DSS) insisted on an independent sex-offender evaluation of Bev's propensity for revictimizing Susan, a common current procedure in such cases today, it is unlikely that he would have been allowed to return home so soon. Current research and clinical practice in the assessment of sex offenders has established an array of methods to distinguish high- from low-risk perpetrators (Abel & Osborn, 2003; Conroy, 2003).

It was not surprising that Susan subsequently lost her virginity to a much older man, became unintentionally pregnant by two men, or began a 5-year pattern of multiple conflicting intimate relationships. Sexual acting-out is a highly frequent outcome of repeated abuse (Kuehnle, 2003; Baker & Hill, 2005). For example, in a sample of more than 2,000 persons, a history of sexual victimization was the best predictor of subsequent sexual acting-out and sexually precocious behavior (Friedrich, 1998).

Epilogue

Susan was evaluated by forensic psychologists and psychiatrists for the prosecution and the defense. All experts came to the same opinion that she was sane at the time of her children's deaths. Though she was clinically depressed, she knew that her acts were legally and morally wrong. The prosecutor filed notice of the death penalty, and the focus of the trial became the sentence Susan might receive: lifetime incarceration or execution. After numerous witnesses for the defense and prosecution testified and Susan's history of parental loss, depression, suicide, and sexual molestation was dissected, the jury unanimously decided that Susan should receive a life sentence. She remains confined within the South Carolina Department of Corrections.

15

Psychotic/Depressed Mother, Suicidal Type

Marilyn

Marilyn and her husband, Charles, entered the hospital hand in hand. The day they had been wishing for had finally arrived: Their first child was about to be born. After two miscarriages since they married 7 years earlier, Marilyn had been able to carry a baby to nearly full term after extensive bed rest during her third trimester. Their baby would be almost a month premature. With anxious smiles on their faces, they met their obstetrician in the lobby of the small, rural hospital. Soon, Marilyn's widowed father arrived, and they took the elevator to the second floor maternity ward. Charles and his father-in-law settled into the waiting area as Marilyn was prepared for her labor and delivery by the hospital nurses. Everything was in order. At home, Charles had put the finishing touches on the baby's nursery just 2 days before—bright, colorful balloons hung from the ceiling to welcome their new member of the family.

The labor and delivery took longer and was more difficult than expected; however, their son appeared to be a normal, healthy newborn when delivered. Three days later, Marilyn, Charles, and William came home.

As she held, fed, and changed her infant son, Marilyn knew that she had never had such joy in her life. When she was a child, she had few friends and often spent many hours alone at home while her parents worked until 6 p.m. at the cotton mill. Shy and retiring, she rarely spoke up in class and did not join after-school activities because she felt awkward and inept when talking with other children. As an elementary and middle school student, she had always believed that she was overweight and unattractive.

Her adolescent world was turned upside down during the summer after ninth grade, when her mother died unexpectedly of a stroke. Marilyn became very depressed. She cried herself to sleep for 2 months, rarely left her bedroom, and gained 25 pounds. She had lost the best friend she'd ever had. For the first time in her life she thought about suicide, but her strong religious convictions, the legacy of her parents, prevented her from killing herself.

With her mother gone, Marilyn's father expected her to manage their household duties of meals and cleaning. She did not object. She felt fulfilled knowing that her father needed her, even though he rarely complimented her on her cooking or housekeeping. Her father was a quiet man who would voice opinions or contribute to family discussions only after her mother's gentle teasing or encouragement. After her mother's funeral, her father retreated into himself even more. He never seemed to recover from his wife's death.

Marilyn graduated from high school and completed training as a licensed practical nurse (LPN). She found employment at a nursing home but continued to live at home and take care of her father. She had little in common with her fellow employees, who enjoyed going to bars and parties. Marilyn had never found alcohol or drugs attractive.

She met Charles through the church they both attended. She was surprised when he asked her to go to dinner after the Sunday afternoon service; it was her first true date. Though Charles had dated a few women before, he'd never had a girlfriend, as he too was socially awkward and shy.

Within a year they were married and planned their first pregnancy shortly after their honeymoon. Marilyn conceived her first child during their first year of marriage; however, she awoke one morning to find that she had miscarried. Marilyn and Charles were distraught by the loss of their baby but were somewhat reassured by her obstetrician's advice that miscarriages during first-time pregnancies were very common. After waiting a few months and obtaining their physician's clearance to try again, Marilyn miscarried once more. Two years passed before Marilyn became pregnant with Billy.

Billy's arrival overcame the anguish they'd felt after each of her previous miscarriages. Marilyn was ecstatic that her husband had agreed to try again to have another child. Charles, who, at 40, was 10 years older than his wife, was also contented with his son's birth. After his wife's miscarriages, he never thought he'd be a father. He was surprised that he adjusted so easily to helping Marilyn care for their son as he learned how to change diapers and understand the meanings of Billy's occasional cries. Billy was not a difficult baby, and soon he was sleeping through the night as he adapted to his parents' methodical schedule of feedings, naps, and bedtimes.

Charles was an accountant with his own business, but his income was often sporadic. To ensure stable revenue for family expenses and health insurance, Marilyn continued her employment as an LPN at the local geriatric nursing home. After 90 days of maternity leave, she returned to work on the day shift, and Billy was placed in day care.

When Billy was about 2 months old, Marilyn and her pediatrician became concerned that he was not progressing normally. He was slow to respond to his mother's voice and could not make a fist or grasp his parents' fingers.

When Marilyn smiled at Billy, he did not reciprocate with pleasant gurgles or giggles.

Despite their worries about their son, Marilyn and Charles had been encouraged by Billy's birth. While her pregnancy was progressing without problems and she was in her last trimester, they made plans to have another child. When their son was 3 months old, Marilyn and Charles had resumed intimacies without birth control pills or condoms. Billy was 9 months old when Marilyn discovered she was pregnant again.

Billy had difficulty reaching for toys and bringing them to his mouth to gnaw on. When he was placed on his stomach, Billy did not seem to have the strength to lift his head and raise his upper body. By the time he was 6 months old, he was unable to pull himself up into a sitting position. His reflexes seemed to be slower than those of other babies his age, and the muscles in his arms and legs were weaker and less well developed. The pediatrician's diagnoses of cerebral palsy and mental retardation devastated Marilyn and Charles. Their hopes for Billy's future were dashed.

In the months that followed, they attempted to be rational and logical about Billy's crisis, though neither could overcome their anguish and sense of hopelessness. Marilyn and Charles began to drift apart as each absorbed the implications of Billy's illness to his and their futures. Marilyn would often cry herself to sleep, and after a while her husband stopped consoling her. Charles had never been a very demonstrative or romantic husband, and after learning of his first son's diagnosis, he became more withdrawn from his wife. Marilyn became the sole caretaker for their son, and soon she no longer asked her husband to help change or feed Billy. As the end of her pregnancy neared, neither voiced their worries about their next child's health.

Edward was born without complications after little labor and an easy delivery. Though depressed over Billy's illness, Marilyn had made sure that she had regular prenatal care during this pregnancy. She would often take her son to her pediatrician, whose office was in the same building as her obstetrician's, so that Billy's developmental progress could be assessed and monitored. Marilyn again took extended maternity leave from the nursing home to care for her children. The contrast between her two sons was enormous: Billy was often unresponsive and passive, whereas Eddie was alert and highly active, giggling freely when Marilyn fed or changed him. As the months passed, Eddie soon exceeded his older brother in walking, speech, and play.

Eddie revitalized his parents' marriage. As he had during Billy's first 2 months, Charles became an active father again, getting up in the middle of the night to feed his infant son and change his diaper. He helped Marilyn take care of Billy without being asked. He and his wife would take weekend drives for picnics at nearby state parks. Neighbors would often see the family walking along the streets, with each parent pushing a baby carriage. They returned to their church and became regular members in the congregation once again. Eddie's birth gave them a feeling of hope that partially alleviated the sorrow they felt for their older child's chronic, severely disabling illness.

Over the next 5 years, Eddie grew into the child they'd wished Billy could have become. Their younger son was a rambunctious, inquisitive, slightly hyperactive, intelligent boy who easily made friends at day care and kindergarten. He was an avid, quick student who learned easily and enjoyed being the center of attention at school, home, and the church. As he got older, he began to understand that Billy was "different" and would challenge any child in the neighborhood who would make fun of his older brother. Because Eddie was so popular, he often had friends who would come to his house to play on the weekends and during the summer months.

As Marilyn turned 37 and Charles reached his 47th birthday, they decided that if they were going to have three children, they needed to do it soon. Marilyn stopped taking birth control pills after Eddie's 6th birthday. Three months later, she discovered that she was pregnant again. Because they were so concerned about birth defects after Billy's illness was discovered, Marilyn and Charles again very carefully monitored her pregnancy and prenatal care. They were overjoyed to find out that they would be having a daughter, whom they decided to name Jane in honor of Marilyn's deceased mother. When Marilyn told her father, it was the first time she had ever seen him cry openly—he hugged her and thanked her profusely.

Marilyn's pregnancy with Jane was uneventful. Eddie and Billy were allowed into their mother's hospital room to see their new sister. Billy was brought into the room in a wheelchair because he was unable to walk on his own. Charles held Jane in the crook of his arm and sat next to Billy so that his older son could see the newest member of the family. Jane was a healthy, happy baby and blended easily into her new family. Marilyn was overjoyed with her newborn child. She loved Billy and Eddie but had wished for a daughter for as long as she could remember. Marilyn wanted to recreate with Jane the special union she'd had with her mother. She loved shopping for little outfits and frilly baby clothes for her infant. For Marilyn, it was the happiest period of her life.

When Marilyn returned to work at the nursing home, Billy's in-home care provider also agreed to take care of Jane because she was such an even-tempered, contented child. Eddie was in the third grade at the nearby elementary school, where he was an avid student and popular with his classmates and teachers. Though Marilyn and Charles had hoped that their children could be raised by a stay-at-home mother, Billy's medical expenses and the family's need for employer-sponsored health insurance mandated that she continue to work outside the home.

Eddie was almost 10 years old when he was struck by a speeding car as he rode his bicycle through an intersection in the neighborhood.

Marilyn was on duty at the nursing home when the traffic policeman called her; she collapsed to the floor. Charles wept in shock when he heard the news. They rushed to the hospital and were overwhelmed by the injuries to their son's face, arms, and legs as he lay still on the emergency room bed. Eddie was whisked away to an operating room. Hand in hand, they walked down the corridor to the hospital's chapel and offered silent prayers for their son's life. Hours later, a nurse found them in the chapel and told them Eddie's surgery was finished.

For the next 2 weeks, Marilyn and Charles alternated the vigil beside their son's bed. Neighbors and fellow congregants took care of Billy and Jane. When Marilyn and Charles left the hospital, they collapsed into bed, exhausted from worry, fear, and anguish. After lingering in a coma, Eddie died peacefully in his sleep. Marilyn was napping on a cot next to him when a nurse awakened her to tell her that her son had passed away. She was too distraught to tell Charles over the telephone, but when he answered her call, he immediately knew Eddie had died. He rushed to the hospital to see his son one last time.

Both parents never recovered from Eddie's death—the light had left their lives. Marilyn's elderly father often visited, along with their pastor and many members in the congregation. For a month, neighbors brought food for dinner, but neither Marilyn nor Charles could eat. They sat in the house in numbed silence. The local hospital nursing staff provided home health care for Billy on a rotating basis, and mothers of Eddie's friends helped with taking care of Jane.

After 3 months of mourning, Charles and Marilyn returned to work without enthusiasm. Their marriage reverted to the way it had been after Billy was diagnosed with cerebral palsy. They both retreated into their own tragic, sad worlds. Though they tried to comfort each other, neither had any emotional energy to spare. Charles stayed at his business later in the evening each night and often ate dinners in restaurants alone before returning home just before bedtime. Marilyn also hid, providing minimal care to Jane other than feeding and changing her. They slept in separate bedrooms because their emotional pain was too overwhelming for physical contact, let alone intimacy. When her daughter would cry in discomfort, Marilyn would bring the child into her bed, then fall into a deep, troubled sleep once again.

Marilyn began to steal sleeping pills from the nursing home during the fourth month after Eddie died. She had concluded late one sleepless night that she could no longer go on living. She recalled her suicidal thoughts as a teenager and remembered how she believed that she could not overcome the loss of her mother, but this tragedy was too much to bear. As she contemplated her death, she realized that she would be leaving the burden of Billy and Jane on Charles, who at 48 was too old to raise an infant daughter by himself, as well as a 10-year-old son with cerebral palsy. She was so depressed that she believed that her husband could better survive the loss of his wife to suicide if the children were also in heaven with her, her mother, and his parents, who had died 2 years before Billy was born.

To keep her plan from being discovered, she stole only one pill each night. Marilyn was responsible for administering the medication to the bedridden patients on her ward, so the theft was easily done. She simply altered the records to show that the pill had been administered, although it had actually ended up in her uniform pocket. When she felt she had a sufficient amount of medication, she planned to crush the pills into powder and mix them into her son's after-dinner dessert and her daughter's evening bottle. She would then retire to her bedroom, take an overdose, and join her sons, daughter, and mother in the afterlife. By waiting until her husband went to bed, she knew that her plan would not be interrupted.

She barely spoke to Charles during dinner on the night she planned to die. As he got up from the table, she kissed him briefly on his cheek before he left the kitchen to retreat to the family den. She washed the dishes and finished cleaning up the rest of the house while her husband watched television alone. She let Jane and Billy sleep that evening. Usually she would keep them up until around 10 P.M. so that they would sleep through the night. Tonight they would sleep forever.

When she heard Charles leave the den and shuffle off to his bedroom, she knew the time had finally come. She took the pills from her purse and crushed them into a fine powder. She made up a bottle for Jane, mixing the milk and sedative together. Marilyn then added the powdered pills into Billy's chocolate pudding, his favorite dessert. She went to her son's room and woke him up. With tears streaming down her face, she fed him spoonful by spoonful. When the pudding was gone, she wiped his face clean, kissed him on the forehead, and waited a few minutes until he was asleep again.

She closed Billy's bedroom door behind her, then walked down the hallway to Jane's nursery. Her daughter stirred as she entered the room. She picked Jane up and held her on her lap as she greedily drank from the bottle. She was soon asleep again. Marilyn sobbed as she kissed her daughter and put her back in the crib. She said a silent prayer asking God to forgive her for what she'd done and was about to do.

Marilyn went to her bedroom, changed into her nightgown, and took the suicide note she'd written last night from her bedside table. The message was as simple and direct as she was: "Please forgive me. All our babies are at peace now." She swallowed the sedative-laced juice, then climbed into bed.

She awakened groggily to an emergency medical technician trying to shake her into consciousness. During the night she had vomited the juice onto her pillow. When she realized she'd survived, she moaned deeply and begged her husband to let her die with their children.

Marilyn was taken to the hospital emergency room and placed in intensive care for the next week. She stayed in the hospital for the following 3 months under strict suicide watch. Her antidepressant medication was carefully monitored. She was never out of sight of one or more of the nurses. When she'd use the bathroom, a female orderly would wait outside the stall. Though her treatment team tried to encourage her to participate in group activities with the other patients, she rarely left her hospital room. She refused to see Charles and would not return his telephone calls. Her pastor came onto her ward during his hospital rounds, but she would not leave her room to see him. She did not talk with her father but sent him a note in a sealed envelope that read: "I'm going to Mama." For the first 2 weeks of her hospitalization, Marilyn barely spoke to her attending psychiatrist, who visited twice each day.

As days turned into weeks, Marilyn gradually became more responsive to her doctor's questions, but the dullness never left her eyes as she answered in a monotone voice. During her third month of hospitalization, she finally accepted her husband's pleadings to visit. In the next two meetings, however, they said little to each other; the wall between them was too wide and high to cross.

She was charged with two counts of murder in the deaths of Billy and Jane. The county prosecutor had known of Billy's illness and had participated in local fund-raising drives to help Marilyn and Charles with their substantial medical bills. The prosecutor also knew of Eddie's death and had attended his funeral as a member of their congregation. Though he had met Marilyn and Charles at many church functions, he did not know them well. He had deep sympathy for the tragic loss of their son, Eddie.

The prosecutor was not surprised by Marilyn's suicide attempt but was shocked to discover that she had killed her children. He accompanied the two detectives to the hospital to inform Marilyn that she was under arrest. The procedure was somewhat of an empty exercise: As a nonaggressive hospital patient, she was never restrained or handcuffed. Because of her tragic story and minuscule flight risk, she was not transferred to the jail. Marilyn offered no protest as the detective read her rights. She signed the form without hesitation and simply declared: "I did it; I killed my children and tried to kill myself. Why am I still alive?"

At the request of her court-appointed attorney, my evaluation of Marilyn occurred during her third month of hospitalization, approximately 3 weeks before she was scheduled to be assessed by a psychiatrist and a psychologist from the state's forensic hospital. When she was evaluated at the state hospital, the staff concurred with her attending psychiatrist's recommendation that she had reached maximum benefit from inpatient care and could be managed adequately with twice-weekly outpatient treatment sessions and continuing antidepressant medication. After her forensic psychiatric evaluation, she was released to her home and the supervision of her husband, who had been insisting that she live with him again. Within a week she had died by her own hand.

Case Analysis

Marilyn's story is an excellent example of a filicide-suicide case, a rather common type of maternal filicide when mothers become significantly depressed. After Eddie died so unexpectedly, Marilyn and her husband never emotionally recovered from his death. The severity and duration of her symptoms in the months after Eddie died were clearly indicative of major depressive disorder, recurrent, severe without psychotic features, with melancholic features (American Psychiatric Association, 2000), the primary diagnosis rendered by all forensic mental health clinicians in Marilyn's case. Marilyn's major depression was recurrent because she had had similar patterns as an adolescent following the death of her mother and after Billy was diagnosed with cerebral palsy.

Although Susan Smith's case also exhibited a suicide pattern, Marilyn's experience was more representative of the deliberate, methodical killings and highly lethal suicide attempts that occur in these types of murders. Susan's filicide plan abruptly came to fruition. She got the idea of drowning her children and herself once she realized the ramp allowed her to roll her car into the water, an option not available to her when she had stopped on the bridge over the Broad River. The impulsive ambivalence of her actions was reflected by her twice stopping her car's movement into the lake before jumping out in fear as a final act of self-preservation.

In contrast, Marilyn's plan of suicide and homicide was much more carefully planned and executed. Her premeditation lasted at least 2 weeks, while she accumulated the pills she would use to complete the tragic end to her life and her children's lives. She also very carefully covered her tracks by falsifying the nursing home's medication records. If her theft were discovered and she were suspended or fired from work, she would not be able to complete the killings as she had planned. She would have had to concoct another filicide-suicide plan, perhaps with a gun or knife. She did not want to use such weapons because shooting or stabbing her children would cause them great pain and also mutilate their bodies. She did not want them to suffer in their last moments on earth. She wanted a painless, sure method of ending their lives, as well as her own.

Marilyn constructed the suicide note on the day before her children died for two reasons. First, she wanted Charles and her father to know why she committed the filicides and suicide. Second, she did not want anything to interrupt the continuity of her acts once she began to mix the powdered pills into the food. She worried that if she stopped to write a note, she would not go through with her plan.

Filicide-suicide cases are also often based in a mother's altruistic motives. Altruistic filicides are those in which a parent kills her child or children to save them from future pain and suffering from an actual or imagined illness. Many clinicians have found such patterns in their research of historical (e.g., Resnick, 1969) and current cases (e.g., Wilczynski, 1997). Marilyn's case had altruistic features that emanated from Billy's severe form of cerebral palsy. She was aware that her son's future was bleak because his illness was incurable. With mental retardation, limited communication skills, and continued inability to control his arms and legs, she feared that he would be institutionalized after Charles died or became infirm.

Her concern for her husband also had altruistic elements. She did not want to burden Charles with such vulnerable children at his advanced age. Billy would need care for the rest of his life. Their son would never be able to live independently because of his illness. Jane would not graduate from high school until Charles was in his middle 70s. She recalled the trauma she experienced as she went through adolescence after her mother died. She did not want Jane to have to suffer those problems.

Marilyn reasoned that because of his children's financial dependence on him, Charles would never be able to retire from work. She did not want that future for the man she loved so deeply. In her severely depressed state, she believed that it would be emotionally better for him to lose his entire family at once than to lose only his wife but have to carry the lifelong obligations of their children. She also thought that as a widower without children, Charles might be able to find another wife who could better care for him than she had after Eddie died. Though she felt guilty at her retreat from her husband, she believed that she had to withdraw for her own sanity and self-preservation. If she had not, she believed she would be committed to a psychiatric hospital for the rest of her life, and Charles would still have the responsibility of Billy and Jane. With these as options, suicide and filicide became a more desirable, acceptable solution to her unending agony.

Maternal Filicide Risk Matrix Analysis

The risk matrix for Marilyn is shown in table 15.1.

Prepregnancy Stage

Marilyn was well into adulthood when she married Charles after her 23rd birthday. By then she had graduated from high school and a 2-year nursing program and was gainfully employed full time as an LPN in a nursing home. Her age, education, and intelligence were therefore individual protective factors for her prior to her pregnancy with all three of her children. Because of her nursing training and because of her concern for the welfare of her children, Marilyn monitored her medical health quite well. During her four pregnancies before Jane, she made sure that she received regular prenatal care. Her miscarriages before Billy were not due to poor health habits. Though she'd been somewhat obese as a child and adolescent, by the time she'd entered her marriage to Charles, she'd gained control of her eating and weight.

Prior to her pregnancy with Jane, Marilyn's emotional status was a protective factor, principally due to the invigorating effects of Eddie's entrance into their family. After he was born and became such a delightful child, Marilyn and Charles were revitalized about having another baby. Although at this time in her life, Marilyn's emotional status was rather stable, she had had a number of traumas prior to Jane's birth. Her mother's death when she was an adolescent had triggered her first major depressive episode and her first thoughts of suicide. Marilyn's two miscarriages before Billy were also unfortunate episodes, though neither apparently resulted in another clinical depression—the couple's decisions not to have a vasectomy or tubal ligation were choices of optimism.

The discovery that Billy had cerebral palsy was clearly a trauma for both parents. For Marilyn, the tragic news precipitated a second depressive episode

Table 15.1
Maternal Filicide Risk Matrix: Marilyn (for Jane)

Factor	Pre-P	P/D	EP	LP	PI
Individual					
Age at current pregnancy	P	P	P	P	P
Intelligence level	P	P	P	P	P
Education level	P	P	P	P	P
Medical status	P	P	P	P	P
Emotional status	P	P	P	P	R
Trauma history	R	P	P	P	R
Maternal attitudes	P	P	P	P	R
Family of Origin					
Mother's parenting	P	P	P	P	P
Father's parenting	P	P	P	P	P
Marital/family stability	P	P	P	P	P
Situational					
Marital/partner status	P	P	P	P	R
Financial status	R	R	R	R	R
Child-care status	R	R	R	R	R
Infant's temperament	P	P	P	P	P

Note: R = Risk; P = Protective; Pre-P = Prepregnancy; P/D = Pregnancy/delivery; EP = Early postpartum; LP = Late postpartum; PI = Postinfancy.

and emotional distancing from her husband. Even though she was depressed by Billy's diagnosis, her maternal attitudes remained strong and positive for both of her sons. Though Charles retreated from helping with Billy, Marilyn continued to care for him, making sure his pediatrician was able to assess her son's illness regularly.

Although Marilyn's mother had died during Marilyn's adolescence, she had a profound, lasting effect on her daughter's maternal attitudes and behavior. Marilyn took care of her widowed father and stayed at home with him until she got married. Marilyn abstained from alcohol, drugs, and premature sexual experimentation as her mother and father had hoped she would. She delayed pregnancy until after she got married, and each of her four pregnancies before Jane was well discussed and planned with her husband.

Her father's parenting influence was also evident in Marilyn's adolescent and young adult years. After his wife died, he remained true to his faith and his family obligations toward Marilyn. Though he was not an emotionally demonstrative man, he was a steady, dependable provider throughout Marilyn's life. To a large extent, Marilyn married a man very similar to her father in attitude, demeanor, and reliability. During the prepregnancy stage prior to Jane's conception, Marilyn and Charles evidenced the marital stability that her parents had displayed. Her parents were never violent toward each other, were never unfaithful during their marriage, and never separated until her mother's death.

During the prepregnancy stage preceding Jane's birth, Marilyn and Charles had a strong, supportive marital relationship. Their union had survived two miscarriages and had weathered the trauma of raising a chronically disabled child. Although they drifted apart somewhat after Billy's diagnosis was confirmed, they did not separate or spiral into self-damaging behavior. Charles did not become violent or abusive to Marilyn or Billy. Rather than acting-out with substance abuse or infidelity, Charles became more withdrawn and reclusive from his family. Though Marilyn could have used his help managing Billy, she did not seem to be too resentful about her husband's absence. As it turned out, by the time Eddie was 4 or 5 months old, Charles had regained his sea legs as a father and was optimistically assisting his wife in child care of their sons.

During this stage, Marilyn's financial status, as always, was on the edge. Without her husband's steady employment, she did not make enough money as an LPN to be able to provide sufficiently for her children. With Charles's erratic income, Marilyn was obligated to keep working at the nursing home for family medical benefits. Though they received some state assistance for Billy's disability, his medical and caretaker bills were still an expensive and ongoing concern to Marilyn and Charles.

Marilyn's child-care obligations prior to her pregnancy with Jane included Billy and Eddie, who by then was just over 6 years old. Because of his cerebral palsy, Billy required extensive help from Marilyn. Fortunately, Eddie was a rather self-sufficient 6-year-old who would play outside with his friends, leaving his mother free to manage his older brother. Apart from Billy's illness, neither son's temperament was problematic for Marilyn or Charles.

Pregnancy/Delivery, Early Postpartum, and Late Postpartum Stages

As described, Marilyn's pregnancy and delivery of Jane were uneventful. Marilyn's individual factors were essentially unchanged or improved through the positive influence of Eddie's buoyant, infectious attitude and behavior. During her evaluations after her arrest, Marilyn consistently described these 2 years as the most personally satisfying and optimistic period of her life. She loved being a mother to her children. Though Billy's limitations and physical challenges were draining at times, Marilyn balanced his burdens with the joys of watching her younger son and daughter grow up. Jane was a delightful child as a newborn and infant. Marilyn began to replicate the life she'd remembered with her mother by somewhat spoiling her daughter with special clothes and dolls.

During these stages, Marilyn's family of origin factors continued to exert a positive influence on her and her marriage to Charles. As Jane finished her

first year of life, her parents' relationship was at its strongest and most supportive point. Financial stability was still an elusive goal for Marilyn and Charles,
though her medical insurance did cover almost all the costs of her pregnancy
and delivery of Jane, as well as her first-year well-baby pediatric appointments.
Jane's easygoing temperament, a match for Eddie's, was a constant source of
pleasure and enjoyment for Marilyn and Charles.

Postinfancy Stage

Marilyn never overcame the traumatic loss of Eddie. Following his death, her
emotional stability deteriorated into a severe, debilitating major depressive
disorder, which persisted until her death by suicide. If Eddie had not died,
Marilyn's tragic acts would likely not have occurred. If Billy had suddenly become sick and died, Marilyn and Charles could likely have survived that loss,
in part because they would have felt that their oldest child would be at rest
from his disabling illness. If Jane had suddenly died, Marilyn would have had
a severe depressive episode from which she might have recovered. She had become a rather resilient woman by the time she was pregnant with her daughter. Though she was strongly bonded to Jane, she did not have as long a positive history with her daughter as she had with her middle child. Marilyn and
Charles both knew that it was through Eddie that they had regained their optimism and rekindled their marriage and family. When he died so suddenly and
unexpectedly, their personal and marital life died with him. Only by accident
did Marilyn survive her suicide by overdose.

Even though she had received months of competent inpatient psychiatric
care and had received Charles's forgiveness for her terrible acts, she never wa-
vered from her goal to end her life once all her children had died. She believed that she had nothing left to live for. After her postarrest release from
the hospital, she'd planned her suicide down to the finest detail: a nightgown
for modesty after death, warm water to ensure that the blood seeping from
her wrists did not clot, and lying in a bathtub so that she would not make a
mess.

Relevant Research: Suicidal Mothers

In the United States, more than 30,000 persons die by suicide each year, approximately one every 20 minutes. The number of attempted suicides is estimated to exceed completed deaths by a ratio of nearly 22 to 1 (Jacobs, 1999;
Sadock & Sadock, 2003). More than 600,000 emergency room visits each year
are attributable to suicidal episodes (Frierson, Melikian, & Wadman, 2002).
Although women attempt suicide approximately three times more often than
men, males complete suicide at significantly higher rates (Safer, 1997). In addition to being male, higher suicide risk has also been associated with age
over 45, divorced or widowed status, unemployment, chronic medical illness,

psychiatric disorders (e.g., severe depression, psychosis, substance abuse, borderline personality disorders), intensity and duration of suicidal ideation, frequency of prior attempts, lethality of method (e.g., hanging, firearm, jumping), low likelihood of rescue, social isolation, and hopelessness (Sadock & Sadock, 2003).

Numerous studies have reported a strong association between psychiatric disorders and death by suicide. For example, in samples of completed suicides, 50–70% of the victims have had a primary diagnosis of major depression (Barraclough, Bunch, Nelson, & Sainsbury, 1974; Murphy, 1986). The completed suicide rate of persons with depressive and affective disorders has been estimated to be almost eight times greater than the rate within the general population (Jacobs, Brewer, & Klein-Benheim, 1999), but suicide victims are often undiagnosed, untreated, or underdiagnosed (Rihmer, Barsi, Arato, & Demeter, 1990).

Researchers have discovered that many suicidal persons, especially mothers, are reluctant to disclose their thoughts of self-harm to their pediatricians or other health care providers because of distrust or fear of being negatively judged (Guttman, Dick, & To, 2004; Heneghan, Mercer, & DeLeone, 2004). One recent study of depressed mothers seeking primary medical care recommended that physicians who enquire about the emotional health of the patients' children increase their opportunities to facilitate mental health care of the mothers (Weissmann et al., 2004).

Although research has generally indicated that being an adult female with children is associated with lower risk for suicide, parents of children who have died by filicide and other causes have much higher risks of taking their lives. For example, in a study of more than 6,000 mothers who had committed suicide between 1981 and 1997, suicide risk was very high in the first month following their children's deaths (Qin & Mortensen, 2003). Additionally, Bourget and Gagne (2002) discovered that 56% of their sample of filicidal mothers committed suicide after killing one of more of their children. Rodenburg (1971) reported that 41% of the filicidal mothers in his sample committed or attempted to commit suicide following their children's deaths. The pattern of maternal filicide followed by suicide has been cited by many researchers. Alder and Polk (2001) found that the two most common patterns in their research were maternal filicide-suicide cases and fatal physical assault cases due to battering or shaking.

This chapter has focused on Marilyn; however, Charles's history of recurrent depression also placed him at higher risk for suicide. In filicide-suicide cases, the pattern of homicide by fathers and mothers has been found to be quite different. Mothers tend to kill one or all of their children, then take their own lives (Daly & Wilson, 1988). In contrast, fathers will more likely kill their children and their spouses before committing suicide (Byard, Knight, James, & Gilbert, 1999; Dietz, 1986; Rodenburg, 1971). For example, in one sample of murder-suicide cases, none of the mothers who killed their children had murdered their husbands before committing suicide, but each of the fathers who committed filicide also killed his spouse before completing suicide (Byard et al., 1999). Dietz (1986) has coined the term "family annihilator" to describe the fathers who kill both their wives and children in a single episode. Rodenburg (1971) reported that in his sample of 35 filicidal fathers, 40% killed both their children and their wives; in his sample of 41 filicidal mothers, not one killed her spouse.

Suggestions for Prevention at Risk Intervention Points

1. Her adolescent world was turned upside down during the summer after ninth grade, when her mother died unexpectedly of a stroke. Marilyn became very depressed. She cried herself to sleep for 2 months, rarely left her bedroom, and gained 25 pounds.

A number of factors contributed to Marilyn's not receiving mental health treatment after her mother's death. Her father was so preoccupied with his own grief that he was unable to appreciate the emotional needs of his daughter. Marilyn was not in school during the summer months and thus did not have contact with other adults who might have recognized her depression and intervened with referrals for counseling. Their family doctor realized that she would be affected by her mother's death but attributed her sadness to the normal process of bereavement. The physician was not aware of Marilyn's extreme social withdrawal, excessive daily crying, and significant weight gains because she and her father were reluctant to voice such complaints to others.

Marilyn's few friends were only acquaintances she knew at school. During the summer she did not have contact with other adolescents who might have alerted their parents or other adults about her depressed mental state. If her mother had died during the academic school year, Marilyn would not have been able to isolate herself for 2 months without her teachers noticing her absence and subsequently arranging mental health services for her. With a history of mental health care, she might have been more receptive to seeking out such community resources when she faced her next personal crises, her miscarriages.

2. After waiting a few months and obtaining their physician's clearance to try again, Marilyn miscarried once more . . . The pediatrician's diagnosis of cerebral palsy devastated Marilyn and Charles . . . Their hopes for their son's future were dashed.

Marilyn and Charles had carefully planned the conception of each of their children; thus the pregnancies were intended and highly anticipated events. When Marilyn became pregnant the first time, she and Charles were ecstatic. An intended pregnancy is more than a simple biological process. When conception occurs, both parents begin to plan their lives around the future event:

deciding whether to know the sex of the baby before delivery, making lists of names, arranging baby showers, buying cribs and other paraphernalia, fixing up the nursery, and attending prenatal medical visits and birthing classes.

With intended conceptions, the bonding between mother (and father) and infant begins during pregnancy and continues after delivery. For these parents, the fetus becomes a member of the family well before delivery. The devastating psychological effects on both parents of a miscarriage have historically been underestimated by medical personnel but are now more widely recognized as significant trauma for expectant mothers and fathers (Sadock & Sadock, 2003).

In addition to the medical advice that Marilyn and Charles received, referral to a psychologist, social worker, or nurse practitioner might have helped them better manage their grief and bereavement. Establishing a therapeutic relationship at this point would have also given them an opportunity to express their unspoken anxieties about having a third miscarriage during Marilyn's pregnancy with Billy.

When Billy's cerebral palsy was discovered, mental health services for Marilyn and Charles would have already been in place to help them overcome the crisis, to educate them about their son's birth defect, and to facilitate arrangement of ancillary services (parent support groups, disability applications, in-home assistance, respite care, etc.). The availability of a mental health clinician might have interrupted their marital estrangement and given them better skills to cope with their grief then and, more important, after Eddie's death.

3. Eddie was almost 10 years old when he was struck by a speeding car as he rode his bicycle through an intersection in the neighborhood . . . After lingering in a coma, Eddie died peacefully in his sleep.

Few experiences are more traumatic for a parent than the unanticipated loss of a child. In addition to grief and depression, the surviving parent's most common reaction is hopelessness, the overwhelming sense that the future will be persistently painful because the child is no longer alive. The relationship between hopelessness and suicide risk has been well established by many studies (e.g., Beck, Brown, & Berchik, 1990; Young, Fogg, & Scheftner, 1996). A number of authors consider hopelessness rather than a diagnosis of depression to be more directly related to suicidal intention (Drake & Cotton, 1986; Jacobs et al., 1999).

Although it was fortunate that Marilyn and Charles had the assistance of neighbors and the hospital staff following Eddie's death, Marilyn's hopelessness might have been lessened through the use of grief and bereavement counseling before and after their son died. Sattler (1998) has recommended that the surviving parents should express to each other their loss of hopes, dreams, and expectations for the deceased child and to focus on what they have lost individually, as a couple, and as a family. Keeping a daily journal of their feelings, openly discussing suicidal thoughts as a common reaction, and encouraging vocalization of rage and anger may also help surviving parents to overcome their tragic loss (Sattler, 1998).

> 4. *When she realized she'd survived (her filicide-suicide attempt), she moaned deeply and begged her husband to let her die with their children. . . . Marilyn was taken to the hospital emergency room and placed in intensive care for the next week. She stayed in the hospital for the following 3 months under strict suicide watch. . . . After her forensic psychiatric evaluation, she was released to her home and the supervision of her husband, who had been insisting that she live with him again. Within a week she had died by her own hand.*

It was unfortunate that Marilyn had not been psychiatrically treated before her despair and hopelessness following Eddie's death drove her to filicide and suicide. Psychotherapy for her previous depressive episodes would have certainly entailed discussions about suicidal thoughts and plans. Those sessions may have subsequently helped her to disclose the intensity of her suicidal wishes after Eddie died. Once her suicidal intentions were known, the clinician could then have asked her Resnick's (1996) classic question: "What are your plans for the children?" That inquiry would have focused on filicide and more likely prevented the deaths of Billy, Jane, and Marilyn.

Epilogue

After her release from the hospital, Marilyn attended one outpatient treatment session with her psychiatrist and promised to continue taking her antidepressant medication as prescribed. Later that evening, after she'd said good night to Charles, she changed into her nightgown, ran water for a bath, climbed in the tub, and cut her wrists with a straight razor. Charles found her dead the next morning.

16

Retaliatory Mother
Olivia

Olivia was holding her 15-month-old daughter, Brittany, on her lap when she heard the knock on her apartment door. Holding her infant's hand, she looked out through the peephole to see who it was. She immediately recognized the two social workers from the county child protective services agency who had arrived for an unscheduled home visit. Olivia looked frantically around the room. Clothes, toys, dirty dishes, and magazines were strewn on the floor and furniture. At 11 in the morning, she was still in her nightgown, and Brittany was wearing only a diaper. The visit was going to be a disaster for her. She was afraid of the social workers' criticism but also furious because she knew that her ex-boyfriend's mother, Brittany's grandmother, had filed another complaint against her.

She opened the door and began apologizing for the condition of her apartment. The social workers looked around the living room and made notes on their clipboards. Olivia knew the visit was not going well. As she picked up clothes and dishes, she angrily explained that Brittany had had a fever the night before and that they finally fell asleep about 4 A.M. Her visitors nodded without comment as they moved into the bedroom and looked at the bathroom.

When they turned to face her, she knew bad news was coming. The senior social worker declared that because she had failed to follow the agency child protection plan, they were going to recommend that Brittany be placed in temporary foster care once more. Olivia demanded that they tell her who had filed a complaint against her, though she knew all complaints were anonymous. As the social workers left the apartment, they handed Olivia a document notifying her of a court hearing next week to determine whether the child protection agency would regain custody of her daughter.

She closed the door and threw the dishes she was holding against the wall. The noise of glasses breaking and Olivia swearing quickly brought the social workers back up the stairs. When they demanded to be let back in, Olivia screamed at them to leave her alone. Brittany continued to cry loudly, but Olivia still would not open the door. She overheard the senior worker on her cell phone calling the police. Before the officers could arrive, the building superintendent unlocked the door, and all three entered. Olivia was clutching her daughter to her chest and yelling at them to get out of her apartment. When they attempted to take Brittany from her mother's arms, Olivia tried to lock herself in the bathroom, but her path was blocked by the younger, male social worker.

Olivia was still swearing loudly when the police officers arrived. They quickly took control of the situation and forcefully removed Brittany from her mother's firm embrace. Her daughter screamed for her mother with her arms outstretched as she was taken away. The other social worker gathered some clothes and diapers for the child and told Olivia that she would be able to see Brittany next week in a supervised mother-child visit at the agency's office. The policemen stood guard over Olivia while she sat sobbing on the couch.

As the social worker left, one officer held Olivia back when she screamed that she "would get that bitch, Ann," Brittany's paternal grandmother, for taking her daughter. The officers told her to calm down, but Olivia continued to curse and cry. After the policemen returned to their car, Olivia grabbed a skillet and made a hole in the wall of her kitchen. It was not the first time she had been unable to control her rage in her 19-year-old life. She had a lot to be angry about.

When Olivia was approximately 2 weeks old, her mother placed her in the care of her maternal aunt and uncle, who had three children of their own. She never felt accepted by her male cousins, who did not want her living with them. Before she went to first grade, they would harass her by breaking her dolls or tearing her books, then claim to their parents that she was at fault. She would be pinched and punched by the youngest of her cousins, who would threaten to hurt her more if she told what he'd done. Olivia was afraid of her cousins, but she would get so frustrated with them that she would break her own toys and dolls.

When Olivia entered first grade, she had difficulty adjusting to school. A sullen, unfriendly child of mixed race, she was not readily accepted by the other girls in her class. Olivia received her first in-school suspension in the first grade when she beat up one of the boys in her class, who had taken a pencil from her desk. After the incident, the other children no longer teased her, but she was even further isolated from them. She was suspended from school for 3 days in the third grade when she pushed a girl classmate into the hallway lockers after the girl said something to her friends that made them laugh at Olivia. During the assault, she tore the girl's shirt and also kicked her in the leg.

When Olivia was 9 years old, her uncle was jailed on his third charge of domestic battery against his wife, having caught Olivia's aunt taking drugs in the bedroom with another man. Olivia was placed in temporary foster care. Six months passed before Olivia's widowed, elderly maternal grandmother agreed to take responsibility for her. Olivia told her what her nephews had done to her, but her grandmother called her a liar because the boys had always been so nice when they'd visited. In the fourth grade, Olivia was suspended from school again when she turned over her desk, threw her books across the classroom, and hit her teacher in the stomach.

Olivia was 11 years old when her birth mother, Candy, abruptly appeared at Olivia's grandmother's house. At first she did not recognize her mother, because the family did not keep pictures of her around the house. Her mother had dropped out of high school in the 10th grade after she got pregnant with one of Olivia's half-siblings, whom Olivia had never met. Olivia did meet the 2-year-old half-sister who was with her mother; the child's birth father had left Candy a month ago. As an unemployed single mother, she'd decided to come home for a loan until she could get back on her feet again. Olivia barraged her mother with questions of where she'd been for the past 10 years, but Candy deflected the inquiries by telling her that what was important now was that they were all together. Candy told Olivia that she could come to the state where she lived and that they'd both take care of Olivia's half-sister, Sissy. Olivia was overjoyed at her mother's news and ran upstairs to decide what to pack for the trip the next day.

When her grandmother came in from running errands and found Candy sitting in the living room, she did not rush to embrace her daughter. She demanded to know what she wanted and why she'd come home. Olivia overheard them arguing but stayed in her room because she did not want her mother mad at her. She wanted to move to her house with her new half-sister.

After her mother and grandmother stopped yelling, Olivia happily declared that she was going to live with Candy and Sissy. Candy remained silent at her own mother's skeptical look. Olivia was oblivious to their exchange: Her mother wanted her again. The next morning, when Olivia discovered that Candy and Sissy had left without her, her grandmother exclaimed, "What did you expect?" Olivia ran to her room crying. Later that morning, her grandmother heard things breaking. The next day, Olivia told her grandmother that she never wanted to see her mother again.

In the seventh and eighth grades, Olivia remained a sullen loner at school but would occasionally associate with some of the more delinquent girls and boys. She had tried a gulp of beer and a puff on a marijuana cigarette but did not like how they tasted. She was still living with her grandmother because her aunt had been convicted of another drug offense and was on probation. Olivia's male cousins had also developed substance abuse problems, which led to troubles with the law.

She was also a sullen, angry child at home. As her grandmother became more infirm, she had become afraid of Olivia and did not want to make her angry. She never told the family about two incidents in the previous year: Olivia had thrown a vase against the living room wall, and a few weeks later she had smashed dishes she was washing because her grandmother had told her to clean her room.

Although she did not have a close relationship with a female friend, Olivia did begin attracting the attention of some of the adolescent boys in her school. When she was 12 years old, a 14-year-old named Del asked if she wanted to go with him to the mall after school. Soon they were meeting daily. Though they never attempted intercourse, their intimacies progressed far beyond petting. Their relationship ended when Del's family moved to another city the following year.

As her interest in the opposite sex increased, Olivia's devotion to school declined. At 15, she lost her virginity to a 20-year-old man, Greg, on their second date. Soon they were having sex regularly. She would occasionally stay overnight after telling her grandmother that she was at a female friend's house.

As Olivia was spending more time away, her relationship with her grandmother, never a close bond, was becoming even more distant. One night, Olivia became so enraged at her grandmother's snide comments that she was like her mother, Candy, that she threatened the elderly woman with a kitchen knife. Her grandmother ran to her bedroom, locked herself in, and called the police. When the officers arrived, the police decided not to file charges, because Olivia's tearful apology appeared to be so heartfelt. Her grandmother did not object because she was afraid of Olivia's retribution. Following that incident, Olivia came and went from the house as she wished.

After dating Greg for nearly 3 months, Olivia wanted to have a baby, but she did not want to ask him. She knew that he did not want children yet and had very carefully used a condom whenever they'd had intercourse. She wanted to have someone who would be totally dependent on her, a child who would always need her every day. Olivia told Greg that she had begun to take birth control pills and that they no longer needed to use condoms when they had sex. He accepted her lie uncritically, because by now they virtually lived together. When she told him that she was pregnant, he was furious that she had lied to him and yelled at her to leave. Their relationship was dead.

Olivia moved back into her grandmother's home. Because she was 15, her grandmother was still legally obligated to care for her. In any event, she felt she could not protest because Olivia would explode once again. Olivia did not tell her grandmother that she was pregnant. When Olivia discovered that she'd had a miscarriage, she did not tell her grandmother what had happened, but she did revisit the clinic for medical care.

Olivia was 16 when she told her grandmother that she was dropping out of school. Her grades were well below what she was capable of achieving, and she no longer had any interest in going to classes. She discovered that she could be declared an emancipated minor at age 16 if she could get her grandmother's permission and the approval of a family court judge. She was soon working in a store and had enrolled in a GED program to appear more mature to the judge.

She filed for emancipation status, which was granted without serious investigation because of her grandmother's endorsement. The following month, she moved into her own apartment within walking distance of her job—she never attended GED classes again.

Two months later she met Scott, a young man of 18 who often visited the store where she worked. He was a freshman at the university who lived in the dormitory. Olivia and Scott would meet at her apartment after she was off work and he'd finished his classes for the day. He thought she'd graduated from high school and was also 18. Olivia did not correct his misimpression. Within weeks, Scott was sleeping at her apartment every night. Olivia still wanted to have a child, and once again she told her lover that she was taking birth control pills.

She became pregnant for the second time at age 16. Scott ran from the apartment after she told him he was going to be a father. She'd expected that he would not stay around. In any case, she did not want anyone to interfere with her relationship with her baby—he'd just be in the way. When she did not see or hear from him for the next 2 weeks, Olivia thought that he had drifted out of her life.

Scott's mother, Ann, called Olivia one evening to tell her that she and her husband would visit her the next weekend. Olivia did not like the demanding tone of Ann's phone call but agreed to meet them at a restaurant near her apartment. Olivia realized that Ann knew that she was pregnant and was coming to talk about terminating her pregnancy. Olivia had no intention of either having an abortion or giving up her child for adoption.

Ann and her husband, Scott's stepfather, were in full agreement that she should give birth to the baby and asked what arrangements she'd made for prenatal care. Olivia knew that Scott's parents were well off, and she agreed to go with them to be examined by an obstetrician at the university medical school.

For the next 7 months, Ann would take Olivia to her doctor's appointment. Scott and Olivia had stopped seeing each other, but he would accompany them to her prenatal visits. At his mother's urging, Scott would ask the physician numerous questions about the fetus's health. Although Olivia appreciated her help, she felt smothered by Ann's invasive assistance: Ann was the one calling the shots, not the expectant mother of the baby. When Ann once made a seemingly innocuous remark about the dust in the apartment's living room, Olivia exploded and ordered her to leave. Ann returned the next day to accompany Olivia to her appointment as if nothing had happened the day before. Ann did not want to say anything that would disrupt her plan to gain custody of the baby.

Olivia gave birth to Brittany without any complications. Scott stayed in the labor and delivery room until his daughter arrived. The first time he held Brittany, he passed her to his mother, who then gave her back to Olivia. The new mother was too exhausted to protest, but she never forgot the incident that foreshadowed their conflicts over the next 15 months. During Olivia's hospitalization, Ann was a constant presence, walking the corridors with Olivia and assisting her with feeding and diaper changes. Olivia felt smothered again by Ann's help and had another verbal eruption near the nurses' station.

For the following 2 months, before she had to return to her job, Olivia devoted herself to Brittany's care. Though she would become tired by the night-time feedings, Olivia reveled in being a new mother. Brittany was a bright, happy child who actively responded to her mother's attention. Olivia's grandmother arrived during the first week to see Brittany, but there were no other visitors from the family. Ann called frequently, but Olivia would not answer the messages. She wanted to exclude Ann from the relationship she was consolidating with her new daughter. Ann visited unannounced twice, but Olivia would not let her in. She would return Ann's packages for Brittany unopened.

When Olivia had to return to full-time employment, she found a woman in her apartment complex who provided day care that she could afford. When the woman increased the number of children in her care, however, Olivia would find Brittany in a wet diaper and dirty clothes. She tried another woman's day care but was enraged when her daughter developed a bruise on her face. The woman claimed that a toddler boy had done it, but Olivia did not believe her. She took Brittany back to the other babysitter.

Olivia was fired from her job for insubordination when Brittany was just 6 months old. She had had the second of two explosive arguments with her supervisor over the span of just 3 weeks. When Ann discovered that Olivia had lost her job, she offered to take her and the baby into her own house. Olivia refused. She asked to move in with her grandmother but was rebuffed. Two weeks went by before Ann called again. This time she offered to pay Olivia's rent and expenses until Brittany's first birthday. With few other options, she accepted Ann's offer. She also agreed that Ann could visit her only grandchild as often as she wished.

Brittany was 9 months old when Olivia was investigated for child abuse and neglect for the first time. Ann had filed a complaint with the county protective services agency, alleging that Olivia's angry outbursts toward her daughter placed the child in danger. When the agency social workers arrived unannounced at her apartment, Olivia was furious and demanded to know who had called them. At the emergency hearing, Ann offered to take care of Brittany and allow Olivia unlimited supervised visits. Over Olivia's angry profane objection, the judge ruled that the child would live with Ann until Olivia satisfactorily completed a child protection plan developed by the agency.

Olivia was ordered to attend weekly parenting classes for the next 3 months. She was distraught at losing custody of Brittany but completed the classwork assignments promptly. When she saw Brittany at Ann's house, her daughter would not leave Olivia's lap and had to be pried from her embrace when the visit was over. Each visit was heartbreaking and infuriating, but Olivia managed to remain icily civil with Ann. At the next court hearing, Brittany was allowed to return to her mother's apartment because Olivia had complied with the court's orders.

During the emergency hearing 3 months later, the social workers testified about Olivia's explosive, profane anger during their most recent visit. The police officers and apartment supervisor corroborated their reports. The judge ordered Brittany to be placed in a local foster home but allowed Olivia weekly supervised visits. Although Ann was not at the hearing, Olivia knew that she had orchestrated the entire procedure. Before her first visit with Brittany at the foster home, she received a copy of a letter from Ann's attorney, urging the judge to place the child with Ann again. Olivia believed that if the judge granted Ann's petition, she would never have unfettered access to her daughter again. If she could not have Brittany, then no one could.

Olivia arrived at the foster home on time. Brittany rushed to her arms, and they held each other tightly. For the next half hour, she played on the floor with her daughter as the foster parents sat in the kitchen drinking coffee. Olivia told them that Brittany wanted to use the potty and obtained their permission to go with her to the bathroom. With the door closed, Olivia told Brittany that she would always love her and pressed her face to her breast until her daughter stopped breathing.

She walked out of the bathroom with Brittany in her arms and told the foster parents to call the police.

Case Analysis

Olivia's case has a number of features that have appeared in other women's stories in this book. When a child under 2 years old dies at the hands of its teenage mother, issues of distorted attachment and bonding such as those that categorize detached mothers are an initial consideration. There is no indication that Olivia attempted to deny her pregnancies, as she quickly informed the prospective father each time. She was neither resentful nor ambivalent about becoming pregnant, because she had, with deception, deliberately planned to conceive each child. She did not appear to have become exhausted by the demands of new motherhood, having only one even-tempered child in her care.

Olivia's history of rage suggested that Brittany might become a victim of recurrent child abuse; however, there was no evidence that Olivia ever directed her aggression at her daughter. Though the social workers found that her apartment was a mess, she had never been previously cited for child neglect. Indeed, Brittany's pre-and postnatal medical records documenting normal height and weight showed that Olivia was a very responsible expectant and new mother. Olivia's above-average intelligence and conscientious care of Brittany precluded her case from being designated as an example of the inadequate type in this maternal filicide category.

Although there was no indication that Olivia had ever experienced psychotic symptoms, the loss of custody of her daughter at 9 months and at 15 months could have resulted in major depressive episodes. Instead, Olivia externalized her emotions toward Ann rather than becoming recurrently depressed and suicidal, as in Susan's and Marilyn's cases. Further, there was no indication that Olivia suffered from depression after the birth of Brittany or following the miscarriage of her first pregnancy.

In the rare maternal filicide cases of retaliatory mothers, the perpetrator has a recurrently conflicting relationship with at least one other adult whom she believes is trying to take her child or children from her. As indicated in other chapters of this book, retaliatory filicides are more characteristic of fathers who consider their spouses' wishes to leave them as a narcissistic insult. These men see their wives and children as extensions of their own identities. Retaliatory filicidal males cannot tolerate the thought of some other man supplanting them as a father or husband. In the extreme case, the result is a familicide-suicide in which the entire family is eradicated.

Olivia was clearly in recurrent conflict with Ann over custody of Brittany. The battle began during her early months of pregnancy and continued until her daughter died. The origin of Olivia's plan to get pregnant was to have a child who would always need and love her, experiences that she had not had with Candy, her aunt, or her grandmother. When Scott dropped out of the picture, Olivia believed that she had achieved her goal, only to be confronted by Scott's mother, Ann, a much more formidable and well-funded foe.

After Brittany was born, Olivia was able to consolidate her bonding to her daughter while keeping Ann at bay. However, Olivia's limited resources, lack of meaningful family support, and concern for her daughter's immediate welfare put her back under Ann's influence. As Ann's intentions became clearer through her complaints to child protective services, the intensity of their rivalry for Brittany increased. When Olivia lost the second court hearing, she knew that Ann had finally won. Going to prison for murder became an acceptable price to pay for giving her "mother-in-law" the eternal emotional pain of never having Brittany again.

Maternal Filicide Risk Matrix Analysis

Table 16.1 depicts the risk and protective factors in Olivia's case.

Prepregnancy Stage
Olivia became pregnant for the first time at age 15 and arranged to become pregnant a second time when she was just 16 years old. Teenage pregnancies, even intended conceptions as in Olivia's case, have been associated with higher risks for neonaticide and infanticide, as indicated in previous chapters. Her young age was a risk factor throughout all her stages. She had dropped out of school after the 10th grade; limited formal education has also been linked to higher maternal filicide risk. Her medical status was a protective factor in that she had prenatal care during her first pregnancy and made sure she had no medical complications from her miscarriage; these decisions reflected her above-average intelligence as an additional protective factor. Her emotional status during this stage comprised both risk and protective elements. Although she displayed a history of numerous intermittent explosive disorder (IED)

Table 16.1
Maternal Filicide Risk Matrix: Olivia

Factor	Pre-P	P/D	EP	LP	PI
Individual					
Age at current pregnancy	R	R	R	R	R
Intelligence level	P	P	P	P	P
Education level	R	R	R	R	R
Medical status	P	P	P	P	P
Emotional status	R	R	R	R	R
Trauma history	R	R	R	R	R
Maternal attitudes	P	P	P	P	R
Family of Origin					
Mother's parenting	R	R	R	R	R
Father's parenting	R	R	R	R	R
Marital/family stability	R	R	R	R	R
Situational					
Marital/partner status	P	R	R	R	R
Financial status	P	P	P	R	R
Child-care status	—	—	—	—	—
Infant's temperament	—	P	P	P	P

Note: R = Risk; P = Protective; Pre-P = Prepregnancy; P/D = Pregnancy/delivery; EP = Early postpartum; LP = Late postpartum; PI = Postinfancy.

episodes at school and home, there was no evidence that she suffered from a psychotic disorder. She did not use alcohol or drugs. She was not indiscriminate in her sexual experimentation and had protected intercourse until she decided she wanted to become pregnant.

Olivia had a number of traumas in infancy, childhood, and adolescence stemming from her mother's abandonment and the physical abuse she suffered from her male cousins. Fortunately, she was not sexually assaulted by them or physically abused by her violent uncle with whom she had lived. Olivia's maternal attitudes were a mixture of risk and protective features. Although she carefully arranged to become pregnant, thus having an intended conception, her reasons were highly narcissistic: The baby would fulfill her own need to be loved and cherished, an unsurprising desire after years of familial rejection.

Olivia's family of origin elements for all stages of Brittany's life were uniformly risk factors. Olivia's mother, Candy, was an inadequate parent who had abandoned her at 2 weeks and subsequently had a number of children who were raised in foster care. When Olivia finally met her birth mother, Candy deceived her into believing that they would be reunited, only to reject her once more. Olivia's aunt and grandmother appeared to grudgingly provide parenting by default. Olivia never knew her father, grew up in the home of a domestically violent uncle, and lived her late childhood and adolescent years with a widowed grandmother. She never experienced the benefits of a dependable, reliable, emotionally protective father or father figure, which likely led to her wish to have a child without the continuing presence of a male.

At the prepregnancy stage immediately prior to her conception of Brittany, Olivia appeared to have a positive relationship with Scott. There was no evidence that he was an abusive man, nor did he dabble in excessive alcohol or drug use. In terms of financial stability at this stage, Olivia was gainfully employed in a full-time job with good health benefits and was living independently from her grandmother as an emancipated minor.

Pregnancy/Delivery Stage and Early Postpartum Stage

Because Olivia got pregnant with Brittany at age 16, her youth and still-limited education continued to be risk factors. Her trauma history was also a risk factor, as she had not had mental health treatment to overcome its effects. Although she had deceived Scott to become pregnant, she displayed careful concern for the welfare of her fetus by receiving regular medical and prenatal care. Unexpectedly, Ann entered her life, but fortunately both had the same goal for the pregnancy. As her pregnancy progressed, the two women's relationship did become strained, with Olivia having additional explosive, though nonviolent, episodes before and after Brittany's birth.

Olivia's family did not assist her at all through this period, nor in the months following Brittany's birth, risk factors that contributed to Olivia's filicide. Had her family supported her, Olivia would have had other options than Ann. Because of the way in which she arranged to become pregnant, Olivia destroyed the relationship she had with Scott. Though he would accompany her to her prenatal appointments, his involvement was principally due to his mother's urging. Like Gregg, Scott also rejected Olivia, though both chose to do so. Either could have put his baby's well-being above his own, forgiven her deception, and actively assumed the role of expectant father.

At these two stages, Olivia's financial status was still a protective factor, as she had employment and health benefits. Olivia did not have any other children in her care when Brittany was born; thus she could devote her energies exclusively to her newborn baby. Her bonding was also facilitated by her health care policy, which allowed 2 months of postpartum leave from work. Fortunately, her daughter was a healthy, happy, even-tempered baby. Had Brittany been a more difficult baby, Olivia might have had IED outbursts that could have threatened her child's health and life.

Late Postpartum Stage and Postinfancy Stage

During these stages, Olivia's plan to be the sole provider and caretaker of her baby began to unravel. She had rejected Ann's help during the early postpartum stage, which made her more vulnerable to Ann's arrangement after Olivia was unable to find reliable, safe child care. Her emotional status became more unstable, resulting in recurrent explosive episodes that led to the termination of her employment.

After losing her job, and because she still received no help from her own family of origin, Olivia had few other choices than Ann's offer. Olivia was able to stay at home with Brittany on a full-time basis, but Ann's invasive presence reactivated Olivia's emotional conflicts about her mother, Candy. Her unresolved traumatic history of abandonment likely fueled her resentment of Ann's help. She saw the assistance as more smothering than it actually might have been. When she was investigated by child protective services, Olivia's history of IED incidents before and after Brittany's birth and at both court hearings was damaging evidence against her, which led to the baby's placement with Ann.

In terms of marital/partner status, the conflict between Ann and Olivia was heightened by the absence of Scott, Brittany's father. Although he was in school, he still resided in the same city where Olivia and his daughter lived. Scott's absence reactivated Olivia's traumatic history with her father and other male parent figures. These negative past experiences impaired her judgment and kept her from seeking help from Scott to minimize his mother's intrusion into their relationship. Had their relationship been more pleasant and supportive, Olivia's risk of filicide would likely have been substantially lower.

Relevant Research: Intermittent Explosive Disorder

According to the American Psychiatric Association (2000), intermittent explosive disorder (IED) is characterized by: (1) a recurrent failure to prevent expression of aggressive impulses, resulting in assaults or property damage; and (2) a degree of aggressiveness during the episodes that is grossly out proportion to the precipitating psychosocial stressors. IED is considered to be a relatively rare disorder, with a prevalence of less than 2%, though its occurrence may likely be underreported (Sadock & Sadock, 2003). One recent study (Coccaro, Schmidt, Samuels, & Nestadt, 2004) reported that IED was far more common than previous studies had demonstrated, with a possible lifetime prevalence of nearly 10 million persons in the United States. IED is typically diagnosed more frequently in men than in women, consistent with numerous studies that report lower overt physical aggression in females (Cale & Lilienfeld, 2002). For males and females, IED is usually first evident in childhood and preadolescence, continues into adulthood, then declines after age 50.

The behavior displayed during an IED episode may include physical and/or verbal aggression, as well as property destruction. Alcohol-related settings (e.g., bars, restaurants, sporting events, etc.) and domestic and marital situations are frequent locations for IED episodes, though aggressive drivers have also been the subjects of research studies. Galvoski and Blanchard (2002), for example, found that aggressive drivers with IED reported higher levels of assaultiveness, resentment, and impatience than aggressive drivers who did not meet IED diagnostic criteria.

Many persons suffering from IED report a characteristic course before, during, and after their acts. McElroy, Soutullo, Beckman, Taylor, and Keck (1998) discovered that, in their sample of IED-diagnosed participants, 88% described feeling pre-event tension against their impulses, 75% indicated a feeling of relief after acting, and 48% acknowledged experiencing pleasure after their episodes. These participants also reported that they had been additionally diagnosed with mood disorders (93%), substance abuse disorders (48%), and/or anxiety disorders (48%), as well as with high rates of migraine headaches. Other research has demonstrated comorbidity of IED with border-line personality disorder (Zlotnick, Rothschild, & Zimmerman, 2002), bipolar disorder (Davanzo et al., 2003), and eating disorders (Lejoyeaux, Arbaretaz, McLoughlin, & Ades, 2002; McElroy et al., 1998).

The precise origins of IED have not been clearly delineated, though authors have emphasized combinations of biological and genetic factors, childhood-familial environmental experiences, and recurrent psychological processes (Sadock & Sadock, 2003). The therapeutic use of various psychiatric medications such as clozapine (Kant, Chalansani, Chengappa, & Dieringer, 2004), Celexa (Reist, Nakamura, Sagart, Sokolski, & Fujimoto, 2003), De-pakote (Hollander et al., 2003), and Tegretol (Mattes, 1990) suggest that bi-ological factors may contribute to IED. First-degree relatives of patients with IED have been found to have higher rates of impulse-control disorders and histories of more frequent explosive episodes.

Persons who grow up with one or more physically and verbally abusive parents often develop patterns of rage and aggression that are directed at their spouses and children (Schoenfield & Eyberg, 2005; Suinn, 1998). To high-light the generational origins of an individual's current aggressive and other behavior patterns, for example, many mental health clinicians will develop a genogram from the patient's self-reported history and interviews with other family members. A genogram is a multigenerational family tree in which members' symptoms, intrafamilial conflicts, emotional problems, and psy-chiatric disorders are depicted. Family members' difficulties are illustrated by a standard set of symbols denoting sexual/physical abuse, alcohol/drug problems, serious mental disorders, sexual orientation, miscarriages, foster or adopted status, and divorce (Petry & McGoldrick, 2005). The genogram may be employed for assessment and treatment by the mental health clinician in individual, marital, and/or family therapy and may be adapted for effective treatment of children (Gil, 2003).

Psychological explanations of IED have focused on the person's anxiety and fear, which often precede a verbal or physical episode. From a psycholog-ical perspective, outbursts of anger may occur as a preemptive self-protective defense against narcissistic injury (Sadock & Sadock, 2003); that is, individuals with IED erupt because they anticipate that they will be demeaned or rejected by the persons with whom they are interacting. These explanations are consistent with the McElroy et al. (1998) research previously cited. Non-medication-based treatment programs that emphasize anger management through relaxation training, focused imagination of anger-inducing situations, and enhancement of assertiveness skills highlight psychological contributions to the development of IED symptoms (Deffenbacher, Filetti, Lynch, & Oetting, 2002; Suinn, 1998).

Unfortunately, few persons with IED voluntarily seek treatment for their disorder. For example, in the Coccaro et al. (2004) community sample, only 12.5% of the participants diagnosed with IED reported that they had sought help. More frequently, the outbursts have resulted in brushes with the law in the form of child abuse, domestic violence, or charges of assault; in these situations, treatment is more commonly rendered under court order (Brodsky, 1998; Galvoski, Blanchard, & Veazy, 2002). In such situations, Brodsky (2005) has emphasized the importance of establishing three- or four-session treatment contracts focused on realistic self-coping skills to enhance the involuntary client's continued attendance in psychotherapy sessions. Safran (2005) has recommended that an enduring, productive therapeutic alliance is more likely to occur when the patient is encouraged to voice and resolve his or her negative feelings about therapy.

Suggestions for Prevention at Risk Intervention Points

1. *Olivia received her first in-school suspension in the first grade when she beat up one of the boys . . . in the third grade when she pushed a girl classmate into the hallway lockers . . . In the fourth grade, Olivia was suspended from school again. . . .*

Physical violence in a primary-grade girl is a very rare occurrence and a strong signal that a school-based intervention should be initiated involving the student's parent(s) and guidance counselor. In Olivia's case, apparently nothing was done. She recalled that her violence in the third and fourth grades resulted in only suspensions from school. She could not recall seeing any counselors with her aunt and uncle or with her grandmother. Her aggressive behavior appeared to have been a replication of how she was being treated by her male cousins. The vigor of her attacks on her classmates reflected the anger toward her cousins that she'd been unable to express in their presence. Had the school initiated an intervention into Olivia's family life after either of her transgressions, the cousins' abuse would likely have become known, and protective services for Olivia could have been rendered. Those services, in turn, may have resulted in an earlier and safer placement with her grandmother.

2. *After her mother and grandmother stopped yelling, Olivia happily declared that she was going to live with Candy and Sissy. . . . when Olivia*

*discovered that Candy and Sissy had left without her, her grandmother
exclaimed, "What did you expect?"*

Olivia's grandmother missed an opportunity to acknowledge and alleviate Olivia's pain at being rejected by her mother again. Rather, she treated
her granddaughter as an ignorant, naïve child who should have known not
to trust the words of her own mother. Her grandmother's dismissive response
to Candy's disappearance likely had its origin in her own unresolved feelings
of guilt and regret at having a daughter who could so callously abandon Olivia
and her other children. Episodes such as these are often the foundation of
alienation and anger in adolescents (and younger children) when they begin
to realize that they are vulnerable to and unprotected from the adults who are
supposed to care for them.

In Olivia's case, she evolved into an angry, resentful teenager who could
fly off the handle at the slightest provocation. In the months subsequent to
her mother's leaving, Olivia began to direct her rage toward her grandmother.
Had intervention services been initiated in response to Olivia's earlier violence,
perhaps she and her grandmother would have had a treatment resource for
help with their current and subsequent crises.

*3. Olivia . . . discovered that she could be declared an emancipated minor
at age 16 . . . [with] the approval of a family court judge.*

Although Olivia had the intelligence, literacy, and employment skills to be
considered an adult, she was a pseudo-mature adolescent with serious emotional and behavioral problems. She became an emancipated minor to gain
control of her life, to be free of adult supervision. Her wish for this legal status
is not surprising, given the poor parenting she had received to this point in her
life. It is unfortunate that the family court judge simply accepted the endorsement of Olivia's grandmother and did not order a thorough psychological,
psychiatric, and social work evaluation of Olivia and her family situation. The
results of those assessments may have readily identified her IED, her recurrent
conflicts with her grandmother and others, and the necessity for psychotherapy and perhaps medications for Olivia. She might have also received helpful
family planning advice that would have prevented or at least delayed her next
pregnancy until she was truly a mature adult competent to make wiser decisions for her long-term benefit.

*4. Ann and her husband, Scott's stepfather, were in full agreement that she
should give birth. . . . At his mother's urging, Scott would ask the physician
questions about the fetus's health.*

Ann and her husband failed to provide adequate parenting to Scott by
allowing him to escape his obligations as Brittany's father. Even though he was
a college student, it was his responsibility to provide for his baby and assist
Olivia. Many other young men in Scott's situation have delayed their academic

careers, found employment, and financially provided for their unexpected family. Though Scott and Olivia may not have lived together, he could have been Olivia's first-choice child-care option once her maternity leave ended. If he had been more responsible to the family he created, Brittany would not have experienced the inadequate child care she received when Olivia did go back to work. If Scott had accepted his responsibility as a new father and supported Olivia as the mother of his child, his assertiveness might have diminished the conflicts between Ann and Olivia. With Scott as an ally, Olivia might have been less retaliatory to her baby's grandmother and might not have taken Brittany's life.

> 5. *Brittany was 9 months old when . . . the judge ruled that the child would live with Ann . . . At the emergency hearing 3 months later . . . the judge ordered Brittany to be placed in a local foster home . . .*

As it turned out, these were the last opportunities for interventions that might have saved Brittany. Because Olivia had not had any treatment for IED before, it was not surprising that the stress of the court hearings would provoke her angry outbursts, which only confirmed to others that she was a danger to her child and others. The child protective services agency did not arrange for psychological and psychiatric evaluations of Olivia as part of their investigation. They were therefore deprived of valuable information that might have helped them develop a protection plan that incorporated psychiatric care for Olivia's IED and a more productive resolution of the Ann-Olivia conflict. Unfortunately, as it is with virtually every child protection services agency in the United States, these workers were overwhelmed by the volume of cases and lack of resources with which they had to cope each day. As a result, a well-developed protection plan, valid for Olivia's treatment needs, was not completed. The final, tragic outcome was Brittany's death.

Epilogue

Olivia confessed to the police that she had killed Brittany. She was confined in the county jail until trial. I was retained by her public defender and found that, although she suffered from intermittent explosive disorder, she was able to recognize right from wrong at the time of her daughter's death. Because the defense did not enter an insanity plea, Olivia was not evaluated by the state's forensic psychological or psychiatric examiners. The public defender agreed with her client's request to plead guilty and contacted the prosecutor to bargain for the best possible case disposition. Olivia received a 15-year sentence.

17

Psychopathic Mother, Financial Type

Pauline

Pauline hung up the telephone after the caller threatened her life. She was afraid because she knew the man well. They had once been lovers, and he had loaned her money many times over the years to cover her gambling debts and other expenses. She had promised to pay him back but never had. He said she owed him $10,000 and had 30 days to pay off her loan. She believed his threats because he had severely beaten her when they had lived together. She had protested that she was broke after she'd sold her car to settle her other debts, but the man told her that was her problem. He had said that she was being watched each day in case she tried to escape the city. She *was* broke and had no idea how she was going to pay.

As she nervously smoked a cigarette and had a second glass of whiskey, her 12-year-old son, Benjamin, entered their apartment. He was home from school. When he saw his mother drinking again in the afternoon, he went to his bedroom to leave her alone. He knew if he criticized her drinking as he had done before, his mother would get angry and hit him again. He told Pauline he had homework for a test tomorrow, a lie that she accepted without comment. She was too preoccupied with how she was going to find enough money to survive.

The next day after she got home from work at the casino restaurant, Benji was not there, even though it was nearly dinnertime. She knew that he was often at the arcades playing video games or hanging out on the beach with some of his friends. At 9:00 in the evening, he still was not home. She thought that Benji might have run away again, as he had twice earlier in the year after they had had arguments about her drinking and the men she would sometimes bring home late.

They had fought that morning when she did not get out of bed to fix him breakfast. They had not spoken since. She was about to call the police to report her son missing again when Benji walked in. She demanded to know where he had been, but he did not reply. She asked again, and her son screamed "What do you care, you're never home!" In truth, she really did not care about him and had not for as long as she could remember.

Benji had come back into her life nearly 4 years previously after her parents, who had raised him from birth, had died in an automobile accident. The money that Pauline had inherited from their estate had long since disappeared in vacations, parties, and the pockets of some of her previous live-in boyfriends. Benji did, however, have a $50,000 trust fund, which he would receive when he was 21. Pauline was prohibited from withdrawing from the account but was the beneficiary if her son died before he reached adulthood.

Pauline was an only child. Her father, who'd become a wealthy business executive, and her mother, a former airline attendant, had married later in life. Growing up, Pauline was spoiled by her parents. She had lived in a huge house with a live-in maid and had all the toys, dolls, and clothes she wanted. Pauline loved being the center of attention and knew that her girlfriends were jealous of the wealth that her family had.

In the elementary and middle grades of the local private school she attended, Pauline was the leader of her childhood and adolescent girlfriends. She was always the first of her group to try whatever she thought would be a new, exciting experience. Pauline would then brag to her friends about what she had done and challenge them to copy her. She thought it was fun to manipulate them by designating which would be her best friend on the basis of their duplicating her latest adventure.

Pauline was 9 when she shoplifted for the first time. Her girlfriends soon followed suit. Pauline was still 9 years old when she was caught by an employee. Pauline's father met alone with the store owner, a business associate of his, and persuaded him that it was all a misunderstanding that would be very embarrassing to the family. He offered to reimburse the store's losses. Pauline was punished by being grounded in her bedroom for the entire weekend. She did not complain because there she had her own television, popular movies on tape, private telephone line, and video games. Her mother had wanted a more severe consequence for Pauline, but her father called her crime a childhood prank.

Pauline was 11 years old when she sampled her mother's predinner mixed drink of vodka with orange juice. She liked it. Pauline told her girlfriends about her cocktail and challenged them to drink with her at the next pajama sleepover at her house. At the party, Pauline became intoxicated. Though she had a headache the next day, she had liked the effects of the alcohol.

She was 12 years old when she was the first in the group to have a real boyfriend and begin sexual experimentation. He had wanted to have intercourse, but Pauline refused; that was too fast for her at 12. Three boyfriends later, at age 14, she became the first in her group to get pregnant. She did not tell her friends about that adventure. She felt she had been stupid to get pregnant and did not trust her classmates to keep it a secret. When she told her parents of her condition, they exploded at her, then began blaming each other for failing to keep her a virgin. She told them she had not informed the adolescent boy of her pregnancy. Her parents decided to keep the pregnancy a secret and arranged an out-of-town abortion.

Over the next 2 years, Pauline's parents would have heated arguments with her over curfew violations or late-night escapes from their home. When she came home drunk and disheveled one morning at 3 A.M. during the Christmas holidays, they'd had enough. Her parents enrolled her in a boarding school the following semester. In retribution, Pauline became pregnant within 3 months. She was 16 when she discovered she'd conceived Benjamin. By the time she told her parents of her condition, the time limit for a legal termination of the pregnancy had passed. She was surprised at their reaction: They were not going to bail her out. She would have to give birth.

Pauline was 17 when she gave birth to Benji. Although her pregnancy became the subject of much gossip at the country club, her parents tried to minimize the damage to their family reputation by having Pauline admitted to an out-of-town hospital. At her parents' insistence, she received excellent prenatal care. Pauline did not like being pregnant; it was not the adventure she thought it would be. When she delivered Benji, she was glad that her ordeal was over, but she found that she was not overwhelmed with maternal feelings. She held her baby in her arms but was pleased when her mother would feed or change him.

Pauline returned to the boarding school to finish the last three semesters of her high school education while her mother took care of Benji. Thomas, the 18-year-old father of the baby, was relieved when Pauline's parents told him that they preferred to raise Benji because they could give him all the advantages of their wealth. He never told his parents.

Pauline saw her son on holidays and long weekends when she was home from school. During the summer, she made up the credits she'd failed during the academic year. She was content to let her parents raise Benji; he was the son they'd never had. They spoiled him just as they had their daughter. Pauline finally graduated from high school with mediocre grades, but when she received F's in three of her four college courses, she dropped out of college. Her parents were not surprised.

Pauline did not return home to stay. She spent a month with her parents, occasionally taking care of Benji, who by then was almost 4 years old. She declared that she wanted to move to one of the state's beach communities because she wanted to get a full-time job and get her own place to live. She told her parents that once she was settled in, they could bring Benji to live with her. By now, her parents realized that Pauline had little interest in caring for their grandson. They suggested that Benji could stay with them and that Pauline could visit whenever she liked. Pauline agreed to their plan and moved out the next day. Benji did not live with his mother on a full-time basis for the next 6 years, but he and Pauline would see each other during holidays and occasional weekends when Pauline's parents would bring him to visit the beach.

Pauline did not receive any financial help from her parents once she moved away except for occasional never-repaid loans that she requested when she was between paychecks. As she had so few vocational skills but was an attractive, superficially personable woman, she was employed at a series of restaurants and retail stores that dotted the coastal highway. She usually would work for a few months before she would be accused of stealing money or merchandise from her employer. Often she was able to talk her way out of trouble; however, at age 23, she did receive a disposition of fines and restitution for petty theft. A year later she was charged with larceny under $5,000 when she assisted one of her boyfriends in the burglary of the store where she worked. She and her public defender worked out a plea agreement to a misdemeanor and a fine. Once her criminal record appeared on preemployment background checks, local employers refused to hire her.

She was too broke to move to another city, and her parents had stopped giving her loans that they knew would never be repaid. Pauline turned to topless dancing. She already knew many of the people who worked in the clubs. She never told her parents how she now paid her bills because she hoped that after a while they would lend her money once again. Pauline was always short of cash; she loved video poker.

After work, which would end around 2:00 A.M., she would go parties where alcohol and drugs were in full supply. Although she was not a steady drinker, she would occasionally drive home intoxicated and was cited twice for driving under the influence. She became more enmeshed in the adult entertainment culture and would often have brief relationships with men who worked as bouncers, assistants, or managers of the clubs where she would dance. Some would live with her for periods of time. Many of the men had serious drug problems and would steal from her to feed their addictions.

Though she never really enjoyed topless dancing, she did like the easy money she could make. One month when she did not have enough money for rent, she finally agreed to have sex for money; soon she had regular male clients, until she was arrested for prostitution by an undercover policeman. Pauline would refuse to perform in pornographic videos that would be offered to her; she did not want a permanent record of what she was doing during this phase of her life.

Pauline was 28 when her parents died in an automobile accident. Benji, who had not been in the car, was now 10 years old. As she drove home, she thought of what she might inherit. Her parents' death would solve her financial troubles and allow her to stop dancing in clubs. She began spending the money in her head: a new car, a beachfront condominium, and vacations like the ones she had had as a child.

The attorney calculated that the estate was worth about $150,000, considerably less than Pauline had expected. It was in this meeting that she discovered that her parents had established a trust fund for Benjamin. The bank was designated as the executor of the trust until his 21st birthday, when the money would be his. Until he reached that age, Pauline was the beneficiary. When the papers for the house and estate were finally signed, Pauline and Benji moved to the condominium she bought with her inheritance.

Pauline put Benji in the local public elementary school and spent most of her days on the beach, gambling in the casinos, or hanging out with her friends from the clubs in the afternoons. Though her son liked living in the new condo for the first year they were together, he began to be oppositional and sullen with his mother. He was an intelligent boy who had done well in school, but without his mother's reliable supervision and direction, his grades began to drop.

Benji would often come home from school to find his mother sitting on the balcony smoking cigarettes with a new boyfriend, who'd often be smoking marijuana. Sometimes, Benji would enter an empty apartment and then not be able to find Pauline at the condo's pool or beach. At first she would apologize for not being home after he got out of school, but by their second year living together, he knew her promises to be a better mother were empty.

Pauline's money ran out about 2 years after her parents died. When she had to sell the condominium because she could not afford the monthly payments, the sale left her with less than $10,000. She owed more on her luxury car than it was worth. Benji was not happy when she told him they had to move to a smaller, less elegant apartment. That night he ran away for the first time. Pauline and her son were living parallel lives just as they had when she was at the beach and Benji was residing with his grandparents.

When Pauline was forced to go back to work after her money ran out, she did not return to topless dancing. She found work as a waitress at one of the casino's restaurants. On smoke breaks, between shifts, and after work, Pauline could be found in the casino playing the video poker machines.

Benji was expelled in the fifth grade for repeated truancy and talking back to his teachers. He was now 12 years old. When the principal reached Pauline on her cell phone, she told the woman that her son would not obey her, either. It was the truth: He barely responded to her furtive efforts to reestablish her parental authority by yelling at him. He would just tune her out and leave the apartment sullenly. He'd become even more oppositional over the previous 2 months because he despised his mother's newest live-in, unemployed, drug-smoking boyfriend, Cal. Cal felt the same way about Benji, whom he considered to be a spoiled, whiny brat.

Two days after Pauline received the life-threatening phone call, she was lying in bed with Cal worrying about how she was going to pay off her debts. He knew about Benji's trust fund; she had told him one night when she was drunk. Although she wanted to resolve her financial dilemma, Cal just wanted to make money.

Even after Pauline was incarcerated for Benji's death, she insisted that Cal was the one who first proposed to kill her son and split the trust fund. She adamantly maintained that he devised the plan and then forced her to go along with it. After they were arrested, however, Cal produced a secretly recorded audiotape revealing Pauline's step-by-step discussion of what they would do to her son.

They thought their plan was lethally simple. First, Pauline and Cal would stop living together so that they would not appear to be coconspirators. Then late one night, they would meet at Pauline's apartment, take her sleeping son from his bed, drown him in the surf of the ocean, dress him in one of his bathing suits, and leave the body on the beach to make his death look like a swimming accident. Before his body could be discovered in the morning, Pauline would call the police and report that her son had not slept at the apartment the previous night and that she was afraid he had run away from home again.

Cal and Pauline would establish alibis by deliberately being seen by others before and after the brief period it would take them to drown the boy. Cal would hang out in a bar with friends all night, and Pauline would work a 16-hour shift, leaving only for an hour on the pretense of checking to make sure her son was safely asleep at home. It would be during this interval that the murder would occur.

They thought that once the body was discovered, the medical examiner would not be able to establish an accurate time of death; thus their alibis would hold up. They anticipated that once the coroner had declared the death an accident, not a homicide, the bank would release Benji's trust fund to Pauline, and she would give Cal his share.

Pauline left the restaurant between her shifts and quickly drove to her apartment. She found that Cal had already arrived. Benji was soundly asleep in his bed. They wrapped him in a blanket, and Cal slung him over his shoulder. The boy was undersized for his age and easy to carry. He did not awaken when they laid him in the back seat of the car and drove to a remote section of the beach. Pauline carried a plastic bag containing his swimming suit.

Cal stopped the car, took Benji from the back seat, and walked toward the surf. Pauline hesitated at the shore. When the cold water hit Benji, he began to struggle with Cal, who turned and hissed at Pauline that he was not going to do this alone. Pauline grabbed one of Benji's arms and, without looking at him, pushed him deeper into the water. Cal put his hand on the back of the boy's neck and held him down. After Benji stopped moving, Cal told Pauline to get his swimming suit. She ran to the car, grabbed the bag, and returned to her son's body. She stared dumbly at his naked body. Cal yanked the bag from her hand, put the swimming suit on Benji, and demanded that she help him carry the boy back into the shallow surf. They left him face down in the sand.

Benji was found early that morning by beach walkers. The police and the medical examiner were immediately suspicious and thought that he had been killed. After many heated questions by the detectives, Pauline burst into tears and said that Cal had forced her to kill her son so that he could get Benji's trust fund. She told them that Cal terrified her and had threatened to kill her after she got the inheritance if she did not go along with his plan.

The police arrested Cal that morning at his motel room. When they arrived, he knew that Pauline had implicated him in Benji's death and that he would be arrested. He was an experienced criminal who had been in prison twice before. He knew what the next few hours would be like, but he was prepared: The audiotape he'd secretly made of his planning with Pauline was locked in the courtesy safe of his room. The tape was his leverage to cut the best deal he could. When he got to the police station, he was formally arrested on suspicion of murder. He refused to make a statement and requested an attorney. When a public defender arrived, he gave the attorney his room key and the combination to the safe. Cal would become the state's star witness if the case ever came to trial.

Case Analysis

The women who come under the category of psychopathic mothers display much darker, more sinister motives for their filicidal behavior than mothers in other categories. In cases such as Pauline's, once the reason for the child's murder is known, it is difficult to understand how a mother could have so coldly, deliberately, and selfishly terminated the life of her child. It is extremely difficult to have sympathy for a woman (or man) who kills his or her child for financial gain; indeed, intense anger at the perpetrator is the most common reaction of our society in these cases. To my knowledge, Nadeau (1997) was the first to propose this motive in a classification of maternal filicide. The antisocial patterns of the women in this category are antithetical to our society's notions of traditional feminine, maternal characteristics of mothers and women. Analysis of Pauline's case, and those of Samantha and Rhonda in the next two chapters, may provide some explanations for these heinous filicides and point to interventions that might have prevented their murders of their children.

Maternal Filicide Risk Matrix Analysis

The risk matrix for Pauline is shown in table 17.1.

Prepregnancy Stage
Prior to her pregnancy with Benji, Pauline had become pregnant and had a parent-endorsed abortion when she was only 14 years old. Her precocious sexual activity was a prominent risk factor; however, termination of her first pregnancy eliminated the possibility of Pauline committing maternal neonaticide or infanticide. Although she did show some self-protective behavior by refusing to have intercourse at age 12 with her first boyfriend, she did not maintain her resistance over the next 2 years, as she broadened her sexual experience. It is notable that Pauline felt that she had been stupid to become pregnant at

Table 17.1
Maternal Filicide Risk Matrix: Pauline

Factor	Pre-P	P/D	EP	LP	PI
Individual					
Age at current pregnancy	R	R	R	R	P
Intelligence level	P	P	P	P	P
Education level	R	R	R	R	P
Medical status	P	P	P	P	R
Emotional status	P	P	P	P	R
Trauma history	P	P	P	P	P
Maternal attitudes	R	R	R	R	R
Family of Origin					
Mother's parenting	P	P	P	P	R
Father's parenting	P	P	P	P	R
Marital/family stability	P	P	P	P	
Situational					
Marital/partner status	P	R	R	R	R
Financial status	R	R	R	R	R
Child-care status	—	—	—	—	P
Infant's temperament	—	P	P	P	P

Note: R = Risk; P = Protective; Pre-P = Prepregnancy; P/D = Pregnancy/delivery; EP = Early postpartum; LP = Late postpartum; PI = Postinfancy.

14. Her reaction to her unintended pregnancy suggested that her maternal attitudes were then negative and narcissistic: A baby would be an inconvenience to her lifestyle, which involved the selfish pursuit of immediate gratification. If she had given birth following her first pregnancy, it is likely that the indifferent, negative attachment that she subsequently displayed toward Benji would have been manifested with the fetus she carried at age 14.

Although Pauline's emotional stability did not reflect serious mood disorders, substance use or abuse, or childhood-adolescent psychotic patterns, there were early signs of antisocial-psychopathic behavior in the way in which she manipulated her girlfriends and sought excitement through orchestrated shoplifting and other delinquent activity. Pauline did not experience any significant traumas during her childhood and adolescent years, such as child abuse or neglect, parental loss or abandonment, serious medical problems, or physical or sexual violence.

Pauline's parents might be faulted for overindulging and spoiling their only child; however, each acted in ways that he or she thought were best for their daughter. Having been informed that they could not have any more children, it was not surprising that they used their financial resources to give Pauline the kind of childhood that neither of them had had. Throughout Pauline's childhood and adolescence prior to her pregnancy with Benji, her mother and father remained together and demonstrated for her a model of marital stability and unity. According to Pauline, neither parent had significant difficulties with substance abuse, nor were they verbally or physically violent with each other. In contrast to the mothers and fathers that have been described in many other cases in this book, Pauline's parents provided a stable, dependable, protective environment for her. Although there were things that they might have done differently at various points in Pauline's life prior to her pregnancy with Benji, her family of origin elements were protective factors for her.

Pauline's situational factors during her prepregnancy stage were consistently negative. Prior to her conception of Benji, she had become intimate with three adolescent boys, resulting in her first pregnancy at age 14. Once she discovered she was pregnant, however, she did not tell the prospective father; rather, she first disclosed her condition to her parents. She agreed with them that they would keep her conception a family secret. Pauline's decision not to tell the partner who impregnated her reflected the superficial, distrusting relationship she had with him. It is also noteworthy that she did not turn to her girlfriends for emotional support by telling one or more of them that she was pregnant. She did not trust her friends to keep quiet, indicating that she saw them as girls who would be vindictive and vicious toward her—not the basis of true friendship. Prior to her pregnancy with Benji, at age 16, Pauline would not have been able to provide monetarily for herself solely on her own efforts; thus her lack of financial stability would have been a risk factor for her.

Pregnancy/Delivery Stage
Pauline was only 16 when she discovered she had conceived for the second time. A second pregnancy before age 17 has been associated with increased risks for neonaticide and infanticide. Fearing her parents' rage at her becoming pregnant again, she delayed disclosing her condition to them until she was in her second trimester. She had planned to terminate this pregnancy as she had before, an indication that Pauline was not ready yet to be a mother. When her parents told her they would not allow her to terminate her pregnancy, Pauline appears to have transferred her anger at her parents onto her fetus.

It was fortunate that she did tell her parents that she was pregnant. Being away at school, she could have, like Edna in chapter 7, avoided contact with her parents through the semester and holidays, then delivered the child without their knowledge. Because she would have still been a minor when Benji was born, she would have needed parental consent to have the child adopted, thus increasing the likelihood of neonaticide as the tragic outcome to her pregnancy. In contrast to Edna, who struggled with ambivalence throughout her pregnancy, Pauline had no such dilemma: She had no interest in carrying her fetus to full term. If she had been unable to obtain an abortion, she likely would have either discarded Benji in a remote location or committed neonaticide shortly after his delivery. By telling her parents she was pregnant, Pauline was forced to ensure that she had adequate prenatal medical care, which she likely would not have sought on her own. Throughout her pregnancy, her negative reaction toward her fetus never changed.

When Pauline disclosed her pregnancy to her parents, they acted responsibly and protectively toward their grandchild's health and well-being. They immediately had Pauline examined by their family physician, who confirmed that she was pregnant and well into her second trimester. In contrast to her first pregnancy, this time her mother and father decided to weather the embarrassment of having an unwed, pregnant teenage daughter.

By this stage in Pauline's life, her parents appeared to have had inklings that their daughter had become a self-centered, self-absorbed, immature adolescent who would not accept responsibility for her mistakes and failures. Their perceptions of their daughter's poor maternal attitudes toward Benji were confirmed during the early and late postpartum stages of their grandson's life. Returning Pauline to boarding school provided a justification for her parents to avoid a confrontation about her indifferent bonding to her newborn.

Pauline's relationship with Thomas, the father of Benji, was as deficient as had been her relationship with the first young man by whom she had become pregnant. Thomas's relief at being able to avoid his paternal responsibilities suggested that he might not have been a reliable, nurturing parent to Benji nor a supportive partner to Pauline. Her financial stability had not changed from the preceding stage, as she was still reliant on her parents for her subsistence. If she had had to care for Benji by herself as a high school dropout without job skills, she would have had to rely on public assistance or minimum-wage employment to survive—financial factors that have been associated with risks of maternal infanticide and filicide.

Early Postpartum and Late Postpartum Stages

As illustrated in table 17.1, Pauline's individual, family of origin, and situational factors during Benji's first year of life did not change from her pregnancy/delivery stage. Though her intelligence, health, and emotional stability were protective factors during these stages, she never did develop positive maternal attitudes toward her infant son. Until Benji's first birthday, Pauline continued her boarding school education; thus she and Benji had few opportunities to develop a mother-baby relationship. Pauline did not appear to be in a rush to take care of her infant. She did not protest when her parents suggested that she return to school. She could have come home on weekends to see her son rather than waiting until semester breaks and holidays. She was able to avoid additional interaction with Benji by attending summer school to make up the classes she had deliberately failed during the regular semesters.

Pauline's mother and father became the parents to Benji as they arranged for their daughter to continue her high school and college education. Because they assumed parental responsibility for Benji, their grandson was exposed to loving, supportive, nurturing adults. Though their enthusiastic care of Benji was good for his well-being, by taking over the child care of their grandson they may not have been acting in the best interests of their daughter. When their daughter became a mother, her parents indulged her once again by preventing her from facing the natural consequences of her unintended pregnancy.

Her parents' assumption of parenting responsibility for Benji also had consequences for their relationship with Pauline. She felt her parents' shift in preference away from her and toward Benji. As a child and adolescent who had been spoiled and overindulged, to be supplanted in her parents' favor by her own baby did not engender positive maternal feelings in Pauline: Her son was a competitor with her for her parents' love. Unfortunately for Pauline during Benji's first year, she did not confront her parents about the issue. Instead, she retreated to the boarding school, which for her was a much more enjoyable, carefree existence. However, her absence only distanced her more from Benji, and, as her parents' relationship with her son deepened, she became more resentful and rejecting of her baby. During the early and late postpartum stages of Benji's life, he and his mother became more like distant, rival siblings than parent and child. After Pauline's parents became Benji's de facto parents, Pauline was treated as the older sister to her mother and father's late-life surprise baby.

Pauline had no relationship with her baby's father, Thomas, who had jumped at the chance to voluntarily terminate his parental rights to Benji. According to Pauline, they never dated again. She stated that they had never intended to marry nor discussed long-term plans. Neither was in an educational, vocational, or financial position to start and maintain a family. Benji was an entirely unintended pregnancy. Apart from their physical couplings, they had few other shared interests. Their relationship was what would be expected of adolescents that age, essentially two high school children temporarily dating. When Pauline became pregnant, they did not discuss marriage with her parents, and Thomas never told his parents. There would be no joint family discussion of how Benji's birth and life would be managed and nurtured. Pauline's parents took charge of the crisis, and Benji's mother and father returned to being the irresponsible teenagers they were before he was born.

Postinfancy Stage
Before Benji was 4 years old, her mother and father had realized that Pauline was not going to be a dependable, nurturing mother. Once she moved to the beach, the frequency of her contact with her son followed the pattern she had established when she was in high school and college. As she became an adult with full-time employment, she often used the false excuse of work to escape having to return to her parents' house and be with Benji. By her repeated absence and avoidance, Pauline ensured that she and her son would continue to live emotionally distant, parallel lives. Given her inadequate, negative maternal

attitudes, it was likely best for Benji that he was raised by relatives who loved, nurtured, and indulged him.

When Pauline's parents died, the flaws that were evident in her absent, indifferent bonding to Benji became readily apparent. Over the years following her son's birth, Pauline's emotional stability deteriorated as she became more involved with alcohol and pursued a self-indulgent irresponsible lifestyle. Much of her behavior suggested the development of antisocial personality disorder: stealing from employers, criminal conspiracy and accessory to burglary, deliberate nonpayment of debts, association with socially marginal groups and individuals, and episodic prostitution. By engaging in serial promiscuity with drug-abusing men who likely also were indiscriminately promiscuous, she substantially increased her risk of contracting sexually transmitted diseases that would have jeopardized her health and medical well-being.

After Benji was born, Pauline was assaulted more than once by the man who had threatened her life prior to her son's death. Notably, she did not characterize the previous attack by the man as a trauma. Rather, she saw his assault and subsequent threats as normal exchanges between men and women within the culture in which she lived. Though she did indicate being scared by the man's threats, she did not otherwise display or report symptoms suggestive of posttraumatic stress disorder during her evaluation with me.

When she was told that her parents had died, she estimated the extent of her inheritance, then thought of her parental obligations to Benji. She resolved her dilemma of unexpected motherhood by deciding that Benji would prefer the same lifestyle that she would now have with her parents' money. She did not contemplate what her son wanted or needed to become a mature, responsible adult. After they returned to the beach, she purchased a luxury car and expensive condominium. Rather than carefully managing their inheritance, Pauline used the money to take a 2-year vacation from work and responsibility. At first, Benji seemed to enjoy living with her, though after years of living with his dependable, responsible grandparents, he quickly appreciated that his mother was only interested in herself.

To the outside observer, it was difficult to see how Benji's arrival had altered Pauline's behavior at all. When he was at school, she slept in late, drank alcohol with her friends, or wasted the day gambling on video poker machines. She continued to bring home men and was indifferent to the impact of her promiscuity on her young son. When he rather quickly realized that his mother was not dependable or self-sacrificing for him, Benji's resentment of Pauline flourished. He began acting-out at elementary school, engaged in truancy, and argued with his mother about her drinking and live-in boyfriends. Pauline did not seriously contemplate what she was doing wrong.

Pauline's postinfancy situational factors remained unchanged from the preceding stages. She associated with partners with whom it was unlikely she could develop productive, long-lasting relationships. When she was in high school and college, she had liaisons with men who might have developed into mature, responsible partners for her and her son. However, once she became an adult living on her own, the quality of the men with whom she associated deteriorated as her antisocial patterns became more pronounced. Although the men she lived with would steal from and occasionally beat her, she would continue to link up with the same sorts of partners. Her financial stability never improved from previous stages and was now jeopardized by her compulsion for gambling. Ultimately, her maternal filicide was based in situational risk factors: financial panic facilitated by a criminally oriented, greedy partner who was as psychopathic as Pauline was.

Relevant Research: Women With Antisocial Personality Disorder

Antisocial personality disorder (ASPD) is defined by the American Psychiatric Association (2000) as a pervasive pattern of disregard for and violation of the rights of others since the age of 15, as illustrated by a number of different behaviors that include criminal acts, deceit and repeated lying, impulsivity, repeated physical aggression, reckless disregard for others' safety, repeated failures to honor financial and/or work obligations, and/or lack of remorse for hurting or victimizing others. The individual must be at least 18 years old at the time of diagnosis and must also have displayed, prior to age 15, symptoms of conduct disorder (e.g., aggression against persons or animals, property destruction or theft, serious violations of parental/school rules before age 13, etc.).

Within the general population ASPD is diagnosed in approximately 3% of males, roughly three times the rate that has been determined in female samples. Among personality disorders found within the American culture, ASPD ranks third in prevalence, behind obsessive-compulsive and paranoid types (Grant et al., 2004). ASPD is considered to have a chronic course that may abate somewhat in the individual's fourth decade of life.

Because the diagnosis requires the presence of certain symptoms prior to and after age 15, a number of researchers have attempted to track the pathway of early childhood behavior problems into adulthood. For example, among an urban sample of late adolescent boys and girls, 29% of those who had had at least one contact with the police had been under age 13 at the time (White & Piquero, 2004). Smith and Farrington (2004) found that across three generations there were continuities of antisocial behavior; that is, antisocial males tended to partner with antisocial females, who in turn tended to produce children with behavior and conduct problems. Foley et al. (2004) discovered that mothers who had had stepfathers had higher rates of antisocial personality disorder and alcoholism than mothers from intact families.

In another national study of three-generation households, Black et al. (2002) reported that among adolescent mothers, maternal abuse and clinical depression were significantly associated with childhood externalizing behavior problems characteristic of conduct disorder. In a prospective study of boys and girls followed longitudinally from ages 12 to 42 months, the interaction between child noncompliance and rejection as a maternal parenting style resulted in significantly higher acting-out patterns among the young children of both genders (Shaw et al., 1998).

Because the diagnosis of ASPD includes many criteria that involve the legal system, significantly higher prevalence rates for both men and women have been found among prison inmates, substance abuse treatment center clients, and forensic hospital patients (Cottler, Price, Compton, & Mager, 1995; Hesselbrock, Meyer, & Keener, 1985; Salekin, Rogers, & Sewell, 1997). For example, in a sample of male and female alcoholics, Hesselbrock et al. (1985) discovered that nearly 50% of the men and 20% of the women met the diagnostic criteria for ASPD. In a study of homeless individuals, North, Smith, and Spitznagel (1993) found ASPD prevalence rates of 25% and 10% for men and women, respectively. Among a sample of cocaine-dependent women, 76% met diagnostic criteria for ASPD (Rutherford, Alterman, Cacciola, & McKay, 1999).

Women and mothers with ASPD are an understudied population, especially within the general community (Cale & Lilienfeld, 2003). Some authors have argued that ASPD has been underdiagnosed in females because the criteria for conduct disorder and ASPD reflect aggressive behavior, which is more characteristic of men than of women. Numerous studies of homicide and other violent acts have demonstrated that men commit such crimes at significantly higher rates. For example, in a review of the literature on gender differences in children and adolescents, girls between ages 5 and 13 displayed fewer conduct problems when compared with boys within the same age range (Silverthorn & Frick, 1999); thus the girls would be much less likely to subsequently qualify for an adolescent diagnosis of conduct disorder or an adult diagnosis of ASPD.

In contrast to the criminal and violence-based criteria of the DSM-IV-TR for the diagnosis of ASPD (American Psychiatric Association, 2000), other descriptions of the disorder have emphasized the individual's attitudes, emotional expression, superficial interpersonal relationships, social learning deficits, and characteristic defense mechanisms in addition to patently aggressive behavior. For example, the World Health Organization's International Classification of Diseases (World Health Organization, 1992) specifies the diagnostic criteria for dissocial personality disorder as lack of empathy, persistent attitude of irresponsibility and disregard for social norms, incapacity to maintain enduring relationships, low tolerance for frustration, failure to profit from prior experience and punishment, persistent irritability, and marked proneness to blame others when caught or criticized in a social situation. These characteristics appear to be consistent with the childhood, adolescent, and adult patterns displayed by Pauline in her relationships with her girlfriends, middle school and high school boyfriends, and transient live-in male partners after she gave birth to Benji.

A second approach to the description and classification of antisocial behavior has been the characterization of psychopathy, a term first proposed by Cleckley (1941/1998). Psychopathic individuals have been described along interpersonal, affective-emotional, and behavioral dimensions (Hemphill & Hart, 2003). Interpersonally, such persons display manipulative, deceitful, and arrogant patterns. Their emotional and affective expressions are highly variable and superficial. Psychopathic individuals have great difficulty developing close, meaningful feelings for others. They do not seem to experience anxiety, guilt, or empathy as others do. Behaviorally, their actions are typically impulsive, sensation seeking, and irresponsible. These descriptors appear to apply closely to Pauline's behavior in childhood, adolescence, and adulthood.

Over the past 20 years, the clinical, empirical, and psychometric study of psychopathy has been a central feature in the understanding, explanation, prediction, and treatment of antisocial behavior in males and females. A number of psychological tests and/or specialized scales have been developed to empirically assess the presence of psychopathy, including the Hare Psychopathy Checklist-Revised (PCL-R; Hare, 1991), the Antisocial Practices (ASP) content scale of the Minnesota Multiphasic Personality Inventory-2 (MMPI-2; Butcher, Dahlstrom, Graham, Tellegen, & Kaemmer, 1989), the Antisocial Features (ANT) scale of the Personality Assessment Inventory (PAI; Morey, 1991), and the Psychopathy Personality Inventory (PPI; Lilienfeld & Andrews, 1996).

Almost all of the research on psychopathy has focused on adult males (Cale & Lilienfeld, 2002; Salekin, Rogers, Ustad, & Sewell, 1998). There have been a few studies involving females and mothers. For example, in a sample of 103 adult female prison inmates assessed with the PCL-R, 15% could be categorized as psychopaths using the cutoff score for males recommended by the test's author (Salekin et al., 1997). The Antisocial (ANT) and Aggression (AGG) scales of the PAI were found to be among the best predictors of future criminal recidivism in a sample of adult female inmates (Salekin et al., 1998).

When the PPI was administered to a sample of university undergraduate men and women, no gender differences were found (Hamburger, Lilienfeld, & Hogben, 1996). However, in another PPI study with a similar undergraduate sample, men scored significantly higher than women on the following PPI subscales: Machiavellian Egocentricity, Coldheartedness, Fearlessness, Impulsive Nonconformity, Stress Immunity, and Blame Externalization (Lilienfeld & Andrews, 1996). Mothers of children under 2 years old who were categorized as antisocial on the basis of high scores on the ASP scale of the MMPI-2 were observed to be less understanding and more hostile and harsh in their parenting practices than mothers who scored lower on the scale (Bosquet & Egeland, 2000). Summarizing the literature on the psychometric measurement of psychopathy in females, Cale and Lilienfeld (2003) concluded that much work remains to be done before confident conclusions can be drawn.

Persons with antisocial and psychopathic disorders have generally been considered to be very difficult to treat successfully, principally because they experience little guilt or anxiety that might prompt them to seek mental health services (Hemphill & Hart, 2003). Commonly, persons with psychopathy and ASPD are involuntarily referred for treatment following involvement with the legal system; as a result they often have little motivation to change their behavior (Brodsky, 2005). Most authors recommend that the most successful interventions will be those that are implemented when early signs and symptoms are initially observed.

Kazdin (2002) has described a variety of empirically validated treatments for childhood and adolescent conduct disorder that emphasize retraining the parents' behavior (parent management training; PMT), coordinating and altering the various interpersonal and institutional environments of the child (multisystemic therapy; MST), modifying the problem-solving and interpersonal perceptions of the child (problem-solving skills training; PSST), and changing the communication and interaction patterns within the child's family (functional family therapy; FFT). PMT approaches appear to be most effective when they are provided to small groups of parents who reside within the same neighborhood (Kazdin, 2002), though they are less effective with severe and chronic forms of conduct disorder (Ruma, Burke, & Thompson, 1996).

MST approaches have also shown promise, even with seriously disturbed groups of juvenile offenders and abusive/neglectful families (Henggeler, Schoenwald, Borduin, Rowland, & Cunningham, 1998). PPST approaches have also demonstrated reductions in children's aggressive and conduct-disordered behaviors at home, in school, and within the community (Kazdin, 2000; Pepler & Rubin, 1991). FFT approaches have not been studied as extensively as PMT, MST, and PPST have, but some research has reported alterations in conduct problems among delinquent youths (Gordon, Arbuthnot, Gustafson, & McGreen, 1988; Morris, Alexander, & Turner, 1991). Regardless of the treatment approach, however, it is critical for the clinician to engage the child's parents and family in the therapeutic process. Without such involvement, it is unlikely that the child will attend, participate, or profit from the therapy (Kazdin, 2002).

Suggestions for Prevention at Risk Intervention Points

1. *Pauline's father met alone with the store owner, a business associate of his, and persuaded him that it was all a misunderstanding that would be very embarrassing to the family. He offered to reimburse the store's losses. Pauline was punished by being grounded in her bedroom for the entire weekend.*

Although Pauline's mother wanted a more severe consequence for her daughter, her husband interpreted the event in light of his own (male) history. As indicated in the section on relevant research, delinquent behavior by girls under age 13 is a significant risk factor for subsequent adolescent conduct disorder, which is in turn the precursor of adult antisocial personality disorder. At age 9, it is unlikely that Pauline would have been perceived as a budding criminal, but her father's solution of protecting her (and his family) from a more public disposition of the crime taught Pauline that money and influence could be used to escape responsibility for misdeeds.

A common resolution that many parents employ when their child shop-lifts is to have their son or daughter apologize directly to the store manager or owner, then pay restitution from their allowance or extra household chores. Pauline's weekend in her room was actually a brief vacation. Time-out and grounding work as punishments only if they are undesired consequences for the child. If her father had conducted a more thorough investigation and discovered that Pauline was there with her friends, he might have contacted their parents and uncovered the children's shoplifting ring. If he had put his daughter's long-term well-being ahead of his own temporary embarrassment, Pauline might have learned a valuable lesson in personal responsibility.

2. Three boyfriends later, at age 14, she became the first in her group to get pregnant . . . her parents . . . arranged an out-of-town abortion.

If her parents had been tougher with Pauline's shoplifting, that conse-quence would not have necessarily prevented her first pregnancy. However, their reaction (and what Pauline was learning) was highly similar: Protection of the family's public image is paramount. Pauline realized that she could ex-ploit her parents' self-induced vulnerability by using disclosure of her delin-quency as leverage against parental controls. As illustrated by her subsequent irresponsible behavior, she felt immune to her parents' limits. Although she believed that she won these adolescent-parent conflicts, she unfortunately lost the long-term benefits of becoming a law-abiding, socially responsible adult. Her parents' efforts to protect their public image also had ripples beyond their immediate family.

By keeping her pregnancy a secret from the prospective father's family, Pauline's parents were depriving them of the opportunity and right to decide the fetus's fate. The prospective father's family might have vigorously opposed termination of the pregnancy and offered to raise the child as a viable alter-native to abortion. Pauline's parents perhaps assumed that the other family would want to keep the secret hidden, just as they did. Instead, the boy's par-ents might have wanted to teach their child a more important lesson of per-sonal responsibility.

If Pauline's parents had been less concerned about their public image, a series of family therapy sessions might have helped them become aware of the severity of their daughter's delinquency and their role in its development. Be-cause of the seriousness and duration of Pauline's irresponsible behavior, pro-fessional services would have been warranted as an intervention. In the ses-sions, Pauline and her parents could have decided on reasonable birth control solutions to her precocious sexuality, which might have prevented her second pregnancy as an adolescent.

3. *Her parents enrolled her in a boarding school the following semester. In retribution, Pauline became pregnant within 3 months. . . .*

Once her parents finally acknowledged that Pauline was out of control, they unfortunately resolved their family crisis by further alienating their daughter through exile to a boarding school. Pauline punished them once again with the public embarrassment of having an unwed pregnant teenage daughter. To her surprise, they did not cave in and agree to her plans for abortion. Their decision to make Pauline carry the baby to full term did make her experience the natural consequences of her irresponsible act. They ensured that she and the fetus received excellent prenatal care.

By weathering their public embarrassment, her parents taught Pauline that they would no longer be blackmailed by her outrageous behavior. Unfortunately, they did not arrange for her to have prenatal mental health services, which might have helped her to resolve the bitter feelings toward her parents that she displaced onto her fetus. The negative maternal attitudes that she carried throughout her pregnancy were never altered once Benjamin was born. To this extent, Pauline's case is similar to that of Francine, the detached mother, resentful type, in chapter 8. If Pauline had been abandoned by her parents without support or resources, she might have resorted to infanticide as a solution to the weeks-long inconvenience of new motherhood. Fortunately for Benji, though not for the long-term moral development of Pauline, his grandparents assumed custody of his welfare.

Even though Pauline had her education to finish, she did not need to return to the boarding school. By sending her away, her parents were depriving her of many important learning opportunities. Her mother and father could have provided ample assistance to Pauline as the primary caretaker of her son, helping her out when she was at the local school, studying, or sleeping through the night. Her mother could have demonstrated many techniques of newborn care. Keeping Pauline at home would have given all three of them the shared project of Benji.

If Pauline had had daily contact with her son during his infant, toddler, preschool, and school-age years, it would have been very difficult for her to remain emotionally detached from her child. She and Benji would have had some positive experiences during those years, from which she might have developed more empathy for her son's welfare—an antidote to antisocial traits and attitudes. Additionally, Pauline would have had more opportunities to experience a sense of accomplishment and enhanced self-esteem as she learned that she could become a competent adult mother. Had her parents assisted Pauline's continuous mothering of Benji, they might have lessened the devastating impact of their premature deaths when Benji was 10. Both mother and child survivors would have had an existing relationship to help them overcome their loss.

> 4. *A year later she was charged with larceny under $5,000 when she assisted one of her boyfriends in the burglary of the store where she worked. She and her public defender worked out a plea agreement to a misdemeanor and a fine.*

Pauline's felony burglary and earlier thefts from the stores that had employed her were much more serious reenactments of the shoplifting she'd done as a preteen. By allowing her to plead to a misdemeanor and simply pay a fine, the court was unknowingly repeating her parents' shortsighted solution to her criminal behavior. Most important, another opportunity was lost to teach Pauline prosocial behavior.

As an alternative to a fine, Pauline might have learned more if the judge had sentenced her to an extended period of community service helping less fortunate persons. For example, she might have been ordered to complete 100 or 200 hours as a Head Start aide for underprivileged, indigent children or as an orderly in a pediatric burn unit. Compulsory assignments such as these would have had the additional benefit of placing her with responsible, caring adults who routinely put others' needs ahead of their own—another antidote to antisocial attitudes and traits. These experiences in turn might have altered her perception of her relationship with her son, prompted her to become a more responsible mother to Benji, and restored her relationship with her parents.

Epilogue

Pauline and Cal were charged as codefendants in the murder of Benji. Notably, Pauline is the only case in this book in which the filicidal mother had an accomplice. Because the child's murder for profit might have qualified as a capital offense, Cal bargained for a life sentence in exchange for his testimony and corroborating audiotape, which would convincingly implicate Pauline. Under the statutes in force at that time, he could be paroled from prison after serving less than 20 years. For 32-year-old Cal, this was an acceptable alternative to the death penalty or a life-without-parole sentence.

I conducted a forensic psychological assessment of Pauline at the request of her defense attorney. However, when the evaluation results confirmed her antisocial personality disorder, the lawyer decided not to rely on a mental health defense of insanity. She received a life-without-parole sentence. Pauline will die in prison.

18

Psychopathic Mother, Addicted Type

Samantha

Samantha rummaged through the dirty dishes and half-eaten food on the kitchen counters feverishly looking for her lighter. She wanted to have a few more hits on her crack pipe before her 9-year-old daughter, Camille, came home from school. She had been smoking crack all day and had left her apartment three times to get more drugs to smoke. She had gone through the money she'd made last night turning tricks in the cars of men that she would meet in the bars a few blocks away. They did not know Samantha had syphilis and HIV. Only her drug dealer, Stanley, knew her secret. When Samantha had told him she'd contracted the sexually transmitted diseases, he had refused to continue to exchange crack for sex with her. Because she could no longer use her body to get crack from Stanley, the preceding 6 months of Samantha's life had been a desperate search for money. Prostitution with strangers was the most reliable source of quick cash.

Samantha knew that her daughter was disgusted with her drug use. She had tried to quit many times, only to start up again after 1 or 2 days of self-imposed abstinence. In the preceding year her addiction had gotten worse, and her demand for crack had been out of control. There were times when she'd go for 2 days without food, smoking crack continuously until the rocks were gone.

About 3 hours later after Camille came home, Samantha was getting desperate. Her crack high was wearing off. She wanted more drugs, though she had no money. She had to call Stanley. Samantha hoped he'd give her a couple of rocks for manual sex—it was all she had to offer him.

She begged Stanley to come over with some crack, but when he refused, she said she'd do anything to get high. It was almost 11 P.M. by the time he knocked on her door. She rushed to let him in and grabbed his arm, which held a plastic bag of rock cocaine. He pulled away and told her he could not just give away $300 worth of drugs to her. He wanted something in return.

She stopped pacing the room and began to take off her clothes, but Stanley shook his head and walked to the door to leave. Samantha yelled out for him to stop and ran to grab him again. This time he turned and hit her across the face, threatening to beat her if she ever touched him again. He put his hand on the doorknob but hesitated to see whether she'd offer her last valuable asset: Camille. She told Stanley to stop again and told him that she'd do anything he wanted. He turned slowly, looked directly at her then nodded toward her daughter's bedroom door. Samantha furiously shook her head no. Stanley shrugged his shoulders, opened the door, and left.

Samantha held out for another 2 hours before she called Stanley again. He told her he would not come to her apartment unless he could get what he wanted. She told him to hurry up. When he arrived, angry but aroused, he moved toward Camille's bedroom door but stopped before entering. He looked back at Samantha, then tossed her a bag of crack cocaine after she nodded.

He went into Camille's room. Samantha rushed to the kitchen for her crack pipe and quickly lit up. She heard her daughter shout as she tried to fend off Stanley's advances, but Samantha didn't move. Soon Camille's bedroom was quiet. Samantha smoked all of the rocks before she peeked into her daughter's room. Camille was huddled in the corner with blood streaks on her thighs. Stanley was snoring in the bed. Samantha approached her daughter, but Camille shrank from her and swore at her to leave her alone. Samantha went to the couch and fell asleep, exhausted from her 3-day binge.

It was only 5 hours later when Samantha felt her daughter pushing her onto the floor. Camille was furious at her mother for sending Stanley into her room. She hit her mother on the face and screamed that she was going to school to tell her teacher what Samantha had done to her. As Camille opened the front door, Samantha leaped toward her and yelled that she wasn't going to tell anyone anything. She was terrified of being sent to prison. Camille was on the stair landing just outside the apartment when she told her mother again that she'd tell her teacher. In an agitated, anxious rage, Samantha lunged at her and pushed her down the stairs. Camille screamed as she tumbled down the steps but then was silent. The fall had broken her neck and killed her.

The elderly woman in the apartment next door, who would subsequently tell police she'd heard the entire argument, rushed to the top of the stairs and saw Camille's still, crumpled body on the landing below. She turned to see Samantha sitting on the floor of her apartment sobbing. Stanley, sleeping deeply, never left Camille's bedroom.

When the police arrived, Samantha quickly declared that Camille had had a terrible accident. The officers entered the apartment, found Stanley naked in Camille's bed, searched his clothes, and arrested him on charges of possession of crack cocaine. Later, he would also be charged with statutory rape of Camille following the forensic pathologist's examination of her body. The detectives interviewed Samantha, who repeated that her daughter's death was an accident. After the elderly neighbor told them what Camille had said before her mother pushed her down the stairs, Samantha was charged with murder and promoting prostitution of a minor.

Ten years earlier it would have been difficult to foresee the lives of Samantha and Camille ending so tragically. Samantha was the youngest of three children born to college-educated parents, who had been happily married for 34 years until her father's death 6 years earlier. During her pretrial evaluation with me, Samantha recalled that she had had a very happy childhood and adolescence. Samantha's older brother and sister had been excellent students, and she followed in their academic footsteps. She loved school and learning.

In high school she had had her first serious relationship with a young man. Roy was a year older than Samantha when they began dating in her sophomore year of high school. They dated until he left for college in another state. Though she went out on a few dates in her senior year, Samantha avoided developing any serious relationships because she looked forward to entering an out-of-state university.

When she started her freshman semester, she easily adapted to the academic demands of the school. She had a much more difficult time adjusting to the unsupervised, unlimited freedom that she had as a young adult college student.

Samantha lost her virginity at the end of her freshman year at the university. After the Christmas holidays, she'd begun to date Carter, a sophomore she'd met at a bar. He was more sexually experienced than she was, but he did not pressure her into intercourse until she said that she was ready. They rented a downtown hotel room away from the campus as part of a romantic weekend together. She recalled during her pretrial evaluation that the weekend was one of her most pleasant memories of her university years. Carter was a gentle and patient lover the first few of the many times they had sex that weekend. He wore condoms every time because he'd been clear with her that he was not interested in any surprise pregnancies. Samantha and Carter dated exclusively until they mutually ended their relationship when he decided to transfer to a college in his home state.

For the next 3 years, Samantha dated a number of other young men at the university, occasionally being intimate with some. When she had returned for her sophomore year, Samantha obtained a prescription for birth control pills, which she took without fail on a daily basis. Until she graduated at age 21, Samantha had only one unpleasant episode while she was dating. She had gone to a hotel with another young man in her class, and he attempted intercourse with her without using a condom. She refused. He became angry and tried to force himself into her, but she was able to escape into the hotel bathroom, then call the front desk for assistance with her luggage. Though she had no luggage other than an overnight case, she left with the porter, then took a taxi back to campus. The senior student never bothered her again.

After she graduated from college, she obtained employment as a salesperson in a company located in a large city in another state. Though she was well paid for her work, the job required long hours and a lot of travel. She spent many nights on the road alone in hotel rooms. She found that after a long days' work alcohol would help her to relax. She would sometimes worry that she might be drinking too much.

Samantha had her first experience with cocaine when she was 23 years old. She'd gone to a house party with Dexter, a fellow salesperson in the company whom she'd been dating for about 2 months. Samantha had heard of cocaine when she was at the university but had not ever seen anybody use it. Her classmates had told her that cocaine gave a pleasant rush of increased energy but was otherwise harmless. After Dexter snorted a line of cocaine, he offered Samantha a small spoon of white powder. She hesitated for a moment and then inhaled the cocaine quickly. The drug hit her system immediately. Her whole body tingled pleasantly, and she felt a rush of energy. She wanted to try again as the effects of the cocaine began to wear off. After the second sample, she found that the party had become much more fun. People laughed at her jokes, men vied for her attention, and she became much more amorous with Dexter. Samantha wanted to try cocaine again the next weekend and asked Dexter if he knew where he could get some. He did.

For the next 6 months, she and Dexter would snort lines of cocaine on the weekends at parties or at his apartment. She began to worry that she was becoming too involved with cocaine. One weekend morning, she declared to Dexter that she was going to stop using drugs for a month to see if she could do it. After a month's abstinence, Samantha was surprised to find that she could live without cocaine and decided to be drug-free for another 2 months. Dexter did not stop snorting cocaine, and after a few arguments about his continued drug use, they agreed that their relationship was over.

Samantha was 24 when she began dating the man who would become Camille's father. Ned had moved into the city a few years ago as a salesman at a rival company, but they'd struck up a relationship after meeting at a local business convention. He was almost 30, and after dating a few months, they realized that they were ready to settle down and get married.

Ned and Samantha decided to start their family quickly, and within 2 months of the marriage, she was pregnant with Camille. Ned earned enough that Samantha was able to stay home with her daughter for almost 6 months by using up all of her vacation and additional medical leave. When Samantha returned to work, she found that she could not keep up the pace she had before she became pregnant with Camille. Shortly after Camille's first birthday, Ned's company told him that he would have to do more out-of-state travel. Over the next year, Ned was gone throughout the workweek, which resulted in Samantha providing all of the care to Camille.

Camille was almost 2 years old when Ned told Samantha that he'd met another woman in a distant city during his business travels and had ended up sleeping with her. They'd been having an affair for more than 3 months. He said he had been offered a more lucrative position in another company there and wanted to relocate to that city. Samantha told Ned that she wanted a divorce. She would not stay in a marriage with a man she could not trust. Ned agreed to provide child support for Camille and did not contest Samantha's request for sole custody of their daughter.

With Ned gone, Samantha continued on as a single mother as she had for the past year. Camille was an even-tempered child who could become feisty if she did not get her way as a 2- and 3-year old. Samantha, however, liked her spunk, and they rarely had significant conflicts.

After her divorce, Samantha had little interest in dating men. Her waking hours were filled with long hours of work and travel within the city to sales appointments. She would spend evenings reading to Camille before her bedtime. Samantha would watch television for an hour or so, but she often awoke in the middle of the night to find that she'd fallen asleep on the couch once more. She could not see how she could squeeze another relationship into her cramped, though well-organized, schedule.

Samantha was completely unprepared when she was told that the new owners of her company had given her sales territory to another employee. Samantha was out of a job. It took her 5 months to find new work. She accepted a straight-commission sales position with a company that at least had good fringe benefits. Samantha figured that if she was productive, she could almost equal her previous salary. Because she would not have a regular paycheck, however, she would have to work even more hours to achieve the same income she'd had with her prior company.

After 6 months in the new sales position, Samantha was exhausted and overstressed with work and parenting demands. She was one of the older salespersons in her section of the company. Most of her colleagues were young single adults without children who had unlimited time devote to their jobs. They worked hard and played hard. As she became familiar with the other salespersons, she could recognize the signs of cocaine use in some of them: itchy noses, brief bursts of activity and faster speech, and groggy, somewhat disheveled appearances at early morning sales meetings.

One Friday afternoon following a very draining week, she asked another female employee if she had access to cocaine. At first the woman objected to her inquiry but quickly realized that Samantha knew what she was talking about. The woman nodded and gave her a small packet, which she slipped into her purse. That night Samantha snorted her first cocaine in nearly 7 years. The euphoric, energizing effects were equal to those she'd had so long ago. She relished the rush. She thought that cocaine could give her the extra edge she'd need to make her sales quotas and take care of Camille on the weekends.

Over the next month she bought cocaine packets through the woman at work. When the woman employee began to get nervous as Samantha's go-between, she introduced her to Stanley, her supplier. She purchased two packets from him, one for that night and another for the weekend. In addition to the drugs, Stanley gave her his beeper number.

Within 6 months, Samantha was buying three packets a week and sometimes arranging for additional bags on the weekends. Although she was aware that her drug use was accelerating, Samantha still believed that she could stop again, just as she had when she was with Dexter. Stanley was always available, prompt, and reliable with his deliveries. He was a good salesperson, too.

Camille enjoyed her mother's newfound energy, though she did not know its origin. Camille had inherited the gift of gab from her parents and appeared to be unafraid to speak directly and frankly about what she wanted. Samantha got a kick out of her daughter's precocious conversations but found that, as Camille got older, she had to negotiate more often with her about bedtimes and other activities during the weekends. Most of the time, they would come to an agreement after brief debates; however, as Samantha's use of cocaine increased, she was more irritable at her daughter's arguments.

Although Samantha now had more energy throughout the week, her enthusiasm and activity did not translate into additional sales, as she'd hoped. Ever since she'd taken the job, her income had been sporadic. She'd gone through her savings and had refinanced her apartment to make ends meet. When she had a good month, she found that she would buy more cocaine from Stanley rather than pay her mounting credit card bills. Soon she had creditors calling frequently. Stanley knew that she was running out of cash and offered to let her have a few packets on credit.

About a year before Camille died, Samantha experienced crack cocaine for the first time. She had called Stanley for a delivery, but when he arrived he told her all he had was crack. Though she used cocaine often, Samantha still did not believe that she was addicted to it. Stanley told her that crack was just cocaine in another form. He assured her that, as she was not addicted to powder cocaine, she would not become hooked on crack. He showed her how to smoke it. He pulled out a small pipe, put it to her lips, lit a rock of cocaine in the bowl, and told her to inhale. The drug exploded in her brain and gave her a high much greater than she'd ever experienced. She immediately felt better and laughed with him as he smiled at her. Before he left, Stanley allowed her to have another sample and the crack pipe, all free of charge.

Within 3 months, Samantha had been fired for excessive absenteeism and nonproductivity. Desperate with craving and out of money, she went to bed with Stanley for the first time in exchange for crack. A few weeks later, Stanley brought one of his male friends when he made a delivery. As soon as they arrived at her apartment, Samantha knew what they expected. She went into her bedroom with the stranger while Stanley watched television. When she later discovered she had syphilis and was HIV-positive, Samantha did not know who had infected her with the sexually transmitted diseases.

Case Analysis

Maternal Filicide Risk Matrix Analysis

Table 18.1 depicts the risk and protective factors for Samantha. In contrast to most of the other women's histories, all of her risk matrix stages before Camille's first birthday were positive and protective factors against commission of maternal neonaticide and infanticide. Therefore, discussion of her risk matrix focuses on the postinfancy stage.

Postinfancy Stage

Samantha's life spiraled out of control when she became more heavily addicted to powder and crack cocaine when Camille was approximately 7 years old. In terms of Samantha's individual factors, her repeated use of cocaine interfered with her intellectual capacity to make reasoned, deliberate choices. Her judgment and decision making became increasingly impulsive and drug-

Table 18.1
Maternal Filicide Risk Matrix: Samantha

Factor	Pre-P	P/D	EP	LP	PI
Individual					
Age at current pregnancy	P	P	P	P	P
Intelligence level	P	P	P	P	R
Education level	P	P	P	P	P
Medical status	P	P	P	P	R
Emotional status	P	P	P	P	R
Trauma history	P	P	P	P	R
Maternal attitudes	P	P	P	P	R
Family of Origin					
Mother's parenting	P	P	P	P	P
Father's parenting	P	P	P	P	P
Marital/family stability	P	P	P	P	P
Situational					
Marital/partner status	P	P	P	P	R
Financial status	P	P	P	P	R
Child-care status	—	P	P	P	P
Infant's temperament	—	P	P	P	P

Note: R = Risk; P = Protective; Pre-P = Prepregnancy; P/D = Pregnancy/delivery; EP = Early postpartum; LP = Late postpartum; PI = Postinfancy.

influenced as her addiction deepened. Due to her addiction, she engaged in indiscriminate sexual exchanges for money and drugs, which resulted in infections with sexually transmitted diseases.

During the last year of Camille's life, Samantha's emotional functioning was severely impaired as she desperately sought ways to feed her body's insistent cravings for cocaine. By the time her daughter was 9 years old, Samantha's once-admirable maternal attitudes were a distant memory as she physically and emotionally neglected Camille. Samantha did not have a nurturing, supportive relationship with an adult partner. Once Ned moved out of town and remarried, he disappeared from Samantha's and Camille's lives. At the time of her daughter's death, Samantha was financially and morally bankrupt.

Samantha did not have the long history of childhood, adolescent, and adult antisocial behavior and attitude that exemplified Pauline's case. As a result, at the time of Camille's death, Samantha did not meet the diagnostic criteria for antisocial personality disorder (ASPD). She had, however, become so selfishly altered by her substance dependence that she led a criminal lifestyle, prostituting herself and repeatedly buying illegal drugs with the proceeds from her acts.

Her addiction led her to consort with others who committed daily felonies of illegal drug possession and who lived in a violent world in which their lives were often shortened by gunfire. In contrast to a person addicted to alcohol, who can obtain beer and liquor without worry of arrest, Samantha committed unlawful acts simply to purchase, possess, and consume cocaine to satisfy her dependence.

Samantha neglected her parental and personal responsibilities because of her addiction to crack cocaine. When she was confronted with the choice of feeding her addiction or Camille's welfare, she sacrificed her daughter's innocence to her drug dealer. When she was confronted by the possibility of going to prison, she pushed Camille to her death.

Relevant Research: Mothers With Cocaine Dependence

According to surveys within the United States, approximately 10% of respondents have reported using cocaine at least once, with the highest prevalence among young adults between the ages of 18 and 25 (American Psychiatric Association, 2000; Sadock & Sadock, 2003). Although cocaine use has declined over the past 10 years, approximately 2% of the U.S. population will develop either dependence on or substantial abuse of the drug. Among cocaine users, males are approximately twice as likely as females to develop abuse or dependence.

Because highs from cocaine typically last less than an hour, cocaine addicts who smoke crack will continue to ingest the drug to maintain their intoxication. During binges of crack use, a person with cocaine dependence may spend extremely large amounts of money within a short period of time to obtain more cocaine. Many crack addicts, after exhausting all of their financial resources, will turn to illegal ways to acquire money through stealing, prostitution, and drug dealing (American Psychiatric Association, 2000). Samantha's rapid progression from use to dependence is a common pattern among crack smokers.

Because of the high prevalence of drug use among women ages 18 to 36, a woman's primary childbearing years, cocaine-abusing expectant mothers pose significant risks to their babies. One recent survey found that nearly 6%, or 230,000, infants are born each year to mothers who use illegal drugs, principally marijuana, cocaine, and heroin (Butz, Lears, O'Neil, & Lukk, 1998). This survey discovered that the newborns had significantly decreased birth weight, length, and head circumference, as well as high rates of infectious diseases and subsequent developmental problems. The drug-using mothers had numerous social and health problems, in addition to limited knowledge about parenting, understanding signs of infant illness, basic nutrition, and infant development. These results have been repeated in many other studies (Delva, Mathiesen, & Kamata, 2001; Schuler & Nair, 1999; Wohl et al., 1998).

Mothers with crack dependence often have significant comorbid medical and social problems. For example, in one 7-year study, crack-using mothers were significantly more likely than other drug-using mothers to have traded sex for drugs, had more sexual partners, and had more sexually transmitted diseases, as well as high rates of unemployment, single motherhood, and receipt of public assistance (Wohl et al., 1998). These findings were recently replicated in a study by Lam, Wechsberg, and Zule (2004), which also found that crack-using mothers who lost custody of their babies were more likely to have higher rates of drug-for-sex exchanges, risky sexual activity (e.g., promiscuity, unprotected intercourse, etc.), homelessness, psychological distress, histories of childhood victimization, and lack of health insurance.

Children born to cocaine-using mothers have numerous deficits in the early postpartum, late postpartum, and postinfancy stages. In a recent 9-year retrospective U.S. study that compared cocaine-exposed and drug-free babies, the children of cocaine-using mothers had significantly higher rates of mortality, congenital syphilis, premature rupture of membranes, premature delivery, and respiratory distress syndrome and longer hospital stays (Ogunyemi & Hernandez-Loera, 2004). Of the 200 cocaine-exposed babies studied, 38% suffered from neonatal cocaine withdrawal syndrome, and 75% were placed into foster care or adoption.

Similar studies in the United States have reported significantly decreased birth weight and head size (Shankaran et al., 2004), increased breast-feeding precautions to prevent cocaine transmission (England et al., 2003), increased necessity for neonatal intensive care (Shankaran et al., 2003), higher rates of AIDS (Bauer et al., 2002), and an array of early motor-developmental problems, including lower arousal, higher excitability, and lower reflex sensitivity (Lester et al., 2002). Those mothers with higher rates of cocaine abuse and dependence were much more likely to give birth to a developmentally damaged baby (Frank et al., 2005; Myers et al., 2003; Shankaran et al., 2003).

Studies of older children who were cocaine-exposed prior to delivery have shown that their developmental problems may persist through childhood and into adolescence. For example, children at ages 18 and 36 months were found to have lower rates of secure attachment to their cocaine-using mothers (Seifer et al., 2004), somewhat higher deficits in expressive and receptive language development (Morrow et al., 2004), and abnormal neurological examinations (Lewis, Misra, Johnson, & Rosen, 2004). In a study of 3-year-olds' maternal attachment, cocaine-exposed children were observed to be less responsive to their mothers, who tended to be less nurturing and less emotionally available and to use more maladaptive coping mechanisms (Singer et al., 2001). Seven-year-old boys and girls with prenatal cocaine exposure were significantly more likely than same-age drug-free boys and girls to display delinquent and problematic behavior (Norstrom-Bailey et al., 2005). Adolescent girls who were prenatally exposed to cocaine have been found to display more deviant, delinquent behavior than same-age girls who had drug-free mothers at birth (Stanger et al., 2002).

Samantha was drug-free during her pregnancy, but Camille was still the tragic victim of crack-fueled maternal behavior. By the time of her daughter's death, Samantha had lost everything in order to feed her addiction. She had, however, many positive attributes (higher education, intelligence, lengthy work history, etc.), which might have improved her prognosis if she had been forced into a therapeutic program. Unfortunately, cocaine users rarely enter treatment voluntarily (Sadock & Sadock, 2003).

Although treatment of cocaine addicts is very difficult, an array of therapeutic methods that include combinations of psychotherapy and medications have been reported in the literature. For example, cognitive-behavior therapy (CBT) that focuses on abstinence and relapse prevention has been found to be an effective, empirically validated intervention for cocaine-abusing adults (Chambless, 2005). Coyer (2003) discovered that treatment that focuses on issues of abandonment, impatience/anger, lack of parenting knowledge, and interrupting dysfunctional patterns from the patient's family of origin were helpful for cocaine-addicted mothers in maintaining their abstinence. Sterk (2002) found that psychotherapeutic treatment that improved patients' decision-making ability and assertiveness skills in sexual and drug-use encounters can be effective in treating crack-using mothers and women.

Young mothers with cocaine and heroin dependence who were placed in a 3-year-long treatment program in which they were paid to work or receive training if they demonstrated continuing drug-free urine samples showed significantly higher duration of abstinence than addicted mothers who received only traditional therapy and case management (Silverman et al., 2002). Psychotherapeutic programs that incorporate same-site child care while the cocaine-dependent mothers are in daily group therapy and educational programs may result in higher rates of treatment success (Conners, Bradley, Whiteside-Mansell, & Crone, 2001; Volpicelli, Markman, Monterosso, Filing, & O'Brien, 2000).

Many drug abuse treatment programs also incorporate medications to block the positively reinforcing effects of cocaine (Kleber, 1995). Although research has produced mixed results with many medicines, some drugs do appear to show promise. For example, among less severely abusing cocaine users, Norpramine and Tofranil may be effective in reducing cocaine-induced cravings, euphoria, and depression (Kolar et al., 1992; Nunes et al., 1995). Fluanxol has also been shown to enhance abstinence and decrease cravings in crack smokers with poor prognoses (Khalsa, Jatlow, & Gawin, 1994). More recently, Antabuse has produced longer cocaine abstinence and/or greater decreases in frequency and amount of cocaine use in patients who also were receiving weekly outpatient therapy contact (Carroll, Nich, Ball, McCance, & Rounsaville, 1998; Petrakis et al., 2000).

With a variety of interventions that were then available to her, it is unfortunate that Samantha did not pursue, or was not court-ordered into, drug abuse treatment that might have saved her daughter's life.

Suggestions for Prevention at Risk Intervention Points

1. *Samantha had heard of cocaine when she was at the university but had not ever seen anybody use it. Her classmates had told her that cocaine gave a pleasant rush of increased energy but was otherwise harmless.*

Samantha's case occurred well before the Internet was a readily available source for scientifically verified information about drug and alcohol abuse and dependence. When she was in college during the mid-1980s, many adults believed that cocaine was a harmless drug with little potential for addiction. The popular press glorified some nightclubs where cocaine was openly traded and used in the presence of others. In the early 1990s, more than 25 million persons in the United States disclosed that they had experimented with cocaine, and cocaine dependence was found to be almost twice as prevalent as manic-depressive disorder (Sadock & Sadock, 2003).

The widespread self-report of cocaine use attested to this country's ill-informed acceptance of the drug. When Samantha was in college, crack cocaine had not yet become as readily available as it was during the 1990s after she became addicted. Since the late 1990s and the early 21st century, the medical and lethal risks of cocaine have become well publicized through systematic community drug prevention education programs. As a result, current cocaine use has been on the decline over the past few years (Sadock & Sadock, 2003).

2. *She began to worry that she was becoming too involved with cocaine. . . . One weekend morning, she declared to Dexter that she was going to stop using drugs for a month to see if she could do it. After a month's abstinence, Samantha was surprised to find that she could live without cocaine and decided to be drug-free for another 2 months.*

Cocaine abusers rarely seek treatment voluntarily for a variety of reasons. Many fear being arrested and forced to reveal the names of their suppliers to avoid felony incarceration. Fear of violent retaliation by drug dealers is another significant disincentive. Most cocaine users do not enter therapy simply because their experience with the drug is too positive and because the negative effects of withdrawal are relatively mild during the early stages of abuse. When their dependence becomes severe and they experience serious medical crises such as seizures, cardiac abnormalities, and respiratory depression, cocaine users often appear at hospital emergency rooms seeking help (American Psychiatric Association, 2000).

Samantha's self-imposed abstinence was admirable, but without the treatment assistance of knowledgeable drug counselors, she was unaware that she could easily relapse into another period of cocaine abuse later in her life. Unfortunately, her success at this point gave her a false sense of security over her control of her drug use. Had she entered an outpatient drug treatment program of weekly psychotherapy, she might have acquired the knowledge and resistance skills to avoid cocaine use in the months prior to her daughter's death.

3. *Though she used cocaine often, Samantha still did not believe that she was addicted to it. Stanley told her that crack was just cocaine in another form. He assured her that, as she was not addicted to powder cocaine, she would not become hooked on crack.*

At this point in her life, Samantha's denial regarding the severity of her addiction to cocaine was substantial and life-threatening. One measure of her dependence was her reliance on her drug dealer for product (crack cocaine) information—Stanley was not bound by "truth in advertising" laws. He wanted another woman addict as a customer, someone who would do whatever he wanted her to do. His pedophilic interest in Camille suggests that he likely had other cocaine-dependent mothers with young children with whom he had sex. He did not count on Camille's refusal to remain silent about his sexual assault of her. Tragically, her courageous threat to speak out led to her death.

4. *When she later discovered she had syphilis and was HIV-positive, Samantha did not know who had infected her with the sexually transmitted diseases.*

By the time she had contracted syphilis and HIV, Samantha's medical condition had deteriorated significantly due to cocaine addiction. During her pretrial evaluation with me, Samantha remembered that the county health department worker had encouraged her to return for counseling at the community mental health center and had made an appointment for her with a local physician. She recalled that she had told the worker she would return but had no intention of obtaining treatment services. She declared that she was childless to prevent the worker from contacting the county's protective services department. Samantha was realistically afraid that if she was investigated, Camille would be taken from her and she would be arrested for child neglect or abuse. She knew by then that she was addicted to crack and saw no alternative path for her life.

It was unfortunate that her siblings were not informed about her cocaine addiction, but Samantha would have never given the staff her permission to contact them. She would have been too embarrassed for them to see how her life had turned out. If the staff member had called Samantha's brother or sister, their immediate response would have likely been to protect Camille while simultaneously arranging for substance abuse and mental health treatment for Samantha. Her siblings would likely have consulted with Ned and his wife. If they had deferred to Samantha's family's decision, her brother or sister would most probably have readily welcomed Camille into their home, an intervention that would have saved her life.

Epilogue

At Samantha's request, her public defender called her sister and brother to inform them of Camille's death and her arrest for murder. They kept the news from their ailing mother but called Ned to tell him what had happened. He was devastated and furious. He told Samantha's siblings that he had no interest in seeing his ex-wife but would attend his daughter's funeral.

Because of the heinous circumstances surrounding Camille's death, the prosecutor considered filing capital charges against Samantha. Her siblings and Ned successfully persuaded him to spare their families the embarrassment of the public disclosures of the life that Samantha had finally led.

Evaluations by the state's forensic clinicians were consistent with my findings. Although Samantha's diagnosed cocaine dependence had severely disrupted her personal, vocational, and parental functioning, she did have the capacity to know right from wrong at the time of her crime: She had attempted to prevent disclosure of her prostitution of her daughter by pushing her down the staircase. After receiving all of the experts' reports, the prosecutor agreed to allow her to plead guilty to manslaughter. Samantha was sentenced to 20 years of incarceration. She remains in prison today.

The trial judge ordered Stanley's felony sentences to run consecutively for a total of 30 years.

19

Psychopathic Mother, Narcissistic Type

Rhonda

Rhonda yelled to a day-care teacher's aide to call an ambulance immediately. She knelt over the 2-year old girl, who was lying on the floor struggling to get her breath. Rhonda snapped at the children who had clustered at the doorway, telling them to go outside and play. Looking over her shoulder to see that she was alone again with the toddler, she calmly placed her hand over the child's mouth once more. When the day-care manager entered the room, Rhonda bent over and pretended to use mouth-to-mouth resuscitation to save the child's life. She looked up with tears in her eyes and shook her head, telling the manager that the girl might not survive. The manager asked what she could do to help. Rhonda suggested that she tell the other aides to keep the other children in the playground and call the child's parents, then go to the corner to flag down the ambulance. She informed the manager that it would be best if the child were not moved and that she'd stay with the girl until the paramedics could take over. As the woman left the room, Rhonda returned to suffocating, then reviving the child.

By the time the paramedics rushed into the room, the toddler's eyes were dull and listless, though she was still breathing. They quickly checked her respiration and other vital signs, then carried her out of the center. Rhonda ran outside to the driveway and pleaded with the paramedics to let her go with them to the emergency room. Getting their permission, she jumped into the back of the ambulance, grasped the child's near-lifeless hand, and pretended to pray. Hours later, Rhonda would be lauded by the hospital staff and local newspaper for saving the asthmatic girl's life. She accepted the accolades with grace and modesty. Rhonda had had a lot of practice.

Rhonda had first come to the attention of the day-care manager when the manager read in her resume that Rhonda had experience managing children with respiratory problems because her own children had suffered from asthma and sleep apnea. The manager conducted an Internet search as part of her employment background check and came across a newspaper article describing how Rhonda had recently saved the life of an infant child from an accidental drowning. She was named "Hero of the Week" by the newspaper and had her picture taken with the mayor. After reading the article, the manager decided to hire her. She had been saddened to learn that Rhonda's first son had died from sudden infant death syndrome when he was 6 months old. The manager did not know that Rhonda had been previously investigated, but cleared, in the crib death of an infant girl she'd been babysitting.

The girl whom Rhonda "saved" at the day-care center did survive but suffered irreversible brain damage. Suspicions would not be raised about Rhonda's culpability until her second son, Marlin, died nearly 9 months later.

Rhonda's childhood had been far from idyllic. Her mother, an alcoholic with severe respiratory problems as a result of her drinking, had been married and divorced four times. Rhonda was not an only child. She was the youngest of her mother's four children, two of whom were fathered by different alcoholic and drug-abusing men who had long since left the families they'd created. She never knew her biological father, and it was never resolved whether her parents had been married when she was born. Her mother would tell her only that her father was a "loser" and that they were all better off because he had disappeared before Rhonda's first birthday.

Rhonda had known little stability in her life before she entered kindergarten. Her mother was frequently hospitalized for ill health. At first, she was afraid to visit her mother on the ward, but she soon began to enjoy the friendly medical staff she met at the hospital. The nurses' aides would let her keep the toys they gave her, and once she received a child's nursing kit complete with a plastic stethoscope.

If Rhonda's mother happened to be unmarried or unattached when she was hospitalized, the children would be left to fend for themselves without adult supervision. Rhonda and her siblings were often in and out of temporary foster homes because of their mother's frequent neglect of them.

Rhonda was a sickly child who suffered from periodic bronchitis. When she would have a breathing attack because her mother was too intoxicated or hung over to make sure she got her medication, Rhonda would be rushed to the emergency room and often hospitalized for a few days' observation. After a number of trips to the ER, Rhonda began to look forward to her next medical crisis because her days in the hospital were so much more enjoyable than her life at home. All the nurses and doctors seemed to be so loving and caring to her.

As she grew older, her conflicts with her mother increased. Rhonda was almost 11 years old the first time she ran away from home. Her stepfather had begun to take an interest in her and asked her to sit on his lap. He was intoxicated at the time, and they were alone in the house. Rhonda refused to come near him, and when he yelled at her, she ran out the back door. She slept in a car that night but returned the next morning for breakfast. Her mother happened to be awake early and confronted her at the door. She accused Rhonda of talking back to her husband and raised her hand to hit her. Rhonda kicked her mother in the shin, ran to the kitchen, and threatened to stab her parents in their beds if they ever hit her again. Rhonda's mother was enraged at her outburst and called the police to arrest her for being incorrigible. After the officers arrived, they took Rhonda to an emergency children's shelter for the next few days. When her child protective services case came to court, the agency social workers recommended that Rhonda be assessed and treated by the university's child and adolescent mental health clinicians.

Rhonda was hospitalized for observation and evaluation at the university's psychiatric facility. As in the other hospital, she found that the doctors and nurses were caring and concerned for her. She wanted to stay. Rhonda did not have to embellish her history of child abuse and neglect; her mother's inadequacies were well known to the county's child protection services agency. As Rhonda interacted with the other children in the center, she learned what to say to ensure that she was not discharged.

She would fabricate threats of suicide and made scratch marks on her arm when she saw how compassionately the staff reacted to her self-mutilation. By guile and deceit, Rhonda was able to stay in the hospital and after-care residential center for almost 2 years. Because her discharge options were either placement in foster care or return to an unstable alcoholic mother who had never visited her, the residential treatment team was content to let her remain. Rhonda was not a behavior problem to them. She often helped the new child patients to adjust to the center's milieu.

Rhonda was surprised and angry when, at age 13, she was told she would be discharged to a foster home. Rhonda remained with her foster parents for the next 5 years, until she graduated from high school. Because she was the only child in the home, her retired foster parents were able to devote their time and resources toward her emotional and medical well-being. Rhonda would continue to have many health-related complaints and receive numerous pediatric examinations because of her self-reported irregular menses, abdominal cramping, and incapacitating headaches. She was occasionally hospitalized for brief periods of observation, though the physicians could not establish specific reasons for her ailments.

Rhonda had little interest in dating boys when she was in high school. She had never liked being pawed by her mother's boyfriends and did not want to be groped by overeager dates who would try to pressure her into sexual experimentation. Rhonda discovered that she liked situations with young men in which she was in control and could boss them around. She graduated from high school as a virgin, a condition she planned on maintaining until she was married.

To make extra money, Rhonda would take babysitting jobs for the parents who lived in her neighborhood. She did not like taking care of infants, but there were few other employment opportunities available to her at that point in her life. Her foster parents encouraged her to take the jobs as a way of earning money and learning how to work. Grudgingly, Rhonda agreed to the temporary employment until she entered the U.S. Army at age 19.

An army recruiter who had visited the high school during her senior year had promised that she could get nursing training if she agreed to an extended tour with the armed services. Rhonda thought it was a good opportunity and signed up after talking with her foster parents, who endorsed her decision. By this point in her life, her mother was no longer part of her life and had not been for many years. When her mother would be hospitalized for alcohol-related medical ailments, Rhonda would inform her caseworkers and foster parents that she did not want to see her mother again.

One night while she was babysitting, the 9-month-old girl she was taking care of would not stop crying. Rhonda briefly put her hand over the girl's mouth to silence her. The child choked and sputtered but cried even louder when Rhonda let her breathe again. When she silenced the child again, however, the child struggled for a few minutes, then stopped moving. Rhonda immediately knew that something was terribly wrong: The child had died. The medical examiner would later report that the child had been dead for approximately 4 hours when Rhonda, in tears, had called the baby's parents to report that she had found the infant cold and silent in her crib. After a brief interrogation by a detective, she was cleared of wrongdoing. The medical examiner attributed the infant's demise to sudden infant death syndrome. A few months later, Rhonda entered the military. She did not take care of children again until she gave birth to her first son, Melvin.

Rhonda's basic training in the army was more physically demanding than she thought it would be. When she would try to avoid morning exercises by claiming to be nauseous, her drill sergeant would ignore her complaints. A few times she forced herself to throw up in the bathroom; on those days, she would be allowed to go to sick call. She made it through her initial training despite many sick call visits and soon began her training as a hospital technician. Rhonda was not selected for the limited number of training slots for nursing but was assigned as an orderly at an armed services hospital. She detested the work of cleaning up patients' messes.

In contrast to her child and adolescent experiences as a patient, these doctors and nurses ignored her while she worked on the wards. Deeply embittered by the army's betrayals of their promises to her, she plotted her discharge. Because of her history of excessive sick call, her claims of illness were dismissed as malingering. She received disciplinary warnings from her supervisors not to fake ailments or she would be dishonorably discharged. Because she wanted to enter nurses' training in the civilian sector, Rhonda did not want to be kicked out of the army for disciplinary reasons. She decided she would have to get pregnant.

She chose an older man whom she'd met at the base grocery store. Like her high school dates, Henry was a timid man who was surprised by Rhonda's attention to him. In contrast to her high school years, Rhonda encouraged his sexual advances and suggested that they have intercourse on their third date. She assured him that she was taking birth control pills. She was not. Their first coupling was not romantic or satisfying to her, but after a few weeks of intercourse, Rhonda discovered she was pregnant.

Henry was surprised at her pregnancy; she said she must have miscounted her pills. Henry proposed marriage, Rhonda accepted, and they were quickly married by the justice of the peace in a small ceremony. Rhonda called her foster parents after her wedding and told them of her impending delivery. When she talked with her commanding officer about her pregnancy and marriage, he told her that she would be discharged for medical reasons. Rhonda did not object.

Melvin was born 7 months later. Though Rhonda cared little about the fetus she carried, she did like the attention she received as her pregnancy became more noticeable to others. She had an uneventful pregnancy and delivery. She and Melvin were healthy. She was able to stay in the hospital for 5 days after giving birth. She was in no rush to leave. As a patient, she was once again treated as royalty. Her newborn child was only a mild inconvenience for her. When she would hold Melvin, she felt little bonding with him. He was a placid, contented baby who was the center of attention for the nurses because there were few other mothers on the ward at the time. Melvin would be brought into her room, and Rhonda would act like a caring, compassionate mother when the nurses and medical staff were present.

Because Henry was able to provide for his wife and son, Rhonda did not have to work outside the home after she gave birth to Melvin. Now that she was out of the army, Rhonda wished to pursue her nurses' training, but she felt burdened by her newborn son. He was in the way of her dreams. Melvin was 2 months old when Rhonda created her son's first medical crisis. After smothering and reviving him in his crib a few times, she alerted Henry that Melvin needed to go to the emergency room. They rushed out the door for the hospital. Melvin was kept overnight for observation. Rhonda insisted that she stay by her baby's side until he was ready for discharge. She sent Henry home, and he left without complaint. Rhonda refused to leave her baby's crib. The staff complimented her on her vigil and brought her a blanket and pillow so that she could sleep next to him. During the night, Rhonda pressed the alarm button three times because Melvin had stopped breathing. She kept silent about the true cause of her son's distress.

Melvin was given a diagnosis of sleep apnea. Rhonda was sent home with a monitoring device that would track his breathing and also signal an alarm if his breathing became critical. The first few nights, Melvin slept soundly until morning. Two weeks later, however, he had multiple crises for 5 nights in a row. Rhonda brought her son to the emergency room again, and he was re-hospitalized for further tests and observation.

Rhonda returned to her 24-hour post by her son's crib. Two days later, the hospital pediatrician informed her that the tests were inconclusive and that Melvin would be discharged the following morning. Rhonda became irritated with the physician's abrupt demeanor and insisted on a second opinion. She declared that she did not want her son's medical problems to become worse at home. She wanted her child to stay at the hospital until the doctors figured out what was wrong with him. She informed them again of the two episodes he'd had the previous 2 nights. She did not reveal that she was the cause of her infant's crises. The pediatrician agreed to delay his discharge for another 2 days.

Over the next 4 months, Rhonda became very well educated about infant sleep apnea. Melvin was hospitalized once more, but after the hospital pediatrician began to question the baby's slow recovery from treatment, Rhonda took her infant to another hospital in a nearby city. She told them it was Melvin's first hospitalization. As before, she camped out in her son's room and received condolences from the nursing staff. When Henry questioned why she'd switched hospitals, Rhonda told him that the pediatrician was incompetent and that the staff at the new hospital was better. Henry shrugged and, as always, let Rhonda have her way.

One morning, Henry was awakened by Rhonda's screams. Melvin had died during the night, and his cold, lifeless body was covered by the blanket in his crib. Henry did not know that his wife, bored by motherhood and resentful of her son's disruption to her nursing career, had suffocated Melvin in his crib. After reviewing the baby's medical records and his body, the county medical examiner declared that Melvin had died from sudden infant death syndrome complicated by infant sleep apnea.

Rhonda enrolled in her first-year nursing courses at the local community college 4 weeks later. Though Henry had encouraged her to take her time before going to school, Rhonda insisted that she needed to stay busy to keep from being overwhelmed by the loss of her son.

She was enraged to discover that she was pregnant again at the end of her first year of training. She had seriously considered terminating the pregnancy, but Henry insisted that she deliver their child. He refused to discuss an abortion, and Rhonda relented after he said that he would work additional hours so that she could stay in school until the baby was born. Rhonda had another uneventful pregnancy. Marlin was delivered without complications. Soon, however, he began having the same respiratory problems as his recently deceased brother, caused by the same perpetrator, his mother.

Because of Marlin's birth, Rhonda had to delay her nursing training once more. When Henry was unable to get overtime work, Rhonda agreed to start a day care and babysitting service in their home. She figured that as long as she had to be home with Marlin, she might as well make a few dollars. She soon had five other preschool children in her care. After a few months of being stuck in her home with little daytime contact with other adults, Rhonda felt isolated from the outside world. She did not enjoy constantly picking up the messes her toddlers would make and had had enough of wiping bottoms. She wanted to return to school and be the center of attention once again.

Rhonda concocted the story of the little girl falling into the plastic swimming pool. In reality, she had precipitated the child's medical crisis by holding her face in the shallow water, then resuscitating the infant. She had brought her portable telephone outside to be able to call for an ambulance as she knelt next to the child. Rhonda knew that the dispatcher's audiotape would record her desperate pleas for the emergency medical technicians to hurry.

She did not anticipate that the newspaper would publish a story about the episode, but she did not shy away from the reporter or his photographer. During the interview, she mentioned that her nursing training had been interrupted and emphasized how important it was for parents and child-care providers to learn infant lifesaving techniques such as mouth-to-mouth resuscitation. She was very surprised when she received a call from the mayor's office for a meeting and photograph.

Rhonda was pleasantly surprised when the day-care center manager offered her a part-time well-paying position and daily care of Marlin while she finished her education at the local community college. After she lost her job at the day-care center and had to again take care of Marlin, Rhonda felt that she was cut off from the world once more. Each day was a boring routine of housekeeping, laundry, and changing Marlin's diapers.

When she took Marlin to the emergency room twice in the following month, the hospital staff became increasingly skeptical of her explanations for her son's medical crises. They began to question her more closely about his symptoms before she brought him to the hospital. Rhonda was angered by the doubts the pediatricians and nurses had about her. She was so upset by their response during those first two visits that she went to another hospital for help after she initiated Marlin's third crisis.

The emergency room nurses at the hospital recognized her from the newspaper stories but did not respond sympathetically to her. Instead, the nurse and doctor requested her permission to obtain her son's medical records from the other hospital, as well as the records from Marlin's pediatrician. This reaction was not what Rhonda had expected at all. Physicians and nurses were supposed to accept her uncritically and believe her without doubt. This was entirely different. She left the ER in a huff, yelling over her shoulder that she might file a complaint against the hospital for their failure to treat her son.

When Rhonda awoke her husband 2 months later bawling that Marlin had died in his sleep, Henry became skeptical, too. This time, the medical examiner very carefully examined the child's body and thoroughly questioned Rhonda and Henry. She insisted that she had awakened for breakfast, gone into her son's bedroom, and found him dead in his crib. She adamantly denied any responsibility for his death and collapsed in Henry's arms when the detectives suggested that Marlin had been murdered.

Rhonda was arrested for homicide by child abuse 1 month later. The police department had received information from the state in which she had been investigated in the death of the 9-month-old girl she had babysat years before. The police departments began sharing information, interviewing hospital personnel, and reviewing the medical records of Melvin and Marlin. They concluded that Rhonda was likely responsible for the deaths of three children. Both states charged her with murder.

Case Analysis

Rhonda's case amply demonstrates the narcissistic and psychopathic attitudes found in persons with Munchausen syndrome by proxy (MBP). Few of us can imagine someone who could deliberately and repeatedly injure a child and then deceptively thwart the well-intentioned efforts of medical personnel to successfully treat the highly vulnerable victim.

Rhonda's story stands out in other ways, as well. In contrast to the other cases presented in this book in which more than one child died at the hands of the mother, this case exemplifies a woman who kills as a serial murderer. She is the only woman discussed in this book who had killed someone before she murdered one of her own children.

Maternal Filicide Risk Matrix Analysis

The Maternal Filicide Risk Matrix for Rhonda is presented as table 19.1. The factors that were present before Melvin's death are incorporated in the prepregnancy stage for Marlin.

Prepregnancy Stage

Before her pregnancy with Melvin, Rhonda had few positive markers but numerous individual risk factors that foreshadowed future crises and difficulties as a parent. Her only protective factors within the individual domain were her delaying of her pregnancy until she was nearly out of her teenage years and her completion of high school, with some postsecondary training in the army. Though she possessed intelligence in the upper limits of the average range, her reasoning, judgment, and insight were significantly distorted by her traumatic childhood and adolescent experiences, as well as her own homicidal actions as a babysitter.

Her medical status was a negative marker for almost all of her life before her first pregnancy, because she frequently induced illness in herself as a child, adolescent, and adult in hopes of being hospitalized and treated by nurses and physicians. Once she became pregnant, she narcissistically reveled in prenatal care, not for the benefit of her fetus but for the attention from medical and nonmedical individuals that she received as an expectant mother. Although Rhonda did not display psychotic or major affective signs or symptoms, her persistent wish to be a patient—the primary way in which she sought and received love—significantly distorted her childhood and adolescent emotional status before her marriage to Henry.

Rhonda's childhood history was certainly traumatic due to her mother's emotional instability and chronic neglect of her and her siblings, which led to

Table 19.1
Maternal Filicide Risk Matrix: Rhonda (for Marlin)

Factor	Pre-P	P/D	EP	LP	PI
Individual					
Age at current pregnancy	P	P	P	P	P
Intelligence level	R	R	R	R	R
Education level	P	P	P	P	P
Medical status	P	P	P	P	P
Emotional status	R	R	R	R	R
Trauma history	R	R	R	R	R
Maternal attitudes	R	R	R	R	R
Family of Origin					
Mother's parenting	R	R	R	R	—
Father's parenting	R	R	R	R	—
Marital/family stability	R	R	R	R	—
Situational					
Marital/partner status	P	P	P	P	P
Financial status	R	R	R	R	R
Child-care status	P	—	—	—	—
Infant's temperament	P	P	P	P	P

Note: R = Risk; P = Protective; Pre-P = Prepregnancy; P/D = Pregnancy/delivery; EP = Early postpartum; LP = Late postpartum; PI = Postinfancy.

frequent foster-care placements and alternative caretakers. Indeed, the hospital became a reliable refuge for Rhonda during her formative years: She could always count on the nurses and doctors to take care of her without complaint or rejection. Although Rhonda did deliberately plan to become pregnant with Melvin, her motives were hardly maternal. Rather, she used her fetus (and Henry) as a way of escaping her obligations to the army.

She did not develop a nurturing bonding with her first baby and acted like a caring mother only when the performance would be to her benefit with the hospital staff. Once Melvin was delivered, she continued to induce illness in him to receive the attention of emergency room physicians, pediatricians, and nurses. She maintained her ongoing contact with medical personnel by making her son sick, then lying about his symptoms.

Rhonda's selfish attitudes evolved out of the pathological parenting she received from her own abusive, alcoholic mother and her absent father, as well as her family's continuing instability. During my postarrest evaluation of Rhonda, there were indications that her childhood respiratory problems may not have been exclusively the result of bronchitis. Rhonda recalled that the times she would be rushed to the emergency room were late at night, after she'd awakened abruptly with her mother standing over her. Rhonda's childhood and adolescent medical records did not indicate that she had had such respiratory attacks when she was in foster care or at the inpatient psychiatric hospital. Perhaps her mother had made her sick.

Prior to her pregnancy with her second child, Marlin, Rhonda's situational factors were generally positive. Though her financial status was dependent on Henry, he appeared to be a steady, reliable, supportive partner to Rhonda. He was not abusive to her or to Melvin, and there were no indications that he shirked his responsibilities as a father or husband. He was a passive, quiet individual who allowed Rhonda to have her way almost all the time, with the exception of her wish to terminate her unexpected pregnancy with Marlin. Until Melvin's death at 6 months, his pediatric records indicated that he was a pleasant, complacent infant when he was hospitalized, in contrast to his mother's description of his demeanor and sleep patterns when he was exclusively in her care.

Pregnancy/Delivery, Early Postpartum, Late Postpartum, and Postinfancy Stages

Because there were no changes in Rhonda's individual, family of origin, and situational factors during Marlin's brief life, the stages have been condensed. The stability of her risk factors in each of the domains reflects the duration of her MBP disorder. As described in greater detail in the subsequent section on relevant research, individuals with MBP are extremely resistant to treatment. They commonly drop out of contact with clinicians if confronted with the accusation that they might be inducing illness in themselves and/or others to maintain their status as patients. Like other MBP individuals who actively avoid psychotherapy, Rhonda never attempted to resolve her traumatic history of family instability, her alienation from her mother, the absence of her father, or her own self-induced illnesses. Although individuals with MBP are reluctant to enter treatment, Rhonda's resistance was likely also deepened by her fear that she might reveal her secret that she had killed the neighbor's baby.

After Melvin's death, Rhonda thought that she was free of parental obligations so that she could pursue her nursing training. She enjoyed being a nursing student, but it was not clear that she necessarily wanted to become a nurse. As a person with Munchausen syndrome and subsequently MBP, she wanted to be the recipient, not the provider, of care. Though she reported being upset when she unexpectedly became pregnant, she might have deliberately stopped taking her birth control pills. Her motives were not likely motherly. Instead, by being pregnant she could deliver another object she could exploit, as she had done with Melvin, while also having a reason for not being able to complete her nursing degree.

Once Marlin was born, he also had mysterious respiratory problems, just as his older, deceased brother had. To Rhonda, children were replaceable parts in her ongoing quest for attention and love.

Relevant Research: Munchausen Syndrome by Proxy (MBP)

Munchausen syndrome by proxy (MBP) is a severe form of child abuse in which a parent or caretaker "persistently fabricates symptoms on behalf of another so causing that person to be regarded as ill" (Meadow, 1995, p.5). The diagnosis has been widely accepted by clinicians in many medically related fields since the original descriptions of the disorder in the mid-1970s (Meadow, 1977; Money & Werlwas, 1976). Although MBP has not yet been officially recognized as a fully researched disorder for inclusion in the American Psychiatric Association's *Diagnostic and Statistical Manual* (American Psychiatric Association, 2000), the APA has recommended continued inquiry into this very severe form of abuse of children and other vulnerable persons.

The prevalence of MBP is unknown, and most of the research on the disorder comprises single case studies or small samples of patients (Galvin, Newton, & Vandeven, 2005). Because MBP entails deliberate injury to the victim through life-threatening methods such as poisoning and suffocation, the disorder has been considered to have extremely high mortality rates for a psychiatric diagnosis (Galvin et al., 2005; McGuire & Feldman, 1989). Meadow (1990) reported that in a study of 27 children who had been repeatedly suffocated by their mothers, 9, or 33%, had died. Also, there are case reports of serial MBP perpetrators, such as Mary Beth Tinning and Beverly Allitt, who, over a period of time, may have killed as many as nine and four children, respectively (Alexander, Smith, & Stevenson, 1990; Eggington, 1989; Meadow, 1995). Even though the victim might not die initially, the child or vulnerable adult is still at grave risk for death: The persistent and repetitive inducement of serious illness and injury is a commonly reported characteristic of MBP perpetrators (Rosenberg, 1995).

Although the original descriptions of the disorder appeared in American and British journals, MBP cases have been found in many other countries, including Canada (Yonge & Haase, 2004), Oman (Bappal, George, Nair, Khusaiby, & DeSilva, 2001), Brazil (Moreira & Moreira, 1999; Pires & Molle, 1999), India (Somani, 1998), Israel (Ben-Cherit & Melmed, 1998), France (Absolut de la Gastine, Penniello, Le Truest, Grujard, & Guillois, 1998), and Australia (Single & Henry, 1991).

Within the MBP literature, mothers have been found to be the most common perpetrators (Levin & Sheridan, 1995), but case reports have also described MBP abuse by fathers (Praaken et al., 1991; Single & Henry, 1991), as well as by caretaker daughters of elderly parents (Ben-Cherit & Melmed, 1998). Almost all of the MBP cases in the literature describe children as the victims of their caretaker; however, more recently the diagnosis has been extended to vulnerable adults as well, particularly when the victim is unconscious, demented, financially dependent, or frightened by the perpetrator (Sigal & Altmark, 1995).

The breadth of illnesses and symptoms induced in the victim is vast, and MBP may present as virtually any medical condition, including respiratory disorders (apnea, asthma, etc.) gastrointestinal ailments (vomiting, diarrhea, etc.), hematological conditions (anemia, bleeding, etc.), infections and fever, skin rashes and bruising, allergies, renal and urinary dysfunction, ocular diseases (conjunctivitis, pupil abnormalities, nystagmus, etc.), and neurological crises such as seizures and disorders of consciousness (Sheridan & Levin, 1995).

Diagnosis and detection of MBP perpetrators is a professionally daunting venture for a number of reasons. Confrontation of a suspect caretaker amounts to accusing the person of a criminal felony punishable by imprisonment. A misdiagnosis may be grounds for a malpractice suit (Ostfeld, 1995). The clinical picture is often complicated because many symptoms and illnesses seen in MBP cases are genuine medical diseases. True seizures can be produced by poisoning or suffocation; the clinical presentation reflects MBP only if the etiology is actually confirmed (Levin & Sheridan, 1995). Also, the caretaker may not necessarily be the perpetrator of the child's illness: In a summary of 53 children under age 18 with fevers or infections, the symptoms were discovered to be self-induced by the child in 22 (42%) cases (Mian & Huyer, 1995).

MBP perpetrators, when challenged by skeptical medical personnel, commonly take their children from the hospital against their physicians' advice, briefly cease their abuse to demonstrate their innocence, or seek additional physicians' opinions, which may complicate the diagnostic picture. Cases of the misdiagnosis of MBP have been reported, though the rate may be less than 5% (Rand & Feldman, 1999).

The best evidence to validate MBP may be to catch the perpetrator in the act by procedures such as covert videotaping during hospitalization (Ostfeld, 1995; Thomas, 1996). In one study of videotaped surveillance, 18 of 19 cases resulted in confirmatory evidence of intentional suffocation (Samuels, 1993). Because such practices place the clinician in a dual role of therapist and detective, a number of authors have raised ethical and clinical concerns about such practices, including invading the privacy of the parent and child, increasing the subsequent risk of harm to the child, and postponing intervention by child protective services agencies (Williams & Bevan, 1988).

In an effort to clarify detection, Lasher and Sheridan (2004) have suggested that MBP perpetrators: (1) are often the primary caretakers, (2) present clinically as normal and good caretakers, (3) may be accomplished liars and manipulators, (4) may appear to be overanxious or overprotective, (5) may have a background in a health profession, (6) may seek attention from a variety of people, (7) may deny culpability despite overwhelming evidence, (8) do not necessarily stop when suspected or caught, (9) may have a personal history of symptom falsification, and (10) are often the only persons consistently present at or in association with the onset of the victim's symptoms. Although this list of characteristics is similar to others (e.g., Rosenberg, 1995; Sheridan & Levin, 1995; Ludwig, 1995), there are no empirical data that specify that a suspected perpetrator of MBP necessarily has any one or any given number of characteristics (Lasher & Sheridan, 2004).

Treatment of persons with MBP is challenging for many reasons, not the least of which may be the involuntary, court-ordered status of the perpetrator-patient and the significant risks to the child victim with premature reunification of the family. Most researchers in MBP recommend a multidisciplinary team composed of the attending pediatrician, social worker, and nurse, in affiliation with the hospital administrator, legal staff, and security, as well as consulting psychiatrist, psychologist, and child protective services worker (Mian, 1995; Schreier & Libow, 1993). If the perpetrator-parent and victim(s) are subsequently reunited, continued monitoring of the child or children is strongly recommended to prevent recidivism and relapse (Mian, 1995; Ragaisis, 2004).

Suggestions for Prevention at Risk Intervention Points

1. *By guile and deceit, Rhonda was able to stay in the hospital and after-care residential center for almost 2 years. Because her discharge options were either placement in foster care or return to an unstable alcoholic mother who had never visited her, the residential treatment team was content to let her remain.*

The hospital and after-care residential center provided an excellent opportunity for a thorough investigation of Rhonda's personal history and mother-daughter relationship. Establishing a therapeutic alliance with the family through home visits and nonconfrontational contacts might have led to the revelation of her mother's Munchausen syndrome, which has often been found to be a precursor to MBP in the parent and also in her offspring when they become parents. Broadening the clinical picture beyond Rhonda and her needs for placement might have led to a longer term treatment plan to prevent her subsequent MBP.

2. *Rhonda would continue to have many health-related complaints and receive numerous pediatric examinations because of her self-reported irregular menses, abdominal cramping, and incapacitating headaches. She was occasionally hospitalized for brief periods of observation, though the physicians could not establish specific reasons for her ailments.*

Rhonda's medical history, in retrospect, was replete with signs of Munchausen syndrome. Her wish to be hospitalized as a child and adolescent and to receive numerous examinations should have raised warning flags for the series of treatment teams that provided medical care until her adulthood. She apparently reveled in being a patient and was eager to go through invasive evaluations so that she would be admitted for observation and treatment. Although many adolescents engage in attention-seeking behavior through suicide threats and low-risk attempts, few adolescent girls actively volunteer for repeated examinations or wish to be confined in a hospital away from friends and classmates.

3. Because of her history of excessive sick call, her claims of illness were dismissed as malingering. She received disciplinary warnings from her supervisors not to fake ailments or she would be dishonorably discharged.

This RIP highlights the similarities and differences between malingering and Munchausen syndrome. Both are similar in that the patient fabricates physical or psychological symptoms. However, in malingering, the patient's intention is to obtain some secondary gain such as money, avoidance of duties, or escape from criminal culpability (American Psychiatric Association, 2000). The Munchausen syndrome patient's motivation is solely to obtain uncritical medical nurturance and support as a medical or psychiatric patient. Referral for a psychiatric or psychological evaluation may have uncovered Rhonda's true intentions and led to more appropriate treatment than the threat of disciplinary action (e.g., demotion) or dishonorable discharge. Establishing a diagnosis of Munchausen syndrome at this point in her life might have alerted her future physicians to the possibility that Rhonda was at risk to become an MBP perpetrator.

4. Melvin was kept overnight for observation. Rhonda insisted that she stay by her baby's side until he was ready for discharge. She sent Henry home, and he left without complaint. Rhonda refused to leave her baby's crib. . . . During the night, Rhonda pressed the alarm button three times because Melvin had stopped breathing.

As illustrated in the foregoing section on relevant research, Rhonda's actions during Melvin's initial hospitalization were consistent with many MBP perpetrator characteristics. Because mothers with MBP present themselves to the uninformed medical staff as "supermoms," nurses and physicians without experience with this patient population often miss critical signals for accurate diagnosis. Many authors have commented that the best screening for MBP is the clinician's low threshold of suspicion and willingness to consider that a mother may be a perpetrator (Mian & Huyer, 1995).

5. After reviewing the baby's medical records and his body, the county medical examiner declared that Melvin had died from sudden infant death syndrome complicated by infant sleep apnea.

A number of MBP researchers have highlighted factors that may differentiate sudden infant death syndrome (SIDS) from recurrent child abuse and MBP, including the child's age, history, apnea history, and autopsy findings, as well as the characteristics of the child's mother and father (Light, 1995). Because MBP was not previously suspected and then recorded in progress notes or discharge summaries during Melvin's prior hospitalizations, it was difficult for the medical examiner to gain a true picture of the infant's medical history.

Certainly Rhonda was not a source of reliable information. For her to disclose her MBP perpetration would be equivalent to a confession to a serious felony, then homicide after Melvin died. If MBP had been suspected and a child protective services investigation been initiated prior to Melvin's death, he likely could have survived his mother's violence by placement in foster care. When Rhonda became pregnant with Marlin, her name on the state's central registry for child abuse perpetrators would have alerted the community's hospitals to her risk of MBP when she presented her second son at an emergency room.

> 6. *When she took Marlin to the emergency room twice in the following month, the hospital staff became increasingly skeptical of her explanations for her son's medical crises. They began to question her more closely about his symptoms before she brought him to the hospital. Rhonda was angered by the doubts the pediatricians and nurses had about her.*

Because Rhonda had come to the same hospital so many times with children displaying the same symptoms, the staff became skeptical of her intentions. When she was confronted by the staff, she went to another hospital after precipitating her son's third crisis, a common pattern among MBP perpetrators. As noted previously, if there had been a consistent, well-informed medical record for Melvin and Marlin, notification to child protection may have ultimately saved both children's lives.

Many authors have commented that the principal barriers to clinicians' discovery of MBP are a lack of knowledge of the disorder, an unwillingness to believe that a parent is capable of such acts, an underestimation of the scope and severity of the perpetrator's crime, and a belief that factitious disorders such as Munchausen syndrome and MBP are not serious (Kaufman, Coury, & Pickrel, 1989; Mian, 1995; Yorker & Kahan, 1991). However, as we have seen in Rhonda's case and in others described in the preceding literature review, MBP is a very lethal disorder with a high mortality rate. The chronic course and sequential victims of Rhonda's undetected MBP place her at the top of the list as the most dangerous filicidal mother in this book.

Epilogue

Rhonda was extradited to the other state to face a charge of capital murder in the death of the 9-month-old girl she babysat when she was 19. The state in which Melvin and Marlin died did not have the death penalty, so the local district attorney deferred prosecution and had Rhonda transported to her home state. If she were found not guilty in that death, the prosecutor believed he still had sufficient evidence to prove her culpability in Marlin's and perhaps Melvin's deaths.

After a jury trial, Rhonda was convicted in the death of the 9-month-old girl. Conflicting expert testimony about the child's cause of death was presented by prosecution and defense witnesses. Though the prosecutor had sought the death penalty based on the young age of the victim and the child's manner of death, the jury spared Rhonda's life. She was sentenced to life without parole. She subsequently pled guilty in the deaths of Marlin and Melvin.

20

Final Thoughts

What Have We Learned
and What Do We Need to Do?

This casebook has illustrated that maternal neonaticide, infanticide, and filicide are worldwide public health problems that are being actively investigated
by researchers in many different countries. The cases in this book took place
in the United States; however, these women's stories could be found in many
other cultures. This final chapter summarizes what the research and clinical
literature has discovered and highlights what might be done to reduce the likelihood of these child homicides.

What Have We Learned?

The research and case study chapters in this book have illustrated that each
year: (1) hundreds of infants and very young children die at the hands of their
mothers; (2) thousands of newborns are abandoned in public and private hospitals because their mothers are unwilling to care for them; (3) hundreds of
newborns are likely discarded by their mothers and left to die undiscovered;
(4) mothers kill their children for a variety of reasons, but (5) many newborns'
and infants' deaths may be preventable if the mothers, their partners, and their
families are adequately educated to recognize signs of elevated filicidal risk.
Each point is summarized briefly.

Newborn, Infant, and Early Childhood Deaths

As indicated in chapter 2, national statistics suggested that in 2001 more than
1,300 children died due to abuse or neglect by their caretakers in the United
States. Approximately 390 children, or one child each day, were killed by their

mothers. The children who died were very young and vulnerable: 85% were less than 6 years old, and 41% had not reached their first birthdays.

Abandoned Babies

Every year, thousands of newborns are voluntarily left by their mothers at public and private hospitals throughout the United States—almost 31,000 in 1998 (U.S. Department of Health & Human Services, 2004a). Two-thirds of the mothers reported that they were willing but unable to provide for their newborns. However, in more than 8,600 cases (28%), the mothers reported that the children were unwanted and that they were not willing to retain custody of their babies. The numbers of unwanted babies is even more staggering considering that the estimates are based only on known abandonment of live children.

Discarded, Undiscovered Newborns

Hundreds of newborns likely die undiscovered after being abandoned by their mothers without care or supervision. Some babies are, fortunately, found alive; however, the mortality rate of these discarded babies is extremely high. In a survey of newspaper accounts of discarded babies, the U.S. Department of Health and Human Services' Administration for Children and Families found that, in 1998, 33 of 105, or 31%, of the babies were dead on discovery (U.S. Department of Health & Human Services, 2004a). More recently, in just one county in California over a period of 27 months, 73% of the abandoned newborns were discovered deceased ("Safe Havens," 2003).

The true annual prevalence of discarded newborns is unknowable, but estimates suggest that the number may be in the hundreds. For example, the annual rate of known infant abandonment due to being unwanted is approximately 8,600. If the prevalence of discarded babies is even just 5% of that total, the annual number of undiscovered, deceased newborns would exceed 430, which would more than double the yearly maternal filicide rate.

Newborn and Infant Deaths May Be More Preventable

Pregnancy is a relatively easy condition to detect, especially by the second or third trimester. Human gestation takes many months; thus there is a prolonged opportunity to identify and prevent neonaticides and infanticides by surrounding the prospective and new mothers with family- and community-based services during the pregnancy/delivery and early postpartum stages. One recent national effort to reduce neonaticide and first-week infanticide has been the passage of "safe haven" legislation in almost every state. Unfortunately, very few new or prospective mothers are taking advantage of the statute. For example, as of September 2001 only 33 babies nationally had been legally relinquished (National Conference of State Legislatures, 2003).

In a 2-year period following their state's implementation of the law in 2000, however, New Jersey reported a 63% reduction in infant abandonment. California indicated that 20 newborns were saved under the statute (National Conference of State Legislatures, 2003). "Safe haven" laws are not without controversy (Daliard, 2000), but the legislation does focus on the most critical period for maternal neonaticide and infanticide: the first month of the baby's life. Clearly, these statutes need to be more vigorously advertised in public service announcements on radio, television, and the Internet.

Maternal Filicide Reasons and Prevention

The purpose of this book is to help prevent neonaticide, infanticide, and filicide by explaining the variety of reasons why mothers kill their children. Although the scholarly research and clinical literature are important in understanding the factors associated with maternal child homicide, I adopted a case-study format to show the numerous simple family- and community-based interventions that can be implemented to help keep newborns and infants alive. Under the variety of circumstances that are illustrated in this casebook, I hope that the reader will realize that many child homicides by mothers (and fathers) may be preventable.

What Do We Need to Do?

Since 1998, at least five textbooks and numerous journal articles have been published about maternal neonaticide, infanticide, and filicide. Research is now being actively conducted by investigators in many different fields, including psychologists, psychiatrists, pediatricians, sociologists, social workers, criminologists, and attorneys. Although answers to these tragic events are being clarified, many mental health, protective services, medical, and law enforcement professionals are likely faced with at-risk cases on a near-weekly basis. Confronted with decisions that might drastically alter the life course of their clients and patients, these professionals need well-validated risk analysis and prevention methods that will protect the children and their families.

Maternal filicide is a significant, tragic public health problem affecting hundreds, if not thousands, of persons each year. Although research and clinical practice are important, these efforts are only two legs of the risk-analysis-and-prevention tripod. Equally important to the prevention of maternal filicide is public education. Indeed, public education, clinical practice, and research are interwoven, each informing and clarifying the efforts of the other. For example, through public education, people become knowledgeable about problems and seek help from the professional community of clinicians whose methods have, ideally, been refined by systematic research. The following proposals are offered to enhance the prevention of maternal filicide and deepen our understanding of these tragic events.

Primary Prevention Programs

It is critical that public education programs are developed in a manner that will most likely affect those prospective and new mothers most at risk for neonaticide and infanticide. One of the primary benefits of public education is that many people can be simultaneously informed about a particular issue at a relatively low cost. At present, the bulk of research in maternal filicide exists in academic textbooks and scholarly journals that are actively shared among investigators in this field. Through those studies, clinicians and other professionals are educated about the indicants of maternal filicide risk. The clinician's knowledge is then applied in the services he or she provides to new or prospective mothers on a case-by-case, site-by-site basis. Because this approach often relies on the at-risk mother coming to the attention of the professional, many cases, especially neonaticides and first-week infanticides, are likely undetected.

Most of what the general public knows about maternal child homicide, however, comes from newspaper and television accounts of high-profile cases such as Andrea Yates and Susan Smith. The difficulty with this form of public education is that these cases are atypical; that is what makes their stories newsworthy. As a result, the public often obtains a distorted view of the reasons why mothers kill their children. Because the high-profile cases are unusual, the at-risk mother (and/or her family) may say "that's not me" and thus ignore signs and signals that she may be on a course for neonaticide, infanticide, or filicide. As illustrated through the case studies in this book, telling the women's stories may be a broadly effective way to inform and educate the public about maternal child homicide.

At-risk mothers who are teens and young adults, however, may be unlikely to attend a public lecture, read an academic textbook on maternal neonaticide and infanticide, or peruse the latest scholarly journal. Rather, these women often get their information from the visual media, specifically television and the movies. To teach these women about the risks of maternal filicide, we need to tell them in ways that will encourage them to watch and listen.

The cases in this book are accounts of ordinary women who have resolved their child-care crises in tragic ways. Telling these and other women's stories through made-for-television movies or documentaries, cable interviews, and/or case-study series in teenage girls' or women's magazines may have a broader community and national primary prevention impact. As the public becomes better informed, many more prospective and new mothers (and their families) may seek help from the professional community, and thus a higher number of infant lives may be saved.

An Interdisciplinary Panel of Experts

Formation of an interdisciplinary panel of experts from the professions of psychology, medicine, law, law enforcement, nursing, social work, criminology, and public health may result in an integrated and structured research program of retrospective and longitudinal risk assessment and prevention studies of maternal neonaticide, infanticide, and filicide. Research in this area has faced many difficulties, including small sample sizes, lack of adequate control groups, and lack of primary-source data (e.g., direct-contact interviews, psychometric test results, etc.). The current research also suffers from a lack of uniformity in selection and measurement of perpetrator risk and protective factors, as well as victim and crime characteristics. These problems have hampered progression of knowledge in this field.

If a "blue ribbon" panel of experts could be established and obtain consensus on an integrated research plan, substantial gains could be made in our understanding and prevention of these tragedies. For example, in the clinical practice arena for psychologists and psychiatrists, the panel's "best practices" evaluation procedures might follow the forensic mental health assessment model of Heilbrun (2001) and his colleagues (Heilbrun, DeMatteo, & Marczyk, 2004). These model evaluations, in turn, could be exemplars for the pragmatic-psychology "psycholegal Lexis proposal" of Fishman (2003), which might be applied to insanity and other forensic evaluations of women charged with neonaticide and infanticide (Dobson & Sales, 2000). Consensus on these methods might create the foundation for the research studies described next.

Large Sample Studies of Convicted Filicidal Mothers

Large-sample, multisite, multistate clinical assessment studies of mothers who were convicted of child homicide will be of great benefit. These evaluations would include one or more individual interviews with structured and semi-structured questions to obtain data on the women's childhood, adolescent, familial, educational, medical and childbirth, mental health and substance abuse, criminal, sexual, partner/marital, interpersonal, and vocational histories. As well, each woman would be administered a battery of personality tests, and in addition a collateral interview of her family members would be done.

Control groups for these studies could be established of women inmates who were incarcerated for nonfilicidal murder (e.g., spouse, parent, victim outside the family) and similar crimes (e.g., attempted murder, assault and battery with attempt to kill, etc.). As I have indicated previously, many studies of maternal filicide involve very few participants because the detected base rate of the act is relatively low compared with other crimes by females. The larger the sample size, the more confidence can be attached to the conclusions drawn from the data. By developing multisite, multistate samples, researchers may more clearly and reliably identify those factors that might best describe mothers who kill.

Large-sample, multisite studies will also overcome another common problem of maternal filicide research: the limited applicability of results to other settings due to sample-specific bias. For example, if the investigators examine only women in a pretrial forensic hospital (e.g., McKee & Shea, 1998), it is more likely that the participants will be mentally ill because insanity has been raised as a legal defense.

In contrast, the women convicted of maternal filicide will likely display a wider array of characteristics. Though some will be mentally ill, many more may exemplify the features of neonaticidal, abusive and neglectful, and psychopathic mothers who kill. Larger sample sizes will also produce larger numbers of rarer forms of maternal filicide, in particular from the category of retaliatory mothers, which in turn will allow for stronger conclusions about these women's characteristics and risk factors.

Studies of Mothers of Newborns

Conducting large-sample, multisite, multistate clinical assessment studies of mothers who abandoned their newborns in the hospital or other public service locations will also be critically important. Little is known about the characteristics of these women; indeed, many states with "safe haven" laws forbid asking the mother for any information (National Conference of State Legislatures, 2003). The evaluation paradigm described previously could also be employed with these research participants. The value of these studies would be in understanding why these women, who were at-risk mothers for neonaticide and infanticide, instead chose a safe alternative for their newborns.

Follow-up interviews with repeated administration of the personality test battery at 6 months, 1 year, and 2 years postpartum (early postpartum, late postpartum, and postinfancy stages) would provide valuable data regarding the changes over time in the women's individual, family of origin, and situational maternal filicide risk and protective factors. Control groups for the women in these studies would be assessed with the same evaluation methods as those mothers in the site-hospitals who chose to keep their newborns. From these and other large-sample studies, risk analysis devices such as the Maternal Filicide Risk Matrix in this book might be refined and improved.

Therapeutic Jurisprudence Analysis of "Safe Haven" Laws

Therapeutic jurisprudence (Wexler, 1993) is a relatively new interdisciplinary field that brings together specialists from law and the social sciences to analyze whether a particular legal rule or practice enhances the psychological and physical well-being of those to whom the law applies (Slobogin, 1995). "Safe haven" laws have been designed specifically to prevent neonaticide and infanticide by providing mothers of newborns a simple, legal way of voluntarily abandoning their babies. The content of these laws, however, varies on many dimensions, and this variation provides many opportunities for therapeutic jurisprudence analysis.

Some statutes allow the mother to relinquish her child within 72 hours of birth (e.g., Arizona, Alabama, California, Colorado), whereas others permit the mother to wait as long as 30 days (e.g., Arkansas, Connecticut, Idaho) to 45 days (Indiana) or up to 1 year postpartum (North Dakota). The statutes vary as well on the issue of maternal liability for abandonment (Child Welfare League of America, 2002). For example, the mother is immune from prosecution (except for evidence of abuse or neglect) in as many as 20 of the states (e.g., Florida, Georgia, North Carolina, North Dakota, Ohio, and South Carolina), but in other states (e.g., Oregon, Mississippi, Texas, West Virginia) the law is only an affirmative defense to prosecution. Some "safe haven" laws allow the mother to maintain her anonymity and do not require collecting information about her (e.g., medical history, drug use, etc.), whereas others do not (National Conference of State Legislatures, 2003). Therapeutic jurisprudence analysis might provide information to help states improve utilization of their statutes and ultimately reduce the prevalence of maternal neonaticide and infanticide.

References

Abel, G. G., & Osborn, C. A. (2003). Treatment of sex offenders. In R. Rosner (Ed.). *Principles and practice of forensic psychiatry* (pp. 705–716). London: Arnold.

Abidin, R. (1995). *Parenting stress index: Professional manual.* Odessa, FL: Psychological Assessment Resources.

Abramowitz, J. S., Schwartz, S. A., Moore, K. M., & Luenzmann, K. R. (2003). Obsessive-compulsive symptoms in pregnancy and the puerperium: A review of the literature. *Journal of Anxiety Disorders, 17*(4), 461–478.

Absolut de la Gastine, G., Penniello, M. J., Le Truest, M., Grujard, D., & Guillois, B. (1998). Urinary calculi and Munchausen syndrome. *Archives of Pediatrics, 5*(5), 517–520.

Agrawal, H. R., Gunderson, J., Holmes, B. M., & Lyons-Ruth, K. (2004). Attachment studies with borderline patients: A review. *Harvard Review of Psychiatry, 12*(2), 94–104.

Ainsworth, M., Blehar, M., Waters, E., & Wall, S. (1978). *Patterns of attachment: A psychological study of the Strange Situation.* Hillsdale, NJ: Erlbaum.

Alder, C., & Polk, K. (2001). *Child victims of homicide.* Cambridge, UK: Cambridge University Press.

Alexander, R., Sato, Y., Smith, W., & Bennett, T. (1990). Incidence of impact trauma with cranial injuries ascribed to shaking. *American Journal of Diseases of Childhood, 144*(6), 724–726.

Alexander, R., Smith, W., & Stevenson, R. (1990). Serial Munchausen syndrome by proxy. *Pediatrics, 86*(4), 581–584.

American Academy of Pediatrics. (1999). Committee on child abuse and neglect and committee on community health services: Investigation and review of unexpected infant and child deaths. *Pediatrics, 104,* 1158–1160.

American Psychiatric Association. (2000). *Diagnostic and statistical manual of mental disorders* (4th ed., text rev.) Washington, DC: American Psychiatric Association.

Andrews, A. B. (1995). *Excerpts from social history of Susan Vaughan Smith.* Unpublished manuscript.

Appleby, L., Warner, R., & Whitten, A. (1997). A controlled study of fluoxetine and cognitive behavioural counseling in the treatment of postnatal depression. *British Medical Journal, 314,* 932–936.

Arieff, A. I., & Kronlund, B. A. (1999). Fatal child abuse by forced water intoxication. *Pediatrics, 103,* 1292–1295.

Atwal, G. S., Rutty, G. N., Carter, N., & Green, M. A. (1998). Bruising in non-accidental head injured children: A retrospective study of the prevalence, distribution, and pathological associations in 24 cases. *Forensic Sciences International, 96*(2–3), 215–230.

Bacon, D. (2004). Sudden unexpected death and covert homicide in infancy. *Archives of Disease in Childhood, 89*(5), 433–437.

Bagge, C., Nickell, A., Stepp, S., Durrett, C., Jackson, K., & Trull, T. (2004). Borderline personality disorder features predict negative outcomes 2 years later. *Journal of Abnormal Psychology, 113*(2), 279–288.

Baker, J. (1991). *You can't let your children cry: Filicide in Victoria 1978–1988.* Unpublished master's thesis, University of Melbourne, Victoria, Australia.

Baker, J., & Hill, S. S. (2005). The APSAC study guides. In G. P. Koocher, J. C. Norcross, & S. S. Hill (Eds.), *Psychologists' desk reference* (2nd ed., pp. 416–422). New York: Oxford University Press.

Bakken, J., Miltenberger, R.G., & Schauss, S. (1993). Teaching parents with mental retardation: Knowledge versus skills. *American Journal of Mental Retardation, 97*(4), 405–417.

Bappal, B., George, M., Nair, R., Khusaiby, S. A., & DeSilva, V. (2001). Factitious hypoglycemia: A tale from the Arab world. *Pediatrics, 107*(1), 180–181.

Barley, W. D., Buie, S. E., Peterson, E., Hollingsworth, A., Griva, M., et al. (1993). Development of an inpatient cognitive-behavioral treatment program for borderline personality disorder. *Journal of Personality Disorders, 7,* 232–240.

Barraclough, B. M., Bunch, J., Nelson, B., & Sainsbury, P. (1974). A hundred cases of suicide: Clinical aspects. *British Journal of Psychiatry, 125,* 355–373.

Bauer, C. R., Shankaran, S., Bada, H. S., Lester, B., et al. (2002). The maternal lifestyle study: Drug exposure during pregnancy and short-term maternal outcomes. *American Journal of Obstetrics and Gynecology, 186*(3), 487–495.

Beck, A. T., Brown, G., & Berchik, R. J. (1990). Relationship between hopelessness and ultimate suicide: A replication with psychiatric outpatients. *American Journal of Psychiatry, 147,* 190–195.

Bell, S., & Ainsworth, M. (1972). Infant crying and maternal responsiveness. *Child Development, 43,* 1171–1190.

Ben-Cherit, E., & Melmed, R. N. (1998). Recurrent hypoglycemia in multiple myeloma: A case of Munchausen syndrome by proxy in an elderly patient. *Journal of Internal Medicine, 244*(2), 175–178.

Berger, R. P., Kochanek, p. m., & Pierce, M. C. (2004). Biochemical markers of brain injury: Could they be used as diagnostic adjuncts in cases of inflicted traumatic brain injury? *Child Abuse and Neglect, 28*(7), 739–754.

Berkowitz, L. (1993). Towards a general theory of anger and emotional aggression: Implications of the cognitive-neoassociationist perspective for the analysis of anger and other emotions. In R. S. Wyer & T. K. Krull (Eds.), *Advances in social cognition: Vol. 6. Perspectives on anger and emotion* (pp. 1–46). Hillsdale, NJ: Erlbaum.

Berlin, H., & Rolls, E. (2004). Time perception, impulsivity, emotionality, and personality in self-harming borderline personality disorder patients. *Journal of Personality Disorders, 18*(4) 358–378.

Bibring, G. (1959). Some considerations of the psychological processes in pregnancy. *Psychoanalytic Study of the Child, 14,* 113–121.

Black, D., Blum, N., Pfohl, B., & Hale, N. (2004). Suicidal behavior in borderline personality disorder: Prevalance, risk factors, prediction, and prevention. *Journal of Personality Disorders, 18*(3), 226–239.

Black, M. M., Papas, M. A., Hussey, J. M., Hunter, Dubowitz, H., Kotch, J. B., et al. (2002). Behavior and development of preschool children born to adolescent mothers: Risk and 3-generation households. *Pediatrics, 109*(4), 573–580.

Blackman, J. S. (2004). *101 defenses: How the mind shields itself.* New York: Brunner-Routledge.

Bongar, B., & Sullivan, G. R. (2005). Treatment and management of the suicidal patient. In G. P. Koocher, J. C. Norcross, & S. S. Hill (Eds.), *Psychologists' desk reference* (2nd ed., pp. 240–245). New York: Oxford University Press.

Bosquet, M., & Egeland, B. (2000). Predicting parenting behaviors from Antisocial Practices content scale scores of the MMPI-2 administered during pregnancy. *Journal of Personality Assessment, 74*(1), 146–162.

Bourget, D., & Bradford, J. M. W. (1990). Homicidal parents. *Canadian Journal of Psychiatry, 35,* 233–237.

Bourget, D., & Gagne, P. (2002). Maternal filicide in Quebec. *Journal of the American Academy of Psychiatry and the Law, 30*(3), 345–351.

Bowlby, J. (1961). Processes of mourning. *International Journal of Psychoanalysis, 42,* 317–340.

Bowlby, J. (1973). *Attachment and loss: Vol. 2. Separation.* New York: Basic Books.

Bowlby, J. (1980). *Attachment and loss: Vol. 3. Loss.* New York: Basic Books.

Brandes, M., Soares, C. N., & Cohen, L. S. (2004). Postpartum onset obsessive-compulsive disorder: Diagnosis and management. *Archives of Womens' Mental Health, 7*(2), 99–110.

Braverman, P., & Strasburger, V. (1994, January). Sexually transmitted diseases. *Clinical Pediatrics,* 26–37.

Brazelton, T. B., Koslowski, B., & Main, M. (1974). The origins of reciprocity. In M. Lewis & L. A. Rosenbaum (Eds.). *The effects of the infant on its caregiver.* New York: Wiley.

Briere, J. (1997). *Psychological assessment of adult posttraumatic states.* Washington, DC: American Psychological Association.

Bright, P. (1987). Adolescent pregnancy and loss. *Maternal-Child Nursing Journal, 16,* 1–12.

Brodsky, S. (1998). Psychotherapy with reluctant and involuntary clients. In G. P. Koocher, J. C. Norcross, & S. S. Hill (Eds.), *Psychologists' desk reference* (pp. 306–313). New York: Oxford University Press.

Brodsky, S. (2005). Psychotherapy with reluctant and involuntary clients. In G. P. Koocher, J. C. Norcross, & S. S. Hill (Eds.), *Psychologists' desk reference* (2nd ed., pp. 257–262). New York: Oxford University Press.

Brody, J. E. (1999, March 15). Earlier work with children steers them from crime. *New York Times,* p. A16.

Brown, G., Newman, C., Charlesworth, S., Crits-Christoph, P., & Beck, A. (2004). An open clinical trial of cognitive therapy for borderline personality disorder. *Journal of Personality Disorders, 18*(3), 257–271.

Brown, S., & Eisenberg, L. (Eds.). (1995). *The best intentions: Unintended pregnancy and the well-being of children and families.* Washington, DC: National Academy Press.

Bugental, D. (1992). Affective and cognitive processes within threat-oriented family systems. In I. E. Sigel, A. V. McGillicuddy-DeLisi, & J. J. Goodnow (Eds.), *Parental belief systems: The psychological consequences for children* (2nd ed., pp. 219–248). Hillsdale, NJ: Erlbaum.

Bureau of Justice Statistics. (1997). *Homicide trends in the United States.* Retrieved October 25, 2005, from http://ojp.usdoj.gov/bjs/homicide/homtrnd.htm

Bureau of Justice Statistics. (2000). *Homicide trends in the United States.* Retrieved October 25, 2005, from http://ojp.usdoj.gov/bjs/homicide/children.htm

Burgess, A. W., & Holmstrom, L. L. (1979). *Rape: Crisis and recovery.* Bowie, MD: Brady.

Burt, V. K., Suri, R., Altshuler, L., & Stowe, Z. (2001). The use of psychotropic medications during breast-feeding. *American Journal of Psychiatry, 158*(7), 1001–1009.

Butcher, J. N., Dahlstrom, L., Graham, J. R., Tellegen, A., & Kaemmer, B. (1989). *Minnesota Multiphasic Personality Inventory-2.* Minneapolis: University of Minnesota Press.

Butz, a.m., Lears, M. K., O'Neil, S., & Lukk, P. (1998). Home intervention for in utero drug-exposed infants. *Public Health Nursing, 15*(5), 307–318.

Byard, R. W., Knight, D., James, R. A., & Gilbert, J. (1999). Murder-suicides involving children: A 29-year study. *American Journal of Forensic Medical Pathology, 20*(4), 323–327.

Byrne, C. P., Velamoor, V. R., Cernovsky, Z. Z., Cortese, L., & Losztyn, S. (1990). A comparison of borderline and schizophrenic patients for childhood life events and parent-child relationships. *Canadian Journal of Psychiatry, 35*(7), 590–595.

Cale, E. M., & Lilienfeld, S. O. (2002). Sex differences in psychopathy and antisocial personality disorder: A review and integration. *Clinical Psychology Review, 22,* 1179–1207.

Cale, E. M., & Lilienfeld, S. O. (2003). What every forensic psychologist should know about psychopathic personality. In W. O'Donohoe & E. Levensky (Eds.), *Handbook of forensic psychology: Resource for mental health and legal professionals* (pp. 395–428). San Diego, CA: Elsevier.

Calzada, E. J., Aamiry, A., & Eyberg, S. M. (2005). Principles of treatment with the behaviorally disordered child. In G. P. Koocher, J. C. Norcross, & S. S. Hill (Eds.), *Psychologists' desk reference* (2nd ed., pp. 401–405). New York: Oxford University Press.

Campbell, J. C. (Ed.). (1995). *Assessing dangerousness: Violence by sexual offenders, batterers, and child abusers.* Thousand Oaks, CA: Sage.

Carlson, K. (1998). *Physiology of behavior* (6th ed.). Needham Heights, MA: Allyn & Bacon.

Carroll, K. M., Nich, C., Ball, S., McCance, E., & Rounsaville, B. J. (1998). Treatment of cocaine and alcohol dependence with psychotherapy and disulfram. *Addiction, 93,* 713–728.

Case, M. E., Graham, M. A., Handy, T. C., Jentzen, J. M., & Monteleone, J. A. (2001). Position paper on fatal abusive head injuries in infants and young children. *American Journal of Forensic Medical Pathology, 22*(2), 112–122.

Casiano, M. E. (1990). Outpatient medical management of postpartum psychiatric disorders. *NAACOGS: Clinical Issues in Perinatal Womens Health Nursing, 1*(3), 395–401.

Cassem, N. H. (1988). The person confronting death. In A. M. Nicholi (Ed.). *The new Harvard guide to psychiatry* (pp. 728–758). Cambridge, MA: Harvard University Press.

Cates, W. (1991). Teenagers and sexual risk taking: The best of times and the worst of times. *Journal of Adolescent Health, 12,* 84–94.

Centers for Disease Control and Prevention. (2004). Alcohol use among adolescents and adults. *Morbidity and Mortality Weekly Report, 53*(8), 174–175.

Chambless, D. L. (2005). Compendium of empirically supported therapies. In G. P. Koocher, J. C. Norcross, & S. S. Hill (Eds.). *Psychologists' desk reference* (2nd ed., pp. 183–192). New York: Oxford University Press.

Chandra, P. S., Venkatasubramanian, G., & Thomas, T. (2002). Infanticidal ideas and infanticidal behavior in Indian women with severe postpartum psychiatric disorders. *Journal of Nervous Mental Disorders, 190*(7), 457–461.

Chasten, S. E. (1991). *Making effective referrals: The therapeutic process.* New York: Gardner.

Chaudron, L. H. (2000). When and how to use mood stabilizers during breastfeeding. *Primary Care Update Obstetrics and Gynecology, 7*(3), 113–117.

Chess, S., & Thomas, A. (1986). *Temperament in clinical practice.* New York: Guilford Press.

Cheung, P. K. T. (1986). Maternal filicide in Hong Kong, 1971–1985. *Medicine, Science, & the Law, 26,* 185–192.

Child Welfare League of America. (2002). *Baby abandonment project.* Retrieved on October 31, 2004, from http://www.cwla.org/programs/pregprev/flocrittsafehaven .htm

Clark, L., Brasseux, C., Richmond, D., Getson, P., & D'Angelo, L. (1998). Effect of HIV counseling and testing on sexually transmitted diseases and condom use in an urban adolescent population. *Archives of Pediatric and Adolescent Medicine, 152,* 269–273.

Clarkin, J., & Foelsch, P. (2005). Principles in the treatment of borderline personality disorder. In G. P. Koocher, J. C. Norcross, & S. S. Hill (Eds.), *Psychologists' desk reference* (2nd ed., pp. 255–257). New York: Oxford University Press.

Clarkin, J., Hull, J., & Hurt, S. (1993). Factor structure of borderline personality disorder criteria. *Journal of Personality Disorders, 7,* 137–143.

Cleckley, H. (1998). *The mask of sanity.* St. Louis, MO: Mosby. (Original work published 1941)

Cloninger, C. (1987). Neurogenetic adaptive mechanisms in alcoholism. *Science, 236,* 410–416.

Coccaro, E. F., Schmidt, C. A., Samuels, J. F., & Nestadt, G. (2004). Lifetime and 1-month prevalence rates of intermittent explosive disorder in a community sample. *Journal of Clinical Psychiatry, 65*(6), 820–824.

Cohen, J. A., & Mannarino, A. P. (1998). Factors that mediate the treatment outcome of sexually abused preschool children: 6 and 12 month follow-up. *Journal of the Academy of Child and Adolescent Psychiatry, 37,* 44–51.

Cohle, S. D., Trestrail, J. D., Graham, M. A., Oxley, D. W., Walp, B., & Jachimczyk, J. (1988). Fatal pepper aspiration. *American Journal of Diseases of Childhood, 142*(6), 633–636.

Comitz, S., Comitz, G., & Semprevivo, D. M. (1990). Postpartum psychosis: A family's perspective. *NAACOGS: Clinical Issues of Perinatal Womens Health Nursing, 1*(3), 410–418.

Connell, J. (1992, April 5). Seeking common ground. *Oregonian,* B1–B4.

Conners, N. A., Bradley, R. H., Whiteside-Mansell, L., & Crone, C. C. (2001). A comprehensive substance abuse treatment program for women and their children: An initial evaluation. *Journal of Substance Abuse Treatment, 21*(2), 67–75.

Conroy, M.A. (2003). Evaluation of sexual predators. In A. M. Goldstein (Ed.), *Handbook of psychology: Vol. 11.Forensic psychology* (pp.463–484). Hoboken, NJ: Wiley.

Cordner, S. M., Burke, M. P., Dodd, M. J., Lynch, M.J., Ranson, D. L., & Robertson, S. D. (2001). Issues in child homicide: 11 cases. *Legal Medicine, 3*(2), 95–103.

Cottler, L. B., Price, R. K., Compton, W. M., & Mager, D. E. (1995). Subtypes of adult antisocial behavior and drug abusers. *Journal of Nervous and Mental Disease, 183,* 154–161.

Coyer, S. M. (2003). Women in recovery discuss parenting while addicted to cocaine. *American Journal of Maternal Child Nursing, 28*(1), 445–449.

Cramer, B., Robert-Tissot, C., Stern, D., Serpa-Rusconi, S., de Muralt, M., Besson, G., et al. (1990). Outcome evaluation in brief mother-infant psychotherapy: A preliminary report. *Infant Mental Health Journal, 11,* 278–300.

Crimmins, S., Langley, S., Brownstein, H. H., & Sprunt, B. J. (1997). Convicted women who have killed children: A self-psychology perspective. *Journal of Interpersonal Violence, 12,* 49–69.

Crittenden, P. M. (1985). Social networks, quality of child rearing, and child development. *Child Development, 56,* 1299–1309.

Crittenden, P. M. & Craig, S. E. (1990). Developmental trends in the nature of child homicide. *Journal of Interpersonal Violence, 5,* 202–216.

Crooks, R., & Bauer, K. (1999). *Our sexuality* (7th ed.). Pacific Grove, CA: Brooks/Cole.

Crouch, J., & Behl, L. (2001). Relationships among parental beliefs in corporal punishment, reported stress, and physical child abuse potential. *Child Abuse and Neglect, 25,* 413–419.

Cummings, P., Theis, M. F., Mueller, B. A., & Rivara, F. (1994). Infant injury and death in Washington state, 1981–1990. *Archives of Pediatric and Adolescent Medicine, 148,* 1021–1026.

Currid, T. (2004). Issues relating to puerperal psychosis and its management. *Nursing Times, 100*(17), 40–43.

Curtis, G. B., & Shuler, J. (2001). *Your pregnancy: Questions and answers* (3rd ed.). Cambridge, MA: Perseus.

Daliard, C. (2000, August). The drive to enact "infant abandoment" laws: A rush to judgment? *The Guttmacher report on public policy, 3*(4). Retrieved October 31, 2004, from http://www.guttmacher.org/pubs/tgr/03/4/gr030401.html

Daly, M., & Wilson, M. (1988). *Homicide.* Hawthorne, NY: Aldine de Gruyter.

Davanzo, P., Yue, K., Thomas, M. A., Belin, T., Mintz, J., Vekatraman, T. N., et al. (2003). Proton magnetic resonance spectroscopy of bipolar disorder versus intermittent explosive disorder in children and adolescents. *American Journal of Psychiatry, 160*(8), 1442–1452.

Deblinger, E., Steer, R., & Lippman, J. (1999). Two-year follow-up study of cognitive behavior therapy for sexually abused children suffering post-traumatic stress symptoms. *Child Abuse and Neglect, 23,* 1371–1378.

Deffenbacher, J., Filetti, L., Lynch, R., & Oetting, E. (2002). Cognitive-behavioral treatment of high anger drivers. *Behavior Research and Therapy, 40,* 895–910.

Delva, J., Mathiesen, S. G., & Kamata, A. (2001). Use of illegal drugs among mothers across racial/ethnic groups in the United States: A multi-level analysis of individual and community level influences. *Ethnology and Disease, 11*(4), 614–625.

Dietrich, D., Berkowitz, L., Kadushin, A., & McGloin, J. (1990). Some factors influencing abusers' justification of their child abuse. *Child Abuse and Neglect, 14*(3), 337–345.

Dietz, P. E. (1986). Mass, serial, and sensational homicides. *Bulletin of the New York Academy of Medicine, 62,* 477–491.

Dobson, V., & Sales, B. (2000). The science of infanticide and mental illness. *Psychology, Public Policy, and Law, 6,* 1098–1112.

Dowdney, L., & Skuse, D. (1993). Parenting provided by adults with mental retardation. *Journal of Child Psychology and Psychiatry, 34*(1), 25–47.

Downs, W., Capshew, T., & Rindels, B. (2004). Relationships between adult women's alcohol problems and their childhood experiences of parental violence and psychological aggression. *Journal of Studies in Alcoholism, 65*(3), 336–344.

Drake, R. E., & Cotton, P. G. (1986). Depression, hopelessness, and suicide in chronic schizophrenia. *British Journal of Psychiatry, 148,* 554–559.

Eggington, J. (1989). *From cradle to grave.* New York: Morrow.

Ehlers, C. L., Frank, E., & Kupfer, D. J. (1998). Social zeitgebers and biological rhythms. *Archives of General Psychiatry, 45,* 948–952.

Emerick, S. J., Foster, L. R., & Campbell, D. T. (1986). Risk factors for traumatic infant death in Oregon, 1973–1982. *Pediatrics, 77,* 518–522.

Emery, J. L. (1993). Child abuse, sudden infant death syndrome, and unexpected death. *American Journal of Diseases of the Child, 147,* 1097–1100.

England, L., Brenner, R., Bhaskar, B., Simons-Morton, B., Das, A., Revenis, M., et al. (2003). Breastfeeding practices in a cohort of inner-city women: The role of contraindications. *BMC Public Health, 3*(1), 28.

Ewigman, B., Kivlahan, C., & Land, G. (1993). The Missouri child fatality study: Underreporting of maltreatment fatalities among children younger than five years of age, 1983–1986. *Pediatrics, 91,* 330–337.

Feldman, M. A., Ducharme, J. M., & Case, L. (1999). Using self-instructional pictorial manuals to teach child-care skills to mothers with intellectual disabilities. *Behavior Modification, 23*(3), 480–497.

Feldman, M. A., & Walton-Allen, N. (1997). Effects of maternal mental retardation and poverty on intellectual, academic, and behavioral status of school-age children. *American Journal of Mental Retardation, 101*(4), 352–264.

Fishman, D. (2003). Background on the "psycholegal Lexis proposal": Exploring the potential of a systematic case study database in forensic psychology. *Psychology, Public Policy, and Law, 9,* 267–274.

Foley, D. L., Pickles, A., Rutter, M., Gardner, C. O., Maes, H. H., Silberg, J. L., et al. (2004). Risks for conduct disorder symptoms associated with parental alcoholism in stepfather families versus intact families from a community sample. *Journal of Child Psychology and Psychiatry, 45*(4), 687–696.

Fonagy, P., Steele, M., & Steele, H. (1991). The capacity for understanding mental states: The reflective self in parent and child and its significance for security of attachment. *Infant Mental Health Journal, 12,* 201–218.

Fraiberg, S. H. (1980). *Clinical studies in infant mental health: The first year of life.* New York: Basic Books.

Fraiberg, S. H., Adelson, E., & Shapiro, V. (1975). Ghosts in the nursery: A psychoanalytic approach to the problem of impaired infant-mother relationships. *Journal of the American Academy of Child Psychiatry, 14,* 387–422.

Frank, D. A., Rose-Jacobs, R., Beeghly, M., Wilbur, M., Bellinger, D., & Cabral, H., et al. (2005). Level of prenatal cocaine exposure and 48-month IQ: Importance of preschool enrichment. *Neurotoxicology and Teratology, 27*(1), 15–28.

Friedman, S. H., & Rosenthal, M. B. (2003). Treatment of perinatal delusional disorder: A case report. *International Journal of Psychiatry Medicine, 33*(4), 391–394.

Friedrich, W. N. (1998). *Child sexual behavior inventory manual.* Odessa, FL: Psychological Assessment Resources.

Frierson, R. L., Melikian, M., & Wadman, P. C. (2002). Principles of suicide risk assessment. *Postgraduate Mdicine, 112*(3), 65–71.

Gale, S., & Harlow, B. L. (2003). Postpartum mood disorders: A review of clinical and epidemiological factors. *Journal of Psychosomatic Obstetrics and Gynaecology, 24*(4), 257–266.

Galvin, H. K, Newton, A. W., & Vandeven, A. M. (2005). Update on Munchausen syndrome by proxy. *Current Opinions in Pediatrics, 17*(2), 252–257.

Galvoski, T. E., & Blanchard, E. B. (2002). The effectiveness of a brief psychological intervention on court-referred and self-referred aggressive drivers. *Behavior Research and Therapy, 40*(12), 1385–1402.

Galvoski, T., Blanchard, E. B., & Veazy, C. (2002). Intermittent explosive disorder and other psychiatric comorbidity among court-referred and self-referred aggressive drivers. *Behavior Research and Therapy, 40*(6), 641–651.

George, C., Kaplan, N., & Main, M. (1985). *The Adult Attachment Interview.* Unpublished manuscript, University of California at Berkeley.

Gil, E. (2003). Play genograms. In C. F. Sori & L. L. Hecker (Eds.), *The therapist's notebook for children and adolescents: Homework, handouts, and activities for use in psychotherapy* (pp. 97–118). New York: Haworth Press.

Glasser, M., Dennis, J., Orthoefer, J., Carter, S., & Hollander, E. (1989). Characteristics of males at a public health department contraceptive service. *Journal of Adolescent Health Care, 10,* 115–118.

Gober, P. (1997). The role of access in explaining state abortion rates. *Social Science Medicine, 44,* 1003–1016.

Gordon, D. A., Arbuthnot, J., Gustafson, K. E., & McGreen, P. (1988). Home-based behavioral-systems family therapy with disadvantaged juvenile delinquents. *American Journal of Family Therapy, 163,* 243–255.

Grant, B. F., Hasin, D. S., Stinson, F. S., Dawson, D. A., Chou, S. P., Ruan, W. J., et al. (2004). Prevalence, correlates, and disability of personality disorders in the United States: Results from the national epidemiologic survey on alcohol and related conditions. *Journal of Clinical Psychiatry, 65*(7), 948–958.

Grohol, J. M. (2005). Top Internet sites for psychologists and their clients. In G. P. Koocher, J. C. Norcross, & S. S. Hill (Eds.), *Psychologists' desk reference* (2nd ed., pp. 491–494). New York: Oxford University Press.

Gruskin, S. (2001, April 16). Porcelain deliveries a crisis as teens seek to hide pregnancies. *South Florida Sun-Sentinel.* Retrieved on June 17, 2004, from http://www.vachss.com/help_text/archive/porcelain.html

Guscott, R. G., & Steiner, M. (1991). A multidisciplinary treatment approach to post-partum psychosis. *Canadian Journal of Psychiatry, 36*(8), 551–556.

Guttman, A., Dick, P., & To, T. (2004). Infant hospitalization and maternal depression, poverty, and single parenthood: A population-based study. *Child Care Health Development, 30*(1), 67–75.

Hamburger, M. E., Lilienfeld, S. O., & Hogben, M. (1996). Psychopathy, gender, and gender roles: Implications for antisocial and histrionic personality disorders. *Journal of Personality Disorders, 10,* 41–55.

Hare, R. D. (1991). *The Hare Psychopathy Checklist, Revised.* Toronto, Ontario, Canada: Multi-Health Systems.

Harris, E. A., & Bennett, B. E. (2005). Sample psychotherapist-patient contract. In G. P. Koocher, J. C. Norcross, & S. S. Hill (Eds.), *Psychologists' desk reference* (2nd ed., pp. 255–257). New York: Oxford University Press.

Hart, S. N., Brassard, M. R., & Karlson, H. C. (1996). Psychological maltreatment. In J. Briere, L. Berliner, J. A. Bulkley, C. Jenny, & T. Reid (Eds.), *The APSAC handbook on child maltreatment* (pp. 72–89). Thousand Oaks, CA: Sage.

Hasin, D. & Grant, B. (2004). The co-occurrence of DSM-IV alcohol abuse in DSM-IV alcohol dependence: Results of the national epidemiologic survey or alcohol and related conditions on heterogeneity that differ by population subgroup. *Archives of General Psychiatry, 61*(9), 891–896.

Heilbrun, K. (2001). *Principles of forensic mental health assessment.* New York: Kluwer Academic/Plenum.

Heilbrun, K., DeMatteo, D., & Marczyk, G. (2004). Pragmatic psychology, forensic mental health assessment, and the case of Thomas Johnson: Applying principles to promote quality. *Psychology, Public Policy, and Law, 10,* 31–70.

Heilbrun, K., Marczyk, G., & DeMatteo, D. (2002). *Forensic mental health assessment: A casebook.* New York: Oxford University Press.

Hemphill, J. F., & Hart, S. D. (2003). Forensic and clinical issues in the assessment of psychopathy. In A. M. Goldstein (Ed.), *Handbook of psychology: Vol. 11. Forensic psychology* (pp. 87–107). Hoboken, NJ: Wiley.

Heneghan, A. M., Mercer, M., & DeLeone, N. L. (2004). Will mothers discuss parenting stress and depressive symptoms with their child's pediatrician? *Pediatrics, 113*(3), 460–467.

Henggeler, S. W., Schoenwald, S. K., Borduin, C. M., Rowland, M. D., & Cunningham, P. D. (1998). *Multisystemic treatment of antisocial behavior in children and adolescents.* New York: Guilford Press.

Herman-Giddens, M. E., Brown, G., Verbiest, S., Carlson, P. J., Hooten, E. G., Howell, E. G., et al. (1999). Underascertainment of child abuse mortality in the United States. *Journal of the American Medical Association, 282*(5), 463–467.

Hesselbrock, M. N., Meyer, R. E., & Keener, J. J. (1985). Psychopathology in hospitalized alcoholics. *Archives of General Psychiatry, 42,* 1050–1055.

Hicks, R. A., & Gaughan, D. C. (1995). Understanding fatal child abuse. *Child Abuse and Neglect, 19*(7), 855–863.

Hildyard, K. L., & Wolfe, D. A. (2002). Child neglect: developmental issues and outcomes. *Child Abuse and Neglect, 26*(6–7), 679–695.

Hipwell, A. E., Goossens, F. A., Melhuish, E. C., & Kumar, R. (2000). Severe maternal psychopathology and infant-mother attachment. *Developmental Psychopathology, 12*(2), 157–175.

Hipwell, A. E., & Kumar, R. (1996). Maternal psychopathology and prediction of outcome based mother-infant interaction ratings. *British Journal of Psychiatry, 169*(5), 655–661.

Holden, C. E., Burland, A. S., & Lemmen, C. A. (1996). Insanity and filicide: Women who murder their children. In E. P. Benedek (Ed.), *Emerging issues in forensic psychiatry: From clinic to courtroom* (pp. 25–34). San Francisco: Jossey-Bass.

Hollander, E., Tracy, K. A., Swann, A. C., Coccaro, E. F., McElroy, S. L., Wozniak, P., et al. (2003). Divalproex in the treatment of impulsive aggression: Efficacy in cluster B personality disorders. *Neuropsychopharmacology, 28*(6), 1186–1197.

Ide, J. (2001). *Shaken baby syndrome—leading cause of child abuse case deaths in U.S.* Retrieved on November 3, 2003, from http://www.afmc.wpafb.mil/HQ-AFMC/PA/news/archive/2001/jun

Jacobs, D. G. (Ed.). (1999). *The Harvard medical guide to suicide assessment and intervention.* San Francisco: Jossey-Bass.

Jacobs, D. G., Brewer, M., & Klein-Benheim, M. (1999). Suicide assessment: An overview and recommended protocol. In D. G. Jacobs (Ed.), *The Harvard medical guide to suicide assessment and intervention* (pp. 3–39.). San Franciso: Jossey-Bass.

Jamison, K. R. (1999, Spring/Summer). A world apart. *Newsweek,* p. 79.

Jason, J., & Andereck, N. D. (1983). Fatal child abuse in Georgia: The epidemiology of severe physical child abuse. *Child Abuse and Neglect, 7*(1), 1–9.

Jones, E., Forrest, J., Goldman, N., Henshaw, S., Lincoln, R., Rosoff, J., et al. (1985). Teenage pregnancy in developed countries: Determinants and policy implications. *Family Planning Perspectives, 17,* 53–63.

Jones, I., & Craddock, N. (2001). Familiality of the puerperal trigger in bipolar disorder: Results of a family study. *American Journal of Psychiatry, 158*(6), 913–917.

Kant, R., Chalansani, R., Chengappa, K. N., & Dieringer, M. F. (2004). The off-label use of clozapine in adolescents with bipolar disorder, intermittent explosive disorder, or posttraumatic stress disorder. *Journal of Child and Adolescent Psychopharmacology, 14*(1), 57–63.

Kaplan, H., & Sadock, B. (1990) *Comprehensive textbook of psychiatry.* Baltimore: Williams & Wilkins.

Kaufman, K. L., Coury, D., & Pickrel, E. (1989). Munchausen syndrome by proxy: A survey of professionals' knowledge. *Child Abuse and Neglect, 13,* 141–147.

Kazdin, A. E. (2000). *Psychotherapy for children and adolescents: Directions for research and practice.* New York: Oxford University Press.

Kazdin, A. E. (2002). Psychosocial treatments for conduct disorder in children and adolescents. In P. E. Nathan & J. M. Gordon (Eds.), *A guide to treatments that work* (2nd ed., pp. 57–85). New York: Oxford University Press.

Kendell, R. E., Chalmers, J. C., & Platz, C. (1987). Epidemiology of puerperal psychoses. *British Journal of Psychiatry, 150,* 662–673.

Khalsa, E., Jatlow, P., & Gawin, F. (1994). Flupenthixol and desipramine treatment of crack users: Double-blind results. In NIDA Research Monograph 141, *CPDD Problems of Drug Dependence,* Department of Health and Human Services 438, NIH Publication No. 94–3794. Washington, DC: National Institutes of Health.

Kleber, H. D. (1995). Pharmacotherapy, current and potential, for the treatment of cocaine dependence. *Clinical Neuropharmacology, 18* (Suppl. 1), S96–S109.

Klompenhouwer, J. L., & van Hulst, A. M. (1991). Classification of postpartum psychosis: A study of 250 mother and baby admissions in The Netherlands. *Acta Psychiatric Scandanavia, 84*(3), 255–261.

Koenigsberg, K., Woo-Ming, A., & Siever, L. (2002). Pharmacological treatments for personality disorders. In P. E. Nathan & J. M. Gorman (Eds.), *A guide to treatments that work* (2nd ed., pp. 625–641). New York: Oxford University Press.

Kolar, A. F., Brown, B. S., Weddington, W. W., Haertzen, C. C., Michaelson, B. S., & Jaffe, J. H. (1992). Treatment of cocaine dependence in methadone maintenance clients: A pilot study comparing the efficacy of desipramine and amantadine. *International Journal of the Addictions, 27,* 849–868.

Korbin, J. E. (1986). Childhood histories of women imprisoned for fatal child maltreatment. *Child Abuse and Neglect, 10,* 331–338.

Koss, M. P. (1993). Detecting the scope of rape: A review of prevalence research methods. *Journal of Interpersonal Violence, 8,* 198–222.

Krugman, R. D. (1983). Fatal child abuse: Analysis of 24 cases. *Pediatrician, 12*(1), 68–72.

Kuehnle, K. (2003). Child sexual abuse evaluations. In A. M. Goldstein (Ed.), *Handbook of psychology: Vol. 11. Forensic psychology* (pp.437–460). Hoboken, NJ: Wiley.

Kuehnle, K. (2005). Treatment of child sexual abuse. In G. P. Koocher, J. C. Norcross, & S. S. Hill (Eds.), *Psychologists' desk reference* (2nd ed., pp. 430–435). New York: Oxford University Press.

Kumar, C., McIvor, R. J., Davies, T., & Brown, N. (2003). Estrogen administration does not reduce the rate of recurrence of affective psychosis after childbirth. *Journal of Clinical Psychiatry, 64*(2), 112–118.

Kunz, J., & Bahr, S. J. (1996). A profile of parental homicide against children. *Journal of Family Violence, 11*(4), 347–362.

Lam, W. K., Wechsberg, W., & Zule, W. (2004). African-American women who use crack cocaine: A comparison of mothers who live with and have been separated from their children. *Child Abuse and Neglect, 28*(11), 1229–1247.

Lasher, L. J., & Sheridan, M. S. (2004). *Munchausen by proxy: Identification, intervention, and case management.* New York: Haworth Press.

Lejoyeaux, M., Arbaretaz, M., McLoughlin, M., & Ades, J. (2002). Impulse control disorders and depression. *Journal of Nervous Mental Disorders, 190*(5), 310–314.

Lester, B. M., Tronick, E. Z., LaGasse, L., & Seifer, R., Bauer, C. R., Shankaran, S., et al. (2002). The maternal lifestyle study: Effects of substance exposure during pregnancy on neurodevelopmental outcome in 1-month-old infants. *Pediatrics, 110*(6), 1182–1192.

Levin, A. V., & Sheridan, M. S. (Eds.). (1995). *Munchausen syndrome by proxy: Issues in diagnosis and treatment.* New York: Lexington Books.

Levitsky, S., & Cooper, R. (2000). Infant colic syndrome—maternal fantasies of aggression and infanticide. *Clinical Pediatrics, 39,* 395–400.

Lewis, C. F., Baranoski, M. V., Buchanan, J. A., & Benedek, E. P. (1998). Factors associated with weapon use in maternal filicide. *Journal of Forensic Sciences, 43*(4), 613–618.

Lewis, C. F., & Bunce, S. C. (2003). Filicidal mothers and the impact of psychosis on maternal filicide. *Journal of the American Academy of Psychiatry and the Law, 31*(4), 459–470.

Lewis, M. W., Misra, S., Johnson, H. L., & Rosen, T. S. (2004). Neurological and developmental outcomes of prenatally cocaine-exposed offspring from 12 to 36 months. *American Journal of Drug and Alcohol Abuse, 30*(2), 299–320.

Lieb, K., Zanarini, M., Schmahl, C., Linehan, M. M., & Bohus, M. (2004). Borderline personality disorder. *Lancet, 364,* 453–461.

Light, M. J. (1995). Respiratory manifestations. In A. V. Levin & M. S. Sheridan (Eds.), *Munchausen syndrome by proxy: Issues in diagnosis and treatment* (pp. 103–119). New York: Lexington.

Lilienfeld, S. O., & Andrews, B. P. (1996). Development and preliminary validation of a self-report measure of psychopathic personality traits in noncriminal populations. *Journal of Personality Assessment, 66,* 488–524.

Linehan, M. M. (1993). *Cognitive-behavioral treatment for borderline personality disorder.* New York: Guilford Press.

Locke, T., & Newcomb, M. (2004). Child maltreatment, parent alcohol and drug-related problems, polydrug problems, and parenting practices: A test of gender differences and four theoretical perspectives. *Journal of Family Psychology, 18*(1), 120–134.

Ludwig, S. (1995). The role of the physician. In A. V. Levin & M. S. Sheridan (Eds.), *Munchausen syndrome by proxy: Issues in diagnosis and treatment* (pp. 287–294). New York: Lexington.

Maguire, K., Pastore, A., & Flanagan, T. (Eds.). (1993). *Sourcebook of criminal justice statistics 1993.* Washington, DC: U.S. Department of Justice.

Main, M., Kaplan, N., & Cassidy, J. (1985). Security in infancy, childhood and adulthood: A move to level of representation. *Social Research Child Development, 50*(1–2), 66–106.

Main, M., & Solomon, J. (1986). Discovery of a new, insecure-disorganized/disoriented attachment pattern. In T. B. Brazelton & M. Yogman (Eds.), *Affective development in infancy* (pp. 95–124). Norwood, NJ: Ablex.

Mammen, O., Kolko, D., & Pilkonis, P. (2002). Negative affect and parental aggression in child physical abuse. *Child Abuse and Neglect, 26,* 407–424.

Mattes, J. A. (1990). Comparative effectiveness of carbamazepine and propranolol for rage outbursts. *Journal of Neuropsychiatry and Clinical Neuroscience, 2*(2), 159–164.

McClain, P. W., Sacks, J. J., Froelke, R. G., & Ewigman, B. G. (1993). Estimates of fatal child abuse and neglect, United States, 1979 through 1988. *Pediatrics, 91*(2), 338–343.

McDonough, S. (1993). Interaction guidance: Understanding and treating early infant-caregiver relationship disturbances. In C. Zeanah (Ed.), *Handbook of infant mental health* (pp. 414–427). New York: Guilford Press.

McElroy, S. L. (2004). Bipolar disorders: Special diagnostic and treatment considerations in women. *CNS Spectrum, 9*(8), 5–18.

McElroy, S. L., Soutullo, C. A., Beckman, D.A., Taylor, P., & Keck, P. E (1998). DSM-IV intermittent explosive disorder: A report of 27 cases. *Journal of Clinical Psychiatry, 59*(40), 203–210.

McGrew, M., & Shore, W. (1991). The problem of teenage pregnancy. *Journal of Family Practice, 32,* 17–25.

McGuire, T. L., & Feldman, K. W. (1989). Psychologic morbidity of children subjected to Munchausen syndrome by proxy. *Pediatrics, 83,* 289–292.

McKee, G. R., & Shea, S. J. (1998). Maternal filicide: A cross-national comparison. *Journal of Clinical Psychology, 54*(5), 679–687.

McKee, G. R., Shea, S. J., Mogy, R. B., & Holden, C. E. (2001). MMPI-2 profiles of filicidal, mariticidal, and homicidal women. *Journal of Clinical Psychology, 57*(3), 367–374.

Meadow, R. (1977). Munchausen syndrome by proxy: The hinterland of child abuse. *Lancet, 2,* 343–345.

Meadow, R. (1990). Suffocation, recurrent apnea, and sudden infant death. *Journal of Pediatrics, 117,* 351–357.

Meadow, R. (1995). The history of Munchausen syndrome by proxy. In A. V. Levin & M. S. Sheridan (Eds.), *Munchausen syndrome by proxy* (pp. 3–11). New York: Lexington Books.

Meadow, R. (1999). Unnatural sudden infant death. *Archives of Disease in Childhood, 80*(1), 7–14.

Meesand, P., & Turchin, W. (2003). The mother-infant relationship: From normality to pathology. In M. Spinelli (Ed.), *Infanticide: Psychosocial and legal perspectives on mothers who kill* (pp. 209–233). Washington, DC: American Psychiatric Association.

Melton, G., Petrila, J., Poythress, N., & Slobogin, C. (1997). *Psychological evaluations for the courts* (2nd ed.). New York: Guilford Press.

Meyer, C. L., & Oberman, M. (2001). *Mothers who kill their children.* New York: New York University Press.

Mian, M. (1995). A multidisciplinary approach. In A. V. Levin & M. S. Sheridan (Eds.), *Munchausen syndrome by proxy: Issues in diagnosis and treatment* (pp. 271–286). New York: Lexington.

Mian, M., & Huyer, D. (1995). Infection and fever. In A. V. Levin & M. S. Sheridan (Eds.), *Munchausen syndrome by proxy: Issues in diagnosis and treatment* (pp. 161–179). New York: Lexington.

Miller, W., Andrews, N., Wilbourne, P., & Bennett, M. (1998). A wealth of alternatives: Effective treatments for alcohol problems. In W. R. Miller & N. Heather (Eds.), *Treating addictive behaviors* (2nd ed., pp. 203–216). New York: Plenum Press.

Money, J., & Werlwas, J. (1976). Folie a deux in the parents of psychosocial dwarfs: Two cases. *Bulletin of the American Academy of Psychiatry and the Law, 4,* 351–361.

Moreira, E. C., & Moreira, L. A. (1999). Hypochondriasis by proxy in children: Report of two cases. *Journal of Pediatrics, 75*(5), 373–376.

Morey, L. C. (1991). *The Personality Assessment Inventory professional manual.* Odessa, FL: Psychological Assessment Resources.

Morris, S. M., Alexander, J. F., & Turner, C. W. (1991). Do reattributions reduce blame? *Journal of Family Psychology, 5,* 192–203.

Morrow, C. E., Vogel, A. L., Anthony, J. C., Ofir, A. Y., Dausa, A. T., & Bandstra, E. S. (2004). Expressive and receptive language functioning in preschool children with prenatal cocaine exposure. *Journal of Pediatric Psychology, 29*(7), 543–545.

Morrow, P. L. (1987). Caffeine toxicity: A case of child abuse by drug ingestion. *Journal of Forensic Sciences, 32*(6), 1801–1805.

Murphy, G. E. (1986). The physician's role in suicide prevention. In A. Roy (Ed.), *Suicide* (pp. 171–179). Baltimore: Williams & Wilkins.

Murray, L., Cooper, P., & Hipwell, A. (2003). Mental health of parents caring for infants. *Archives of Womens Mental Health, 6*(2), 71–77.

Myers, B. J., Dawson, K. S., Britt, G. C., Lodder, D. E., Meloy, L. D., Saunders, M. K., et al. (2003). Prenatal cocaine exposure and infant performance on the Brazelton Neonatal Behavioral Assessment Scale. *Substance Use and Misuse, 38*(14), 2065–2096.

Nadeau, M. (1997, August). *A taxonomy of maternal filicide*. Paper presented at the meeting of the American Psychological Association, Chicago.

Nadelson, C. C., Notman, M. T., & Carmen, E. (1986). The rape victim and the rape experience. In W. J. Curran, A. L. McGarry, & S. A. Shah (Eds.), *Forensic psychiatry and psychology* (pp. 339–362). Philadelphia: Davis.

National Abandoned Infants Assistance Resource Center. (2003). *Boarder babies, abandoned infants, and discarded infants July 2002*. Retrieved June 15, 2004, from http://www.aia.berkeley.edu/publications/fact_sheets/boader_defs.html

National Center on Child Abuse and Neglect. (1996). *Child maltreatment 1994: Reports from the states to the National Center on Child Abuse and Neglect*. Washington, DC: U.S. Government Printing Office.

National Center on Shaken Baby Syndrome. (2005). *Please, don't shake me*. Retrieved November 14, 2004, from http://www.dontshake.com

National Conference of State Legislatures. (2003). *Update: Safe havens for abandoned infants*. Retrieved October 31, 2004, from http://www.ncsl.org/programs/cyf/ai laws.htm

Nolte, K. B. (1993). Esophageal foreign bodies as child abuse: Potential fatal mechanisms. *American Journal of Forensic Medical Pathology, 14*(4), 323–326.

Nonacs, R., & Cohen, L. S. (1998). Postpartum mood disorders: Diagnosis and treatment guidelines. *Journal of Clinical Psychiatry, 59*, 34–40.

Norstrom-Bailey, B., Sood, B. G., Sokol, R. J., Ager, J., Janisse, J., & Harrigan, J. H., et al. (2005). Gender and alcohol moderate prenatal cocaine effects on teacher-report of child behavior. *Neurotoxicology and Teratology, 27*(2), 181–189.

North, C. S., Smith, E. M., & Spitznagel, E. L. (1993). Is antisocial personality a valid diagnosis among the homeless? *American Journal of Psychiatry, 150*, 578–583.

Nunes, E. V., McGrath, P. J., Quitkin, F. M., Ocepek-Welikson, K., Stewart, J. W., Koenig, T., et al. (1995). Imipramine treatment of cocaine abuse: Possible boundaries of efficacy. *Drug and Alcohol Dependence, 39*, 185–195.

Oates, M. (2003). Perinatal psychiatric disorders: A leading cause of maternal morbidity and mortality. *British Medical Bulletin, 67*, 219–229.

Oberman, M. (1996). Mothers who kill: Coming to terms with modern American infanticide. *American Criminal Law Review, 34*, 1–110.

Oberman, M. (2003). Mothers who kill: Cross-cultural patterns in and perspectives on contemporary maternal filicide. *International Journal of Law and Psychiatry, 26*(5), 493–514.

Ogunyemi, D., & Hernandez-Loera, G. E. (2004). The impact of antenatal cocaine use on maternal characteristics and neonatal outcomes. *Journal of Maternal Fetal and Neonatal Medicine, 15*(4), 253–259.

O'Hara, M. W., Stuart, S., & Gorman, L. L. (2000). Efficacy of interpersonal psychotherapy for postpartum depression. *Archives of General Psychiatry, 57*, 1039–1045.

Oldham, J. M. (2002). A 44-year-old woman with borderline personality disorder. *Journal of the American Medical Association, 287*, 1034.

O'Leary, B. J., & Norcross, J. C. (1998). Making successful referrals. In G. P. Koocher, J. C. Norcross, & S. S. Hill (Eds.), *Psychologists' desk reference* (pp. 524–526). New York: Oxford University Press.

Olsen, S. J., & Durkin, M. S. (1996). Validity of hospital discharge data regarding intentionality of fatal pediatric injuries. *Epidemiology, 7*(6), 644–647.

d'Orban, P. (1979). Women who kill their children. *British Journal of Psychiatry, 134,* 560–571.

Orr, C. J., Clark, M. A., Hawley, D. A., Pless, J. E., Tate, L. R., & Fardal, P. M. (1995). Fatal anorectal injuries: A series of four cases. *Journal of Forensic Sciences, 40*(2), 219–221.

Orr, D., Langefeld, C., Katz, B., Caine, V., Dias, P., Blythe, M., et al. (1992). Factors associated with condom use among sexually active female adolescents. *Journal of Pediatrics, 120,* 311–317.

Ostfeld, B. M. (1995). The role of the hospital administrator. In A. V. Levin & M. S. Sheridan (Eds.), *Munchausen syndrome by proxy: Issues in diagnosis and treatment* (pp. 355–367). New York: Lexington.

Overpeck, M. D. (2003). Epidemiology of infanticide. In M. Spinelli (Ed.), *Infanticide: Psychosocial and legal perspectives on mothers who kill* (pp. 19–31). Washington, DC: American Psychiatric Association.

Overpeck, M. D., Brenner, R. A., & Cosgrove, C. (2002). National underascertainment of sudden unexpected infant deaths associated with deaths of unknown cause. *Pediatrics, 109,* 274–283.

Overpeck, M. D., Brenner, R. A., & Trumble, A. C. (1998). Risk factors for infant homicide in the United States. *New England Journal of Medicine, 339,* 1211–1216.

Pagano, M., Skodol, A., Stout, R., Shea, M., & Yen, S. (2004) Stressful life events as predictors of functioning: Findings from the collaborative longitudinal personality disorders study. *Acta Psychiatric Scandanavia, 110*(6), 421–429.

Paris, J. (2004). Borderline or bipolar? Distinguishing borderline personality disorder from bipolar spectrum disorders. *Harvard Review of Psychiatry, 12*(3), 140–145.

Pedersen, C. A. (1999). Postpartum mood and anxiety disorders: A guide for the nonpsychiatric clinician with an aside on thyroid associations with postpartum mood. *Thyroid, 9*(7), 691–697.

Pepler, D. J., & Rubin, K. H. (1991). *The development and treatment of childhood aggression.* Hillsdale, NJ: Erlbaum.

Petrakis, I. L., Carroll, K. M., Nich, C., Gordon, L. T., McCance-Katz, E. F., Frankforter, T., et al. (2000). Disulfram treatment for cocaine dependence in methadone-maintained opioid addicts. *Addiction, 95,* 219–228.

Petry, S. S., & McGoldrick, M. (2005). Genograms in assessment and therapy. In G. P. Koocher, J. C. Norcross, & S. S. Hill (Eds.), *Psychologist's desk reference* (2nd ed., pp. 366–373). New York: Oxford University Press.

Pfulman, B., Franzek, E., Beckmann, H., & Stober, G. (1999). Long-term course and outcome of severe postpartum psychiatric disorders. *Psychopathology, 32*(4), 192–202.

Pires, J. M., & Molle, L. D. (1999). Munchausen syndrome by proxy: Two case reports. *Journal of Pediatrics, 75*(4), 281–286.

Pistella, C., & Bonati, F. (1998). Communication about sexual behavior among adolescent women, their family, and peers: Families in society. *Journal of Contemporary Human Services, 79,* 206–211.

Pizarro, R., & Billick, S. B. (2003) Forensic evaluation of physically and sexually abused children. In R. Rosner (Ed.), *Principles and practice of forensic psychiatry* (pp. 377–395). London: Arnold.

Pollanen, M. S., Smith, C. R., Chiasson, D. A., Cairns, J. T., & Young, J. (2002). Fatal child abuse-maltreatment syndrome: A retrospective study in Ontario, Canada, 1990–1995. *Forensic Science International, 126*(2), 101–104.

Pope, K. S., & Vasquez, M. J. T. (2005). Assessment of suicidal risk. In G. P. Koocher, J. C. Norcross, & S. S. Hill (Eds.), *Psychologists' desk reference* (2nd ed., pp. 63–66). New York: Oxford University Press.

Poppen, P. (1994). Adolescent contraceptive use and communication: Changes over a decade. *Adolescence, 29,* 503–514.

Qin, P. & Mortensen, P. (2003). The impact of parental status on the risk of completed suicide. *Archives of General Psychiatry, 60*(8), 797–802.

Ragaisis, K. (2004). When the system works: Rescuing a child from Munchausen's syndrome by proxy. *Journal of Child and Adolescent Psychiatric Nursing, 17*(4), 173–176.

Rand, D. C., & Feldman, M. D. (1999). Misdiagnosis of Munchausen syndrome by proxy: A literature review and four new cases. *Harvard Review of Psychiatry, 7*(2), 94–101,

Rapkin, A. J., Mikacich, J. A., Moatekef-Imani, B., & Rasgon, N. (2002). The clinical nature and formal diagnosis of premenstrual, postpartum, and perimenopausal affective disorders. *Current Psychiatry Report, 4*(6), 419–428.

Ray, N. K., Rubenstein, H., & Russo, N. J. (1994). Understanding the parents who are mentally retarded: Guidelines for family preservation programs. *Child Welfare, 73*(6), 725–743.

Reece, M., & Kirschner, R. H. (2004). *Shaken baby syndrome/Shaken impact syndrome.* Retrieved November, 13, 2004, from http://dontshake.com.

Reed, P., Sermin, N., Appleby, L., & Faragher, B. (1999). A comparison of clinical response to electroconvulsive therapy in puerperal and non-puerperal psychoses. *Journal of Affective Disorders, 54*(3), 255–260.

Reid, W. H., & Stout, C. E. (2003). Terrorism and forensic psychiatry. In R. Rosner (Ed.), *Principles and practice of forensic psychiatry* (pp. 661–668). London: Arnold.

Reist, C., Nakamura, K., Sagart, E., Sokolski, K. N., & Fujimoto, K. A. (2003). Impulsive aggressive behavior: Open-label treatment with citalopram. *Journal of Clinical Psychiatry, 64*(1), 81–85.

Rekers, G. (1996). *Susan Smith: Victim or murderer.* Lakewood, CO: Glenbridge.

Resnick, P. J. (1969). Child murder by parents: A psychiatric review of filicide. *American Journal of Psychiatry, 126*(3), 325–334.

Resnick, P. J. (1970). Murder of the newborn: A psychiatric review of neonaticide. *American Journal of Psychiatry, 126,* 1414–1420.

Resnick, P. J. (1996, June). *Clinical prediction of violent behavior.* Paper presented at Hall Psychiatric Institute, Columbia, SC.

Rhode, A., & Marneros, A. (1993). Postpartum psychoses: Onset and long-term course. *Psychopathology, 26*(3–4), 203–209.

Rihmer, Z., Barsi, J., Arato, M., & Demeter, E. (1990). Suicide in subtypes of primary major depression. *Journal of Affective Disorders, 18,* 221–225.

Robling, S. A., Paykel, E. S., Dunn, V. J., Abbott, R., & Katona, C. (2000). Long-term outcome of severe puerperal psychiatric illness: A 23-year follow-up study. *Psychological Medicine, 30*(6), 1263–1271.

Rodenburg, M. (1971). Child murder by depressed parents. *Canadian Psychiatric Association Journal, 16*(1), 41–48.

Rogers, R. (2000). The uncritical acceptance of risk assessment in forensic practice. *Law and Human Behavior, 24*(5), 595–605.

Rosenberg, D. (1995). From lying to homicide: The spectrum of Munchausen syndrome by proxy. In A. V. Levin & M. S. Sheridan (Eds.), *Munchausen syndrome by proxy: Issues in diagnosis and treatment* (pp. 13–37). New York: Lexington.

Rosenberg, R., Greening, D., & Windell, J. (2003). *Conquering postpartum depression.* Cambridge, MA: Perseus Books.

Roye, C., & Balk, S. (1997). Evaluation of an intergenerational program for pregnant and parenting adolescents. *Maternal-Child Nursing Journal, 24,* 32–36.

Rubenstein, A. K. (1998). Guidelines for conducting adolescent psychotherapy. In G. P. Koocher, J. C. Norcross, & S. S. Hill (Eds.), *Psychologists' desk reference* (pp. 265–269). New York: Oxford University Press.

Ruma, P. R., Burke, R. V., & Thompson, R. W. (1996). Group parenting training: Is it effective for children of all ages? *Behavior Therapy, 27,* 159–169.

Russell, L. (2000). *My daughter Susan Smith.* Brentwood, TN: Authors Book Nook.

Rutherford, M. J., Alterman, A. I., Cacciola, J. S., & McKay, J. R. (1999). Gender differences in the relationship of antisocial personality disorder criteria to Psychopathy Checklist—Revised scores. *Journal of Personality Disorders, 12,* 69–76.

Ryle, A. (2004). The contribution of cognitive analytic therapy to the treatment of borderline personality disorder. *Journal of Personality Disorders, 18*(1), 3–35.

Sadock, B. J., & Sadock, V. A. (2003). *Kaplan and Sadock's synopsis of psychiatry* (9th ed.). Philadelphia: Lippincott Williams & Wilkins.

"Safe havens" for babies questioned. (2003, March 10). Retrieved on October 10, 2004, from CBS News website http://www.cbsnews.com/stories/2003/03/10/national/main543359.shtml

Safer, D. J. (1997). Adolescent/adult differences in suicidal behavior and outcome. *Annals of Clinical Psychiatry, 9,* 61–66.

Safran, J. D. (2005). Repairing ruptures in the therapeutic alliance. In G. P. Koocher, J. C. Norcross, & S. S. Hill (Eds.). *Psychologists' desk reference* (2nd ed., pp. 216–219). New York: Oxford University Press.

Salekin, R. T., Rogers, R., & Sewell, K. W. (1997). Construct validity of psychopathy in a female offender sample: A multitrait—multimethod evaluation. *Journal of Abnormal Psychology, 106,* 576–585.

Salekin, R. T., Rogers, R., Ustad, K. L., & Sewell, K. W. (1998). Psychopathy and recidivism among female inmates. *Law and Human Behavior, 22,* 109–128.

Sammons, R. A. (1987, October). *Psychotic mothers who kill their children.* Paper presented at the semiannual forensic symposium of the Institute of Law, Psychiatry, and Public Policy, Charlottesville, VA.

Samuels, M. (1993, October). *ALTEs and Munchausen syndrome by proxy.* Paper presented at the annual conference on Apnea in Infancy, Rancho Mirage, CA.

Saternus, K., Kernbach-Wighton, G., & Oehmichen, M. (2000). The shaking trauma in infants: Kinetic chains. *Forensic Sciences International, 109*(3), 203–213.

Sattler, J. (1998). *Clinical and forensic interviewing of children and families.* San Diego, CA: Author.

Schmitt, B. D. (1987). Seven deadly sins of childhood: Advising parents about difficult developmental phases. *Child Abuse and Neglect, 11*(3), 421–432.

Schoenfield, L. J., & Eyberg, S. M. (2005). Parent management training for childhood behavior disorders. In G. P. Koocher, J. C. Norcross, & S. S. Hill (Eds.), *The psychologist's desk reference* (2nd ed., pp. 327–332). New York: Oxford University Press.

Schopf, J., & Rust, B. (1994). Follow-up and family study of postpartum psychoses. *European Archives of Psychiatry and Clinical Neuroscience, 244*(2), 101–111.

Schreier, H. A., & Libow, J. A. (1993). *Hurting for love: Munchausen by proxy syndrome.* New York: Guilford.

Schuler, M. E., & Nair, P. (1999). Brief report: Frequency of maternal cocaine use during pregnancy and infant neurobehavioral outcome. *Journal of Pediatric Psychology, 24*(6), 511–514.

Schwartz, L. L., & Isser, N. K. (2000). *Endangered children: Neonaticide, infanticide, and filicide.* Boca Raton, FL: CRC Press.

Scott, P. D. (1973). Parents who kill their children. *Medicine, Science, and the Law, 13*(3), 120–127.

Seagull, E. A., & Scheurer, S. L. (1986). Neglected and abused children of mentally retarded parents. *Child Abuse and Neglect, 10*(4), 493–500.

Sears, W., & Sears, M. (2001). *The attachment parenting book.* Boston: Little, Brown.

Sedlak, A. J., & Broadhurst, D. D. (1996). *Third national incidence study of child abuse and neglect.* Washington, D.C.: U.S. Department of Health and Human Services, National Center on Child Abuse and Neglect.

Seifer, R., LeGasse, L. L., Lester, B., Bauer, C. R., Shankaran, S., Bada, H. S., et al. (2004). Attachment status in children prenatally exposed to cocaine and other substances. *Child Development, 75*(3), 850–868.

Seitz, V., & Apfel, N. (1993). Adolescent mothers and repeated childbearing: Effects of a school-based intervention program. *American Journal of Orthopsychiatry, 63,* 572–581.

Seyfried, L. S., & Marcus, S. M. (2003). Postpartum mood disorders. *International Review of Psychiatry, 15*(3), 231–342.

Shankaran, S., Bauer, C. R., Bada, H. S., Lester, B., Wright, L. L., & Das, A. (2003). Health-care utilization among mothers and infants following cocaine exposure. *Journal of Perinatology, 23*(5), 361–367.

Shankaran, S., Das, A., Bauer, C. R., Bada, H. S., Lester, B., Wright, L. L., et al. (2004). Association between patterns of maternal substance use and infant birth weight, length, and head circumference. *Pediatrics, 114*(2), 226–234.

Sharma, V. (2003). Pharmacotherapy of postpartum psychosis. *Expert Opinion in Pharmacotherapy 4*(10), 1651–1658.

Shaw, D. S., Winslow, E. B., Owens, E. B., Vondra, J. I., Cohn, J. F., & Bell, R. Q. (1998). The development of early externalizing problems among children from low-income families: A transformational perspective. *Journal of Abnormal Child Psychology, 26*(2), 95–107.

Sheridan, M. S., & Levin, A. V. (1995). Summary. In A. V. Levin & M. S. Sheridan (Eds.), *Munchausen syndrome by proxy: Issues in diagnosis and treatment* (pp. 433–443). New York: Lexington.

Sieving, R., Resnick, M., Bearinger, L., Remafedi, G., Taylor, B., & Harmon, B. (1997). Cognitive and behavioral predictors of sexually transmitted disease risk behavior among sexually active adolescents. *Archives of Pediatric and Adolescent Medicine, 151,* 243–252.

Sigal, M., & Altmark, D. (1995). Adult victims. In A. V. Levin & M. S. Sheridan (Eds.), *Munchausen syndrome by proxy: Issues in diagnosis and treatment* (pp. 257–267). New York: Lexington.

Silverman, K., Svikis, D., Wong, C. J., Hampton, J., Stitzer, M. L., & Bigelow, G. E.

(2002). A reinforcement-based therapeutic workplace for the treatment of drug abuse: Three-year abstinence outcome. *Experimental Clinical Psychopharmacology, 10*(3), 228–240.

Silverthorn, P., & Frick, P. J. (1999). Developmental pathways to antisocial behavior: The delayed-onset pathway in girls. *Development and Psychopathology, 11,* 101–126.

Singer, L., Arendt, R., Minnes, S., Farkas, K., Yamashita, T., & Kleigman, R. (1995). Increased psychological distress in postpartum cocaine-abusing mothers. *Journal of Substance Abuse, 7*(2), 165–174.

Singer, L. T., Hawkins, S., Huang, J., Davillier, M., & Baley, J. (2001). Developmental outcomes and environmental correlates of very low birthweight, cocaine-exposed infants. *Early Human Development, 64*(2), 91–103.

Single, T., & Henry, R. L. (1991). An unusual case of Munchausen syndrome by proxy. *Australia and New Zealand Journal of Psychiatry, 25*(3), 422–425.

Slobogin, C. (1995). Therapeutic jurisprudence: Five dilemmas to ponder. *Psychology, Public Policy and the Law, 1,* 193–219.

Smith, C. A., & Farrington, D. P. (2004). Continuities in antisocial behavior and parenting across three generations. *Journal of Child Psychology and Psychiatry, 45*(2), 230–247.

Smith, D. (1995). *Beyond all reason: My life with Susan Smith.* New York: Pinnacle Books.

Smithey, M. (1998). Infant homicide: Victim/offender relationship and causes of death. *Journal of Family Violence, 13*(3), 285–297.

Soderberg, S., Kullgren, G., & Salander, R. (2004). Childhood sexual abuse predicts poor outcome seven years after parasuicide. *Social Psychiatry and Psychiatric Epidemiology, 39*(11), 916–920.

Somani, V. K. (1998). Witchcraft's syndrome: Munchausen's syndrome by proxy. *International Journal of Dermatology, 37*(3), 229–230.

Spinelli, M. G. (2001). A systematic investigation of 16 cases of neonaticide. *American Journal of Psychiatry, 158,* 811–813.

Spinelli, M. G. (Ed.). (2003). *Infanticide: Psychosocial and legal perspectives on mothers who kill.* Washington, DC: American Psychiatric Association.

Stanger, C., Kamon, J., Dumenci, L., Higgins, S. T., Bickel, W. K., Grabowski, J., et al. (2002). Predictors of internalizing and externalizing problems among children of cocaine and opiate dependant parents. *Drug and Alcohol Dependence, 66*(2), 199–212.

Sterk, C. E. (2002). The health intervention project: HIV risk reduction among African-American women drug users. *Public Health Reports, 117,* S88–S95.

Stern, D. (1995). *The motherhood constellation.* New York: Basic Books.

Stevens-Simon, C., & White, M. (1991). Adolescent pregnancy. *Pediatric Annals, 20,* 322–331.

Stevenson, J., & Meares, R. (1992). An outcome study of psychotherapy for patients with borderline personality disorder. *American Journal of Psychiatry, 149,* 358–362.

Stevenson, J., & Meares, R. (1999). Psychotherapy with borderline patients: A preliminary cost benefit study. *Australian and New Zealand Journal of Psychiatry, 33,* 473–477.

Stiffman, M. N., Schnitzer, P. G., Adam, P., Kruse, R. L., & Ewigman, B. G. (2002). Household composition and risk of fatal child maltreatment. *Pediatrics, 109*(4), 615–621.

Stocky, A., & Lynch, J. (2000). Acute psychiatric disturbance in pregnancy and the puerperium. *Ballieres Best Practice Research in Clinical Obstetrics and Gynaecology, 14*(1), 73–87.

Stone, R., & Waszak, C. (1992). Adolescent knowledge and attitudes about abortion. *Family Planning Perspectives, 24,* 52–58.

Strauss, M. A., & Mouradian, V. E. (1998). Impulsive corporal punishment by mothers and antisocial behavior and impulsiveness of children. *Behavioral Sciences and the Law, 16*(3), 353–374.

Suinn, R. M. (1998). Anxiety/anger management training. In G. P. Koocher, J. C. Norcross, & S. S. Hill (Eds.), *Psychologist's desk reference* (pp. 318–321). New York: Oxford University Press.

Susman, J. L. (1996). Postpartum depressive disorders. *Journal of Family Practice, 43*(6), 17–24.

Sutherland, S., & Scherl, D. (1970). Patterns of response among victims of rape. *American Journal of Orthopsychiatry, 40*(3), 503–511.

Taylor, C. G., Norman, D. K., Murphy, J. M., Jellinek, M., Quinn, D., Poitrast, F. G., et al. (1991). Diagnosed intellectual and emotional impairment among parents who seriously mistreat their children: Prevalence, type, and outcome in a court sample. *Child Abuse and Neglect, 15*(4), 389–401.

Terp, I. M., Engholm, G., Moller, H., & Mortensen, P. B. (1999). A follow-up study of postpartum psychoses: Prognosis and risk factors for readmission. *Acta Psychiatric Scandanavia, 100*(1), 40–46.

Thomas, T. (1996). Covert video surveillance: An assessment of the Staffordshire protocol. *Journal of Medical Ethics, 22*(1), 22–25.

Turner, H., & Ornstein, N. (1983). Distinguishing the wicked from the mentally ill. *California Lawyer, 3*(March), 40–45.

Tymchuk, A. J., Yokota, A., & Rahbar, B. (1990). Decision-making abilities of mothers with mental retardation. *Research on Developmental Disabilities, 11*(1), 97–109.

Tymchuk, T. A. (1992). Predicting adequacy of parenting by people with mental retardation. *Child Abuse and Neglect, 16*(2), 165–178.

U.S. Department of Health and Human Services. (2003). *Child abuse prevention and treatment act as amended by the keeping children and families safe act of 2003.* Retrieved October 25, 2005, from http://www.acf.hhs.gov/programs/cb/laws/capta2003.index.htm

U.S. Department of Health and Human Services. (2004a). *Administration for Children and Families News: Abandoned babies—Preliminary national estimates.* Retrieved October 31, 2004, from http://www.acf.dhhs.gov/news/stats/abandon.htm.

U.S. Department of Health and Human Services. (2004b). *Administration for Children and Families News: Child maltreatment fatalities 1998.* Retrieved June 17, 2004, from http://www.acf.dhhs.gov/news/stats/fatalities.htm.

Valliant, G. E. (1988). Defense mechanisms. In A. M. Nicholi (Ed.), *The new Harvard guide to psychiatry* (pp. 200–207). Cambridge, MA: Harvard University Press.

Verdoux, H., & Sutter, A. L. (2002). Perinatal risk factors for schizophrenia: Diagnostic specificity and relationships with maternal psychopathology. *American Journal of Medical Genetics, 114*(8), 898–905.

Videbech, P., & Gouliaev, G. (1995). First admission with puerperal psychosis: 7–14 years of follow-up. *Acta Psychiatric Scandanavia, 91*(3), 167–173.

Visscher, H. C., & Rinehart, R. D. (1990). *Planning for pregnancy, birth, and beyond.* New York: Dutton/Penguin.

Vock, R., Meinel, U., Geserick, G., Gabler, W., Muller, E., Leopold, D., et al., (1999). Lethal child abuse through the use of physical force in the German Democratic Republic: Results of a multicenter study. *Archives of Criminology, 204*(3–4), 75–87.

Volpicelli, J. R., Markman, I., Monterosso, J., Filing, J., & O'Brien, C. P. (2000). Psychosocially enhanced treatment for cocaine-dependent mothers: Evidence of efficacy. *Journal of Substance Abuse Treatment, 18*(1), 41–49.

Vungkhanching, M., Sher, K., Jackson, K., & Parra, G. (2004). Relation of attachment style to family history of alcoholism and alcohol use disorders in early adulthood. *Drug and Alcohol Dependence, 75*(1), 47–53.

Walther, V. N. (1997). Pospartum depression: A review of perinatal social workers. *Social Work Health Care, 24*(3–4), 99–111.

Webb, R. T., Howard, L., & Abel, K. M. (2004). Antipsychotic drugs for non-affective psychosis during pregnancy and postpartum. *Cochrane Database Systems Review, 2*, CD004411.

Weissmann, M. M., Feder, A., Pilowsky, D .J., Olfson, M., Fuentes, M., Blanco, C., et al. (2004). Depressed mothers coming to primary care: Maternal reports of problems with their children. *Journal of Affective Disorders, 78*(2), 93–100.

Wexler, D. B. (1993). Therapeutic jurisprudence and the criminal courts. *William and Mary Law Review, 35*, 279–299.

White, N. A., & Piquero, A. R. (2004). A preliminary empirical test of Silverthorn and Frick's delayed-onset pathway in girls using an urban African-American, U.S.-based sample. *Criminal Behavior and Mental Health, 14*(4), 291–309.

Wilczynski, A. (1997). *Child homicide.* London: Greenwich Medical Media.

Wilk, A., Jenson, N., & Havighurst, T. (1997). Meta-analysis of randomized control trials addressing brief interventions in heavy alcohol drinkers. *Journal of General Internal Medicine, 12*, 274–283.

Williams, C., & Bevan, V. T. (1988). The secret observation of children in hospital. *Lancet, 2*, 780–781.

Willman, K. Y., Bank, D. E., Senac, M., & Chadwick, D. L. (1997). Restricting the time of injury in fatal inflicted head injuries. *Child Abuse and Neglect, 2*(10), 929–940.

Winans, E. A. (2001). Antipsychotics and breastfeeding. *Journal of Human Lactation, 17*(4), 344–347.

Wisner, K. L., Gracious, B. L., Piontek, C. M., Peindel, K., & Perel, J. (2003). Postpartum disorders. In M. G. Spinelli (Ed.), *Infanticide: Psychosocial and legal perspectives on mothers who kill* (pp. 35–60). Washington, DC: American Psychiatric Association.

Wisner, K. L., Peindl, K., & Hanusa, B. H. (1994). Symptomatology of affective and psychotic illnesses related to childbearing. *Journal of Affective Disorders, 30,* 77–84.

Wohl, A. R., Lu, S., Odem, S., Sorvillo, F., Pegues, C. F., & Kerndt, P. R. (1998). Sociodemographic and behavioral characteristics of African-American women with HIV and AIDS in Los Angeles County, 1990–1997. *Journal of Acquired Immune Deficiency Syndrome and Human Retrovirology, 19*(4), 413–420.

World Health Organization. (1992). *International classification of diseases and related health problems* (10th ed.). Geneva, Switzerland: Author.

Yen, S., Shea, M., Sanislow, C., Grilo, C., & Skodol, A. (2004). Borderline personality disorder criteria associated with prospectively observed suicidal behavior. *American Journal of Psychiatry, 161*(7), 1296–1298.

Yonge, O., & Haase, M. (2004). Munchausen syndrome and Munchausen syndrome by proxy in a student nurse. *Nurse Education, 29*(4), 166–169.

Yorker, B. C., & Kahan, B. B. (1991). The Munchausen syndrome by proxy variant of child abuse in the family courts. *Juvenile Family Court Journal, 42*, 51–57.

Young, M. A., Fogg, L. F., & Scheftner, W. A. (1996). Stable trait components of hopelessness: Baseline and sensitivity to depression. *Journal of Abnormal Psychology, 105*, 155–165.

Zanarini, M., Frankenburg, F., Hennen, J., Reich, D., & Silk, K. (2004). Axis I comorbidity in patients with borderline personality disorder: 6-year follow-up and prediction of time to remission. *American Journal of Psychiatry, 161*(11), 2108–2114.

Zlotnick, C., Rothschild, L., & Zimmerman, M. (2002). The role of gender in the clinical presentation of patients with borderline personality disorder. *Journal of Personality Disorders, 16*(3), 277–282.

Index